D1305010

The Authors

HERBERT M. JELLEY is a professor of business education at Oklahoma State University. In addition to teaching at the high school and university level, Dr. Jelley has also taught courses in life insurance at the home office of a life insurance company. He has served as consultant to business firms and as economic education consultant to the Oklahoma City public schools. His research study, "A Measurement and Interpretation of Money Management Understandings of Twelfth-Grade Students," received the National Business Education Research Award, which is sponsored annually by Delta Pi Epsilon. As a specialist in consumer education, Dr. Jelley has contributed many articles to professional journals and has addressed numerous teachers' groups.

ROBERT O. HERRMANN is a professor of agricultural economics at The Pennsylvania State University. Before joining the faculty there, Dr. Herrmann was a member of the Department of Home Economics at the University of California at Davis. In addition to teaching, Dr. Herrmann has conducted research in family economics and consumer behavior and has served on the Board of Directors of Consumers Union. He is former president of the American Council on Consumer Interests, a national association of professionals in the fields of consumer education and consumer affairs, and recently became editor of its journal, *The Journal of Consumer Affairs*. Dr. Herrmann has contributed many articles to professional journals on subjects such as the development of the consumer movement, consumer behavior of young adults, consumer bankruptcy, and food consumption.

THE AMERICAN CONSUMER
Issues and Decisions

Herbert M. Jelley
Robert O. Herrmann

THE AMERICAN CONSUMER
Issues and Decisions

Second Edition

Gregg Division
McGraw-Hill Book Company
New York St. Louis Dallas San Francisco Auckland Bogotá Düsseldorf
Johannesburg London Madrid Mexico Montreal New Delhi Panama Paris
São Paulo Singapore Sydney Tokyo Toronto

EVERMAN
PUBLIC LIBRARY
641

Library of Congress Cataloging in Publication Data

Jelley, Herbert M
  The American consumer.

  SUMMARY: A consumer education textbook emphasizing
controversial consumer issues and the daily problems
of today's consumers.
  1. Consumer education—United States. [1. Consumer
education] I. Herrmann, Robert O., joint author. II. Title.
TX335.J44 1978   640.73   77-25422
ISBN 0-07-032341-0

The American Consumer: Issues and Decisions, Second Edition

Copyright © 1978, 1973 by McGraw-Hill, Inc. All rights reserved. Printed in the United States
of America. No part of this publication may be reproduced, stored in a retrieval system, or
transmitted, in any form or by any means, electronic, mechanical, photocopying, recording, or
otherwise, without the prior written permission of the publisher.

  3 4 5 6 7 8 9 0 V H V H   8 5 4 3 2 1 0

The editors for this book were Phyllis D. Lemkowitz and Alice V. Manning, the
designer was Emily Harste, the cover designer was Eileen Thaxton, the art
supervisor was George T. Resch, and the production supervisors were S. Steven
Canaris and May Konopka. It was set in Caledonia by Waldman Graphics, Inc.
Printed and bound by Von Hoffman Press, Inc.

Contents

Preface

Consumer protection has never had as much publicity and attention as it has in the past few years. But the more legislation is enacted in this area, the more it becomes clear that the most effective consumer protection law is still the original one the ancient Romans gave us: *Caveat emptor . . . Let the buyer beware. The American Consumer: Issues and Decisions, Second Edition,* is designed to help young adults acquire the skills they need to obey that law intelligently and become successful, discerning consumers.

We've tried to make the text interesting to young adults by dealing with topics that they may be thinking about already, such as buying a car or renting an apartment. Important concepts are illustrated with examples that are almost certain to be within their experience, such as the purchase of records and tapes. The result is a text students can understand and enjoy.

INSTRUCTIONAL CONTENT

Recent Changes in the Field

- New laws and revamped government regulatory agencies
- Innovations in the market place, and in business practices
- New attitudes toward energy and conservation
- The effects of inflation and rising taxes
- The ongoing movement toward metrication
- The changes brought about by new technology
- New knowledge in the social sciences, home economics, consumer behavior, and marketing

Comprehensive Coverage

The text covers all the most important topics in consumer education:

- Understanding the role of consumers, business, and government in our economic system
- Managing personal resources—money, credit, time, and talents
- Improving buying skills—judging product quality and identifying the product which relates best to one's needs and resources
- Evaluating consumer information from different sources and using it in making decisions

- Identifying and understanding one's values and developing personal goals as a consumer
- Analyzing consumer issues—recognizing problems which confront us as consumers and evaluating alternative solutions

TEACHING AND LEARNING AIDS

The teaching and learning aids provided with *The American Consumer: Issues and Decisions, Second Edition,* emphasizes the practical solution of real-life consumer problems.

End-of-chapter Activities

"Checking Your Reading" is a series of questions designed to check basic comprehension of the material in each chapter. And those questions are followed by "Consumer Problems and Projects," a series of practical, problem-solving activities designed to give students the opportunity to apply what they've read.

Student Activity Guide

The *Student Activity Guide for The American Consumer: Issues and Decisions, Second Edition,* supplements the text in two important ways. First, it gives students an opportunity to review new concepts and terms from their reading of the text. Second, it maintains the emphasis on practical problem solving with interesting and useful projects for students on all levels.

Teacher's Resource Manual

The *Teacher's Resource Manual* contains answers to all questions in the text and the *Student Activity Guide* and offers suggestions for activities, projects, demonstrations, and discussions. In addition, it includes transparency masters and achievement tests, ready to duplicate and use.

ACKNOWLEDGMENTS

Many teachers have shared their time and knowledge with us, and their suggestions made an important contribution in shaping this new edition.

Experts in business and government contributed their expertise by checking on the text's accuracy and by making guarantees and other documents available.

The assistance from all these people was extremely helpful, and we acknowledge it with thanks.

Herbert M. Jelley
Robert O. Herrmann

PART ONE
Planning and Decision Making

1

Consumers in the American Economy

How would you spend a half million dollars? Believe it or not, *you* are going to have to decide. You can expect to earn and spend this much, or more, over a working lifetime. You are not going to get your half million right away, of course. You are going to have to earn it—a little at a time. Earning a half million dollars means a lot of work. But spending it wisely means a lot of work and a lot of choices too.

How well you make your choices will have a good deal to do with how satisfying your life is. What do you want out of life? An education that leads to a good job? A car? Travel? A happy and secure family life? Most of these things are within reach for all of us, but only if we manage our money well and spend it carefully.

BEING A CONSUMER MEANS CHOOSING

Few of us ever have enough money to do all the things we would like or buy all the things we would like to have. The list of things we want seems almost endless, but the money we have to spend is limited. Clearly, we have to make some choices.

As consumers we have to make three important kinds of choices. To be good consumers, and successful ones, we have to make all three kinds of choices well. First, we have to make choices as money managers. We have to fit our spending to our incomes, and we have to decide how to direct our spending so that we get the things we want most. This may mean, for example, a decision to spend less on records and magazines so we can save money for a class ring or the class trip.

The second kind of choice which we must make as consumers is buying decisions. We have to consider which product meets our needs best and offers best value for the money. We make buying decisions every day. We choose between a hamburger and a cheeseburger at McDonald's. We choose between all cotton and cotton-polyester blend jeans. We decide between the gas station on the corner and the one across the street. To make these kinds of buying decisions well, we have to know what we really need. We also have to know the different kinds of products available and how they perform.

The third kind of choices we must make is less familiar. But these

As consumers, we have to decide how much we can afford to spend on a car, determine which model is the best buy for our money, and consider how our choice relates to pollution, energy shortages, and other public problems. *(Andrew Sacks, Editorial Photocolor Archives)*

choices are important too. They are choices about how our economic system should work and how it should serve customers. To make these choices well, we have to be informed citizens who can voice our opinions on the economic issues that affect us as consumers, workers, and taxpayers. We also have to be prepared to let our elected representatives and government officials know how we feel about these issues. Should autos be made safer even if this raises prices? Should ads for candy be banned on television programs for children? Should the government cut the number of regulations controlling business in hopes of encouraging competition? Should the government put extra taxes on large cars to encourage people to buy smaller cars and conserve on gasoline? These are important issues and ones that affect us all.

This book was written to help you make all three kinds of consumer choices better—choices as a money manager, as a buyer, and as a citizen. Let's begin our study of the roles of consumers by looking at their place in our economic system and how their decisions affect it.

OUR ECONOMIC SYSTEM

We, as consumers, are an important part of the American economic system. It is our choices which set the rest of the system in motion. Our choices provide new sales opportunities for business. Business, in turn, looks for new workers and money to build new factories to produce the things consumers want.

Markets—Where Buyers and Sellers Meet

Whenever buyers and sellers get together to make agreements about buying and selling, economists call this a *market*. Our economic system is made up of a series of markets in which consumers, business, workers, and investors buy and sell. As consumers we get together with business so that we can buy the things we need; this is the *market for consumer goods and services*. Business, in turn, looks for workers to help produce these things. When business and workers get together to make agreements about jobs and wages, we call this the *labor market*. Business also needs money to finance new equipment and new factories. When it gets together with people who have money to invest, we call this the *capital market*.

All these markets are interrelated. Whatever happens in one will affect the others. If sales to consumers are poor, business may lay off workers. When workers' earnings are cut, they will have less money to spend and they, in turn, will buy fewer consumer goods. If sales begin to decline, business may decide not to build the new factories it had planned and will borrow less from investors.

These four key groups make up our economic system: consumers, businesses, workers, and investors. We have seen that they get together to form the three different kinds of markets: the market for consumer goods and services, the labor market, and the capital market. Our economic system also includes the government. The government has four important functions which affect how our economic system works:

- It sets rules and enforces them to keep the dealings in different markets fair and honest and to maintain competition.
- It adjusts taxes and government spending to help keep economic activity and employment at a high level.
- It provides services which are most conveniently financed by tax dollars or run by government.
- It provides welfare payments to people who need help including the aged, the unemployed, and others who are unable to work.

Our decisions as consumers have an important effect on our economic system. Our decisions as buyers, that is, decisions about what we will buy, affect the market for consumer goods and services. Our decisions as money managers about whether to spend or save and whether or not to borrow affect the capital market. Our decisions as money managers about how much income we need affects the labor market. Our desire for income brings us into the labor market. The desire for more income may lead us to consider the idea of a second job or to look for a better-paying job. Our decisions as citizens help decide how government will regulate the markets which make up our economic system. Our decisions as citizens affect how government goes about fighting unemployment and keeping business activity at a high level. Our decisions as citizens also affect how much and what kinds of services the government provides. Clearly, our decisions as consumers reach into every part of our economic system.

Profits—a Signal

When buyers and sellers get together in a market, they all are hoping for personal financial gain. Everyone is hoping to get the most they can for what they have to sell and to pay as little as possible for what they want to buy.

When they meet in a market, both buyers and sellers have in mind the amounts they are willing to buy or sell at a particular price. Economists call the amounts sellers are willing to sell at different price levels *supply*. They call amounts buyers are willing to buy at different price levels *demand*.

After offers and counteroffers, buyers and sellers arrive at a price at which the supply available equals the amount demanded. This price is called the *market price*. It is the price at which the amount sellers are willing to sell just equals the amount buyers are willing to buy.

Changes in prices keep supply and demand in balance. For example, if the supply available at a particular price is too large, the price must fall before it can be sold. The lower price brings new buyers into the market. This is why auto dealers lower prices at the end of an automobile model year. If there are leftover stocks of cars, lower prices help attract buyers. Car dealers know this and reduce prices just enough to attract buyers for the cars they have left. The lower price brings demand into line with the available supply of cars.

Changes in price (sale prices) keep supply (overstock of sweaters at the end of the season) and demand (buyers) in balance. *(Alex Webb, Magnum Photos)*

Sometimes consumers want to buy more than is immediately available. When this happens, prices rise. This is what happens when a new clothing style becomes especially popular. Manufacturers who have made the item are able to get top prices for what they have made. When prices more than cover costs, the extra income above costs is *profit*. If the profits are sizable and opportunities for more sales look good, other manufacturers will begin to make the item too.

Profits are the signal that brings new sellers into the market. Profits are not the result of dishonesty or sharp dealing, except in a few special cases. Instead, they are the way the market signals that more sellers are needed to provide the amounts that consumers want to buy.

We can see that the action of the market will determine how much of a particular product is made. If profits are being made, more will be produced. If sellers have losses, less will be made. All the different markets which make up our economic system work in much the same way. The way they work determines the answers to three important questions:

- What goods and services will be produced and what quantities of each will be made?
- Who will make these goods and provide these services?
- How will earnings, interest payments, and profits be distributed so that people will be able to buy the things which have been produced?

In this country these questions are decided chiefly by the working of different markets. Because our economy is guided mostly by what happens in different markets, it sometimes is called a *market economy*.

We can contrast the way our economic system works with what happens in countries in which the government plays a major role in running the economic system. In these countries, the plans of the government, rather than the operation of markets, guide the economic system. This type of economic system sometimes is called a *planned economy*.

We should be careful not to confuse the type of economic system which a country has with its political system. Some countries which have a market economy are controlled politically by a dictator. Other countries have planned economies and are democratic, such as Sweden and several other Western European countries. Communist countries also have planned economies but are run by one-party political systems.

Free Enterprise and Competition

An important value which guides our economic system is the idea of *free enterprise*. We call it a value because it is something we feel is good and desirable. The idea of free enterprise emphasizes the importance of freedom for business, workers, and consumers to make their economic decisions without interference. Free enterprise means freedom for business people to make new types of products, to compete with other businesses, and to seek profits. It also means freedom for workers to look for the best job and highest pay they can find. For consumers it means the freedom to look for the product which suits them best.

The reason many people favor free enterprise is because they believe it encourages competition. They believe our economic system works best when there is competition in the markets which make it up. With free enterprise, businesses can move into new markets when profits signal the need to increase the supply. The increased supply they provide will help to hold prices down.

Because competition is so important for keeping our economic system working well, we need to know how to protect it and promote it. Experience shows that competition works best when there are a number of firms all competing vigorously to make sales. If there is only one firm or only a few in a market, they can raise prices or reduce supplies to suit themselves. Let's look at an example of how this might work in your own school. Suppose you had control of all the tickets for the biggest football game of the season. (Economists would say you had a *monopoly*.) You could choose to set a price for the tickets that would just cover the costs of the game—lights, ticket takers, referees, and other expenses. You might, however, be tempted to charge more, and anyone who wanted a ticket would have to pay your price.

Now suppose that instead of your having a monopoly, the tickets were divided evenly among 20 students. If some students tried to charge too much, others could take away their customers by charging less. The ticket sellers might try to agree on a price they all would charge. This probably would not work for long. Some sellers would be tempted to cut prices to make more sales, and then others would do the same. This example shows how having a large number of sellers in a market encourages competition.

If consumers are well informed about the products they want to buy, this also encourages competition. When consumers know how to judge different brands, they are able to find the best value for their money. Sellers who offer the best values gain customers, while the others lose. When some sellers begin to lose customers, the only thing they can do to win them back is to improve their product or lower their prices. But when consumers cannot figure out which brands are the best buy, there is no real competition among sellers. Consumers are not able to shift to the brands which offer better value, and there is no reason for any seller to try to improve their product quality.

To keep competition working well, dealings in the marketplace also must be fair and honest. Otherwise, dishonest business people may trick consumers into buying with false or exaggerated claims. When this happens, consumers end up paying too much for what they get. Dishonest businesses lure customers away from the others with lies instead of with better products.

Keeping Competition Working

Sometimes it is necessary for the government to step in to protect competition and make certain that it is working well.

If a market has come under the control of one or only a few sellers, government action may be necessary. Our federal government has power to bring action to break up monopoly control of a market. It also has power to act if there is danger that a market is coming under the control of one or only a few sellers. These powers are called *antitrust powers*. They get this name from the term *trust*, used to describe a group of companies under the control of a single management which decides their activities, prices, and production. This kind of control of an industry or a group of companies is designed to reduce competition. When the government takes action against trusts or agreements between companies to set the prices they all charge, this is called *antitrust action*.

The government also takes action to fight dishonesty in the marketplace because it injures consumers and honest business people and interferes with competition. Attempts to deliberately deceive buyers with untrue product claims, or *frauds*, are a particular concern. In the past, government officials were not so concerned about exaggerated claims. Most of their concern was focused on outright frauds. In recent years exaggerated claims have gotten more attention and some advertisers have been asked to provide proof of their claims.

The government also has taken action to protect competition by helping consumers to get more product information. In recent years there have been a number of new laws and regulations designed to make certain that important information is available to consumers. Examples include:

- *Truth-in-lending.* A requirement that interest rates for loans be stated in a standard way so that different lenders' interest charges can be compared more easily.
- *Care Labeling of clothing.* A requirement that clothing items carry a permanent label indicating how they should be cleaned.
- *Energy Efficiency labeling.* A requirement that autos and major appliances carry labels with information on their energy use so that consumers can compare their operating costs more easily.

Even with more information, consumers cannot always determine a product's quality or whether it is safe. For this reason the government sets standards for a number of products. *Standards* are rules or models against which something—for example, a product's characteristics—can be judged. Government standards affect the way products are made, how they perform, how they are sold, and how they are used. The types of standards include:

- Rules about how products are made—for example, rules setting sanitary procedures which must be followed in food plants.
- Rules about how a product performs—for example, rules for determining whether a medicine is safe and effective, and rules about what information must be provided on a food package.
- Rules about selling products—for example, rules describing the kinds of advertising claims which will be considered deceptive.
- Rules about how a product can be used—for example, rules about the testing and licensing of automobile drivers.

We have described a number of approaches the government uses in protecting competition:

- Antitrust action
- Controlling frauds
- Ensuring product information is available
- Setting product standards

There is still another approach the government uses. This is to help consumers get assistance, or *redress*, when they have problems. It does this in several ways. One way is to help inform consumers of their rights in dealing with businesses. The government may also receive consumers' complaints and work with business and consumers to find solutions to them. In addition, it operates the court system, in which consumers can take legal action when they have been deceived, when they have been injured by a product, or when a seller has not lived up to the terms of a contract.

CONSUMERS' PROBLEMS TODAY

Earlier we looked at the three kinds of decisions consumers must make: decisions as buyers, as money managers, and as citizens. These decisions are often difficult, and many problems stand in the way of consumers who want to decide wisely. Let's look more closely at some of the problems consumers face in making good decisions.

Consumers' Problems as Buyers

Consumers of today buy a tremendous variety of things: records, hi-fi equipment, cars, sports gear, food, clothing, airline tickets, housing, and electricity. Many of these products are complicated. For most, several different brands or choices are available. It is difficult for consumers to know how to recognize quality and to know which brands offer the best value for the money. When consumers look for solid facts to help them in their decisions, they are hard to find. Labels and packages provide some facts, but it still is difficult to compare different brands. Ads are not much help. Instead of providing facts, most ads concentrate on surrounding the product with glamor and excitement.

When we decide to buy, our purchases are often made in large, impersonal stores. Salesclerks seldom are able to offer much information or advice. We must make our choices pretty much on our own. And after we have made our choice, we may be disappointed. Some products have defects; the socks we have bought may unravel the first time we wear them. Some products may not live up to the hopes we have built up after listening to the ads; the new "miracle" cream really does not seem to help our skin problems very much.

We then are faced with the problem of what to do. Should we try to return the product and ask for our money back? Whom should we talk to? The people at the store? The manufacturer? Is it worth the trouble? What will they say? Ads give a lot of advice about what and where to buy, but who tells you what to do when you are not satisfied?

Consumers' Problems as Money Managers

It never has been easy to manage money, and it seems harder today than ever. Changing economic conditions make it difficult to guess what our financial situation will be in a few weeks or months.

Workers face uncertainty about jobs and incomes. Will there be layoffs? Or will some overtime work be available? What will happen to wages? These questions make income uncertain and make savings and a flexible budget important. But what are the best ways to save and to plan a budget?

Inflation and the rising cost of living create other uncertainties. Will the government be able to slow the rate of price increases? Will our incomes keep up with price increases? And what can we do to protect ourselves from inflation?

The widespread availability of credit to consumers creates other problems. How much can we afford to buy on credit? What amount of payments can we handle? Is it better to postpone some purchases in order to save on interest charges? Many consumers learn from bitter experience that it is not always easy to manage credit well.

Consumers' Problems as Citizens

We have mentioned some of the kinds of decisions consumers are called on to make as citizens. These are decisions about how our economic system should work and how it should serve us as consumers. These decisions often are difficult to make. Often the problems are complicated ones. Facts about the problem are hard to get. It often is difficult to determine whether the problem really is serious enough to merit action. Even after we decide that action is needed, choosing the best solution is difficult. What are the possible solutions? Just how will they work? How much will they cost? How do the costs involved in a particular solution compare to the benefits?

Checking Your Reading

1. What are the three kinds of choices consumers must make?
2. What is a market?
3. What are the three kinds of markets in our economic system?
4. What are the four functions of the government which affect our economic system?
5. Define "supply" and "demand."
6. How is the market price determined?
7. Why do we say that profits are a signal?
8. What are the three economic questions which are decided, in our country, by the working of markets?
9. What is the difference between a market economy and a planned economy?

10. Why do most Americans favor the idea of free enterprise?
11. Why does competition work better when consumers are well-informed?
12. What do we mean when we say the government has antitrust powers?
13. What is fraud?
14. What are standards? Give an example of a standard affecting the way a product is made.
15. What problems do consumers face as buyers? As money managers? As citizens?

Consumer Problems and Projects

1. Could our economic system exist without consumers? Why?
2. What decisions have you made recently? (a) What decisions did you make today as a buyer? (b) What decisions have you made recently as a money manager? (c) What decisions have you made recently as a citizen? For example, have you made decisions about using public services or taken a stand on the need for government action? Have you been satisfied with the results of your decisions? How do you think you could have improved them?
3. What actions has the government taken recently which affect the way the marketplace operates? Check newspapers and magazines and try to find an example of (a) an antitrust action or action to protect competition, (b) an action to provide consumers more information, (c) an action to control fraud and deception, and (d) establishment of new standards. Find out what the government did in each case and the reason for the action.
4. What problems have you had recently as a buyer? For example, what problems have you had (a) getting information to help you choose between different brands, (b) with a product which did not work or was unsafe, or (c) returning products which were unsatisfactory? Do you think your problems are typical of problems other consumers have?
5. Are consumers' problems today different from the problems of consumers in 1900? How? Are they similar in any ways?
6. Give as many arguments for consumer education as you can.

2

Values and Decisions

One of the first things we discover as consumers is that our ability to get the things we want is limited. The money we have to spend cannot be stretched far enough to get us everything we would like to have. Our money is limited, but our wants often seem unlimited. Clearly, some choices are necessary. The whole process of choosing among the different ways we could spend our money is an important part of being a wise consumer. It is not enough to learn how to look for bargains and recognize quality. It is also important to know exactly what we want and what our goals are.

Most of the chapters in this book were written to help you improve your skill in judging products and services and managing your money. This chapter is somewhat different. It will try to help you identify the goals which are most important to you. It then will look at ways to improve the decisions which will help you reach these goals.

How Our Decisions Are Shaped

In this chapter we will look first at some of the things which shape our decisions. These include:

- Our *needs*, which, if they are not met, push us into action to find a solution.
- Our *values*, or those things which we think are most important, which guide us in making decisions.
- Our *resources*, including both our financial resources and our abilities, which can limit our decisions.

Unmet Needs Push Us into Action

Our *needs*, or basic requirements, are much the same regardless of where we live or the color of our skin. Several different lists of needs have been developed. One of the most widely used lists is one by psychologist Abraham Maslow. The list that follows is based on Maslow's.

1. *Biological Needs*—satisfaction of our need for food, drink, activity, and rest.
2. *Security Needs*—safety from physical harm, freedom from worry, and economic security.
3. *Affection Needs*—the giving and receiving of love, acceptance by others, a feeling of belonging.
4. *Self-esteem Needs*—feelings of self-worth growing out of confidence in our abilities and the feeling that we are accepted by others.
5. *Self-realization Needs*—creative self-expression through personal and social achievements, satisfying our curiosity, and understanding the world and our own surroundings.

These needs are basic to our well-being. If they are not at least partly met, we will feel unsatisfied. This feeling, when it becomes strong enough, will push us into action. We begin to look for ways to meet our unsatisfied needs.

Maslow's list of needs has been called a "hierarchy of needs" because the needs at the top are most pressing. Until the basic needs at the top of the list are at least partly satisfied, we have little time or energy for trying to satisfy unmet needs which are lower on the list. If we are always hungry and never can get enough food, we are not likely to put much importance on success in sports or schoolwork. Once the needs at the top of the list are met, we will be able to give our attention to new achievements in school, sports, hobbies, and recreational activities.

Values Guide Us Toward Decisions

Although all of us have the same kinds of needs, we put different priority on filling these needs. We all know people who have to eat the minute they feel hungry because food is very important to them. And we all know others who will put off eating for hours if they find something more interesting to do. This difference is a result of a basic difference in their *values*—the things they think are important, good, or desirable. This example suggests one of the ways our values affect our decisions. Values affect how quickly we recognize that one of our needs is unmet and how much priority we put on satisfying it.

The Different Kinds of Values. People use the word "values" in several different ways. Understanding some of the different ways the word is used will help us to understand just what it means.

We have both general values and more specific ones. General values deal with the way we live our lives, while the specific values include our attitudes toward particular things, such as the products we buy. Our general values can be divided into two different types:

- *Goals.* Our ideas about desirable objectives; some examples are leading an exciting life, financial security, freedom, and happiness.
- *Instrumental Values.* Our ideas and views on behavior and on how we should conduct our lives; some examples are hard work, self-control, thrift, accepting responsibility, honesty, and self-reliance.

Both types of general values guide us in our decisions about our daily lives. Our goals remind us where we are heading; they serve as objectives. Our instrumental values guide us in picking the best ways to get to our goals.

Our *specific values* are strongly held attitudes about more ordinary matters. They include our ideas about what characteristics are important in a friend and our ideas about the characteristics that are important in a car. Our specific values include strongly held attitudes about the things we buy and use as consumers. Our specific values may, for example, include some ideas about the characteristics we consider desirable in clothing. We can see how these values come into play when we look at what happened to Jane Fong. Jane puts a good deal of importance on attractive styling and color in clothing. Price and durability are less important to her. When Jane was shopping for a new

Good health is a goal or objective for many people; exercising could be an instrumental value, or a means of attaining the goal. *(Jim Anderson, Woodfin Camp Associates)*

coat, she found a good-looking one in her favorite shade of blue. The coat had only one drawback. The price was $20 more than the limit she had set for herself. On the basis of what you know about her values, what do you think Jane decided?

Values—Our Own and Others. We can begin to get some idea about people's values when we ask them about the goals they think are important or desirable. Suppose, for example, that we asked a group of high school students to list what goals were most important for them. Some might emphasize the importance of financial success. Others might talk of marriage and having their own family. Some probably would emphasize becoming financially independent of their parents. A few might talk about having new experiences and seeing the world. Because each of us has a unique background and set of experiences, we have different opinions about what goals are important. Five people were asked to make a list of their goals; these, shown on page

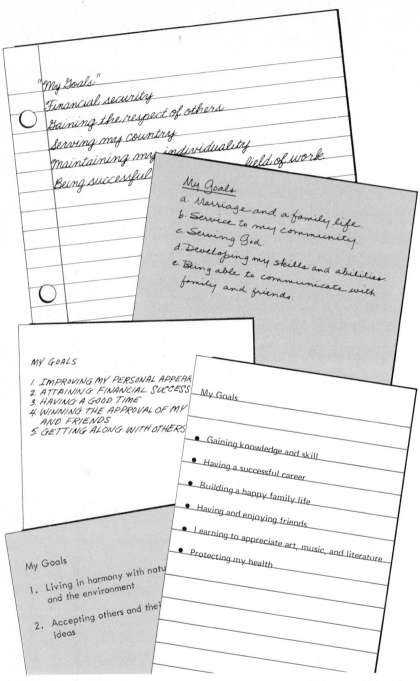

"My Goals"
Financial security
Gaining the respect of others
Serving my country
Maintaining my individuality
Being successful ... field of work

My Goals
a. Marriage and a family life.
b. Service to my community.
c. Serving God.
d. Developing my skills and abilities.
e. Being able to communicate with family and friends.

MY GOALS

1. IMPROVING MY PERSONAL APPEAR...
2. ATTAINING FINANCIAL SUCCESS
3. HAVING A GOOD TIME
4. WINNING THE APPROVAL OF MY ... AND FRIENDS
5. GETTING ALONG WITH OTHERS

My Goals

- Gaining knowledge and skill
- Having a successful career
- Building a happy family life
- Having and enjoying friends
- Learning to appreciate art, music, and literature
- Protecting my health

My Goals

1. Living in harmony with natu... and the environment

2. Accepting others and thei... ideas

If you ask several people to list their goals, the lists you get will be very different from one another because not all people value the same things.

18, reflect their different perspectives. Which list is most like your own? How would you change it to make it represent your own ideas?

We can see that many different lists of goals are possible. Some are long and detailed. Others are short and more general. Since goals are abstract ideas which cannot be seen or observed directly, we have little basis for saying how long or short anyone's list should be.

Where do our values come from? How do we learn them? When we are young, our parents are the people with whom we have the most contact and whom we admire most. We learn our values from them, along with most of our other ideas. As we grow older and enter school, friends, teachers, and religious leaders also begin to influence our thinking. As time goes on, we begin to develop ideas based on our own experiences. We may also be influenced by the media, by the books we read, and by things we see on television.

Conflicts between Values. Sometimes we may find conflicts between our values. Take Jill Johnson's problem, for example. Jill is interested in buying a used car. She feels that both a low price and reliable dealer service are important. These are specific values she rates highest. After checking local dealers, Jill has found that those with the lowest prices do not have reputations for giving reliable service. Clearly she cannot get both the most reliable service and the lowest possible price. Jill is going to have to try to find some balance between these two values which suits her.

Sometimes, however, a decision will satisfy several values. This is what Julie and Don Juarez found when they started thinking about buying a house. Julie and Don put high importance on three goals: a happy family life, financial security, and safe and comfortable housing. They found a chance to buy a duplex in a nice neighborhood, which will help them in moving toward all three goals. The building is a good investment opportunity; one unit will provide rental income while the Juarezes live in the other. The Juarezes like the neighborhood and feel the house will provide a comfortable home for them and their children.

Our Resources Limit Our Range of Choices

The resources which we have available to help us in reaching our goals are limited. Because they are limited, they limit the range of our decisions. This is what Tim Swenson found when he starting thinking about buying a car. Tim had $1000 saved and decided he could afford to borrow another $1500. This limit on his money resources meant, Tim knew, that he had to limit his choices to used cars with $2500 as his top limit. After thinking it over, Tim decided that he really did not know very much about car repairs and that he would be better-off buying a higher-priced car in good condition rather than a lower-priced one which needed work. Tim's decision was limited both by his financial resources and by his lack of skill at car repairs.

This example suggests the two broad categories of resources:

- *Physical Resources* (or physical capital). These include most things we can touch or measure easily. Examples are money, consumer goods such as clothing and cars, houses, factories, and tools. We also can include here our ability to get credit.
- *Human Resources* (or human capital). These include the things we know and can do. Examples are the ability to speak Spanish and the ability to repair cars or make clothes. Good health and the time and energy to do things are also part of our human resources.

Because of the way our resources limit our decisions, we all need to know what resources we have available for use. Often we think only about our physical resources. This is because we can see them and think about them frequently. Since we cannot see our human resources, we often forget them.

Using Physical Resources. The source we are likely to think of first is our *income*, the money we get from a job or perhaps from an allowance. For most of us, the major part of our income comes from our earnings. Some of us also receive investment income from our *capital*, or money accumulated in savings accounts and stock holdings. Some of us depend, at least in part, on social security, welfare benefits, and disability payments distributed by government agencies. These payments are sometimes referred to as *transfer payments*, since they are paid on the basis of need rather than for work or services.

Another important physical resource that we can use in reaching our consumer goals is *credit*, the ability to borrow against our future income. By using credit, we are able to obtain goods and services and pay for them as we use them. The ability to borrow against future income helps us acquire many things that make life more pleasant— houses, cars, appliances, and furniture. Although credit is an important resource and a useful one, like most tools it can be dangerous when it is misused or handled carelessly.

This person's physical resources include the yarn, the loom, and the space for all her weaving equipment. Money or available credit to buy the yarn and loom is also considered a physical resource. The human resources are the time, energy, and skill used to weave a scarf. *(Susan Berkowitz)*

Our *Savings*—money deposited in a savings bank where it draws interest—can also be an important resource. Savings can provide a fund to meet the expense of emergencies such as sickness, or to make possible a more specific goal, such as the purchase of a car.

The things we already have, our possessions, are also important physical resources. If they were well chosen, they provide us with continuing service or satisfaction. Possessions is a broad category and includes household equipment such as furniture and appliances, other durable goods such as automobiles, the house we buy, hobby equipment, and the tools needed for making automobile and household repairs.

Another useful physical resource, one that we sometimes forget, is *community facilities*. The services and facilities provided by a community play an important role in helping the members of the community reach their goals. Schools play a key role in helping families reach educational goals. Libraries provide assistance not only toward educational goals but also toward recreational and occupational goals. Swimming pools, parks, and recreation facilities make it easier for community residents to realize their recreational goals. Other services are important too. Police and fire departments contribute to security goals. What other facilities and services do you have in your community that you would classify as physical resources?

Using Human Resources. Our human resources include all the things we know and can do, that is, our *knowledge* and *abilities*. Our skills at painting a bedroom, changing a tire, and buying a sweater all help us make the best life for ourselves that we can. Skills and knowledge that help us get a job and advance in it are also important resources. These resources and our use of them provide us with income.

Even if we have knowledge and abilities, we need *time* and *energy* to use them. For this reason, time and energy have to be included in the list of human resources. Like our other resources, time and energy are limited too. Time and energy spent on the school yearbook or cheering squad are not available for an after-school job.

Human resources have not always been recognized as important assets. Years ago young people were usually advised to be thrifty and save their money for a "rainy day." This advice was given because savings were regarded as a vital resource and source of security. Nowadays young people are more likely to be advised to develop their job skills and abilities to the fullest extent possible.

Substituting One Resource for Another. Although all the resources that we have are limited in supply, they have another characteristic: to a certain extent one resource can be substituted for another. When you are hired as a baby-sitter, it may seem that all you are doing is taking care of children. In another sense, however, what you are doing is giving up one of your resources (your time) to get another (money). By giving up some of your spare time, you are able to increase the amount of money you have. The parent who hires you is also making a substitution: he or she is giving up money to gain time.

MAKING DECISIONS

Even after we have all our resources clearly in mind, we still need to decide how to use them to achieve our goals. Making decisions always has been difficult and probably is more difficult today than it used to be. The whole range of products and services from which we can choose is wider today, and products and services are more complicated. Another factor that makes the decision process more complex is our improved understanding of the possible results of our choices. As scientific knowledge increases, we learn more about what the results of our choices are likely to be and have to bear them in mind as we choose. When little was known about the effect of diet on health, people did not need to concern themselves about vitamins and calories. Nowadays we must take good nutrition into account along with our food preferences when we decide what to eat.

The Decision-Making Process

The steps in making a decision are much the same regardless of whether the decision is a big one or a small one. The process of purchasing a new notebook includes the same steps involved in purchasing a car. The amount of time and effort devoted to the process of purchasing a car may be greater, but the process itself is much the same. The steps in this process include identifying our goal, identifying the alternatives, gathering information, evaluating the alternatives, and making a choice.

Let's use an example to help us trace the steps in a typical decision. Jim Taylor has just gotten a Saturday morning job in a local clothing store. He knows from experience that he may have trouble waking up early enough to get to work on time. Jim wants very much to be successful in his new job because he hopes to go into the clothing business after he graduates from high school. He feels strongly that promptness and dependability will be important in doing the job well. We can see how Jim's values are pushing him into action on the problem. He wants to be successful in the job (a goal) and wants to be certain he'll wake up so that he can get to work on time (a related goal). He feels promptness and dependability (instrumental values) are important in being successful. Because of his values, he feels the problem is an urgent one.

Identifying the Goal. In solving his problem, Jim will first have to get his goal clearly in mind. Consumers often think only about one particular solution to their problem when, in fact, there are several. After Jim thinks about the problem, he realizes that what he needs is not a particular product, such as an alarm clock. What he needs is the service which an alarm clock can provide—waking him up on time.

Identifying the Alternatives.   When we set out to identify possible solutions, most of us already have some information with which to begin. Both our previous experiences and what we have learned from others help us identify alternatives. Because of what he already knows, Jim quickly thinks of several alternatives. He knows that electric alarm clocks and clock radios both would provide the service of waking him up. He even thinks of asking his friend Jack to call him, but puts this idea aside. He knows Jack has even more trouble waking up in the morning than he does.

Gathering Information.   Once Jim has some alternatives in mind that seem workable, he is ready to begin gathering information. While gathering information, Jim finds another alternative he had forgotten, key-wound alarm clocks. He also discovers that the least expensive clock radios are $25 or more. He decides this is more than he wants to pay and gives up the idea of buying a clock radio.

The information which Jim gathers is of two kinds. Some of the information he collects concerns the *product characteristics* which are important in evaluating alarm clocks. Jim decides that there are several characteristics which should be considered in evaluating alarm clocks.

- *Convenience Features.*   Lighted dial, repeat alarm
- *Durability.*   Sturdy construction, warranty terms
- *Performance.*   Accuracy, reliability
- *Price.* Low

Jim also learns that the operating cost of electric clocks is small; he decides this characteristic is not very important in his choice. He also learns that while there could be electric shock hazards, safety is not a problem in the available models.

The other portion of the information Jim collects concerns the *rating* of each available model on the characteristics he has found are important. This rating is a measure of how much or how little of a product characteristic a model has. Jim finds it easy to get information on the convenience features available and on guarantees and prices. The best measure of reliability, Jim decides, is the power source used. He feels an electric alarm clock would keep ringing until he woke up. A hand-wound alarm might run down. Jim finds that he cannot locate

The decision whether or not to go to college requires careful consideration and more thought than some other decisions. The decision-making process is much the same, however. The process includes identifying the goal, identifying the alternatives, gathering information, evaluating the alternatives, and making the decision. *(Ginger Chih)*

any information on durability. All the models look sturdy, but no specific information on this seems to be available. Jim also would like to have some information on how accurately the different models keep time, but he cannot find any. He decides, after some thought, that he can get along without this information. If the model he chooses is not accurate, he will get it repaired under the guarantee. Jim summarizes the information, shown in Table 2-1.

Evaluating the Alternatives.   As a next step in the decision process it is necessary to develop a ranking of the different choices which are available. Which seems best? Which is second?

TABLE 2-1
Survey of Available Alarm Clocks

Model	Convenience Features	Guarantee	Power Source	Price
Brand A Alarm clock	Lighted dial Repeat alarm	One year	Electricity	$ 9.95
Brand B Alarm clock	Plain dial Repeat alarm	One year	Electricity	$ 7.95
Brand C Alarm clock	Luminous dial	30-day	Hand-wound	$4.95

In developing our ranking we have to consider two things:

- How important are the different product characteristics relative to each other? How much weight should we give to an easy-to-read dial on an alarm clock compared with the price?
- How do different products or models rate on a particular characteristic? If Brand A alarm clock has a lighted dial, how easy-to-read is it compared with Brand B alarm clock?

Jim knows he would like to develop some kind of score or ranking for each model to help him make his decision. He decides he will weight a model's score on a particular characteristic by how important he feels the characteristic is. This, Jim knows, is the same system his teachers use when they calculate final grades. They give different weights to grades on quizzes, exams, and term papers and then add up the weighted scores to get a total score for each student.

Jim decides to begin by setting weights for the different characteristics according to how important he thinks they are. He decides that a lighted dial is not especially important to him; he seldom looks at the time in the dark. Jim feels the repeat alarm feature is more important; it will let him go back to sleep for a few minutes and then will set the alarm off again. After some thought, he decides the guarantee is fairly important. It will protect him if something goes wrong with the clock. It will also be useful if the clock does not keep accurate time. Jim decides the power source is even more important, since he thinks an electric alarm clock would be more reliable than a hand-wound alarm clock. As to price, Jim decides it has to get the highest weight, since he is just beginning on the job and has not been paid yet and is short of money. Jim decides to give each product characteristic a *weight* between 1 (the lowest) and 10 (the highest) depending on how much importance he thinks it should be given.

Characteristic	Weight
Easy-to-read dial	1
Repeat alarm	5
Guarantee	6
Power source	7
Price	10

We can see how the weights Jim chooses relate to his values. The heavy weights he has put on the power source, the guarantee, and the repeat alarm all grow out of his desire to be prompt and dependable (instrumental values) so that he can do well in his new job (a goal). From what we know about Jim, it is not clear whether the heavy weight he put on price shows a continuing concern with spending carefully (an instrumental value). It may be that the heavy weight he put on price is due mostly to the fact he is temporarily short of money. If this is the case, we would have to say that his concern with price is only temporary. It is not the continuing, strong concern that would lead us to label it a value.

As a next step in evaluating the alternatives, Jim decides to give each model a *rating* on each of the five product characteristics he has decided to take into account. He figures that he will give rating scores between 1 (the lowest) and 5 (the highest), depending on how well a model rates on a particular characteristic compared with the others. He begins by rating the three different models on how easy-to-read the dial is. He decides to give a score of 5 if they have lighted dial, a 3 if they have a luminous dial, and 1 if they have a plain dial. Jim then proceeds to give ratings on the other characteristics. When he finishes, his rating sheet looks like Table 2-2.

Finally, Jim is ready to put all his work together and calculate a total score for each model. To do this he multiples each model's rating on each characteristic by the weight of that characteristic. For example, Brand A had a rating of 5 on "easy-to-read dial" and this characteristic has a weight of 1. Multiplying them together Jim gets a weighted score of 5 for Brand A. Jim adds this score to Brand A's weighted scores on the other characteristic and gets a total score of 105. He then repeats the process for Brands B and C. His calculations and the total scores for each brand look like Table 2-3.

TABLE 2-2
Ratings on Product Characteristics

	Product Characteristics				
	Easy-to read Dial	Repeat Alarm	Guarantee	Power Source	Price
Brand A Alarm clock	5	5	5	5	1
Brand B Alarm clock	1	5	5	5	3
Brand C Alarm clock	3	1	1	1	5

We can see that Brand B has the highest total score. It looks like a good first choice, followed in order by Brands A and C. Jim reviews his evaluation and the consequences if he chooses B. Is Brand B really the best choice? It does not have a lighted dial. It does have a repeat alarm, and that still seems important. It has a one-year guarantee. It's run by electricity, so Jim can be sure it will keep on ringing without running down the way a hand-wound alarm would. And there's one very important final consideration: the price is fairly low. Brand B is the next-to-the-lowest-priced of the three alternatives. After this re-

TABLE 2-3
Calculation of Weighted Scores (Weight × Rating) on Product Characteristics and Total Scores

	Product Characteristics					
	Easy-to read Dial	Repeat Alarm	Guarantee	Power Source	Price	Total Score
Brand A Alarm clock	$1 \times 5 = 5$	$5 \times 5 = 25$	$6 \times 5 = 30$	$7 \times 5 = 35$	$10 \times 1 = 10$	105
Brand B Alarm clock	$1 \times 1 = 1$	$5 \times 5 = 25$	$6 \times 5 = 30$	$7 \times 5 = 35$	$10 \times 3 = 30$	121
Brand C Alarm clock	$1 \times 3 = 3$	$5 \times 1 = 5$	$6 \times 1 = 6$	$7 \times 1 = 7$	$10 \times 5 = 50$	71

view, Jim feels sure that he would be pleased with the results of choosing Brand B.

Making a Choice.   After Jim finishes reviewing the consequences of choosing Brand B, he is ready to make his choice. He decides to go ahead and buy a Brand B alarm clock.

Jim heads straight to the store to buy the clock after he has made his choice. He is aware that it is important to put a decision into action after he has made it. He knows that delays in carrying out a decision can result in lost opportunities or can worsen the original problem.

Another good idea when we have made a decision is to review how it turns out. This helps us to learn how to improve our decisions in the future. Jim reviews his decision the very first morning he uses his alarm clock. After waking up early, he looks at his alarm clock but cannot read it. He finally turns on the light to read it. "Should I have gotten the one with the lighted dial?" he wonders. "No, I'd rather have the $2 I saved by not getting it," he says to himself. He turns out the light and goes back to sleep.

Most of us do not make all the calculations that Jim did when we make a decision. Experts who have studied the way consumers make decisions feel that consumers' decision processes resemble the system Jim used. Consumers may not have specific weights and scores in mind, but they do use the same system. They do consider how important different characteristics are to them, and they do rate different models on the characteristics they are concerned about. They use these weights and scores, even if they do not have exact numbers in mind, to rank the alternatives they are considering.

Types of Decisions

Certain kinds of decisions, such as buying toothpaste, come up over and over again. Once we have found a brand that is satisfactory, we are likely to begin skipping over some steps in the decision process when we are choosing toothpaste. Instead of considering all the alternatives each time we buy, we remember that we have been satisfied with the brand we have been using and buy it again. If our experiences continue to be satisfactory, we are likely to put less and less effort into the decision and it becomes more and more a matter of habit.

We rely on habit in many kinds of decisions. In general, there is nothing wrong with this. Being guided by habit can save decision-making time and energy. There is no reason why we need to decide

We often rely on habits in making many kinds of decisions. The decision to buy one particular brand of shampoo that has satisfied you in the past is one such buying habit that can save you time and energy. The decision to buy it in one particular store can also be a habit. Review your buying habits from time to time to make sure they are still good ones. *(Jim Anderson, Woodfin Camp Associates)*

every morning whether or not we should put butter on our breakfast toast. We do need, however, to give some thought to our buying habits from time to time to be certain that they are good ones. We may, for example, have gotten into the habit of buying our toothpaste and toiletries at a particular store. We may not realize that the store down the street sells the same items at lower prices. When we rely on habit, we may save on decision-making effort but we may also be paying higher prices.

We have seen that we can be guided by habit in making decisions about certain kinds of problems. There are other kinds of problems that require more thought. These problems require careful deliberation from beginning to end. Decisions of this type usually involve some kind of new commitment and often are part of major changes in the way we live. They may be the result of a move to a new town, a pay raise, an accident, or the unexpected breakdown of a car. In all these cases, new action to meet the problem is essential, and this action requires careful consideration.

Consumers need to recognize that some decisions are more important than others, and they should give important problems the attention they deserve. Decisions such as the choice of a house or the decision to buy an expensive new car may prove to be major turning points in our life. Poor choices may have unpleasant consequences for years to come.

Checking Your Reading

1. Into what five categories can our basic needs be classified?
2. What do we mean when we say that this list of needs is a "hierarchy of needs"?
3. How do our values guide us in making decisions?
4. What are values? What are the different kinds of values?
5. Where do people learn the values they have?
6. What is meant by saying that for many people getting an education is an instrumental value?
7. Why do our goals sometimes conflict? Is this bad?
8. How do our resources affect the range of alternatives we can consider?
9. What are the two general categories of resources? What things are included in each category?
10. Why can home production of goods and services be an important contribution to family welfare?
11. What are the five main steps in making a decision?
12. How do our values affect the weight we give a particular product characteristic when we are evaluating a product?
13. In the decision-making example, which has more effect on Brand B's final rating: its rating on having an easy-to-read dial or its rating on price?
14. What are the kinds of decisions that we handle by habit?
15. Is it a mistake to be guided by habit in making a decision? Why?
16. How do decisions that require deliberation differ from decisions that we handle by habit?

EVERMAN PUBLIC LIBRARY

Consumer Problems and Projects

1. Collect newspaper and magazine advertisements that illustrate each of the needs in Maslow's hierarchy of needs.
2. Review the lists of different people's values on page 18, and make up a list that represents the goals you think are most important.
3. Suppose you won $50 in a contest. How would you spend it? What do you think this shows about your values?
4. What do you regard as your major goal right now?
    a. What resources will you need in order to reach this goal?
    b. What resources do you now have available?
    c. How do you plan to get the additional resources you will need? What substitutions can you make between the resources you have and those you need?
5. Several kinds of substitutions of one resource for another were mentioned in this chapter. In each of the following cases what resources are used (or given up)? Which ones are gained?
    a. Tom takes money out of his savings account and buys a motorcycle.
    b. Instead of buying a book on auto racing that she wants to read, Carol borrows it from the public library.
    c. Jack opens a charge account and buys a jacket on credit.
    d. Jane helps repaint a friend's bedroom, and in return the friend teaches her how to knit.
6. The kinds of decisions that we handle by habit and the decisions that require deliberation differ in several ways. What kinds of differences do you see between the following examples of a habitual decision and a decision that requires deliberation?
    Habitual: Dan has just bought another bottle of his favorite aftershave for $6.25. He expects it to last for several months.
    Deliberation: Barbara has just bought a new car and hopes she has made the right decision. She has agreed to pay for it in 36 monthly installments of $121 each.
7. Of all the clothing items you own, which one is your favorite? What does your choice show about the specific values you have concerning clothes?
8. What product characteristics do you use to judge a piece of clothing—for example, a sweater? Give a weight to each characteristic. How do these weights relate to your values?

3

Financial Planning and Budgeting

Whether we are rich or poor, we have something in common. We cannot buy everything we want. It may be hard for some of us to imagine certain wealthy people not being able to buy everything they want. But even these persons have limited money. As you learned in Chapter 2, economists call this problem *scarcity*. The problem is universal.

What does scarcity have to do with financial planning and budgeting? If we all have a scarcity of resources (money), then we want to make sure that we use the resources we have to buy the things that will bring us the most satisfaction possible. This requires planning.

WHAT DO YOU REALLY WANT?

Take a simple example. Let's say you really like to listen to music, and one thing you want very much is an 8-track tape player for your car. The tape player you want costs $108. Assume that you do not have $108, and no one will give you or lend you the money. You do, however, have a weekly income of about $18. Unfortunately, your weekly spending is also about $18. Let's say, though, that if you really wanted to, you could get along by spending just $12 a week. That means you could save $6 a week. In 18 weeks, by saving just $6 a week, you could accumulate $108.

If you decided to save $6 a week from your income, however, you would have to change your present spending habits. Is it worth it? Is having an 8-track tape player worth giving up some things each week so you can save $6? What would you be giving up?

BUDGETS SMOOTH THE WAY

Since we all have limited incomes, every time we spend part of that income we sacrifice something else. If you decide to buy an 8-track tape player, you have less money to spend for other things. If you decide to spend more money for movies, you have less for other things. The term used to describe this fact is *the opportunity cost of spending*. Every spending decision you make involves an opportunity cost. When a family decides to buy a microwave oven, they are giving up the opportunity of spending that money for something else. Why? Because we have limited incomes and we face a problem of scarcity.

If we do not have a plan for spending our money and then stick to that plan, we can very easily spend money on things that really do not give us the most satisfaction. That's the purpose of a budget—to help us plan the spending of our money so we buy the things that really count. What really counts? You must decide that. What is important to you? What do you want out of life? The decisions you make when you spend your money determine your whole way of life. Planning a budget and sticking to it forces us to face the fact that we have scarce resources and that every time we buy something we give up the opportunity to spend the money on something else. Perhaps you have already learned that you must do some careful planning if you are to have enough money left for things that really count for you.

Suppose that within a year or two you attend a college in another city and that you have a steady income of $230 a month from an allowance and a part-time job. This is the amount you know you can count on receiving—no more, no less—each month of the school year. With this monthly income, you know that you must pay for your room and board, buy your clothing, books, and other school supplies, and reserve some money "just for spending." How can you be sure that your $230 will last you through each month? Obviously, if you do not have some scheme for spending your income, the last few days of each month are going to be lean indeed.

During your first month in college, for example, you spot a sweater

Every time you spend money, whether it's to see a movie or buy a record, you give up the opportunity to spend that money for something else. Only you can decide what is really important to you. *(Ted Feder, Editorial Photocolor Archives)*

that you would like to own. While looking at the sweater, you also see an attractive college pennant that would look nice in your room. Before you know it, you have spent $25 in the campus store. Later that day, some friends ask you to go out with them to dinner and a movie. This night out costs you another $8. Later in the month when you want to attend an important football game, you do not have enough money to do so. Yet this is the one big event you had looked forward to. You realize that you should have had a plan that would have forced you to spend your monthly income more wisely. Such a plan is called a *budget*.

A LOOK AT THREE FAMILIES

Budgeting is about the same for a family as for an individual. The difference lies in the things budgeted for. The family is a basic economic unit, and its spending is planned in terms of the family group as a whole. Before examining some planning principles for budgeting, let's look at how three families handle their finances.

Each family is made up of a father, a mother, and two children. The three families are remarkably similar in many ways: their ages are comparable, the education of the parents is about equal, their incomes are almost identical, and they live in the same neighborhood. The Able family, the Baker family, and the Cruz family have had dissimilar experiences, however, in handling family finances.

The Ables never seem to be able to stretch the monthly family income long enough to last until the next payroll check arrives. As a result, Mr. Able has had to borrow money from a bank twice during the past two years so that certain bills could be paid on time. This year, the Able family may not be able to go on a vacation trip because the little money they have on hand should be used to help pay a few large bills, one of which is the cost of last year's vacation.

If we examined the way in which the Able family has been handling its financial affairs (like viewing a television replay of the family's financial actions during the past year or two), we would learn that no attempt has been made to plan the use of income. No person in the family knows how much money has been spent on food, clothing, transportation, or entertainment. Mr. Able simply deposits most of his monthly payroll check in a checking account, and when items such as food or clothing are needed, he or Mrs. Able writes a check.

The Able family has never prepared a budget to plan spending for the future. When the family "needs" some new item, it is simply bought. For example, three months ago, the Ables bought a new television set because, as the television repairer said, the old set was finally worn out. Because they had only a few dollars in their checking account at the time, they bought the new television set on time payments arranged by the dealer.

The Able family has not saved money in any systematic way. All the family income is needed for fixed expenses (such as mortgage payments, insurance premiums, taxes, utility bills, and installment payments for various purchases) and for a seemingly endless list of items, such as groceries, gasoline, entertainment, and clothing. The family income does not stretch far enough.

The Baker family got together one day several months ago and discussed the fact that despite their reasonably good income, they did not seem to be doing well financially. They had trouble making ends meet, and they decided that the problem was lack of careful financial planning. Mrs. Baker volunteered to go to the library and check out books on family recordkeeping and budgeting. Among the materials Mrs. Baker found in the library were charts showing how much families with different incomes spend on such things as housing, food, transportation, clothing, and entertainment. The Baker family then made up a detailed list of expenses, covering every item they could think of, and assigned to each item the amount of money they would spend on it each month.

As the Bakers spent money, they recorded the purpose and the amount in a notebook, no matter how small the amount (even 15 or 20 cents for coffee). The Bakers spent time every three or four days going through the book and adding the amounts spent on the various expense categories. They found, first, that the family was spending too much on some of the categories, and long before the month ended they often had exceeded the amounts allowed. So they agreed that no more was to be spent on certain items. Second, they discovered that some family members were forgetting to record the amounts spent on some items. The system was not working well, so for the following month a change in the plan was instituted.

For the second month, an envelope was used for each category. The amount of cash needed for a week's expenditures would be placed in each envelope. When money was needed, it could be removed from the appropriate envelope. Several minor problems arose. For example, when the proper change was not available in an envelope, some quick shuffling of money in other envelopes was necessary. Often the money available for the week was not enough, and money had to be borrowed from one or more of the other envelopes. When money was borrowed in this way, IOU notes were placed in the envelopes from which the money was taken. In many cases the amounts placed in the envelopes were not adequate.

Mr. and Mrs. Baker attempted almost daily to shuffle money from one envelope to another to settle the IOUs, and as the weeks went by they felt harassed and uncomfortable; tempers often flared. Following an agonizing two-hour session of budget work one evening, Mr. Baker emptied the cash from all the envelopes and then threw the envelopes into the fireplace. He decided that budgeting took the joy out of living.

The third family, the Cruzes, always seem to have enough money to take advantage of cash sales for big-ticket or expensive items. For example, just a week or two before the Able family bought a new television set, a discount store, selling for cash, advertised a big discount on a name-brand television set at their warehouse. The Cruz family had been watching for a bargain such as this because they wanted to replace their old set. So they paid cash for a new set.

The Cruzes are able to save money systematically for several different purposes. They successfully match their expenditures with their income. When cash is needed for emergencies, they have the money available. Next month the Cruz family is taking a one-week camping vacation—they have been planning the trip for a long time now, and they have the money for it in a savings account in their bank.

Although the family incomes in these three cases are almost identical, only the Cruz family seems to be experiencing the peace of mind that results from successful matching of outgoes with income. Why the difference? What do the Cruzes do that makes them able to save enough money to take advantage of cash sales for big-ticket items such as television sets? How do they control their income so well? On the other hand, what have the Ables and Bakers done wrong?

The Ables have no plan for spending their money, and without some careful planning, most of us cannot reach the goals that we consider important. Our money will be frittered away on things that we would not have chosen had we taken the time to consider the alternatives. The Bakers made a valiant attempt to plan their family finances, but they became bogged down with plans that were too elaborate and detailed—plans that took the fun out of life, in other words. Also, the Bakers made the common mistake of thinking that their spending habits had to be too much like "average" budget figures.

The Cruz family had examined their interests and their goals in life. They knew what they wanted before they started financial planning. Then, keeping their records as simple as possible, they let their budget plan help them spend their money for the things that bring them the most satisfaction. The Cruzes plan each month's expenditures so that they will not find themselves short of money for things they have decided are important or essential.

After considering some basic principles of financial planning for individuals and families, we will examine in some detail the way in which the Cruz family keeps its records and maintains its budget.

PLANNING PRINCIPLES

Do you think your need for planning the way in which you use your money will decrease as your income increases? It won't. In fact, most persons find that as their incomes increase, their need to plan carefully becomes even more important. One reason for this is that as our incomes increase, so do our wants.

The young woman who gets a substantial salary increase suddenly decides that she wants a better apartment or a newer car or more expensive clothing. When she makes one or more of these buying decisions, she has the same financial problem she had before the salary increase. As her income increases, so do her wants.

What you can do to help you decide what to do with your money is to make out a budget. A budget is a plan. It helps you set realistic financial goals and then takes you toward those goals in systematic, periodic steps.

Some individuals and families keep records of what they spend, and they believe they are budgeting. They are not budgeting; they are just keeping books. These records can be helpful in setting up a budget, or they can help us figure out why an existing budget doesn't work. A budget is a plan for allocating income during a set period of time, usually a month or a year. It is based on an estimate of the funds available.

Business firms and government agencies prepare budgets to serve as guides for expenditures. So do churches, clubs, and other organizations. Millions of individuals regularly make budgets. So if you decide to make a budget, you will be in good company.

Your budget may not look much like the budget prepared by General Motors, yet basically the two are just about the same. No matter who prepares a budget, three important steps are necessary: (1) setting goals, (2) estimating income, and (3) planning the use of income. The latter two steps, estimating income and planning its use, cover a set period of time. To decide whether this set period of time should be a week or a month, you should use as a guide the period covered by your regular allowance, wage, or salary.

Setting Goals

To begin with, decide what goals you wish to reach. Working out the details of a budget makes sense when you know precisely what to expect from your work. In other words, you are budgeting for a purpose. In the case of family budgets, setting a goal should be a group project, with every member old enough to help doing so. If all suggestions are considered, it is more likely that everyone will be satisfied with the results. The most important goals should, of course, be given priority. Income, both present income and future estimates, should be considered carefully so that goals will be realistic.

Many individuals or families find it easiest to begin recording goals by thinking first of long-term goals—those they hope to achieve in 15, 20, or 25 years. Then intermediate goals for the next 5 to 15 years can be decided upon. Finally, short-term goals—goals for the coming year and the next 5 years—are planned.

Long-term goals may include a debt-free home. They may include a vacation cottage on a lake or a houseboat. Long-term goals may also include a sum of money for retirement days.

Intermediate goals may include a vacation trip to Europe, money for education, or a new house in another neighborhood.

Short-term goals for the coming year might include the purchase of a home movie camera or a short vacation trip. Immediate goals might simply be to reduce or pay off certain debts.

Establishing goals is an important first step in the budgeting process, and because individual and family goals change from time to time, they should be looked at regularly. No special form is needed for recording goals. Simply write out the goals under these headings:

- Long-term goals (15 years and longer)
- Intermediate goals (5 to 15 years)
- Short-term goals (coming year to 5 years)

Establishing and recording long-range, intermediate, and short-range goals are the first steps in planning a budget. A vacation you want to take next year, for example, is an intermediate goal. *(UPI)*

Some persons identify their short-term goals (next 5 years) as "needs" or "wants." Then they record the amount of money needed to reach the goal, the date by which the money should be available, and the amount they will have to save each year to reach the goal. Short-term goals for a family might look like Table 3-1.

Estimating Income

The next step to follow in preparing a budget is to estimate all income expected during the period covered by the budget. Most people can be fairly certain of what their income will be during any given period. Even a person who works irregularly can, from past experience, do a fairly good job of estimating future income.

For families, the main source of income is ordinarily salary or wages. An employer withholds from salary or wages income tax and FICA (social security) taxes and, often, insurance and other deductions. It is much simpler for budgeting purposes to consider only the net wages, or take-home pay, that the employee receives after deductions. Then, when listing expenditures, only those items that are spent out of take-home pay are recorded.

In estimating income, it is necessary to include everything that will be received—dividends, interest, bonuses, and any other sources of income. Probably the best way to estimate miscellaneous sources of income is to assume that they will be the same as in the past year. It is best to be conservative in an estimate. If you are not sure that you will

TABLE 3-1
Short-Term Goals

Goal	Amount Needed	Date Needed	How to Save
New washing machine (need)	$ 300	9/1/79	Save $37.50 each month beginning now
Down payment for different car (need)	1,000	7/1/80	Save $300 in 1979; save $700 first part of 1980
Home movie camera (want)	400	12/1/80	Save $100 in 1979; save $300 in 1980
Vacation trip to Bahamas (want)	1,800	1/1/83	Save $600 a year beginning in 1980

get an extra $100 bonus at the end of the year, do not include it. If you do get the bonus, you can easily take it into account; but if you include the $100 and then fail to get it, your whole budget will fall apart.

Planning the Use of Income

Most of the money spent by families goes for fixed, committed expenses over which they have little direct control (for example, car payments set by a bank). The amount of money remaining after these fixed, committed expenses are allowed for can be used for savings and for *variable* living expenses. Variable living expenses include food, clothing, and other items that vary from month to month.

To summarize, individuals and families use their incomes for these three purposes: (1) fixed, committed expenses, (2) savings, and (3) variable living expenses.

Fixed, Committed Expenses. Much of family incomes goes for expenditures that are relatively large and that remain the same size, or about the same size, month after month. Included are such things as rent or mortgage payments, insurance premiums, utility bills, installment payments, and taxes. Once these items exist in our budgets, we are committed to make the payments. When a color television set is bought on an installment plan, the monthly payment represents a large expense item added to the budget for several months. Once the debt is incurred, it must be paid unless the item can be sold. Careful planning of financial resources may force us in the future to examine carefully whether we should make these large purchases.

When planning the use of income, then, these committed expenses must be considered. If you do not prepare for them, they can cause a great deal of hardship when payments are due.

The allowances for large, committed expenses should be spread out so that each monthly allotment of income includes a share of them. For example, if a $300 life insurance premium is due twice a year, the family should put aside $50 every month to meet these semiannual premium payments. By doing this, the family will not run the risk of spending the money for the insurance premiums on a desired but unnecessary item.

If you were a college student with a monthly allowance or income, you should, for example, put aside a certain amount of money for the textbooks that you would have to buy at the beginning of each semester. If you estimated that twice a year you would have to spend $55 for textbooks, then you would put aside $11 a month during each of the ten months you were in school.

Savings. Any person who wants security and independence must save regularly, but no reasonable person wants to save simply for the purpose of piling up money. We save money so that we can take advantage of sales. We save money so that we can pay cash and avoid paying interest charges on time-payment plans. We save money for vacations, for travel, for clothes, for gifts, for education, and for emergencies. The list is endless, just as our wants are endless.

After planning for fixed, committed expenses, we should plan a savings program. For most of us, the first savings fund to be built up is an emergency fund. The main purpose of this fund is to provide for unexpected expenses that always arise but cannot be anticipated. Some financial advisers recommend that a family should have an emergency fund equal to about two months' income.

Variable Living Expenses. After deducting from net income the money for fixed, committed expenses and an amount for savings, the budget planner has remaining an amount that can be used for variable living expenses, such as food, clothing, transportation, gifts, household operation, and personal allowances. These expenses must be covered, but because no advance commitment has been made for them, you can cut down on spending here—tighten your belt, so to speak.

The immediate job of managing income and expenditures is one of watching closely the money available for variable living expenses. It is these uncommitted dollars that the individual or the family must watch carefully and apportion wisely. Possibly only a third of your income will be available for savings and uncommitted spending. So you see why planning large expenditures in the area of fixed, committed expenses must be done with great care.

THE CRUZ FAMILY BUDGET

Now let's return to the Cruz family. This family wanted a budget to do three things: (1) to tell them how much money they would receive each month from various sources; (2) to enable them to provide first for the necessities of life, then for the comforts of life, and then—whenever possible—for the luxuries of life; and (3) to give them a plan for saving money.

After planning for fixed, committed expenses, you should set up a savings program. One of the uses for such savings would be to cover emergency expenses, like unexpected car repairs. *(Susan Berkowitz)*

In order to plan such a budget, the Cruzes devised three different record forms: one form to estimate income for a year; a second form to estimate the family's variable living expenses for about three months; and a third form to record fixed, committed expenses and proposed savings for a year.

Estimating Income

Form I on page 45 is the one that the Cruz family devised to show their estimated income for a year.

Mr. Cruz's take-home pay for his job as a technical engineer at a television station is $1,040 a month, or $12,480 a year. In addition to his salary, Mr. Cruz can count on a bonus of $200 at the end of the year. He repairs radio and television sets in his basement workshop, and this work brings in about $40 every month, except August, when he does not accept any repair jobs. Mrs. Cruz does some consulting work for the marketing research firm for which she used to work. Her income from this consulting work is $310 a month, or $3,720 a year. Finally, they own a bond that pays $60 interest twice a year. Notice that the monthly income varies from $1,350 in August to $1,650 in December. The total annual income is $16,960. Thus, the average monthly income is $1,413.33.

Income

Source	Jan.	Feb.	Mar.	Apr.	May	June	July	Aug.	Sept.	Oct.	Nov.	Dec.	Yearly Total
	1040	1040	1040	1040	1040	1040	1040	1040	1040	1040	1040	1040	12,480
	310	310	310	310	310	310	310	310	310	310	310	310	3,720
Interest					60							60	120
TV + Radio Repairs	40	40	40	40	40	40	40		40	40	40	40	440
Bonus												200	200
Totals	1390	1390	1390	1390	1450	1390	1390	1350	1390	1390	1390	1650	16,960

Variable Living Expenses

Items		Jan.	Feb.	Mar.	Apr.	May	June	July	Aug.	Sept.	Oct.	Nov.	Dec.
Food		268	268	268	268	268							
	Spent	242	264										
Car Expense		55	55	55	55	55							
	Spent	51	62										
Personal Allowances		75	75	75	75	75							
	Spent	75	75										
Clothing		75	75	75	75	75							
	Spent	68	22										
Entertainment		30	30	30	30	30							
	Spent	125	0										
Appliances + Furniture		35	35	35	35	35							
	Spent	15	38										
Bldgs. + Grounds		14	14	14	14	14							
	Spent	0	0										
Gifts + Contrib.		29	29	29	29	29							
	Spent	0	19										
News, Mags, Books		25	25	25	25	25							
	Spent	20	18										

Estimating Variable Living Expenses

Form II on page 45 is the one that the Cruz family devised to show their variable living expenses.

From past experience, the Cruz family knows that monthly food costs average about $268. Similarly, they know that expenses for the other items listed (car expense, personal allowances, clothing, and the like) can be estimated at certain amounts. The estimates are filled in for three months in advance; then, as each month's expenses are recorded in the "Spent" spaces, estimates for another month are added. For example, the month of February has just passed, and the amounts spent have been recorded. Estimates are now recorded for May. At any time, the estimates for any of the items can be changed.

Recording Fixed, Committed Expenses and Proposed Savings

Form III on page 47 is the one that the Cruz family devised to show their fixed, committed expenses and proposed savings.

The Cruzes make seminanual premium payments on three different life insurance policies; premium payments are due in February, April, May, August, October, and November. The car insurance premium is due in March and September, and the license plates must be renewed in March. Notice that the expenses are recorded in the months in which they must be paid; then the total is entered in the Yearly Total column.

Several years ago, the Cruz family borrowed money from a savings and loan association to buy the house in which they live. Each month a payment of $295 is made to the savings and loan association. Part of the $295 is used to reduce the amount owed, part of it is interest on the loan, and part of it is used to buy insurance on the home.

About a year ago, the family bought a new car, and to help finance this purchase, Mr. Cruz borrowed money from the First National Bank. The monthly payment on this debt is $72.

As part of their regular, systematic savings program, the Cruzes are now investing $70 each month in a mutual fund (Chapter 18 discusses mutual funds and other means of investing). In addition, Mr. Cruz contributes to a retirement fund through his employer; his contribution is withheld each month from his salary check, so it does not have to be recorded on the budget sheets. Through July of the current year, the family will add $35 to their vacation fund. Beginning in August

FORM III

Fixed, Committed Expenses and Proposed Savings

Items	Jan.	Feb.	Mar.	Apr.	May	June	July	Aug.	Sept.	Oct.	Nov.	Dec.	Yearly Total
Life Insurance													
Mr. Cruz		362						362					724
Mr. Cruz					138						138		276
Family Policy				76						76			152
Spent													
Car Insurance			89						89				178
Spent													
Taxes													
Real Estate				360						360			720
Auto License			38										38
Spent													
Utilities	95	95	95	95	95	95	95	95	95	95	95	95	1140
Spent	104	101											
Debts													
*Savings + Loan	295	295	295	295	295	295	295	295	295	295	295	295	3,540
1st Nat'l Bank	72	72	72	72	72	72	72	72	72	72	72	72	864
Spent	367	367											
Medical	50	50	50	50	50	50	50	50	50	50	50	50	600
Spent	19	8											
Savings													
X,Y,Z Ins. Fund	70	70	70	70	70	70	70	70	70	70	70	70	840
Spent	70	70											
Vacation Fund	35	35	35	35	35	35	35	15	15	15	15	15	320
Spent	35	35											
Emergency Fund	15	15	15	15	15	15	15	35	35	35	35	35	280
Spent	15	15											
Totals	632	994	759	1068	770	632	632	994	721	1068	770	632	9672
*Mortgage on Home													

(the month during which they will take their vacation), their monthly contribution to this vacation fund will be decreased by $15.

The Cruz family maintains an emergency fund of about $3500. The fund is used for unexpected expenses and for certain buying opportunities, such as the chance they had recently to buy a color television set at a bargain price. During the current year, they are contributing to the fund $15 a month through July and then increasing the contribution to $35 a month for the remaining months of the year. Both the vacation fund and the emergency fund are kept in a savings account.

Through a group plan at Mr. Cruz's place of business, the Cruz family has hospital, surgical, and major medical insurance coverage. Mr. Cruz's contribution to this health insurance coverage is deducted from his salary checks, so the budget forms do not have to show this expense. However, to cover health expenses not included in the group plan, including dental services, the Cruzes set aside $50 a month.

Notice that Form III has rows labeled "Spent" following the major categories. During January, utility bills totaled $104.50 and this amount has been recorded in the appropriate row in the January column. The payments in January to the savings and loan association ($295) and to the bank ($72) total $367 and this figure has been recorded in the "Spent" row under "Debts" in the January column.

The fixed expenses and savings for each month vary from $632 to $1068. The yearly total of $9672 divided by 12 is $806—the amount that must be set aside each month so that money will be available to make the payments when they become due.

Varying the Budget

The Cruz family budget has a feature that is quite important for all budgets—elasticity. If money for a certain item is not used one month, it will accumulate and can be used for the same purpose the following month. For example, the family used only $242 for food during January instead of the allotted $268 (perhaps they used many of the canned goods they had stored). The unused $26 could be added to the February food allotment. The family may plan to cut food costs, but they realize they cannot do it merely by changing a figure in their budget.

If something unusual should cause the Cruzes to spend more on an item during a month than has been allocated for it, the difference can be subtracted from the allotment for the same item for the following month. If it turns out that the allotment for that particular item is too small in the following months, the family will have to increase the allotment for the months to come and find some account from which they can subtract the difference.

COMPARING BUDGETS

The amount of money spent by an individual or family depends on the money available, or income. The way in which the available money is spent depends on how the individual or family wishes to live. For this reason, some families put a greater part of their income into vacations. Other families may wish to put more money into housing, or food, or cars. What is good consumption for one family is not necessarily good consumption for another family.

There is an advantage to be gained, on the other hand, from examining the amounts other families with similar incomes spend on various items. Such an examination may be a signal to the family that it should look again at its goals and perhaps make some changes here and there. Several popular magazines regularly publish family budgeting articles showing what "average" families in different income brackets spend on food, housing, clothing, entertainment, and other items. The Bureau of Labor Statistics sets guidelines for the use of families wishing to make comparisons. Information of this type is available in libraries and can provide valuable examples. But always, the family should form its budget according to its goals, and these goals may be quite different from the goals of the average family.

KEEPING RECORDS

Did you know that most tax accountants, attorneys, and internal revenue officials believe that only wealthy people and others with complex finances need elaborate personal bookkeeping systems? What most of us do need is a system that will tell us what we are spending our money on and how much we are spending.

One of the most valuable recordkeeping tools is the checkbook. When checks are written (see Chapter 17), certain information that will be useful later can be added to the check stub or register. For example, "clothing," or "food," or "gift" can be added to the stub or register to indicate for what purpose the money was used. At the end of the month, the amounts spent for various items can be determined by simply flipping through the check stubs or register and adding the figures. In addition, the canceled checks are both proof of payment and another record of expenses.

Other valuable record information can be added to the check stubs or register. When paying for a magazine subscription, for example, you can indicate the date on which the new subscription will expire. Such a record may be useful as you plan expenditures for such things in the future. Furthermore, if the publisher should bill you early, you have a record to refer to.

In addition to using the checkbook for recordkeeping, many people find it useful to keep a diary of big outlays of cash, such as money spent at a supermarket. Also, when things are bought on charge accounts, a note concerning the purchase can be entered in a diary. What kind of diary should be used? Some families use a loose-leaf notebook; some tie a spiral notebook and pencil to a kitchen bulletin board. Other families have found that placing notes of cash expenditures in a large envelope or shoe box works quite well. The idea is to keep recordkeeping simple. At certain times, the information from the diary (or envelope or shoe box) is combined with the information from the check stubs and a summary of expenditures is made.

A family just beginning to budget its money may want to keep more detailed records for the first several months. In that case, a more detailed record of expenses can be entered on a large sheet known as a *columnar worksheet*. Recordkeeping should be as simple as possible, however.

KEEPING FILES

Families usually need two places to keep records: a home file and a safe-deposit box at a bank. If a regular file cabinet is too large for the home, accordion-type file jackets made from heavy paper are available in many stores. A safe-deposit box can be rented for a few dollars a year, and it is the safest place for valuable items.

A file at home should be used for such things as canceled checks, insurance policies, car records, tax records, investment records, income records, debt records, guarantees, and instruction sheets.

Keeping accurate records for income tax purposes is essential. So keep receipts, canceled checks, and other evidence to prove amounts claimed as deductions. Records that support an item of income or a deduction appearing on the income tax return must be kept for three years after the April 15 filing date, or later if the taxpayer files after the deadline. In cases of tax fraud, there is no time limit—the Internal Revenue Service will dig back farther than three years. Despite this three-year limit, which is called the *statute of limitations* for tax returns, some property and stock records should be kept longer because in some cases profits from the sale of property can be spread over several years so that not all the tax is due the year of the sale.

An easy and convenient way to keep papers is to buy a supply of file folders. A guarantee, pamphlets, receipts, and other data about a stereo system, for example, can be inserted in a folder marked "Stereo System, 19——." Records on the family car would be in a folder marked "Car, 19——."

Most financial records should be filed at home. But papers that are vital, seldom used, and hard to replace should be stored in a safe-deposit box at the bank. Among the records that should be kept in a safe-deposit box are legal records of birth, marriage, citizenship, death, and military service. One copy of wills should also be kept in a safe-deposit box (your lawyer should keep the original). Other items that should be kept in a safe-deposit box include a list of insurance policies and their numbers and an inventory of household items.

A safe-deposit box is the safest place for valuable items like legal records that may be difficult to replace if they are lost, destroyed, or stolen. *(Bruce Anspach, Editorial Photocolor Archives)*

Checking Your Reading

1. Explain what the problem of scarcity has to do with financial planning.
2. Why does every spending decision we make involve the idea of "the opportunity cost of spending"?
3. Give a one-sentence definition of a budget.
4. When preparing a budget, what three important steps should be followed?
5. Give several examples of long-term, intermediate, and immediate goals.
6. How can one best go about estimating miscellaneous sources of income?
7. Explain what is meant by "fixed, committed expenses."
8. Give two examples of "variable living expenses," and explain why they are called variable.
9. What should determine the way an individual or a family spends its money?
10. Explain why a checkbook is a valuable recordkeeping tool.
11. List some of the records that should be kept in a safe-deposit box.
12. List some of the records that should be kept in a file at home.
13. How are accurate records helpful for income tax purposes?
14. When does the statute of limitations expire for income tax returns?

Consumer Problems and Projects

1. Make a list of your goals. Separate them into (1) short-term goals (immediate goals to 5 years), (2) intermediate goals (5 to 15 years), and (3) long-term goals (15 years and longer). Make the list as complete as you can. If you permitted a person who does not know you to examine these goals, do you think the person would know much about your values? Why?
2. Ask credit unions, banks, and savings and loan associations in your neighborhood or community whether they make available budget forms for individuals or families to use. If they do, ask for

a set for your class use. After you have collected the forms (or booklets), answer these questions:

  a. Does the form provide the consumer with enough information so that the budgeting process will be worthwhile?

  b. Is the form simple to use? Will the consumer become so bogged down with detail work that he or she will soon give up?

  c. Does the form suggest percentages for the different items of expenses? Do the instructions say that consumers should make their own choices?

  d. Do you prefer one of these forms? Do you prefer to make your own form based on the suggestions in this chapter and on the ideas you have found in the forms you have gathered?

3. Two families of the same size and with the same income have two entirely different budgets. What might be some of the reasons for these variations?

4. Prepare and present a skit showing a family situation in which there is a need for budgeting. If possible, record the skit on audiotape or videotape for playback.

5. Tom Weldon, who just finished college, plans to be married in a few days. He does not intend to keep a budget. Tom's father had systematically saved money over the years in order to provide a college education for Tom. While Tom was in college, his parents paid directly for his tuition, books, and major supplies, and paid for his room and board in a dormitory. In addition, they sent Tom $80 a month. He spent about $25 a month for clothes and used the rest of the money for miscellaneous expenses. Now Tom will be working in the purchasing department of a manufacturing firm at a salary of $1000 a month, an increase of $920 over the monthly income he had been receiving from his parents. "I got along without budgeting before, so why should I begin now when my income is higher?" asks Tom. Answer Tom's question.

6. Susan and David Buffett would like to trade in their 7-year-old car for a new one, but they do not know whether or not they will be able to make the monthly payment of $126 over a 3-year period. The Buffetts, who have two children, have had difficulty making ends meet on their annual income of $16,800. A friend suggests that budgeting might help them to cut down on their expenditures and make the car payments.

  a. Outline the steps that the Buffetts could take to set up a workable budget.

  b. How will a budget help the Buffetts to solve their problem?

4

Principles of Wise Buying

Doing a good job of managing your money is a lot like planning a trip. First you need to decide where you want to go. Even after you have decided on a destination you still need to make some decisions about how you will get there. Like travelers, consumers need to consider both their goals and a plan for reaching them. In Chapter 2 we talked about identifying our goals. But even after we have identified our goals, we still need a plan to help us reach them.

PLANNING AHEAD FOR PURCHASES

In order to ensure that we reach our goals, we have to make long-range plans. Without careful plans we may end up without the things we need most and with too many things which really are not so important. This would be like the situation of the newlyweds who spent all the money they received as wedding gifts on a large and expensive dining room set and found they did not have enough money left for dishes and silverware so that they could serve their guests.

Determining Your Situation and Needs

The first step in making a long-range plan is deciding exactly what you need. This involves getting your goal clearly in mind and deciding just where you are in relation to it. For example, take the problem of getting together the clothes you need for a part-time job at a supermarket. First, you would need to know what clothes your employer expects you to wear. Once you know this you can go through your wardrobe and decide what you have that meets the rules and what extra things you still need. For many kinds of purchases, including both clothing and food, an inventory of what you already have on hand is an important first step in determining what you need to buy.

Planning a Purchase Program

Many kinds of goals involve a series of smaller purchases that are steps toward a goal. For this kind of program to work, your initial plan must be a good one and it must be kept in mind at each succeeding step. If the plan is forgotten or turns out to be a poor one, you are likely to end up with an assortment of things that really do not go together.

Using Opportunities for Special Purchases

For many kinds of purchases, you can save money by learning when sales or other special purchase opportunities are likely to occur. When you know this, you can plan ahead to take advantage of these opportunities. Certain kinds of sales have become traditional and are held at the same time every year, so it is easy to plan for them. The January white sales, featuring specials on bed linens and bath towels, are an example of this kind of sale.

Seasonal items may be available at special prices either in preseason or postseason sales. Sometimes dealers for seasonal items make special offers well ahead of the season to attract early shoppers. Sales of snow tires in September are one example of this kind of sale. In many cities, Columbus Day and Veterans Day are occasions for preseason sales of winter coats and outerwear. Postseason sales are used to clean out stocks of unsold items that the merchant does not want to keep on hand. Postseason sales on fall and winter clothes and footwear typically come just after Christmas, and the summer sales come just after the Fourth of July. Price reductions on preseason sales are smaller than those for postseason sales, but preseason sales offer better selections.

Taking an inventory of what you have is an important step in deciding what you need to buy. *(Editorial Photocolor Archives)*

Not all sales are held at regularly scheduled times. Smart shoppers should watch advertising and in-store signs for unusual buys. These sometimes may come at unexpected times, even at the peak of the season. Such sales may be held when business is slow.

Several different terms are used to describe the different types of sales. An understanding of these terms will help you know what to expect at sales events. The National Retail Merchants Association suggests the following use of terms to its members:

- *Sale* is used when articles are offered at a reduction from the advertiser's own regular prices or from local prices for identical or comparable merchandise. Ads should make clear which of these bases for comparison is being used. When the term "regularly" or "regular price" is used, it is understood that the merchandise will return to the regular price after the sale period. For merchandise that will not be marked up again after the sale, the terms "were," "formerly," or "originally" should be used.

- *Clearances* or *clearance sales* are sales used to clear out leftover items; prices are reduced from the previous or the original prices. When price comparisons are made, the previous or original price should be clearly indicated. The term "regularly" should not be used for price comparisons for clearance items, since unsold items are not to be returned to their previous prices. Instead, they are marked down until they sell.
- *Special purchase* or *closeout* is properly used to refer to merchandise purchased from the manufacturer on unusually favorable terms. This merchandise is offered to the public at lower prices than they ordinarily would expect to pay in their area.

You should remember that these terms sometimes are used incorrectly. Sometimes they are misused deliberately in order to mislead shoppers.

In planning ahead for sales, it helps to build up some extra savings that you can draw on for your purchases. Staple items you use every day are especially good bargains at sales. You know you will always be able to use some more of your favorite brand of underwear or shampoo. Caution is required for major purchases of clothing and luxury items. Here you will need to consider whether you really like the item on sale or are interested in it mostly because it is cheaper than it used to be.

DECIDING WHETHER TO SHOP AROUND

Shopping costs us both money and time. Because of these costs we need to decide whether we really are going to be able to save enough to make our efforts worthwhile. Our savings from shopping can take two different forms. By shopping around we may be able to get a better product for a particular price or we may be able to get a particular product at a better price.

When Does Shopping Pay Off?

Shopping around is most worthwhile when there are large differences in prices and quality among the brands of a particular product. If prices and quality do not vary much, the easiest-to-find brand or the nearest store is the best choice. If different brands of a product do not all perform equally well, and if prices differ among stores, then shopping for the best price-quality combination will produce worthwhile savings. These savings will be largest for big-ticket items such as cars, appliances, and furniture and for items that are purchased regularly, such as gasoline, food, and toiletries. There are two situations in which shopping is likely to pay off because price and quality differences are great:

- *Situations in Which Sellers Can Practice Price Discrimination.* For some products or services, sellers are able to charge buyers different prices for the same item. This can happen when it is hard for buyers to compare deals. For example, it is hard for car buyers to compare deals because of different trade-ins, models, and options. Price discrimination also can occur when resale of a product by a buyer is impossible. Dentists, for example, can charge different patients different prices since one patient cannot sell another a checkup or a filling.
- *Situations in Which Products Are Differentiated.* Shopping also is worthwhile when different brands of a product, or different sources of a service, offer unique features which keep them from being completely comparable. When such unique features are provided, we say the product or service has been differentiated from others, that is, has been made different. Often the differences are minor. Sometimes they are only the "miracle ingredients" in toothpaste. Or they may be more important; for example, a special type of engine which is available in only one make of car.

When Is Shopping of No Benefit?

For certain products and services the price is fixed and is the same in all stores. In these cases, shopping around provides no savings, since the price is the same everywhere. This may be the result of efforts by a manufacturer to ensure that his brand is sold at the same price everywhere.

In certain cases there is no benefit to shopping, because there is only one seller in the community. This is the situation for utilities such as telephones, electricity, water, and public transportation. For these services there usually is only one seller.

Reducing Shopping Costs

Even in cases in which shopping is likely to be worthwhile, shoppers still will want to hold the time and money costs of shopping to a minimum. One way to save both time and money is to substitute other methods of collecting information for store-to-store shopping trips. You can get information on product availability and prices from newspaper ads. Phone calls also can be used to determine where a particular item is available and its price. You also can use part of the time you spend shopping to collect information about purchases you are planning for the future.

KNOWING WHAT TO LOOK FOR IN A PRODUCT

One of the first steps in buying something is deciding which product characteristics are most important for the use you have in mind. Even after you have decided on the relative importance of these different characteristics, you still will need to know just how to recognize the features that indicate them.

What Product Characteristics Are Important?

There are five product characteristics which are important for judging most products. Their importance will differ from product to product, but they apply to almost every product we buy:

- *Price.* This includes the cost of the item and any service, installation, or delivery charges.
- *Performance.* How well does the product do what it is supposed to do? If it is a food product, does it supply the nutrients it should? If it is a watch, does it keep time accurately?
- *Convenience and Design.* Is the item easy to use and attractive? If it is a sweater, does it fit comfortably? If it is a radio, are the dials easy to read?
- *Durability and Maintenance.* Will the item stand up well in use? If the item is a pair of jeans, how well will they hold up in repeated washings? Will the item require expensive repairs? How expensive is it to operate? What sort of guarantee or warranty is provided?
- *Safety.* Does the product or its use involve any dangers or hazards? If it is a car, how well does it hold up in a crash? If it is an electric appliance, is there a danger of electric shock?

When considering a product, for example, a jacket, different people will put a different weight on each product characteristic. Some people will feel that performance is most important—they want a jacket that is warm. Others will put most weight on design—they want the latest style and color. Still others will be concerned about durability—they want a jacket that will last for several years.

In Chapter 2 we discussed how Jim Taylor chose an alarm clock. We noted that the weight Jim gave to particular product characteristics was related to his values. Advertisers, of course, are very interested in knowing what product characteristics consumers think are important and they want to try to influence their ideas. They may want us to take some new characteristics into account, or they may want us to give more weight to a characteristic which favors them.

Advertisers are not the only source of information on how much weight should be given to particular product characteristics. There are other sources which are less influenced by their own special interests. These sources include government agencies and consumer-supported product-testing organizations such as Consumers Union. We will discuss these information sources in the next chapter.

Even after we have decided how much weight we should give to a particular product characteristic, we still have a problem. We still must decide how to rate the different brands available on that characteristic. It is fairly easy to figure out how a brand rates on some characteristics. It is fairly easy, for example, to decide how easy-to-read the switch on a hair dryer is. But how many of us can judge whether there is a danger of electric shock? Most consumers feel they can use such things as a product's name and its price to judge its quality. In the next section, we will look at some of the things consumers use to help judge quality and how useful they really are.

Looking for Reliable and Useful Indications of Quality

There are a number of ways consumers judge products: by their prices, their brand names, their labels, and their guarantees. Let's look closer at each of these items to see how reliable and useful each one really is as an indication of quality.

Price. Studies of consumer behavior have found that consumers often rely on price as an indication of quality. They seem most inclined to use price as an indication of quality for products whose performance is difficult to judge but which they think vary widely in quality. Stereo equipment is an example. Most of us are convinced that there are important differences in quality among different models and brands, but we are not sure just how to go about detecting them. In such a situation we might be inclined to think that the more expensive models are better.

Consumers may be too convinced of the old saying, "You only get what you pay for." This statement seems to be true for some products, but not for others. Studies of the relationship between the product-testing ratings developed by Consumers Union and actual product prices indicate that, in general, price is *not* a very reliable indication of quality. For many products, lower-priced brands have been almost as likely to get high ratings as the expensive ones. This means that paying a high price does not necessarily assure you of getting a high-quality product. High-quality products have been found at various price levels.

Brand Name. Brand names have developed over the years because manufacturers want to build up a group of customers who will look for their products in the market and buy them again and again. With a brand name to distinguish their products, manufacturers can try to build up a reputation both through the quality of their products and through advertising.

Although most manufacturers try to build up a reputation for the reliable quality of their brand, the quality ranking of particular brands does change over time. Products with a high ranking one year may later lose their position while others gain. When the Consumers Union product ratings of electric appliances in different years were compared, it was found that brands that had a high ranking one year were only to a certain extent the same ones that received high rankings in later tests. It was also found that there was a good deal of variation, over time, in the relative rankings of sunburn lotions. From this we can conclude that a good experience in the past with a brand should be taken into account in making a purchasing decision, but that we cannot count on past experience too heavily.

In considering the full range of brands available, shoppers need to be aware of store brands (sometimes also called private-label brands) as well as the more familiar nationally advertised brands. Store brands often provide good quality at reasonable prices.

For most products, the brand names of large manufacturers who advertise heavily are familiar to us all. We all are familiar with such nationally advertised brands of jeans as Levi's and Wrangler. We may be less familiar with the store brands—products made especially for a retail store or chain, to its specifications, and sold only by the store under its own brand name. An example is Jeans Joint and Roebucks jeans, which are available only at Sears, Roebuck and Co.

Many store brands are made by major manufacturers who also produce their own nationally advertised brands. For instance, Kenmore washers are made for Sears, Roebuck and Co. to its specifications by a washing machine manufacturer that also produces its own brand.

One way to tell whether a product is a nationally advertised brand or a store brand is to check the label to see who makes or distributes the product. Nationally advertised brands use such phrases as "made by" or "processed by," while store brands use the terms "made for" or "distributed by."

Store brands are of special interest to consumers because their quality is often comparable to that of nationally advertised brands, yet they sell at a lower price. This lower price is possible partly as a result of the elimination or reduction of advertising costs. Although the price of a store's own brand often has to cover some expenses for local newspaper advertising, it does not have to cover expensive national television, radio, or magazine advertising.

Label Information. In addition to the brand name, a good label should provide the following information:

- Quantity and/or size
- Composition (ingredients or contents)
- Directions for use and care

Many stores provide unit price information we can use to compare the cost of an item in different sized packages. (*Giant Supermarkets*)

- Warning about any hazards which can arise in use, storage, or disposal
- Name and address of the manufacturer or distributor

Information on quantity and the product price can be useful in calculating the *unit price*. This is the price per ounce for food products. For products sold by count, it is the price per item. For example, suppose we needed to choose between a package with 30 paper clips for 39¢ and one with 50 for 59¢. We can calculate the approximate price per paper clip in each package: 39¢ ÷ 30 = 1.36¢ per clip and 59¢ ÷ 50 = 1.2¢ per clip. Clearly, the larger package is cheaper. With unit price information we can quickly compare the cost of a product in different-sized packages.

Information about the composition of a product can provide some clues about performance and durability. Are the materials used good quality ones, or are they of poorer quality?

Directions for use can provide important clues to performance. Do the directions suggest the item will be difficult to use or that it may be hard to get good results? What about the directions for care of the item? Will it be expensive to keep it in good condition? Will time-consuming work be necessary to maintain it? Are there warnings about hazards? What clues do they provide about product safety? How serious are the hazards involved? Will it be difficult to use the product without danger?

Completeness of label information varies among products and manufacturers. Opinions on exactly what information should be provided also differ greatly. The information that must be provided for food products and textiles is regulated by the federal government. For other products, manufacturers make most of the decisions about what label information will be provided.

Many consumers feel labels should provide more detailed information on product performance. Some leaders in the consumer movement have called for wider use of *informative labeling*. This is labeling which provides information on the performance of a product under a series of standard tests. This information usually is provided in the form of test scores or ratings. Performance test information is available for many industrial products but is seldom available for consumer products. Nutritional labeling of food products is one of the few familiar examples of informative labeling of consumer products. Nutritional labels provide one kind of performance information—information on the amount of important vitamins and minerals in a particular brand. Not all brands provide this information, because nutritional labeling is voluntary for most products. When informative labeling information is available for a number of brands, consumers can more easily compare the brands on the characteristics tested. The usefulness of informative labeling information depends on which characteristics are tested (are they important ones?) and on the tests used (how good are they?).

Grade labeling goes one step beyond informative labeling. With *grade labeling,* the results of the whole set of performance tests are taken into account and an overall quality rating or grade is assigned to the product. The grades used for food products, such as the U.S. Choice grade for beef, are the ones most familiar to us. Developing a system of grade labeling requires decisions about the relative importance of different product characteristics. In assigning an overall grade, should each product characteristic be weighted equally, or are some more important than others? Grades will be most useful to us when the weights given to particular characteristics agree with our own.

Guarantees and Warranties. The words "guarantee" and "warranty" are both used to describe the written statement given by a seller or a manufacturer that promises repair, replacement, or refund if a product fails to perform as specified at the time it was sold. Warranties are provided for a wide variety of items, ranging from automobiles to electric appliances. Warranties differ among brands, and these differences may be an important consideration in choosing a brand.

Even without a written guarantee a manufacturer is responsible for providing a product that works as it is supposed to; a record player, for example, should play records. Under the law, every product should perform as it is intended to. The fact that a manufacturer offers an item for sale for a particular use is regarded as evidence that he is guaranteeing its suitability. In legal terms, his offer to sell the item for a particular use creates an "implied warranty." When an item is sold "as is," this means that there is no implied warranty.

In addition to the "implied warranty," many products also are covered by a written or "express warranty." The written warranty often is used by manufacturers to limit the obligations they might have under the implied warranty rather than to protect buyers. This makes it important for the warranty to be clear and easily understandable. Because warranties can be deceptive, the Federal Trade Commission (FTC) has been given power to regulate the information which is included in written warranties. Manufacturers do not have to offer written warranties, but when they do, they must follow the FTC rules.

```
JCPENNEY RADIO, TAPE RECORDER, TAPE PLAYER,
PORTABLE PHONO, AND WALKIE-TALKIE
```

FULL NINETY DAY WARRANTY

```
This warranty is applicable to all JCPenney Radios, Tape Recorders,
Tape Players, Portable Phonographs, Walkie-Talkies, and combinations
of these products.

Within ninety days of purchase, we will repair, or at our option, will
replace this product if defective in material or workmanship.  Parts
and labor are included.  Batteries are not covered by this warranty.
Just return it to the nearest JCPenney facility for prompt service.

For the addresses of JCPenney facilities in your area, refer to your
local telephone directory.  If there is no JCPenney facility in your
area, write to Carole Winslowe, JCPenney Co., Inc., Product Service
Department, 1301 Avenue of the Americas, New York, New York  10019.

This warranty gives you specific legal rights, and you may also have
other rights which vary from state to state.
```

Manufacturers or retailers provide written warranties for many products, describing what action will be taken if the product is defective. *(Reproduced by permission of JC Penney Company Inc. All rights reserved.)*

Firms which give written warranties on products costing more than $15 must follow the FTC regulations. Other good warranties also follow these guidelines. Warranties must be available to shoppers before they buy. They can be printed on the package, posted near the product, or made available on request, but they must be available. The warranty must be written in simple, easily understood language and must include the following information:

- The name and address of the firm giving the warranty. (Is it the manufacturer or the retailer?)
- The person to whom the warranty is given. (Is it limited to the original purchaser?)
- Exactly what is covered and what is not covered. (Who pays labor and shipping costs?)
- When the warranty begins and the term of coverage on the product or any of its parts. (Are some parts covered longer than others?)
- What will be done in case of a defect or breakdown and at whose expense? This will be repair or replacement if a *full warranty* is provided. If it is a *limited warranty*, the items and services which will and will not be paid for must be indicated.
- What the purchaser must do to get warranty services performed and who must be contacted, with names, addresses, and phone

numbers. (Must the product be returned? Are there locations convenient for you?)
- The time in which the warrantor firm must take action after receiving notice of the problem.
- The fact that an informal mechanism for settling disputes between the firm and the purchaser is available. This may be a panel to arbitrate disputes or other similar arrangements.
- Any requirements or conditions that must be met. Must the registration card be returned in order to have the warranty honored? Is regular maintenance required?

Consumers should be aware that even though the written or express warranty seems to limit their rights, they have many important rights under the implied warranty. When a product is sold, an implied warranty is created that the product will do what it is supposed to do and that it is suitable for the purposes claimed.

Under Federal Trade Commission rules, sellers who promise "satisfaction guaranteed or your money back" or "10-day free trial" should mean that the purchase price will be refunded in full on request by the purchaser. If there are any special requirements which must be met for the guarantee to be honored, they must be made clear at the time of purchase. If there are conditions that are not made clear, the seller is considered to be engaged in a deceptive practice and is subject to the FTC action. So-called "lifetime" guarantees also cause confusion. The FTC specifies that the seller must indicate clearly if the lifetime referred to is a life other than the purchaser's. For example, an auto supply dealer selling a muffler with a "lifetime guarantee" must indicate that the guarantee applies to the life of the car, not the life of the buyer, if that is what is meant.

Consumers should make a habit of saving and filing the guarantees, instructions, and sales receipts that come with the items they purchase. The file does not have to be elaborate; a big envelope or a small box will do. Such a file will save time and problems if difficulties do occur with a product.

COMPARING PLACES TO BUY

Shoppers in larger towns and cities have several choices as to where to shop for clothes, records, and appliances. In some cases, their choice is between two different stores of the same type—for example, two different men's clothing stores. Often, however, the item they want is available in a number of different types of stores. Records, for example, are available at discount stores, drugstores, variety stores, record shops, and department stores. The policies, services, and prices of these different types of stores vary widely. These differences make the decision about a place to buy a complicated one.

Comparing Prices Among Stores

The types of stores range from large discount stores with low prices and a high sales volume to small neighborhood stores with a low sales volume and higher prices. Discount stores gain large sales by emphasizing low prices. They hold costs down by buying in large quantities and limiting the variety of items, the number of clerks, and other services. Smaller stores that cannot compete in terms of price alone survive by providing their customers with other services. Neighborhood stores provide convenience of location and perhaps other services such as easy credit and free delivery. Other smaller shops may emphasize special selections of merchandise, expert assistance, or other special services. In order to make wise decisions, shoppers need to know about the whole range of sellers of items they want and about the extra services each seller provides. Without this information they may not get the combination of product, price, and extra services that would suit them best.

Comparison Shopping. The process of comparing the products, prices, and services offered by different stores is called *comparison shopping.* It is a good habit to form, especially for larger, more important purchases.

Consumer research studies have found that younger and higher-income shoppers visit more stores before making a purchase than do lower-income shoppers. Low-income shoppers seem to prefer to stick closer to neighborhood stores where they are known, where they can be certain about how they will be treated, and where they are certain they can get credit. This is unfortunate because prices in stores serving low-income areas often are a good deal higher than those in stores serving the general market. An FTC study in Washington, D.C., a few years ago estimated that a television set with a wholesale price of $100 would sell for $131 in a store serving the general market, but would sell for $187 in a store serving the low-income market. Many lower-income families were forced to buy at higher prices because they needed credit to make the purchase and could only obtain it from stores in the low-income market. It is worth noting that high prices in the low-income market stores studied were not found to be due to unusual profits. They were a result of higher bad-debt losses and higher outlays for salaries and commissions to sales personnel.

Specials and Average Prices. Comparing price levels among different stores may be difficult because of the frequent use of "specials." Specials are used by many stores to create a "low-price" image which they use to differentiate themselves from their competitors. Such stores constantly shift prices as part of their promotional efforts. Prices of some items are shifted down and emphasized in store ads, while the prices of other items are raised. This procedure, which is common in supermarkets, is called *variable price merchandising.* Because of it, we cannot judge a store just by its specials. Some studies have found that supermarkets with the best specials have higher average prices for other items.

Understanding What Services Are Provided

In order to fully evaluate the price asked for an item, the shopper needs to know exactly what extra services are included in the price

Many businesses are able to offer low prices by eliminating services. Consumers have to decide what services they are willing to pay extra to obtain. (*Left, Raimondo Borea, Editorial Photocolor Archives; right, UPI*)

and the cost of the other services that may be available. In some stores, delivery costs, alterations, installation, and credit charges are included in the price. In other stores there are charges for some of these services.

Another important aspect of a store's services is the policy on returned goods. In general, by law all sales are final unless some serious defect is discovered in an item. In order to maintain customer goodwill, most stores do not insist on the letter of the law. Some stores permit returns for a full refund, while others permit exchanges or give credit on returns. A few permit no returns or exchanges; this is usually the policy for sale merchandise even in more liberal stores. Department stores and specialty shops usually are the most liberal in permitting returns. This is one of the extra services these stores provide in return for the somewhat higher prices they charge.

Consumers should be fair and reasonable in asking stores to accept returned merchandise. Handling returned items is expensive for a store and may involve a substantial loss if the customer has damaged an item. Most retailers have a full set of stories about unreasonable requests for returns. One story that crops up frequently is about the shopper who returned a coat one Monday morning in the fall because "it didn't fit right." On checking the coat over, the storekeeper found mustard stains on the collar and a football ticket stub in the pocket. This type of problem has led some stores to set stricter policies on returns.

Checking Other Sources of Goods

Stores are not the only source for the merchandise that consumers buy. Other possible sources include mail-order houses and door-to-door salespeople. Like regular retail stores, these nonstore sources offer both advantages and disadvantages. It is good to be well aware of both the advantages and disadvantages of buying from these sources.

Mail-Order Sales. Mail-order houses offer consumers an opportunity to obtain specialized merchandise that may not be available in their community because the market is too limited to support a specialty store. This often is the situation for hobby and sports items such as stamps, stereo equipment, or special clothing styles or sizes. The large book and record clubs offer the shopper an opportunity to share in the benefits of large-scale purchasing in return for a promised number of purchases per year.

Because of the distance that separates the buyer and the seller and because of the communication problems involved, mail-order purchases have been a frequent subject of consumer complaints. The most frequent complaint is that merchandise ordered and paid for has not been received.

There are some things which you can do to help avoid problems:

- Read the ad carefully and be sure you understand all the details of the offer before you order.
- Remind yourself that some offers are deceptive. Some firms know they will be able to make a killing before they can be investigated and stopped. Just because an ad is in a magazine or newspaper you respect does not mean the ad is reliable. Many papers and magazines do not check the ads they run.
- Include all the information required in your order and be sure to include your address.
- Send a check or money order—never cash—and keep a record of the firm's address.

FTC rules require mail-order firms to ship orders within 30 days after receiving them or within the time stated in the ad. If an order is not shipped with the 30-day limit, you can demand a refund.

Door-to-Door Sales.   Door-to-door salespeople offer a variety of items including housewares, cosmetics, and cleaning supplies as well as home-improvement products such as aluminum siding. The consumer must proceed especially carefully in door-to-door purchases because of the repeated frauds and abuses that have occurred. Door-to-door salespeople place consumers in a position in which they are especially vulnerable to sales pressure. Most of us find it difficult to end a sales presentation and get rid of a salesperson. Sales pitches are, in some cases, cleverly devised scripts designed to arouse the emotions and interest of the prospective customer.

Salespeople often try to force consumers into making an immediate decision. Insist on time to check other sources, prices, and the reputation of the sales firm. You should never give in and sign a contract just to get rid of a salesperson. Do not let them stay so long that they begin to wear you down. If necessary, you should threaten to call the police. If you find, after signing a contract, that you have made a mistake, you may be able to cancel it. Under FTC rules, it is possible to cancel door-to-door sales contracts for over $25 within 3 business days after they have been signed. The contract must tell the procedures for doing this.

In this chapter we have discussed some of the things consumers can do for themselves in choosing products and the stores in which to make their purchases. Often, however, shoppers will have to turn to other sources for additional information about products or stores. Some of these information sources are discussed in the next chapter.

Checking Your Reading

1. Why is an inventory of what you have often an important first step in planning new purchases?
2. How do clearance sales and special purchase sales differ?
3. Why does the existence of price discrimination among customers create a situation in which it is important to shop around?
4. What is meant by saying that products or services are differentiated?
5. What techniques can consumers use to reduce the time and expense of shopping around?
6. What are the five product characteristics which are important in most products?
7. In what kinds of buying situations are consumers most likely to use price as an indication of quality? How good an indication is it, in general?
8. Why do manufacturers label products with brand names?
9. What are store brands? Why are store brands usually lower in price than manufacturers' brands?
10. How do informative labeling and grade labeling differ?
11. What kinds of information should be included in a guarantee?
12. Why do shoppers need to know the whole range of sellers for the item they want, along with the prices charged and the extra services provided?
13. What is comparison shopping?
14. Why does variable price merchandising make price comparisons among stores difficult for consumers?
15. Do buyers always have the right to exchange or return goods they have purchased? Why do stores differ in their policies on returns and exchanges?
16. What should we do to avoid problems with mail-order purchases? With door-to-door purchases?

Consumer Problems and Projects

1. Long-range planning frequently involves purchasing merchandise during off-season sales. List five items that can be purchased at a saving at certain times of the year. List also some of the disadvantages of this kind of buying. Example: Buying Christmas cards in January. Disadvantage: The cards and envelopes might become discolored before you can use them.

2. What store brands are offered in the drugstore or grocery store where you usually shop? Make a list of five product categories in which the store offers both store brands and manufacturers' brands. Some categories to check are canned peaches, frozen peas, frozen orange juice concentrate, ice cream, cola beverages, aspirin, and rubbing alcohol. List all the brands in each category, along with the price and whether the brand is a store or a manufacturer's brand. Have you ever compared any of these store brands with manufacturers' brands? How would you rate

3. them?
Make a collection of five labels from different products you and your family use. Make your collection as varied as possible— paint, dog food, canned food, toothpaste, clothing, laundry detergent, and so on. What are the good and bad features of each

4. label? What other information would you like to see included?
Obtain a copy of the guarantee for a product in which you are interested. (If necessary, visit a local store and request permission to copy the guarantee.) Does the guarantee provide *all* the information needed? Is it clear? What exactly is covered by the guarantee—the entire product or particular parts? Who pays for

5. replacement parts? Who pays the labor costs for repairs?
Choose a product you would be interested in buying or buy frequently that is sold in several different stores in your area. A hit record or tape, toothpaste, shampoo, or some other toiletry or cosmetic would be a good choice. Prepare a list of places in which the item is offered, along with the price in each store. Also note whether trading stamps or special services are provided. If

6. you were to buy the item, where would you buy it? Why?
What are some of the ways firms differentiate their products or services? Make a list of brands and services and the features which are used to differentiate them. For each, state how important you feel this feature is and why you feel this way.

5

Sources of Information for Consumers

In the last chapter, we discussed a number of kinds of product information which shoppers can find easily. These include product prices, brand names, label information, and guarantee information. As we saw, the information provided by these sources can be useful but does have its limitations. Careful shoppers need more information than these sources are likely to provide. Besides information on selecting products, there are other kinds of information which consumers need. We need information which we can use in better managing our finances. We need answers to such questions as "What kinds of auto loan arrangements are available, and which would suit my needs best?" Consumers also need information on consumer issues and problems. We need information which will help us answer such questions as "Do we need new laws to protect consumers from auto repair frauds?"

JUDGING INFORMATION SOURCES

To answer our questions about buying, financial management, and consumer issues, we need information that we can understand and rely on. In short, we need information that is useful. Just what characteristics should information have to make it useful? Useful information has the following five characteristics:

- *Objective.* To be useful and reliable, information must be objective. It must present the facts without bias or personal prejudice. Some sources slant the information presented in their own favor. They may, for example, exaggerate the importance of product characteristics which favor their brand.

    To be useful, information must be based on facts or reliable evidence. The source of the facts or evidence should be made clear. Are they based on scientific tests or research? Or are they based on individual opinions and judgements? If so, what qualifications do these individuals have? Are they recognized experts?

- *Accurate.* To be reliable, information must be accurate. It must be reported without mistakes. It also must be free of lies, tricks, and misstatements.

- *Complete.* Reliable information sources tell the full story. All the key facts are included. Information can be deceptive when key facts are left out.

- *Provide Critical Evaluations.* When products and services are discussed, both their strong points and their weaknesses should be reported. Comparisons should be made which will help consumers in making their decisions.

    This requirement applies to the discussion of consumer issues too. Discussions of consumer protection proposals should point out both their strengths and their weaknesses.

- *Understandable.* Even if an information source is objective, accurate, and complete and provides a critical evaluation, it will not be very useful if we cannot understand it. To be understandable, an information source should avoid complex language and too many technical terms. Sentences should be clear. Use of legal and technical terms should be held to a minimum. Those terms which are used should be defined or explained.

There are a variety of information sources consumers can use. These include the consumer-supported product-testing organizations, government sources, business sources, and the mass media. In the following sections, we will look at each of these sources and see how they stack up when we judge them against the five characteristics of useful consumer information.

PRODUCT-TESTING ORGANIZATIONS

During the 1920s more and more consumers were buying the new durable goods that were just coming into widespread use. Sales of autos, refrigerators, vacuum cleaners, and radios were brisk. Consumers were flooded with advertising from billboards, electric signs, newspapers, magazines, and a new advertising medium, radio. By the late 1920s many consumers had become aware that they had little useful information to help them with the complicated and expensive purchases they were making.

In 1927 Stuart Chase and F. J. Schlink proposed the idea of a consumer-supported organization that would perform product tests and provide consumers with the technical information they needed to make purchasing decisions. The inquiries from readers of their book, *Your Money's Worth*, soon convinced Schlink that the local Consumers' Club he had organized should be expanded. In 1929 Consumers' Research, Inc. (CR) was organized to perform product testing on a national scale. CR headquarters are in Washington, New Jersey.

Consumers' Research has been outpaced by Consumers Union of United States, Inc. (CU), which split off from CR in 1936 as the result of an employee labor dispute. CU now is by far the larger organization, with a staff of over 300 people. Its headquarters are in Mount Vernon, New York. Both CR and CU issue monthly publications: *Consumers' Research Magazine* is published by CR, and *Consumer Reports* is published by CU. In the late 1970s *Consumer Reports* had a monthly circulation of about 2 million copies.

Before testing a product, the engineers in both organizations decide which product characteristics are most important. They next decide what tests can be used to measure these product characteristics. Each brand is put through the same set of standardized tests, and each brand is given a score on each test. These test scores are multiplied by the weights given to the product characteristics, and a total score for each brand is calculated. These calculations are done just the same way Jim Taylor made his calculations when buying an alarm clock (Chapter 2). After the total scores are calculated, the brands are ranked on the basis of their total scores. This procedure is called *comparative testing*. It provides information on the relative quality of different brands. In this type of testing, brands are compared with each other rather than with some absolute standard.

Both CU and CR know that their reputations depend on the accuracy, reliability, and fairness of their tests. Both organizations make every effort to preserve their independence from all special interests, including product manufacturers. To help them maintain their independence, neither organization's magazine accepts advertising, and neither permits manufacturers to mention their findings. Although both organizations have been accused of playing favorites, no real proof has ever been offered to support such accusations.

What Kinds of Products Are Tested?

Product testing works best with products that consumers can readily identify by brand name and, if necessary, model number. To be useful, the ratings must include the brands that are most widely available and widely used throughout the country. Certain kinds of products do not meet these requirements very well. For example, fresh meat, which usually is sold unbranded, would not meet these requirements. Canned hams and other processed meat products, however, are identified by brand name, and ratings can be developed for these products.

In choosing products to be tested, particular attention is given to items that make up an important part of family budgets: food, automobiles, appliances, and clothing. But attention is also given to hobby and sports items, including a number of items that would be of interest to young adults. One of the special interests of many CU members is stereo equipment, and CU has, over the years, built up a reputation for expertise in this area. Certain products are tested frequently, even annually if necessary, to keep up with model changes. Because of annual model changes, autos are tested each year.

How Are Products Tested?

Both CU and CR use standard testing techniques recognized by both industry and government. In some cases, however, special new tests have to be developed when existing procedures do not cover a situation. To test hair sprays, CU put sprayed swatches of human hair into a high-humidity chamber and measured how much and how quickly each curl drooped.

Each organization does testing in its own laboratories. CU has elaborate special equipment for testing, including a special chamber that shields TV sets from stray electronic signals during testing and a special muffled acoustic chamber to test stereo and other audio equipment. When special tests or information are required, outside testing laboratories with the necessary equipment and special consultants are called on. In addition to being tested in a laboratory, products may also be tested under actual use conditions by panels of consumers who report their experience with the product. A panel of parents with young babies was used recently by CU to test the performance of disposable diapers. They reported on such important performance factors as fit and tendency to leak.

The products that are tested by CU are bought in different cities

This is a Consumers Union test of how quickly the various brands of smoke detectors respond to the "smouldering to flaming" type of fire, which is characterized by a quick flame and diminishing smoke. The experiment was set up very carefully. A bundle of ¾ in × ¾ in wood strips was placed on a grill and lit by a small pan of alcohol. The smoke detectors were attached to the ceiling at a uniform distance. A computer clocked the precise time each detector went off. *(Courtesy of Consumer Reports Magazine)*

around the country by shoppers who do not reveal that the items are to be used for CU tests. For some products, only one sample of a particular brand is tested. In other cases, a number of samples are used.

What Ratings Are Given?

Products are rated on the basis of overall quality. CR rates products on the basis of quality or performance. Products are classified into three categories: (1) recommended, (2) intermediate, and (3) not recommended. CR also assigns price ratings. Thus it could rate a product high in quality but also indicate that it is relatively high-priced.

CU assigns products to two broad categories: (1) acceptable and (2) not acceptable. The products in each category are listed in order of their estimated overall quality. Products that are clearly superior to others in the "acceptable" category are indicated with a check rating. Products that are rated "not acceptable" usually fail because of some safety hazard, such as danger of shock in electric appliances. CU does not assign price ratings but does indicate a "best buy" when a product is rated high and is relatively low in price.

In using the ratings developed by the two product-testing organizations, it is important to be aware of the characteristics on which a product has been rated. CU and CR base the weights they use on their experience and their ideas about the needs of average consumers. You may put different weights on these characteristics than the ones which were used in calculating the ratings. If you have special needs, you may want to study the test reports to determine which of the top-rated products would best meet your own requirements.

What Effect Have the Product-Testing Organizations Had?

The product-testing organizations have had an important impact on government and business, as well as on consumers. Consumers have benefited directly from the money-saving advice offered. Haphazard buying that ignores product-testing information may be more costly than most of us would imagine. This is shown by a study which compared the prices of products given the poorest ratings by CU with the prices of products given the best ratings. It was found that, on the average, the products with the poorest ratings cost 27 percent more than those with the best ratings. Those who bought the lowest-rated products not only spent more but also lost out on quality as well.

Both CR and CU deal with consumer problems that go beyond product testing, and both have published special articles on such issues as pollution and the use of pesticides—issues that are of concern to us all as consumers and as citizens. Both CR and CU also have educational departments that assist schools by providing educational materials. CU, in particular, has tried to help schools develop new consumer education programs. Despite their efforts, CU has had little success in reaching one group of consumers—low-income families.

Manufacturers are well aware of how they stand in the product ratings, and they are sometimes forced to make needed improvements when their products receive unfavorable publicity because of poor test results. They are also influenced by the effect of ratings on sales. Many small and new companies have received their big break when favorable ratings have brought their products to the public's attention.

Even the large car manufacturers can observe the effects of the ratings on the sales of different models.

The government also is affected by the activities of the consumer-supported product-testing organizations. Test results may provide evidence of the need for new laws on product safety or other new legislation. CU has actively assisted in the development of new consumer legislation by providing expert testimony on consumer problems. In contrast, CR does not engage in any legislative activities.

GOVERNMENT AGENCIES

As part of its regulatory and educational activities, the federal government issues a wide variety of consumer information publications. These range from Department of Agriculture pamphlets on food buying to Department of Interior booklets on recreation facilities in the national parks.

Government publications for consumers focus on product characteristics which are important in selecting products and on how we, as consumers, can judge products on these characteristics. They usually avoid naming products by brand name.

Consumer Information Center

The number of government publications is so great that it is difficult to discover what consumer information is available and to keep up with new publications as they appear. The Consumer Information Center was created within the General Services Administration in 1970 to deal with this problem. The center was given responsibility for making existing publications more easily available to consumers and for encouraging the development of new publications based on the product testing done to guide government purchasing and on government research activities. The center issues catalogs four times a year. Each lists about 250 publications of special interest to consumers. Copies of the current *Consumer Information* catalog are available free from the Consumer Information Center, Pueblo, Colorado 81009.

Along with the Consumer Information Center, the General Services Administration also operates Federal Information Centers in a number of major cities. The centers are staffed by people who are prepared to answer or get answers to questions about federal government services, programs, and publications. When problems do not fall into federal jurisdiction, callers are referred to the appropriate local or state agency. In recent years, Federal Information Centers have been operating in 37 major cities. Another 37 cities have free long-distance telephone service linking them to a center. The phone numbers in all 74 cities are listed under "U.S. Government."

Department of Agriculture

One of the largest groups of government publications for consumers is produced by the Department of Agriculture. The publications discuss foods and food buying as well as menu planning and nutrition. Other topics include clothing selection, sewing, and housing. The Yearbooks of Agriculture often are of particular interest to consumers.

National Highway Traffic Safety Administration

The National Highway Traffic Safety Administration of the Department of Transportation also has consumer publications. Its publications provide information on safety aspects of automobile per-

Many government agencies, including the Department of Agriculture, produce pamphlets and other publications that are useful to consumers.

formance. Each year the agency publishes *Performance Data for New Passenger Cars and Motorcycles*. It includes information on acceleration and passing times and distances, on tire reserve loads (the capacity of tires to bear additional weight), and on stopping distances. The data are listed according to make, model, and equipment option. This publication was one of the first to include brand names and model designations. The tables in this report indicate a great deal of variation in performance among makes and models, even for such an important safety factor as stopping distance.

Federal Trade Commission

The consumer education program of the Federal Trade Commission (FTC) is an outgrowth of its responsibility for controlling misleading advertising and deceptive business practices. FTC publications aim to alert consumers to common types of fraudulent claims and deceptive practices. Some of the FTC's concerns are reflected in its recent publication, *Don't Be Gypped,* and a booklet on choosing a vocational school, *Our Vocational Training Can Guarantee You the Job of a Lifetime.* The publication on vocational schools notes that ads often give a glowing picture of a glamorous new career, guaranteed job placement, and top starting salaries. It points out that such claims are deceptive, since schools normally cannot promise specific jobs or starting salaries.

Office of Consumer Affairs

Consumer News, published by the Office of Consumer Affairs in the Department of Health, Education, and Welfare is somewhat different from the other government publications we have discussed. It reports on current government activities in the consumer area. It explains new laws, regulations, and programs. It carries reports of governmental action against individual companies who have violated federal consumer protection laws and regulations and new product recalls and product hazards. It also describes new consumer information publications. Subscriptions to the *Consumer News* are available from the Consumer Information Center.

COOPERATIVE EXTENSION SERVICE

The Extension Service is a cooperative federal, state, and county program of education in agriculture and home economics. It is administered by the land-grant university in each state, such as Cornell University in New York, The University of Illinois, Oklahoma State University, and the University of California. Extension Service programs are carried to the public by field personnel in individual counties throughout each state.

The original goal of the Extension Service was to improve the income and well-being of rural families by providing information on better farming and homemaking practices. As the American population has become more and more urban, the Extension Service has expanded its programs to serve urban as well as rural families.

One of its important services to consumers is its bulletin series. The publications provide information on such varied topics as food selection, sewing, and lawn care. Like the federal government publications, the Extension Service publications do not mention brand names but instead emphasize buying techniques. A current catalog of the Extension Service's consumer publications for your state is available from the Cooperative Extension Service Bulletin Office at your land-grant college or university. Some titles selected from recent catalogs give an idea of the wide range of topics covered:

- *Food for Fitness* (Ohio State University)
- *Electrical Repairs You Can Do* (Michigan State University)
- *Selection and Care of Sweaters and Knit Apparel* (University of Illinois)
- *Be a Better Shopper* (Cornell University)
- *Buy a House . . . Not a Nightmare* (Texas A&M University)
- *Things to Think About Before Buying Vitamin or Vitamin-Mineral Pills* (University of California)

Your local extension service office, usually located in the county seat, has a staff that can answer a wide range of questions.

BETTER BUSINESS BUREAU

The sources of consumer information that we have discussed so far all have provided product information. They provide relatively little help to the consumer who is trying to decide where to buy. There is, however, a source of information on firms in local markets—the better business bureau. In addition to providing information on local firms, the better business bureaus provide booklets with useful tips on buying and many warnings on fraudulent schemes. There are, it should be noted, certain kinds of information the better business bureaus are not set up to provide, including product endorsements and ratings and information on the least expensive places to buy particular items. Another service of the better business bureaus is handling consumer complaints. This part of the work of the better business bureaus will be discussed in Chapter 28.

The beginnings of the better business bureaus date to 1912, when the first local groups were organized by business people to combat exaggerated claims and fraudulent schemes that they felt damaged the public's faith in advertising. There are now over 140 local better business bureaus and branches throughout the United States. These local organizations are all nonprofit and are supported by contributions from businesses.

The local better business bureaus are self-governing and operate independently but are joined together in a national organization, the Council of Better Business Bureaus, Inc. Some local bureaus (BBB) have made outstanding records for their service and information efforts. Others have been less forceful either because of lack of funds and personnel or perhaps because of fear of pressure from local member firms.

In 1970, the national BBB association reorganized with the goal of improving the services of all the local bureaus. The new national organization has sought funds to assist the local organizations and is encouraging them to take a more active role in assisting consumers. The goal of the new national organization is to create a consumer program so effective that new government programs will seem less necessary.

When providing information on local firms, the better business bureaus will not give advice about whom to deal with. They instead give facts from their complaint and information file and leave it up to the individuals to interpret the information and make their own decisions. For example, someone concerned about the reputation of a particular auto dealer might be told:

> The subject company has been identified in a file since 1963. During the past 3 years, we have received complaints that the company has failed to correct repair problems. In connection with these complaints, the company generally has answered with their side of the story and provided substantiation. The company generally has adjusted complaints brought to their attention.

The language used seems a bit legalistic but tells us that in the complaint cases received by the BBB, the firm usually has responded to complaints received from the BBB. Not all do. It also is clear that they have made some effort to resolve the complaints they have received. It is likely, however, that not all the complaints were settled to the customer's satisfaction. There does not seem to be any evidence that the firm is unfair or uses deceptive practices. The decision to buy from the firm or not, however, must be made by each shopper.

The BBB pamphlet series includes a wide variety of subjects, with information on both product choice and kinds of frauds that occur frequently. Some titles from the series are *Tape Recorders and Players, Buying Used Cars,* and *Computer Careers.* The pamphlets are available through local better business bureaus. Many small cities and towns do not have better business bureaus. Those who do not live in an area served by a better business bureau may request publications from the national organization: Public Information Division, Council of Better Business Bureaus, Inc., 1150 17th Street, N.W., Washington, DC 20036. The publications are free; include a stamped, self-addressed envelope with your request.

TRADE CERTIFICATION PROGRAMS

Groups of business firms concerned with improving the durability and safety of consumer goods have joined together to support several different testing organizations. These testing organizations certify products that meet the standards they have set and award these products identifying seals. In cases where the organizations have set high standards that are carefully enforced, their seals have real meaning for consumers. In cases where standards are low or are not enforced, the seals have little significance. Three of the best-known and most useful seals are those of the Underwriters Laboratories Inc., the American Gas Association, and the International Fabricare Institute.

Underwriters Laboratories Inc.

Perhaps the most familiar of these seals is the "UL" symbol of the Underwriters Laboratories Inc. About 2 billion UL seals are used each year on new appliances and other products that the Underwriters Laboratories checks. UL is an independent, not-for-profit organization. It is supported by fees charged manufacturers for its testing services. UL checks not only electric appliances and equipment but also automotive and boat safety equipment, burglar and fire alarms, and fire protection equipment.

UL checks product designs in its own laboratories, visits factories, and checks products purchased in the retail market. The design of

Trade certification seals can be an important source of information for consumers. *(Courtesy associations shown)*

products that are certified has been checked to reduce hazards from fire, electric shock, and other casualties. UL does not, however, judge product quality or performance. Shoppers should look for UL seals when they buy. They should check to be certain that the seal is on the body of the appliance itself.

American Gas Association

The Star Seal seen on gas appliances is the symbol of the American Gas Association (AGA). This seal indicates that the AGA Laboratories have tested a sample of the product and that it meets applicable national standards for safety, durability, and performance. The AGA is a national trade association of natural gas transmission and distribution companies. They do not manufacture or sell gas appliances, and their chief concern is the safety of gas appliance users. Most gas appliances carry the AGA seal. Shoppers should double-check for it before buying.

International Fabricare Institute

Because of their concern that the items they handle stand up well to cleaning, members of the cleaning industry have developed a certification program for clothing and other fabric items. This certification program is conducted by the International Fabricare Institute. After a thorough check proves an item's ability to stand up under typical professional cleaning techniques, the manufacturer is granted permission to use the Institute's "Certified Washable" or "Certified Dry Cleanable" seals. These seals are displayed on hand tags, labels, and in advertising. They can be a useful guide for consumers.

OTHER BUSINESS SOURCES

Individual firms and business trade associations publish a wide variety of booklets and other informational materials about their products and ways to use them. These materials typically are listed in ads. Some home magazines carry special sections listing available informational materials.

Catalogs issued by business firms also may be useful references. In describing items in print, the seller has to point out the quality differences that justify differences in prices. After you cut away the fancy adjectives, catalog descriptions can help you identify key product characteristics and judge a brand's rating on a particular characteristic. Mail-order catalogs also are a useful reference against which local prices can be checked.

MASS MEDIA SOURCES

Until a few years ago, consumer problems and issues were given little coverage in either the print media (magazines, newspapers, and books) or in the electronic media (radio and television). More recently, all the mass media have come to appreciate the public's great interest in the variety of issues that affect us as consumers. Nowadays consumer issues and problems are considered news by the mass media and are the subject of special feature stories, regular columns, and television shows. Stories appear in general-audience magazines such as *Reader's Digest*, home magazines such as *Better Homes and*

Gardens, women's magazines such as *McCall's*, and special-interest magazines such as *New York*.

The new coverage of consumer problems supplements the consumer information that the mass media have provided for years. Such items as movie and play reviews, TV and book reviews, and tips on food buying and recipes have been familiar for many years.

How Reliable Are the Mass Media?

The mass media can be an important source of information for consumers. Just how reliable are they? When we judge them against the five characteristics of useful consumer information, how well do they stack up?

Objective. The public expects the media to report the news without bias or personal prejudice. The facts suggest, however, that the media are sometimes the willing tool of special-interest groups. Public relations people bombard the media with press releases, photos, and ready-to-print editorials on their products and points of view. The media are free to use or ignore these materials. Many of the media do use it and do not seem very concerned about its lack of objectivity. Media which do use this material seldom indicate its source. Instead, the audience is left to think that the information presented is the medium's own objective and independent judgment. Material supplied by heavy advertisers sometimes is given special attention. This practice is said to be especially common on the food and travel pages. The desire to remain independent has led some publications to avoid carrying any advertising.

Accurate. Consumer news stories should be based on facts and reported accurately. The facts should be indicated, and their source and reliability should be made clear.

Consumer news stories also should help consumers put events and problems in perspective. They should make the extent of a problem and its seriousness clear. Sensational treatments of news often exaggerate how serious a problem is or the number of people affected. Stories of unsafe products and product recalls are easily sensationalized. What consumers need is a reliable report on the products involved, ways to identify them, and the action which those who have purchased the product should take. If a story is sensationalized, these vital facts may get lost. Sensational treatment of such news may not be evidence of concern for consumers at all. It may just be a way to sell more papers.

Complete. The media should carry every important news story affecting consumers. Sometimes important stories are neglected. It is often difficult to determine whether this is the result of a decision that the news is not very significant or a desire to protect a favored advertiser or a special interest. Action by government agencies against national, regional, or local firms would seem to qualify as consumer news. However, such stories actually receive only spotty coverage.

Complete coverage of consumer news does not consist just of reports of news events. It also includes reports of problems affecting consumers. Such reports are often the result of investigations conducted locally by reporters. Investigative reports on such local problems as poor sanitation in grocery stores and restaurants and deceptive business practices can play an important role in improving conditions.

Critical. When products and services are discussed, both their strong points and weaknesses should be evaluated. Although the media review books, movies, and television programs critically, many are afraid to make negative comments about consumer products. Some which have made negative comments have had to face open pressure from advertisers and threats that ads would be canceled.

Understandable. Even though the mass media are aimed at the general public, they sometimes forget to explain unfamiliar terms. A story about bait-and-switch deception schemes loses most of its punch if the meaning of "bait-and-switch" is not explained. Do you know what it means? (The term is used to describe the practice of advertising an item at an unusually low price in order to lure shoppers into a store, with no real intention of actually selling it; once shoppers are in the store, salespeople try to "switch" them to higher-priced items.)

In using the mass media as a source of consumer information, we need to remember that they do not always live up to our highest expectations. The five points above will help us to judge how reliable the information provided really is.

Consumer-Oriented Magazines

Among the media, two monthly magazines deserve special mention: *Changing Times* and *Money.* Both are devoted entirely to stories on consumer topics. One major emphasis is money management and financial and career planning. Some typical stories of this type are "Wedding Bills, and How to Peel Them" and "Why You May Be Paying Too Much for Credit." Other stories are on the topic of buying. These stories include such subjects as "Keys to Buying a Piano" and "A Good Buy in a Man's Suit." The stories on buying identify key product characteristics and tell ways to judge them. Both magazines discuss different brands and their features but do not usually rate different brands. Neither magazine conducts product tests. Both call on outside experts to help them in developing their advice. In addition to information on buying, both magazines carry information on product care and maintenance. An example is the story "Help Your Car Battery Last Longer." Both magazines also provide coverage of consumer issues. They discuss consumer problems and current issues as well as new and proposed laws and regulations.

Checking Your Reading

1. What was the basic idea that led to the founding of the consumer-supported product-testing organizations?
2. What is comparative testing?
3. What kinds of products do not lend themselves well to the type of testing performed by Consumers' Research and Consumers Union?
4. How are overall product ratings developed by CR and CU?
5. How do product ratings by CR and CU affect manufacturers?
6. Why was the Consumer Information Center organized?
7. What kinds of product information do government publications usually provide? What kinds of information usually are not provided?
8. What topics do the FTC's publications deal with?
9. What kinds of information does the *Consumer News* carry?
10. How can you contact the cooperative extension service in your state?
11. What kinds of information about local firms do better business bureaus provide?
12. What factors are considered before the Underwriters' Laboratories grants use of its "UL" seal? What factors are not taken into consideration?

13. What do the International Fabricare Institute's seals "Certified Washable" and "Certified Dry Cleanable" indicate?
14. Why are catalog descriptions of products often a useful source of information?
15. How does concern about the reaction of their advertisers affect the mass media in their handling of consumer news?
16. In order to be reliable sources of consumer information, what characteristics should the mass media have?

Consumer Problems and Projects

1. Go to the library and look through some recent issues of *Consumers' Research Magazine,* and *Consumer Reports*. Read carefully about a product that interests you and prepare a report on your findings. Which of the characteristics tested were considered most important and weighted most heavily? How were the products tested on these characteristics? If you were going to buy the product, what brand and model would you choose? Why?
2. Jim Munson was talking to his neighbor about how he had used information from Consumers Union and Consumers' Research in choosing a car. The neighbor said, "I wouldn't believe a word either of them says. You can tell they're taking bribes by the way they always rate the same brand at the top." What could Jim reply?
3. Prepare a report on the activities of Consumers Union using your library as a source of references. You should use both the publications of the organization itself and discussions about the organization in recent periodicals. The *Readers' Guide to Periodical Literature* will be useful in locating current articles. What are some of the criticisms of the organization and what responses have been made to these criticisms? What other activities besides product testing does the organization carry on?
4. Check the catalog of one of the large mail-order firms and select a product that interests you that is offered at several different price levels. Some possibilities are men's T-shirts, jeans, sweat shirts, sneakers, latex interior wall paint, AM-FM table radios, and electric alarm clocks. Make a list of the different items offered by product number. List the materials used and the features, price,

and shipping weight of each item. What are the basic differences among the items offered? Which would best suit your needs? Why?

5. Examine a recent issue of your local newspaper. What examples can you find of the following types of consumer news coverage: (a) news stories on current events; (b) service features such as "how-to" articles, recipes, and home-care hints; (c) investigative reports on consumer problems at the state, local, or national level; (d) critical evaluations of a particular product or service; (e) letters columns which deal with consumer problems and issues. Make a list of the headlines of the articles in each category. What important information is included in each article?

6. Develop comparative ratings for the consumer information in three different publications. Choose each of the publications you rate from a different one of the information sources discussed in this chapter. Rate them on the five characteristics of useful consumer information. Make a chart like Table 5-1 to help you rate them. Change the tests suggested, or add your own, if you wish.

TABLE 5-1
Comparative Testing of Information Sources

| | | Publication | |
| | | *(Insert name)* | |
Characteristic and Test	Weight	Rating	Weighted Score
Objectivity (Carries no advertising; Financially independent of business interests)			
Accuracy (Based on scientific tests or research)			
Completeness (Considers all important product characteristics)			
Critical Evaluation (Discusses both strengths and weaknesses, provides comparative ratings)			
Understandable Easy-to-read; defines technical terms			
Total Score (Total of weighted scores)			

Note: Ratings and weights range from 1 (lowest) to 10 (highest).

6

Understanding the Effects of Advertising

A great deal of money is spent by business to inform and influence American consumers. Information provided by salespeople, public relations offices, and advertising is all part of this effort. Advertising is a major part of it. Each year American business spends an average of $125 per person on advertising designed to influence us as consumers. Advertising is such an important force in the marketplace and in our everyday lives that it is important to understand how it affects us.

ROLE OF ADVERTISING

Advertising has several important roles in our economic system. It provides information about products to consumers, and it helps business to sell its products. It also is an important source of financial support for the mass media.

Informing and Influencing Consumers

A business has several goals in mind when it advertises. It wants, first off, to inform consumers about its product and its characteristics. It does not, however, just want consumers to know about the product. It wants them to have a favorable attitude toward the product. In addition, it wants to move them into action to buy it.

In designing advertising, a business's first consideration is in producing more favorable attitudes toward its product and increasing sales. Sometimes these goals will lead to ads which provide consumers with useful information. They may, however, lead to ads which are eye-catching and effective, but provide little real information.

Consumers, for their part, do not really want to be influenced. They want to make up their own minds. Nor do they want to be moved into action to buy. They want to make up their own minds about that. What they do want is information.

We can see that business and consumers want different things from advertising. Business wants favorable attitudes toward its products and it wants sales. Consumers want information. These differences in what business and consumers expect from advertising have made it a center of controversy.

Providing Support for Mass Media

Advertising also is important because it helps support the mass media, including newspapers, magazines, radio, and television. While consumers pay part of the cost of producing magazines and newspapers, advertisers pay an even larger share. Without advertising revenue to pay part of its operating costs, a newspaper that now costs the consumer 15 cents might cost 50 cents.

Some people are afraid that advertisers may have too much power over media content. In Chapter 5 you have already seen that advertisers sometimes have been guilty of trying to use their financial power to influence the content of the mass media.

THE INFLUENCE OF ADVERTISING

It is hard to ignore advertising. We find it everywhere—in the magazines we read, on television, and in the newspaper. Even when we get in our cars and drive off to get away from it, we find advertising on the car radio and on the billboards we pass. When we finally get home, if we look at the mail, we are likely to find that it is mostly advertising circulars.

How Much Can Advertising Influence Behavior?

Until about 30 years ago, advertising men were convinced that if they kept hitting consumers with a series of ads, they eventually could influence them to buy. Advertising men felt all they needed to do was to find the most effective "sales pitch" and a way to deliver it to the consumer.

More recent research has found that advertising must be related to the needs and concerns of the audience in order to be effective. If it is not, it will be ignored. The audience no longer is thought of as a passive target for whatever the advertiser throws at it. The modern view is that the audience interacts with the ad. Depending on whether or not the ad interests them, they may either ignore an ad or look at it. If they look at it, they may either understand the message or misinterpret it. They then may either remember the message or forget it. And finally, they may choose either to act on the message or disregard it.

Advertising appeals cannot be successful if they conflict with our values and goals. No amount of advertising is ever likely to produce many sales for products that do not fit into our way of life. It seems unlikely that advertising would ever produce many sales for chocolate-covered ants.

Advertising also has little effect on maintaining sales of products outmoded by new technology. The manufacturers of old-fashioned iceboxes could never have successfully competed in the market with manufacturers of electric refrigerators, no matter how much they advertised.

The evidence we have looked at suggests that advertising is not as powerful a force in changing behavior as sometimes has been argued. Claims about the possibility of "brainwashing" the public with advertising are greatly exaggerated. The fact that advertising is not all-powerful does not make misleading advertising any less undesirable. Advertising is an important source of information for consumers, and consumers need and deserve to have it kept honest.

What Are the Appeals Used in Advertising?

Those who write about advertising usually classify ads as either rational or emotional. Ads that supply basic facts and information about product features, prices, and availability are labeled *rational*. Those that provide no facts but instead stress the feelings produced by use of the product are labeled *emotional*. These two categories of ads usually are viewed as direct opposites—either an ad is rational or it is emotional.

With a little thought, we can see that rational and emotional are not really opposites. For example, an ad may be rational and still arouse strong feelings. An ad that says "Accidents Are the Leading Cause of Death Among Young Adults—Drive Safely" has both rational and emotional content. Another problem with classifying ads as either rational or emotional is that, as we saw in the previous section, not all readers react to an ad in the same way. An ad that some consider emotional may produce little reaction in others.

In studying advertising appeal, it may be more useful to focus on the content of an ad and avoid attempting to guess what reaction it will arouse in people who see it. Using this approach we can group ad messages into two broad categories: rational and irrational appeals.

- *Rational Appeals.* The content of the ad has a direct relation to the product. An example would be an ad that describes particular product features, such as the automatic transmission in a new car.

MOM'S APPLE PIE

Remember your mom's apple pie . . . loaded with tender apple chunks, spiced with cinnamon, and topped with a crust that would melt in your mouth? Enjoy that great taste again with our **Mom's Apple Pie.** We use all natural ingredients . . . apples, eggs, sugar, spices. All you have to do is heat and serve. Look for **Mom's Apple Pie** in your grocer's freezer.

The same advertisement may contain both rational and emotional appeals, or may appeal to more than one emotion.

- *Irrational Appeals.* The content of the ad associates a product with something that has no real connection with it. An example is an ad that links a soft drink with a baseball game. While soft drinks are often consumed at ball games, they are more frequently consumed in other types of situations.

We can identify two different kinds of irrational appeals. One type is an *internal association.* In this type of appeal, an association is made between a product and something within the reader, perhaps the need for success or some other personality characteristic. This kind of association is seen, for example, in an ad that reads, "The new car that's free as the wind." In this example, the car is associated with the reader's desire for personal freedom and independence. The other type of irrational appeal is an *external association.* This is an association between the product and things within the reader's environment. An example is an ad showing a new-model car as part of a picnic scene, thus linking it to enjoyable activities.

ADVERTISING—PRO AND CON

There have been many criticisms of advertising over the years and many responses to these criticisms. In this section we will look at some of the most frequent criticisms. Some critics have gone so far as to take the position that no advertising should be permitted at all. This suggestion seems contrary to our basic ideas about freedom of speech. Certainly business people have the right to make their wares known to the public. What is in question is not their right to promote their wares but the way they use advertising to promote them.

Should Ads Be More Informative?

One of the most frequent criticisms of advertising is that it provides little useful information to help consumers in their buying decisions. We have seen that business is not always interested in informing consumers. What they really are interested in is getting consumers to have a more favorable attitude toward their product and influencing them to buy it. This means that business will use irrational appeals containing no real information about the product if they seem to work better than rational appeals. Many ads rely on irrational claims—especially ads for soft drinks, chewing gum, cosmetics and toiletries, and cigarettes. They provide such useful information as the fact that cola drinks can be consumed at picnics, parties, ball games, and other pleasant occasions (big news!).

Most of us, as consumers, would like to have ads which provide more solid facts about the products we are interested in. There does not, however, seem to be any very good way to force advertisers to focus on rational appeals rather than irrational ones.

Is Advertising Wasteful?

A frequent criticism of advertising is that it is wasteful and makes the things we buy more expensive than they otherwise would be. In considering this criticism, we should begin by thinking about what advertising really does cost us. Advertising is not as costly as is often thought. Many people greatly overestimate the portion of a product's price that goes for advertising. What would be *your* estimate?

Some people's estimates of advertising's share of product price run as high as 25 and even 40 percent. In general, advertising's share is far below these figures. Food processors, on the average, spend about 2.2 cents of each dollar of sales on advertising. Manufacturers of tobacco products are among the heaviest spenders and lay out 4.2 cents of each dollar they receive. In contrast, expenditures by motor vehicle manufacturers are only 0.6 cent for each dollar of sales. Of course, this percentage becomes substantial when we consider the prices of new cars—advertising would account for about $30 of the cost of a new $5000 car. We can see that the prices of most products would be reduced relatively little if advertising disappeared altogether.

Supporters of advertising frequently argue that advertising reduces prices. They argue that it replaces more costly methods of providing product information. Most of us probably would agree that it is less costly than relying on door-to-door salespeople and large numbers of store clerks.

Those people speaking for advertising have also argued that advertising expands the market for products and thus permits large-scale production. This, they say, lowers the cost of each unit of output and makes lower prices possible. This argument seems valid for products produced by smaller companies and for new products. However, it probably is not valid for established products produced by larger companies. Most economists believe that after companies reach a certain size, it is difficult for them to improve efficiency and cut costs very much. These economists also point out that as companies become very large, problems of communications and management actually may begin to reduce efficiency and increase costs.

Some critics of advertising argue that advertising is wasteful because ads for one brand only cancel out those for others. For certain types of products this seems to be true. For example, presweetened cereals buyers seem to have little loyalty to particular brands. They are easily switched to others. As a result, cereal manufacturers rely heavily on toys, contests, and advertising to attract and hold customers. Most of us would probably agree this battle for customers is wasteful. There is little question that these expenditures for advertising and promotion do increase the prices that consumers pay. One way to reduce this waste would be to limit the number of brands offered. The dangers and problems of this type of regulation probably would far outweigh the benefits.

Supporters of advertising often argue that advertising is not wasteful because it adds value to products that are advertised. They argue that because of advertising, consumers value products more highly than they otherwise would and gain more satisfaction from them. This argument does have merit. Part of our enjoyment in consuming most products is a result of the feelings they produce. If a particular kind of after-shave makes a man feel more manly and handsome, it actually may give him the self-confidence that will in fact make him more attractive. This effect is something like the *placebo effect* of the sugar pills doctors sometimes give patients. While the sugar pill has no real physical effect, its psychological effect helps to relieve the patient's symptoms.

It should be noted that while advertising can add value to new products, it also can help to destroy the value of things we already own. Ads for new clothing styles may make us value last year's clothes less and may make us more willing to discard them. Thus, ads may increase the *psychological obsolescence* of things we have. They can make us value them less, even though they still are perfectly usable.

Does Advertising Distort Our Values?

We have noted that advertising techniques are not powerful enough to brainwash us into accepting products or ideas that conflict with our basic values. Some critics, however, claim that even though advertising may not be able to completely change our values, it is capable of distorting them. These critics argue that advertising leads us to want the kinds of things we see advertised rather than seek other possibilities. This, they say, leads us to spend more than we might other-wise spend on advertised products and services and less on unadver-tised things such as public recreational facilities and libraries.

A frequent response to this argument is that a consumer's wants have meaning regardless of where they come from. A want created by advertising may be just as strong and just as important as one growing out of more direct experience. One can still wonder, however, what our wants and needs would be like if good nutrition were promoted as heavily as food brands, or if using public parks and swimming pools were promoted as heavily as new motion pictures are.

It should be recognized that the advertising profession has worked to enlist public interest for some important national concerns such as better schools, protection of the environment, and sales of savings bonds. Campaigns dealing with these problems have been developed by the Advertising Council, a nonprofit organization founded and supported by business to conduct public-service advertising cam-paigns. Ads for the council's campaigns are created without charge by advertising agencies, and time and space are donated by the media. Millions of dollars' worth of free ads are run each year as a result of the Advertising Council's efforts.

Does Advertising Interfere with Competition?

Questions about the effect of advertising on competition in the mar-ketplace are heard less often than the questions that we have just discussed. They are, however, important ones. Some economists have expressed concern that advertising gives an unfair competitive advan-tage to larger firms and makes the situation of new firms and small firms more difficult. These economists believe that the advertising costs of launching new products are so high that small firms have difficulty raising the necessary funds. Without advertising, small com-panies cannot win needed customers, since shoppers are likely to rely on more familiar brand names.

In contrast, larger companies have ample funds available to pro-mote new products. They have the added advantage that their company name already is widely known. Larger companies that are high-volume advertisers also have the advantage of getting significant discounts on the time and space they buy in the mass media. Some economists believe that these advantages have been an important fac-tor contributing to the growth of larger firms and their increasing con-trol of the market for many consumer goods.

Critics of advertising have also pointed out that advertising diverts the consumer's attention from the product's price to other aspects of the product. They argue that this tends to reduce competition among companies on the basis of price. Those speaking for advertising admit this and argue that competing on the basis of price is easy. They point out that price cuts by one company can be matched quickly by others. This can end up in a price-cutting war that destroys weaker firms. Supporters of advertising argue that competition that emphasizes product features, service, and warranties also benefits the consumer. It also avoids the problems created by price wars.

Most advertisers emphasize differences in product features and services in the hopes of building a group of customers who will continue to be loyal to their brand. They hope that by using this technique, *product differentiation,* they can insulate themselves from direct competition with other brands.

RECOGNIZING DECEPTIVE APPEALS AND CLAIMS

Certain kinds of deceptive advertising appeals and claims appear over and over again despite continued efforts to stop them. These claims often are used by advertisers who are fully aware that their claims are deceptive and that they may result in government action or pressure from local better business bureaus. Advertisers who use such claims know that they are effective and that they can make a great deal of money before any action can be taken to stop them. Because ads employing deceptive appeals appear repeatedly, we need to learn how to recognize them.

Claims Which Look Like Facts—But Aren't

Ads are full of phrases that at first glance appear to be useful facts. On closer check it is not always easy to understand what these claims really claim.

Unclear Claims and Vague Terms. When claims such as "lasts longer" are made, it is not clear just exactly what the performance of the product is being compared with. Is the comparison being made between the way the present product performs and the way the previous version of the brand performed before it was "improved"? Or is the brand's performance being compared with that of other similar products? Statements of this type are *unclear claims.* They are claims we really cannot evaluate because we cannot be certain what they really mean.

Problems also arise from the use of *vague terms.* These are terms that cover a wide range of meaning or performance. The term "stain-resistant" on the blade of a knife, for example, could be considered vague. Does "stain-resistant" mean that the steel cannot be stained, or does it mean that it stains less than other types of steel blades? Other examples of terms that cover a wide range of performance are "rust-inhibiting," and "wrinkle-resistant."

There is little real protection for consumers from unclear claims and vague terms except to recognize them for what they are. They are not solid facts and cannot be counted on to provide useful information.

Incomplete Information

A second problem area is ads which mislead because they do not provide all the facts. There are certain product facts which are so important that failure to disclose them is considered deceptive. In such cases, the FTC and other government agencies may require that the facts be given, even if the facts make the product less attractive to buyers. This requirement is called *affirmative disclosure.*

One Remedy: Affirmative Disclosure. The kinds of information for which affirmative disclosure is required include changes in the nature or composition of a product. An example is the substitution of a new ingredient for one that had been used for years. Sellers must also provide information on a product's composition when its appearance is deceptive. For example, a belt made of plastic that could be mistaken for leather must be labeled "imitation leather."

Sellers also must warn about dangers in the use of products. For example, they must warn about poisonous vapors, flammability, electric shock, and harmful effects resulting from the misuse of drugs and cosmetics. The warning on cigarette packages is another example of negative product information for which disclosure is required. Sellers also must inform buyers if the items offered are not new and if they are of foreign origin.

An Example of Deception with Incomplete Information—Referral Sales Schemes. Advertising plans that offer purchasers bonuses for providing the seller with the names of other customers have been

The Advertising Council, a nonprofit organization supported by business, conducts public-service advertising campaigns to increase public interest in important national concerns. *(Advertising Council)*

Safety belts, when you think about it, it's a nice way to say I love you.

advertising contributed for the public good

B-52

labeled *referral sales schemes.* These plans have been a repeated source of problems and disappointment for consumers. Under such a scheme, a builder of swimming pools would, for example, offer a pool buyer $50 for each person referred to the builder who decides to buy a pool.

Referral sales schemes usually require the purchaser to pay the full price and in the sales contract promise bonuses for referrals. Few sellers tell buyers how difficult it is for buyers to locate other customers. Most purchasers find that they can produce few real prospects. Although some attempts have been made to outlaw referral sales schemes, they are legal in many areas. In these areas they are considered deceptive only when the seller refuses to make the promised bonus payments. Consumers would be well advised to consider contracts with referral sales promises with care. They should not count heavily on receiving any bonuses.

Affirmative disclosure rules provide us some protection against being deceived by incomplete information in ads. The only sure protection is to ask questions when there seem to be gaps in the information presented and to insist on answers.

Misrepresentation

Another problem area is claims which misrepresent important facts about a product. An ad may, for example, misrepresent how a product rates on a particular characteristic. It may give incorrect or misleading information about its effectiveness or its durability. Ads also can be deceptive because they mislead consumers about the importance of a particular characteristic. This kind of problem led to FTC action against Listerine mouthwash a few years ago. Listerine had advertised for years that it killed germs and that this helped prevent colds. It does, in fact, kill germs, but this does not help prevent colds. Colds are caused by viruses, not germs. Listerine's advertising overemphasized the benefits of killing germs, and as a result, many consumers believe that killing germs is the most important characteristic in a mouthwash. Killing germs is not as important as Listerine advertising suggests. It certainly is not very important in preventing colds.

An Example of Misrepresentation—Fictitious Pricing. A common deceptive practice is the overstatment of the "list price" and "manufacturer's suggested price." These are prices indicated by the manufacturer for use at retail. Often manufacturers and retailers get together and agree on the prices that will be used in "preticketing" goods. The list price used is set high enough so that retailers can discount it and point to the price tag as evidence of what a good buy they are offering.

Not all list prices are fictitious, and offers of price reductions cannot automatically be considered deceptive. The advertising of list-price claims is, however, considered deceptive by the FTC unless the price stated is one at which a substantial amount of sales actually occurred. A clearly deceptive practice would be a watch manufacturer's offer to preticket his watches with any price the retailer wanted.

Another Example—Bait and Switch. Bait advertising is an insincere offer to sell a product or service that the advertiser does not really wish or intend to sell. The offer is, instead, used as bait to lure customers to the advertiser's place of business. Once the customer is in

"Bait-and-switch" advertising is a deceptive practice sometimes used by retailers. The bait is a product that is advertised for sale, but that the advertiser does not really wish to sell. When the customers appear in the store, the retailer tries to switch them to a more expensive item. *(Courtesy Massachusetts Office of Attorney General)*

the store, the advertiser tries to switch the customer to a more expensive and more profitable item than the one advertised. This technique of luring customers with an ad for one item and then trying to switch them to another item is referred to as *bait and switch.* The practice is outlawed by many states and is considered a deceptive practice by the FTC.

Examples of the technique are ads by furniture retailers offering "3 Rooms of Furniture—Only $229." Once in the store, the shopper may find that the items offered include only a bed, a sofa, and a dining table with two chairs, all of which are scratched and in poor condition. The disappointed shopper is quickly shown more expensive items in better condition. Shoppers who still are interested in buying the advertised items are told that they are "already sold" or are not available for some other reason.

The bait-and-switch technique should be distinguished from attempts by salespeople to "trade up" shoppers from advertised models to higher-priced lines. *Trading-up* is an acceptable sales technique in cases where the advertised item is capable of doing the job and where the firm has a reasonable supply that they are willing to sell.

Problems of misrepresentation are covered better by existing laws than the other problems we have discussed. Both the FTC and agencies at the state level have power to move against ad claims which misrepresent the facts. Consumers should remember, however, that these agencies have not checked, and cannot possibly check, all advertising claims. Consumers still need to be on their guard against false claims.

REGULATING ADVERTISING

In the last section, we examined some of the many different kinds of appeals that can deceive consumers. Legal authorities, in general, take the position that as long as an ad does not misrepresent the facts, it should be permitted. The line between exaggerated claims (or "puffery," as it is sometimes called) and misrepresentation is hard to draw. It partly is a matter of degree. Small overstatements may escape legal action while clear exaggerations may not.

Federal Trade Commission

The federal government agency that has the major responsibility for regulating advertising is the Federal Trade Commission. It has the responsibility of taking action against most kinds of deceptive claims appearing in almost any medium, from television to sales brochures and sales talks. The FTC originally was established in 1914 to control unfair methods of competition among business firms. Later its powers were broadened to include deceptive actions as well. Special attention is given to deceptive ads because of the unfair competitive advantage they give dishonest businesses and the financial injury they can do to consumers.

In deciding whether an ad is deceptive, the following things are taken into account:

- Even though every statement in the ad is factually correct, it must not create any misleading impressions.
- Important facts about the product or service advertised must not be concealed.
- Attention must not be shifted away from the actual terms and conditions of the offer.
- False or misleading comparisons with other products are not permitted.

Even in cases where there is no evidence of actual intent to deceive, the FTC can rule an ad deceptive if it is decided that it tends to deceive.

When individual firms employ practices that the FTC considers deceptive, the FTC has the power to order them to "cease and desist" from these activities. The FTC can also go to court to obtain injunctions to temporarily stop firms from using false advertising appeals. This gives it time to hold a regular FTC hearing to decide whether the ad is deceptive.

The FTC relies heavily on the voluntary cooperation of business. It tries to help individual firms and entire industries understand how their advertising and business activities can be brought within the legal guidelines set by the FTC. As part of this effort the FTC issues *trade regulation rules*. These set out the kind of actions required of firms under the laws that the FTC enforces. Violations of these rules are likely to result in FTC action. An example is the trade regulation rule issued in 1971 on grocery store specials. This rule makes it a violation of the law for any retail food store to advertise food or other merchandise at a stated price unless the products advertised are in stock and readily available to customers during the days indicated in the ad.

In recent years the FTC has begun to use some new techniques to control deceptive advertising. In 1971 it began its *ad substantiation program*, which requires advertisers to provide evidence to support their advertising claims. The automobile manufacturers were the first industry group called on to provide evidence. They were asked to supply test evidence for such claims as Ford Motor Company's claim that their LTD was "over 700 percent quieter." The FTC does not try to check every claim made. Instead it focuses its attention on major ad themes which look suspicious and seem most likely to influence buyers.

In recent years the FTC has begun to require advertisiers whose ads have been judged deceptive to provide *corrective advertising*. This advertising is designed to correct the impressions consumers may have gotten from deceptive advertising. The FTC may require corrective advertising when it decides that a deceptive ad is likely to continue to influence consumers even after the ad has been stopped. An example is the ad run after one company's advertising of its vitamins was judged misleading. This ad said, in part:

> Contrary to what I have told you previously, Super B will not make you feel
> better nor make you better to live with nor work better on the job. There is

no need for most people to supplement their diet with vitamins and minerals.

The FTC believes that corrective advertising offers several benefits. It helps to correct false impressions consumers may have received from deceptive advertising. It also helps restore competition in markets where deceptive advertisers may have gained an unfair advantage.

State Laws

The laws which the FTC enforces cover a major portion of all advertising, since they cover all goods and services that are included in interstate commerce. Laws are needed, however, to cover advertising by firms that operate only in a local area or within state boundaries.

Some states have adopted various forms of a new model law, the Unfair Trade Practices and Consumer Protection Law, developed by the FTC. The law gives powers, much like those of the FTC, to control deceptive advertising to state attorneys general. Those who favor the new law believe that "mini-FTCs" at the state level would be better able to give ready assistance to consumers.

The mini-FTC laws list a number of deceptive practices which are unlawful. The list includes, for example, "representing that because of some defect in a consumer's home the lives of his family and himself are in danger if the product or services are not purchased." This deceptive sales tactic is used frequently by furnace salespeople who scare homeowners with stories of "dangerous fumes." The listing of specific unlawful practices is useful because it provides business people guidance on practices they should avoid. As state officials and the FTC identify new problem areas, the list of deceptive practices can easily be extended.

The mini-FTC acts give the Attorney General a wide range of powers. Deceptive advertising can be stopped in several ways. The advertiser may be asked to sign an assurance of voluntary compliance. This is a written promise that the ad will be stopped. Signing such an agreement does not require the advertiser to admit a violation of law but does get the offending ad stopped. The Attorney General also may get an injunction, or court order, stopping a particular ad.

Other states, including Illinois, have laws which deal specifically with consumer frauds. The acts passed by different states usually include lists of specific practices which are made unlawful or put under state regulation. These include referral sales, door-to-door sales, and sales of new and used cars. Under the consumer fraud acts, the Attorney General can use assurances of voluntary compliance and injunctions to stop offending ads and practices.

Other Federal Agencies

Although the FTC has the major responsibility for regulating advertising, certain other federal agencies have responsibilities for particular areas. The Federal Communications Commission (FCC) has certain controls over the content of radio and television advertising as well as the number and length of commercials. As a result of FCC actions, cigarette advertising was removed from both media.

The chief concern of the U.S. Postal Service regarding advertising is with ads sent by mail that involve obscenity, lotteries, or fraud. The Food and Drug Administration regulates the labeling of food and drugs and the content of literature that is included with the items, as well as folders and booklets that might be shipped separately. The Securities and Exchange Commission is responsible for regulating deceptive advertising of investment securities.

Self-Regulation by Business

Business people themselves have played an important role in working to control deceptive claims and bad taste in advertising. Associations of professionals in advertising have worked over the years to fight misleading advertising and develop codes of advertising ethics. The local better business bureaus grew out of early efforts by local clubs of advertising executives to control exaggerated ad claims and fraudulent schemes. The committees organized by the local advertising clubs evolved over time into the present system of better business bureaus.

It should be recognized that there are limits on the effectiveness of self-regulation by business. Business associations have little real power over those who violate their codes of good practice. The only real control these groups have is the power to publicize the activities of violators and the power to expel them from the association.

Many newspapers, magazines, and radio and television stations screen the advertising they carry, both for misleading claims and bad taste. The standards they use and the amount of attention they give to screening advertising appear, however, to vary greatly. In addition to these efforts, many individual firms have established procedures for reviewing their ads before they appear.

Checking Your Reading

1. What major roles does advertising have in our economy?
2. Describe the modern view of how advertising affects an audience.
2. What is an irrational appeal? Give an example. How would you classify your example—as an internal or an external association?
4. How does a business decide whether or not to use rational appeals in its ads?
5. Why do some representatives of advertising argue that advertising adds value to products?
6. Why do some economists believe that advertising gives an unfair competitive advantage to large companies?
7. What is product differentiation? What devices do manufacturers use to differentiate products?
8. Why is the meaning of such claims as "stronger, longer-lasting suds" unclear?
9. How does the bait-and-switch technique work?
10. Why are consumers who participate in referral sales schemes often disappointed?
11. What is meant by fictitious pricing?
12. What four factors are taken into account by the FTC in deciding whether an ad is deceptive?
13. Why does the FTC put so much emphasis on getting the voluntary cooperation of business in controlling advertising claims?
14. Why are state laws regulating deceptive advertising necessary?
15. Why does self-regulation by business of deceptive advertising claims have only limited effectiveness?

Consumer Problems and Projects

1. Make a collection of ads that make rational and irrational appeals and label each. Would you classify the irrational appeals as internal or external associations?
2. Study the ads for a product in which you are interested. (a) What information do they provide? How helpful do you find them? Are they accurate? Complete? Understandable? Do they make com-

parisons between brands? (b) Prepare an ad which provides the kind of information you feel consumers need about a particular brand.

3. Watch the mass media and collect examples of claims you consider deceptive. Can you find examples of unclear claims, vague terms, exaggerated claims that may be false, bait advertising, and referral sales schemes?

4. Visit nearby drugstores and discount stores. What examples of preticketing of merchandise can you find? Are the items being offered for sale at the preticketed price? If not, do you feel deception is involved? Why?

5. Study the advertising in a recent magazine or newspaper. What ad claims can you find that you believe should be supported with scientific evidence? What kind of evidence or tests would be necessary to supply satisfactory proof?

6. Study the ads in publications aimed at purchasing agents (perhaps your principal's office can make some available) and business people (the public library subscribes to such magazines as *Business Week*). Compare the claims in these ads with the claims in ads in general consumer magazines. What differences can you find? What are the reasons for these differences?

7. To be successful an ad must do three things. It must get our attention, be remembered, and move us to action. Check ads in both the print and broadcast media and list some of the techniques used for each one of these three purposes.

8. Watch the mass media for advertising supported by the Advertising Council. It can be identified by a small letter "a" in a circle surrounded by the words "Advertising Council." What are the subjects of the ads you noted? Do you feel these are important public issues? What other issues do you believe should be covered?

PART TWO
Buying the Basics: Clothes, Food, and Cars

7

Going Metric

Most of us have gotten our first introduction to the metric system from watching sports events. We've seen swimmers dive from the 10-meter platform and runners in the 100-meter dash. We know that meters are the unit of length in the metric system and may have figured out that a meter is a little over a yard. There is, however, a lot more to know about the metric system.

The United States and Canada are among the last countries in the world to adopt the metric system. They now are moving rapidly toward its use in all areas of life. Business and commerce are shifting to the use of metric units, making it important for consumers to understand the system and how it works.

THE METRIC SYSTEM

The metric system coming into use is a modified version of the system first developed by French scientists in the 1790s. The new system is called the International System of Units, or SI (from its name in French). Our present system is referred to as the *customary system*, or sometimes the *English system*.

Distances in Olympic events and many other international sports events are measured in meters. *(Bryn Campbell, Magnum Photos)*

One of the appeals of the metric system is its simplicity. Like our money, it uses a decimal system. The units are based on multiples of 10. In our money system we have 10 cents in a dime and 10 dimes in a dollar. In the same way, there are 10 centimeters (a term which means 1/100 of a meter) in a decimeter (a term which means 1/10 of a meter). Ten decimeters, in turn, equal 1 meter. The metric system is built up logically using this approach. In contrast, our present system grew up piecemeal over the years with no logical basis. The result is that we have 12 inches in a foot, 3 feet in a yard, and 1760 yards in a mile.

Only four units of measurement in the metric system are important for everyday use:

	Unit	*Abbreviation*
length	meter	m
weight	gram	g
volume	liter	L
temperature	degree Celsius	°C

Prefixes are used to indicate the division and multiplication of these units by 10, creating smaller and larger units:

Prefix	Term	Abbreviation
kilo	thousand	k
hecto*	hundred	h
deka*	ten	da
deci	one-tenth	d
centi	one-hundredth	c
milli	one-thousandth	m

*seldom used

Combining prefixes and units, we get such units as kilogram (one thousand grams) and milliliter (one-thousandth of a liter). Using this approach, can you figure how many centimeters there are in a meter? How many milligrams are in a gram?

TABLE 7-1
Converting to and from Metrics

If You Know	Multiply By	To Find
Units of Length:		
Inches	2.5	Centimeters
Feet	30.5	Centimeters
Yards	0.9	Meters
Miles	1.6	Kilometers
Centimeters	0.4	Inches
Meters	1.1	Yards
Kilometers	0.6	Miles
Units of Volume:		
Pints	0.47	Liters
Quarts	0.95	Liters
Gallons	3.8	Liters
Liters	2.1	Pints
Liters	1.06	Quarts
Liters	0.26	Gallons
Units of Weight:		
Ounces	28.3	Grams
Pounds	0.45	Kilograms
Grams	0.035	Ounces
Kilograms	2.2	Pounds
Units of Temperature:		
Degrees Fahrenheit	0.55 (after subtracting 32)	Degrees Celsius
Degrees Celsius	1.8 (then add 32)	Degrees Fahrenheit

THE SHIFT TO METRICS

The shift to the metric system, or *metrification* as it is sometimes called, has already produced many changes. Many of the biggest ones are yet to come. What we have seen up to now is mostly what is referred to as *soft conversion*. This is the use of customary measures along with information on the metric equivalent. An example is a quart of milk which also carries the metric equivalent on the label (0.95 liter).

More far-reaching changes will come when package sizes shift to rounded metric units; for example, 1 liter or 5 kilograms. This type of change has been labeled *hard conversion*. When hard conversion comes to the supermarket, you will be buying milk by the liter and meat by the kilogram. A few industries have already made some hard conversions. Soft drinks are now available in 1-liter bottles. Some parts on the Mustang II, Pinto, and Chevette are metric. Yet to come are such changes as clothing sizes in centimeters.

The United States first firmly committed itself to shifting to the metric system in 1975. A bill passed that year made increasing use of

This Pepsi bottle is an example of hard conversion, or changing sizes to even metric units. In this case, the size of the bottle is given in English units (quarts) as well as metric units (liters). *(Courtesy of Pepsico)*

the metric system a national policy. Under this policy each part of our economic system is free to move toward metrification at its own pace. There is no overall national timetable.

An important factor moving us toward metrification is our desire to protect our international trade. Many of our major trading partners have used the metric system for years. When the British and Canadians made the decision to shift to the metric system, it was clear that we should not delay any longer.

CONSUMER ISSUES

Metrification could create problems for consumers. Experience in other English-speaking countries which are ahead of us in the shift indicates that these problems probably are not too serious. As concerned consumers, we do, however, need to be aware of the kinds of problems which could come up.

A major concern is that manufacturers will use the shift to metric sizes to disguise price increases. Consumers must expect to pay their fair share of the cost of converting to the metric system. But as consumers, we have a right to insist that price changes be reasonable.

Some consumers also are concerned about being cheated or deceived because they do not fully understand metric units. This certainly could be a problem until we become familiar with metric measures. Experience in other countries which have shifted to metrics suggests that this problem is not a serious one. There may be some confusion during the changeover period in which some products are available only in metric sizes and some still are available only in customary sizes. During this time, unit pricing using a common measure will be especially important in finding the best buy.

Hard conversion can offer some distinct advantages to consumers. It may provide an opportunity for manufacturers to get rid of unnecessary package sizes and to shift to more logical sizes. Whether this comes about depends on consumers making their wishes known.

Safety is another important concern. Some people are worried that consumers could be confused by medicine dosages or traffic signs in metric units and make dangerous mistakes. One method to avoid this problem is the approach used in Australia. There, use of both metric and customary units (or *dual labeling* as it is sometimes called) has been permitted when there could be dangerous confusion.

Some concern also has been expressed that metrification may be wasteful. Some people are concerned that tools and equipment based on the customary system will have to be discarded before they are worn out. Where possible, it seems better to replace old equipment as it wears out and shift to metric-based equipment then. If we make the shift gradually, we should be able to avoid needless waste.

Metrification will clearly mean changes for all of us. Government, industry, and schools all are making an effort to help us learn the new system. The change will not be too painful if we all make up our minds to master the new system and help explain it to others who find it confusing.

Checking Your Reading

1. Why do some people feel the metric system is more logical and simpler than our customary system?
2. What four metric units of measure are important for everyday use?
3. How are prefixes used in the metric system? What does the prefix "kilo" mean? "Centi"?
4. What is soft conversion? Hard conversion?
5. How could price increases be disguised in hard conversion?

Consumer Problems and Projects

1. What examples of soft conversion can you find around your house? What examples of hard conversion can you find?
2. Using metric measures:

   1 kg equals _____ g   500 g equals _____ kg

   1 L equals _____ mL   200 mL equals _____ L

   2 km equals _____ m   5000 m equals _____ km
3. Make the following conversions:
   a. If your gas tank holds 18 gallons, how many liters will it hold?
   b. If you need a half-pound of hamburger for a recipe, how many kilograms should you buy?
   c. If you are 2 km from the next town, how many miles is this?
   d. If it is 22°C outside, do you need a coat?
4. Select a consumer product, such as toothpaste, which currently is available only in packages based on customary units. What metric sizes do you feel would be appropriate for this product?

8

Buying Clothes

Most of us never think of our clothes in this way, but clothes are really a kind of portable environment which we use to cover ourselves. One of their chief purposes is to provide us with shelter from sun, wind, and cold. Providing a portable shelter is not, however, their only function. If all we wanted from our clothes was shelter from the weather, we might all go around in pup tents with a hole cut out for our heads.

Our interest in clothes goes far beyond their use as a shelter. For most of us, clothes are an expression of our personalities. We express ourselves in the styles and colors we pick and the combinations of clothes we put together. In this country we are so devoted to the idea of clothes as an expression of our individual personalities that one of the things that seems strangest about life in modern China under communism is the uniformity of dress. We find it hard to imagine how people in different walks of life and of different ages and sexes could be happy wearing the same kind of baggy blue suits.

At the same time we use clothes to express our individuality, we also use them to show our membership in special groups. Although high school students pride themselves on the individuality of their clothes, they limit their choices to particular types of clothes. Even the most individualistic students are not likely to choose clothes that will make anyone mistake them for business people or homemakers. Clothes can be used to show group membership in even more direct ways. The athlete shows team membership by wearing a letter jacket. Other students demonstrate their school spirit when they wear clothes in the school colors.

From this discussion you can see that clothes serve several important purposes. This is why, when choosing clothes, we need to keep both functional considerations such as durability, comfort, and ease of care in mind as well as considerations such as style, pattern, and color.

PLANNING YOUR PURCHASES

Some people act as if they think about nothing but what they wear while others hardly seem to think about it at all. Some balance between these two extremes is needed. None of us can really afford to neglect our appearance. Just as we use clothes to express ourselves, other people use them as a way to find out what kind of people we are. If someone looked at the clothes you have on now, how would they judge you? Would they think you are sloppy? Dull? Lively? Athletic? Sociable? Whether we think it is fair or not, others do judge us by the way we look. With effort most of us can make a good appearance. While not everyone can afford to be expensively dressed, there are few people in this country who cannot afford to be neatly dressed.

Determining What You Need

To be well dressed, we need something more than a miscellaneous collection of slacks, sweaters, skirts, and shoes. To really meet our needs, a wardrobe must be planned in relation to the kinds of things we do and the kinds of places we go. Only in this way can it really meet our needs.

To begin with, we must consider all our different activities and the kinds of clothes we need for each. For example, this might be our list:

- School
- Sports
- Informal social events; school events
- Dress-up social events
- Church
- After-school job
- Home chores—cleaning, working on car, yard work

People are judged by the clothes they wear. What are your feelings about these people? *(Left, Ginger Chih; right, Levi Strauss)*

Clothes for one of the categories may also serve another category. Clothes suitable for school usually are also suitable for informal parties. Clothes for dress-up social occasions may be suitable for church.

Our needs vary with the season and changes in the climate. Those people who live in the Midwest and Northeast will need a more varied wardrobe than those who live on the West Coast and in the South.

Taking an Inventory

Once you have some idea about your clothing needs, you will need to evaluate your present situation. In Chapter 4 we discussed the best way to determine one's situation—taking an inventory. Inventory taking is a good time to review the condition of our clothes and a good time to get rid of items that we no longer use and things which are outgrown or beyond repair. You probably will want to get rid of things that you have not worn in the last year. Try on all the items you plan to keep to be certain they still fit—some may be outgrown, and others may need alterations. Once you have sorted things out, you can begin

TABLE 8-1
Clothing Inventory

| | Activities | | |
Seasons	School and Informal Social Events	Dress-up Occasions and Church	Home Chores

to determine the additional things you need—and the things of which you have enough.

Inventory time is also a good time to study our wardrobe to see what it can tell us about the kind of clothes we prefer. Which items have been most useful? Which ones do you feel you look best in? Which ones do you feel most comfortable in? The reasons behind your answers will help you learn why some of your past clothing choices were successful while others fell short.

One of the best ways to get an overview of what you have and what you need is to make up a chart like Table 8-1, which takes account of needs for both different activities and different seasons.

Deciding On Additional Items

When you have your inventory completed, you will be ready to begin deciding what additional items you need to fill out your wardrobe. These decisions will, of course, be limited by how much you can spend. You may not have much to spend right away, so you will need a long-range plan toward which you can work.

Most of us can afford to buy only a few new items each year. This is why it is important to make every choice count. A boy from a typical middle-income family might, for example, buy the following items in a year:

- 3 or 4 pairs of slacks
- 4 or 5 sport shirts
- 1 jacket or sport coat
- 3 or 4 pairs of shoes

We can see that this does not allow much room for errors and poor choices. There are, however, some buying techniques that can help you stretch a limited clothing budget.

Choose Versatile Items   One technique that can help to stretch a clothing budget is to choose versatile items. Versatile items are ones that have several different uses. They may be suitable for more than one season of the year—an example is a raincoat with a zip-in lining for cold weather. Or they may be versatile because they can be worn for different types of occasions—an example would be a basic dress whose appearance can be changed by wearing different accessories.

If you have more money available, you can afford to develop a more specialized wardrobe. You can choose items that are well suited for one special purpose but are not well suited for others. You could, for example, choose a tie that looks great with a particular shirt or a scarf that goes only with one particular blouse without worrying that they do not go well with other items in your wardrobe.

Coordinate Colors and Styles   If your money is limited, you will also want to give some thought to another kind of versatility—the ability of wardrobe items to look good in different combinations. An example would be a sweater that looks good with several different skirts or pairs of slacks. This kind of versatility comes from concentrating your clothing choices on a particular group of colors and styles that go well together. This might mean concentrating your choices on clothes in shades of blue that go well together, plus some clothes in colors that go well with blue—perhaps yellow or red. These items plus some in neutral colors such as white, off-white, and tan will go together well in all sorts of combinations. Such a variety of possible combinations in a wardrobe will make it seem larger than it really is.

Stick to Basic Styles   Many clothing items are discarded long before they are worn out because their style looks out-of-date. If your money for clothing is limited, you will want to choose styles that remain in fashion for several years, especially when you buy expensive items such as a sport jacket or a good dress. Simpler, less extreme designs may never be "the latest thing" but can be counted on to be in good taste and attractive for several years.

If you like the latest styles and have little money to spend, your best bet may be to limit yourself to less expensive items such as sportswear and casual wear. These items usually are expected to give only one or two years' wear, anyway.

SELECTING CLOTHING

A number of product characteristics need to be taken into account in choosing clothing—color, style, fiber and fabrics, durability, and ease of care. Different people weigh these characteristics differently. Those who are especially concerned about their personal appearance are likely to give particular attention to color and style. Others, with limited clothing budgets, may feel they have to pay particular attention to durability and ease of care. In this section on selecting clothing we will give some attention to them all.

Color and Style

We all know that some combinations of colors are more attractive than others. Yet we often forget about our own natural coloring in choosing clothing items. The fact is that each of us has several natural coloring features—the color of our hair, of our skin, and of our eyes. These colors need to be taken into account in choosing clothing colors if the total combination is to be a pleasing one.

Even when we do think about our natural coloring, we often group hair, eye, and skin colors in broad categories without taking full account of all the variations within each category. We say people with brown-green, brown-gold, light-brown, and dark-brown eyes have "brown" eyes. We do the same with skin color—we classify people as either white, black, or yellow. Yet if we look around, we can see that skin colors vary within these three categories.

Among white people, skin tones may vary from very fair, with a hint of blue, to pink. Redheads' skins have orange tones, and those with olive complexions have yellow skin tones. The skins of black people show a similar range of tones. Some are more yellow or orange in tone, while darker skins may have underlying tones of red or blue. Orientals' skin tones also vary widely.

Clothing specialists have developed a number of suggestions about the most pleasing combinations of clothing colors with skin coloring, and you may want to read what they have to say. But once you are aware of your skin coloring, you can begin to do some thinking about clothing colors for yourself. You can study color pictures in magazines to see what colors look best on people with coloring similar to yours. You can note what colors other people with coloring similar to yours seem to look best in. You can also note the colors of the clothes that seem to bring you the most compliments. We all have our own unique natural coloring, and picking clothing colors that go well with it is one way we can emphasize our individuality.

Clothing experts also have developed a number of suggestions about clothing styles that best suit different body types. They suggest, for example, that shorter people choose styles that emphasize vertical lines. This might be done by choosing patterns with vertical stripes or avoiding colors that contrast too sharply above and below the waist. For example, a medium-blue sweater instead of a white one to go with a medium-blue skirt or slacks would be a good choice for a short person. There are other suggestions for heavy people, thin people, and so on.

The teacher who teaches clothing in home economics in your school probably can make helpful suggestions, or if you ask your librarian, he or she will be able to help you find a useful reference book on making style choices.

Fibers and Fabrics

Consumer product-testing information can be a useful guide in selecting many products. There is, however, relatively little test information available on clothing. Only a few items are tested: men's dress shirts, T-shirts, and raincoats; women's hosiery; and children's jeans. Because of the large number of fabrics and fiber combinations used, the large number of manufacturers involved in producing fabrics and clothing, and the use of store brands by many retailers, the number of clothing products to be tested is too large to handle. As a result, testing efforts have focused on products produced by manufacturers that can be readily identified by their brand names. This leaves the consumer without any product-testing information to guide important purchases of wool coats, sport jackets, good dresses, and so on. For these items, then, the consumer must develop some criteria for judging quality.

Consumers must learn to judge clothing quality for themselves. They can be guided in judging quality by the textile fibers and fabric used in a garment and also by the garment's construction. Once consumers have some general information about the characteristics of particular fibers, such as cotton, nylon, and acrylic, they are more able to judge how a fabric made from them is likely to perform, and whether they will be satisfied with their purchases.

Fiber Characteristics The two most familiar natural fibers used in clothing are cotton and wool. Cotton is popular because it is absorbent, comfortable, easy to wash, and easy to care for when treated with permanent-press finishes. Wool is popular because of its warmth, its relatively good resistance to wrinkles, its durability, and its ability to absorb a good deal of moisture without feeling damp.

Rayon and acetate are two of the oldest synthetic fibers. Both are made from cellulose (usually obtained from wood pulp) and both are relatively inexpensive, but the two have somewhat different characteristics. Because of its luster and silky feel, acetate is often used as a substitute for silk. Rayon dyes well and can be made to imitate a variety of fibers. Unlike acetate, it is relatively absorbent. For certain garments this difference can be important.

Nylon is the oldest of the truly synthetic fibers. One of its main assets is its versatility. It can be used in sheer hosiery or to give strength and durability to work clothes. Polyester, in combination with cotton, made modern permanent-press clothing possible. Polyester contributed the important advantages of resistance to shrinking and resistance to wrinkles, and because it is not absorbent, it is fast-drying. One disadvantage of both nylon and polyester is that they may *pill*. This happens when rubbing causes fibers to break and form small balls or "pills" on a fabric's surface. Acrylic is popular because it offers wool-like qualities but is easy to care for and is washable. Triacetate is chemically similar to acetate and has some of the same qualities. It is popular because pleats and creases can be permanently set with heat and it is easy to care for.

The characteristics of these textile fibers are listed in more detail in Table 8-2. In considering the characteristics of individual fibers, you should bear in mind that these can be changed during manufacturing, and that some problems can be overcome with special finishes and treatments.

Blends and combinations of two or more fibers often are used in order to get the best characteristics of each. For example, the popular combination of cotton and polyester provides the comfort and absorbency of cotton and the strength and wash-and-wear qualities of polyester. Many combinations use an absorbent fiber (cotton, wool, or rayon) along with a nonabsorbent one (polyester or acetate). A garment made entirely of an nonabsorbent synthetic fiber seems too warm to many people.

Polyester is also useful in combination with cotton for permanent-press fabrics because the special finish used to get easy-care characteristics seriously weakens cotton. Polyester is used to add needed strength. Experts say that 15 to 20 percent of a fiber is needed for it to

TABLE 8-2
Characteristics of Textile Fibers Used in Clothing

Fibers and Selected Trade Names	Wearing Quality		Appearance Factors		Ease of Care		Uses
	Strength	Resistance to Abrasion	Resistance to Wrinkling	Resistance to Stains	Wash-and-Wear Characteristics	Care Recommendations	
Cotton	Good to excellent	Medium	Fair to poor (unless treated)	Fair to poor (unless treated)	Fair to poor (unless treated)	Machine-wash and tumble dry, or dry-clean	Undergarments, work clothes; in blends with polyester
Wool	Fair to poor	Medium	Good to excellent	Fair to poor	Fair to poor	Dry-clean, or wash by hand with extreme care	Outerwear, suits, dresses, knit goods
Rayon *Avisco Cupioni Celanese*	Fair to poor	Fair to poor	Fair to poor	Fair to poor	Fair to poor	Wash by hand (unless otherwise indicated)	Slacks and suits, women's wear, linings
New Rayons *Avril Avron Zantrel*	Improved in new rayons	Improved in new rayons		Improved in new rayons		Machine-wash and tumble dry, or dry-clean	
Acetate *Acele Avisco Celaperm Chromspun Estron*	Fair to poor	Fair to poor	Fair to poor	Medium	Fair to poor	Hand-launder, if indicated, or dry-clean	Lingerie, dresses; as a substitute for silk

Fiber						Care	Uses
Triacetate *Arnel*	Fair to poor	Fair to poor	Good to excellent	Medium	Good to excellent	Machine-wash and tumble dry	Tricot lingerie and outerwear, knits, permanently pleated garments
Nylon *Antron* *Blue C* *Caprolan* *Qiana*	Good to excellent	Good to excellent	Fair to poor	Good to excellent	Good to excellent	Machine-wash and tumble dry at low temperature	Hosiery, socks, windproof jackets, work clothes; new Qiana has silklike qualities
Acrylic *Acrilan* *Creslan* *Orlon* *Zefran*	Fair to poor	Fair to poor	Good to excellent	Good to excellent	Good to excellent	Machine-wash and tumble dry at low temperature, or dry-clean	Sweaters, knit goods, fake furs; as a substitute for wool
Polyester *Dacron* *Fortrel* *Kodel* *Trevira*	Good to excellent	Good to excellent (some types subject to pilling)	Good to excellent	Good to excellent, but low resistance to oily stains	Good to excellent	Machine-wash and tumble dry, or dry-clean	In blends with cotton for shirts, dresses, sportswear, slacks

Reference: Josephine M. Blandford and Lois M. Gurel, *Fibers and Fabrics*, U.S. National Bureau of Standards Consumer Information Series No. 1.

have a significant effect on a fabric's strength. This is why small amounts of nylon frequently are added to work clothes and jeans. Even smaller amounts of such elastic fibers as rubber or spandex can add stretch qualities to a fabric.

Fiber Labeling   In the years just after World War II a number of new man-made fibers appeared on the market. Each was sold under its own trade name, and consumers had little way of knowing which ones had similar characteristics and which differed. To simplify this problem, family names were developed for man-made fibers with similar chemical compositions. In 1960, when the Textile Fiber Products Identification Act took effect, manufacturers were required to label fabrics with the family (or generic) names of the fibers used. Trade names also may be listed along with the family names. For example, the label on a polyester-cotton blend fabric might say "65% Dacron [the trade name of a polyester fiber made by E. I. du Pont de Nemours & Co.] polyester [the family name], 35% cotton [also a family name]."

Under the terms of the act, all textile products must be labeled, and the labels must list fibers in order by weight and indicate the percent by weight for each fiber for which the weight is 5 percent or more. Fibers that make up less than 5 percent by weight can be listed only if they have some specific function. This is to control attempts to confuse consumers by listing small amounts of expensive fibers. A listing such as "4% spandex for elasticity" is permitted because it states the function of the fiber. In addition, the label must indicate the name or identification number of the firm marketing the product and the country of origin, if the item is imported.

The other major law governing textile labeling is the Wool Products Labeling Act, which became effective in 1941. This act requires that every article of wool clothing must be labeled to indicate the kind of wool used in its manufacture. The label must indicate the amount of wool fiber in the fabric and the percent by weight of new or virgin wool fibers, of reprocessed fibers (wool remanufactured from scraps of wool cloth), and of reused fibers (wool from used clothing). Experts point out that the use of reprocessed wool is not necessarily the sign of an inferior product if the wool is of good quality.

The consumer should bear in mind that while fibers with the same family or generic name perform in a similar way, they are not identical. For example, there are several different types of nylons. Some newer types have antistatic properties; another new type has a silklike appearance. Consumers' problems in learning about these differences

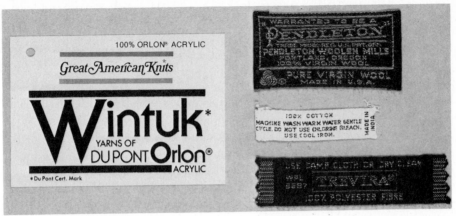

The Textile Fiber Products Identification Act requires manufacturers to identify generic and trade names of fibers and to indicate the percentage by weight of each fiber used.

in characteristics point up the need for more informative fabric labeling.

The most useful kind of information would be ratings of a fabric on such key characteristics as shrinkage, durability, and colorfastness. This would involve the development of generally accepted *standards*, or methods of measuring and rating a fabric on each of these characteristics. Once standards are developed for a characteristic such as shrinkage, fabrics can be rated by how well they resist shrinkage. Fabrics might, for example, be classified into four categories or grades depending on how much they shrink. Those with the least shrinkage would fall in the top grade and be labeled "excellent"; the next group could be labeled "good," the next "fair," and the lowest "poor."

Although grading of textile fabrics has been suggested many times, fabric manufacturers have opposed the idea. They fear that once product-grading information is available, consumers would depend less on brand names. This would weaken the position of large firms that have built up a special reputation for their brand names. No firm with a well-known brand name wants to lose the special advantages that the brand name gives it.

Fabric Construction   There are several different methods of making cloth. The most familiar is weaving. In woven fabrics durability is determined by (1) the closeness and evenness of the weave, (2) the thread count (the number of yarns in both directions in a square inch of fabric), and (3) the thickness of the yarn. Close, tightly woven fabrics are less subject to wear and abrasion, while ones with loose, "floating" yarns may snag.

Another familiar method of fabric construction is knitting. In regular knit fabrics a single yarn is formed into loops that are interlocked. Double knits, which first became popular in the early 1970s, are made somewhat differently. Double knits are made by interlocking loops in two strands of yarn with a double stitch. The result is a fabric with loops on both sides instead of on just one, as in regular knits. Polyester has been especially popular for double knits. The garments produced have been comfortably light and resistant to wrinkling. There have been some problems, however. Double knits are subject to snags, and some people have found them too warm for summer wear. They are also more difficult to alter than garments made of woven fabric, since needle holes remain visible when a garment is let out. This problem can be avoided by buying a large size and taking it in rather than letting out a smaller size.

Fabric Finishes   A variety of special finishes has been developed to improve fabric performance. The most familiar is the *permanent-press finish*, which helps garments retain their shape and pressed-in creases and resist wrinkling when laundered or dry-cleaned. This finish is produced by applying a resin compound to the fabric followed by a heat treatment that permanently sets the fabric in the desired shape. This finish is now used on a wide variety of clothing and is frequently used with polyester-cotton blends. As we noted earlier, the use of polyester helps overcome the finish's weakening effect on cotton fibers. For best results, permanent-press items should be machine-washed, tumbled dry, and removed from the dryer as soon as they are dry and then placed on hangers. Permanent-press finishes are softened by heat. Clothes can pick up wrinkles if they are washed in water that is too hot or dried at too high a temperature without a "cool-down" period at the end. It should be noted that several man-made fibers have permanent heat-set characteristics and resist wrinkling without special finishes; these include nylon, triacetate, polyester, and acrylic.

Stains tend to be a particular problem in cotton-polyester permanent-press fabrics because both polyester fiber and the permanent-press finish have a tendency to attract oily stains. This problem shows up in dark rings around collars and cuffs that cannot be washed out. *Soil-release finishes* that permit soil to be released from the fabric more easily during washing help to solve this problem.

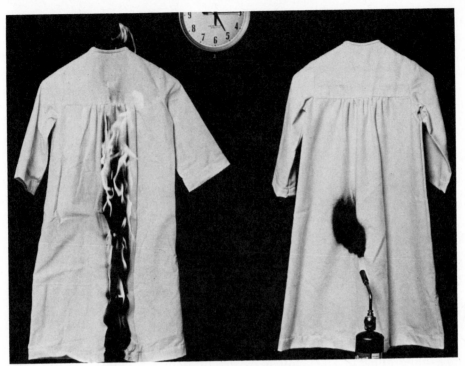

Some fabrics are given flame-retardant finishes. The cotton nightgown on the left was not treated. When touched with a lighted match, the gown became engulfed in flames in 15 seconds. The cotton nightgown on the right has a flame-retardant finish. When touched with a bunsen burner flame, the gown chars, but does not burn. *(Courtesy CIBA-GEIGY)*

Scotchgard Brand Stain Release is an example of a finish which provides both stain resistance and soil-release properties.

Water-repellent finishes also are available. Fabrics treated with *water-repellent finishes* resist the absorption and penetration of water but are not fully waterproof. Scotchgard and Zepel both repel water and resist oily and watery stains. You will want to keep in mind that some fibers such as nylon and polyester have water-repellent qualities without special finishes because they absorb relatively little water.

Shrinkage in fabrics can be controlled by special manufacturing processes, such as the Sanforized process, or by chemical finishes. When shrinkage-control finishes are used, tags should indicate the amount of shrinkage remaining.

In addition to the special finishes mentioned, other finishes provide fire-retardant properties, mothproofing, mildewproofing, and antibacterial properties.

Fabric Flammability Everyone who wears clothes, and that seems to include most of us, should bear in mind that fabric can burn. In fact, some fabrics can burn so rapidly they almost seem to explode. Concern about the use of highly flammable fabrics in clothing led to the passage of the Flammable Fabrics Act of 1953. This law gave the government power to keep highly flammable clothing off the market. Even after the 1953 Act was passed, many people, especially children, continued to be burned in clothing fires. This led to an amendment to the Act in 1967 which gave the federal government power to develop flammability standards for clothing, hats, gloves, footwear, and home furnishings. To date, the only standards put into effect for clothing are those setting limits on the flammability of the fabrics used in children's sleepwear. Regulation of flammable fabrics is a responsibility of the Consumer Product Safety Commission.

Garment Construction

We have seen how important the fabric used in making a garment can be. The way this fabric is put together to form the garment is important too. In making clothes, the basic problem is to shape a two-dimensional piece of cloth to cover a three-dimensional form that, like a landscape, has contours, hills, and valleys.

Shape Garments get their basic shape from the way the pieces of fabric used in making them are cut. As these pieces of fabric are sewn together, they may be further shaped by pressing. Other methods of adjusting to the contours of the body are needed, however, to make a garment fuller in some places and narrower in others. This is done with darts, tucks, and pleats that remove excess fabric in some places and provide extra room at others.

Garments are kept in shape by the resistance of the fabric to stretching and shrinking. A garment made of a fabric that shrinks or stretches quickly loses its original shape. *Interfacings*, the extra pieces of fabric sewn inside the garment at such places as lapels and collars, also help hold a garment in shape. Interfacings give body to lapels and collars and help them lie flat. They prevent stretching at armholes and reinforce areas where buttons are sewn. Garments also get their shape from the padding used in shoulders and from linings used in jackets and skirts that help them to hang smoothly. Although we cannot see the interfacings and padding used, we can see how well they do their job. When lifted out of place or crushed, lapels should snap quickly back into place. Padding should give a smooth contour to the shoulders and should not be lumpy.

Signs of Quality   There are other signs of quality in clothing construction that you can use in judging garments. The garment should be cut on the grain (the yarns in the fabric should run perpendicular and parallel to the floor). If the fabric is cut off the grain, the garment will sag and hang unevenly. The fabric pieces should be securely joined with neat, short stitches that are neither too tight nor too loose. If fabric is sewn too loosely you will be able to see a gap between two pieces when they are pulled apart. Fabric patterns will be matched at the seams in higher-quality garments. Seams should be generous in order to resist strain and to provide fabric in case the garment needs to be let out. Hems should lie flat and be inconspicuous from the outside of the garment. Edges of seams should be finished to prevent raveling.

In the finishing of the garment, points of strain should be reinforced with extra stitching or bar tacks (stitching back and forth in the same place, such as on the corners of jeans pockets). Buttonholes should be neatly made, with the buttons securely sewn. Zippers should be neatly placed to lie flat and should work easily.

The trimming on a garment should be appropriate to the way it will be cleaned. Plastic straps and nonremovable belts are not likely to stand up well in either washing or dry cleaning. Nylon lace or trim on a cotton garment is apt to be melted by the usual ironing temperatures for cotton.

Size and Fit   Although standards have been developed for the sizes of children's clothing and women's clothing and for youth sizes, these standards are voluntary. Many manufacturers make adjustments that they believe are necessary for their particular operation and customers. As a result, the fit of a particular size will vary among manufacturers and, over time, for the same manufacturer.

Poor fits may be the result of the choice of the wrong size or of a garment that is badly proportioned for the build of the wearer. Examples of badly proportioned garments are ones that are too narrow in the hips or too large in the shoulders for the wearer. A well-fitted garment should provide an appropriate amount of *ease*. This is the extra fabric needed to allow for body movements. If there is too little ease, there will be strain marks in the fabric, such as the strain marks seen across the front of skirts and trousers that are too narrow across the hips. If there is too much ease, the garment will seem baggy and too loose.

A well-fitted garment will lie close to the body around the neck, without gaps in front or in back. Shoulder seams should lie in the center of the shoulder. Sleeves should be the correct length, and the garment should be cut so that you can raise your arms without the garment pulling up too much. The waistline of the garment should fall at your natural waistline, except in special designs.

CARING FOR CLOTHES

We spend a good deal of money on clothes, and they deserve to be treated like any other valuable investment—with care. Clothes that are treated with care will last longer, and probably even more important, they will look good for a long time. Good care involves taking care of clothes on a day-to-day basis and using proper cleaning procedures.

Everyday Care of Clothes

Clothes should be hung up at once when you take them off. Wrinkles hang out quickly when clothes are still warm from body heat and slightly damp from body moisture. Use padded or shaped hangers for coats and jackets, not the wire ones that dry cleaners use. This will help these items keep their shape. Clothes should not be crowded too closely in the closet; they should be allowed room to air. Wool, in particular, tends to absorb odors if not allowed to air.

Both clothes and shoes will last longer if you can rotate them instead of wearing the same clothes or pair of shoes several days in a row. Rotating clothes gives them the "rest" they need in order to dry out and resume their original shape. To protect good clothes from spills and stains, change to work clothes before you do chores around the house, work on the car, or help in the kitchen.

Mend clothes promptly. This will keep tears and rips from getting bigger and will keep loose buttons from getting lost. Boys as well as girls should learn how to make simple clothing repairs. Out-of-season clothes should be stored to protect them from dust and moths.

Rainwear should be used when needed to protect clothes. Its use will help save on extra cleaning and pressing bills. Wet shoes should be stuffed with paper (shoe trees might stretch them too much) and allowed to dry slowly away from radiators and hot-air vents.

The FTC requires the manufacturer of this blouse to sew in a fabric care label that provides specific instructions for proper care of the garment. *(Susan Berkowitz)*

100% COTTON MADE IN ITALY

MACHINE WASH WARM IN NEUTRAL SOAP · NO BLEACH - TUMBLE OR LINE DRY-COOL OR STEAM IRON-DO NOT USE THE COIN OPERATED METHOD OF DRY CLEANING

Cleaning Procedures

Stains should be treated before a garment is washed; otherwise they may be set by the heat of the cleaning process. You probably will need a guide on stain removal to help you deal with the variety of stain problems that arise. Techniques differ depending on the type of stain (greasy, nongreasy, or a combination of the two such as gravy or chocolate) and the fabric (washable and nonwashable). One useful guide is *Removing Stains from Fabrics*, available from the U.S. Government Printing Office, 40 cents postpaid. For clothes that are dry-cleaned, identify stains for the cleaners, if possible. This will help them choose the best stain-removal procedures.

You can see from Table 7-2 on the characteristics of textile fibers that the care requirements of different fibers vary a good deal. Some fibers, such as cotton, can be machine-washed and tumbled dry without difficulty. Others such as wool require dry cleaning or special care in washing. Confusion often arises because of the different care requirements of similar fabrics. Many people have ruined articles of clothing by mistakenly machine-washing them when they should have been dry-cleaned. Even experienced cleaners cannot always identify a fabric by just looking at it, and they sometimes make mistakes.

These problems led to pressure for the use of permanent care labels that provide necessary care instructions. The use of permanent care labels was ordered by the FTC, beginning in 1972, for many types of garments—with a few exceptions: (1) articles of clothing that sell for $3 or less at retail and are completely washable under normal conditions—for example, men's cotton T-shirts or handkerchiefs; (2) hats, gloves, and footwear other than hosiery; (3) items whose usefulness or appearance might be spoiled by a label—for example, a lacy blouse. The instructions on the labels give appropriate cleaning procedures for regular care and maintenance. They do not provide any information on spot-removal procedures. The instructions provided are meant to cover all the parts of a garment, unless exceptions are noted.

The FTC regulations indicate that labels should tell both what to do and what not to do with a particular garment. Both kinds of instructions can be seen in these examples of labels that conform to the FTC rules:

- Machine-wash warm. Gentle cycle. Do not use chlorine bleach.
- Hand-wash cold. Do not twist or wring. Reshape. Dry flat. Do not dry-clean.
- Dry-clean only. Do not use petroleum solvents or the coin-operated method of dry cleaning.

Checking Your Reading

1. How can our clothes express both our individual personalities and group membership at the same time?
2. When you make an inventory of your clothes, what else should you do besides just making a list of the things you have?
3. Why is it useful to choose versatile items when buying clothes?

4. Why is polyester used in combination with cotton in many permanent-press items?
5. What label information does the Textile Fiber Products Identification Act require?
6. What are fabric standards?
7. What three factors influence the durability of a woven fabric?
8. What can happen if permanent-press items are washed in very hot water or dried at too high a temperature? Why does this problem occur?
9. How do water-repellent finishes work?
10. How is fabric shaped to fit body contours during the construction of a garment?
11. What is the purpose of interfacings?
12. What key factors can guide consumers in judging the quality of clothing?
13. What two general problems may result in a poorly fitting garment?
14. Why is it best to hang clothes up at once after taking them off?
15. What problems led to the requirement that garments carry permanent care labels?

Consumer Problems and Projects

1. Take an inventory of the clothes you have for the coming season (do not forget to try on every item and to check its condition). What other items will you need? Can you develop a plan to get these items?
2. Study some recent issues of men's or women's fashion and clothing magazines, and identify pictures in which the models have hair, skin, and eye coloring similar to yours. Record (1) your own coloring, (2) the colors of the articles of clothing in the pictures you selected, and (3) the colors that you thought looked best in combination with the models' coloring.
3. Look ahead for a year or two to a new job or role you are likely to have that will require you to have special clothing. This might be a secretarial job, a sales job, or the role of a student at college or a business or technical school. Make a list of the clothes that you will need for your first season on the job or in school. What items do you already have that would be suitable, and what will you

need to buy? Use a mail-order catalog or visit local stores to obtain estimates of the prices of items you will need to buy. What plan can you develop to get the things you will need?

4. Study issues of *Consumers' Research Magazine* and *Consumer Reports* that report tests made on articles of clothing. Select a particular item in which you are interested. What characteristics did they test? Which characteristics did they consider most important? Which characteristics do you think are most important? What brands were given top ratings? If you were to buy this item which brand would you choose? Why?

5. Charley Rogers was considering buying a new coat and was having trouble deciding whether to buy a regular top coat or a raincoat with a zip-out lining. What are the advantages and disadvantages of each alternative?

6. Suzie Samuelson complained that her permanent-press dresses and blouses always need ironing when they come out of the wash. If you were advising Suzie, what questions would you want to ask her about how she was handling her permanent-press clothes?

7. Identify an article of clothing that is available at several different price levels. Check the prices of this item in local stores or in a mail-order catalog. How do the construction, styling, and fabrics used differ among price levels? If you were to buy the item, at which price level would you buy? Why?

8. What information would you like to see on the label when you are buying clothes? Prepare a label for a clothing item you sometimes buy, for example, jeans. Include all the types of information you feel consumers need. On your label, put an asterisk (*) by information which is not provided now.

9. Prepare a report on one of the consumer problems and issues which affect consumers of clothing. These include the following:

- Clothing care and permanent care labeling
- Fabric flammability and flammability standards
- Fiber identification and labeling
- Fabric testing and informative labeling or grade labeling of fabrics
- Clothing sizes

What are the problems in the area, and what laws have been passed or are needed?

9

Buying Food

For most of us, food is partly a luxury and partly a necessity. We could survive on a diet of enriched bread, margarine, nonfat dry milk, potatoes, and cooked dry beans. Would you want to live that way? Few of us are only interested in getting the nutrients we need at the lowest possible cost. What we really want is good food that we can enjoy and that provides us good nutrition without costing too much. This means balancing some of our values against each other. How important is economy compared with enjoyment, or compared with good nutrition? Different people and different families settle on different balance points. But the same values are more or less important to us all.

You already know what foods you like. In this chapter we will look at some things you may not know so much about—good nutrition and wise food buying. First we will look at our nutritional needs and the foods that help provide them. Then we will look at ways to plan menus and shop that will help us get the food we need and want as cheaply as possible.

HOW IMPORTANT IS GOOD NUTRITION?

Good nutrition is closely linked to some of the things we want the most—a good build, physical fitness, and vitality. The payoff for good eating habits does not come right away, however. An extra glass of milk on Thursday is not likely to produce a winning performance on the football field on Friday. Because the payoff for good nutrition develops over time, some people think good nutrition is not important or can be ignored without harm. A good supply of nutrients is essential to keep our bodies functioning, to provide us with the energy we need, and to provide materials for growth and for the continuous job of rebuilding our bones and body tissues.

A Guide for Good Nutrition

To help us in knowing what we need to eat, nutritionists have developed what they call the *Basic Four*. Although the name sounds like a new music group, the *Basic Four* really is a list of essential food groups and the number of servings from each that we need every day.

- *Milk Group.* Whole and skim milk, cottage and cheddar-type cheese, and ice cream. This group is our leading source of calcium needed for bones and teeth. It also provides high-quality protein, riboflavin, vitamin A, and many other nutrients. [Four or more servings each day for teenagers, two or more for adults, two to three or more for children.]
- *Vegetable and Fruit Group.* All vegetables and fruits. Oranges and orange juice, grapefruit, broccoli, and fresh strawberries are good sources of vitamin C. Spinach, tomatoes, potatoes, and sweet potatoes cooked in their jackets and raw cabbage are fair sources of vitamin C. Spinach, carrots, broccoli, sweet potatoes, and turnip greens are good sources of vitamin A. Four or more servings daily.
- *Bread and Cereal Group.* Bread, cooked and ready-to-eat cereals, cornmeal, and spaghetti. Use enriched products when possible. Foods in this group furnish worthwhile amounts of protein, iron, thiamine, riboflavin, and niacin, along with food energy. Four or more servings each day.
- *Meat Group.* Beef, pork, chicken, eggs, fish, and shellfish; as alternates, dry peas and beans, peanuts, and peanut butter. These foods provide protein, iron, thiamine, riboflavin, niacin, and other nutrients. Two or more servings each day.
- *Other Foods.* Some other foods will be needed to round out meals. These can include additional servings from the four groups, as well as other foods not listed in these groups. Such foods include margarine, butter, jelly, seasonings, and salad dressings.

A good supply of nutrients is necessary to keep your body functioning well, and to give you the energy you need. *(Sylvia Johnson, Woodfin Camp & Associates)*

Although it is easier to be well fed if you have a lot of money to spend, it is possible to make good menu plans using the Basic Four at different cost levels. The menu plans in Table 9-1 show how an adequate diet can be provided at different levels of spending. The meals in the high-cost plan cost more than 2½ times those in the low-cost plan.

A Guide for Improving Our Eating Habits

Most people are reluctant to make major changes in the way they eat, even for the sake of good nutrition. There are some easy changes we all could make. Here are a few suggestions:

- *Avoid Skipping Breakfast.* Even taking just a glass of milk, some orange juice, and a piece of toast is better than skipping breakfast. These foods will provide some of the energy we need to start the day. Skipping meals is a poor way to diet. When meals are skipped, it is hard to get a balanced diet. Dieters may end up so

TABLE 9-1
A Day's Menu at Different Costs for a Family of Four

	Low-Cost Menu	High-Cost Menu
Breakfast	Orange juice (canned) Oatmeal with milk Cinnamon toast Milk (nonfat dry) or coffee	Strawberries (fresh) Bacon and eggs Biscuits (frozen) Milk (fresh) or coffee
Lunch	Hard-cooked egg or peanut butter and jelly sandwich Celery sticks or a banana Milk (nonfat dry)	Baked ham on seeded roll with lettuce and tomato Asparagus in cheese sauce (frozen) Milk (fresh)
Snack	Cookies Fruit punch	Pear Chocolate milk (fresh)
Dinner	Fried chicken Carrots (fresh) Mashed potatoes Bread (white enriched) Apple pie (homemade) Milk (nonfat dry) or coffee	Beef rib roast Broccoli with butter sauce Corn on the cob (fresh) Dinner rolls (bakery) German chocolate cake (frozen) Milk (fresh) or coffee

Source: U.S. Department of Agriculture

hungry that they eat too many high-calorie snacks between meals.

- *Get More Exercise.* The energy requirements of modern life are so low that it is hard to get the vitamins and minerals we need while holding calories down. With more exercise we can eat the foods we need without gaining weight.

- *Diet Intelligently.* One way to diet is to choose well-balanced meals and form the habit of eating smaller portions. Substituting skim milk for whole milk is another way to cut down on calories without losing needed nutrients.

- *Choose Better Snacks.* Snacks are a part of our way of life, and few of us would give them up. What we need to do is make our snacks do a better job for us. We can do this by substituting more nutritious foods for typical snack foods that are long on calories and short on the vitamins and minerals we need. A cheeseburger or a hamburger, especially with a slice of tomato, and a glass of milk would be a good snack choice.

SMART MENU PLANNING

In order to get good value for the money we spend on food, we have to make a two-step attack on the problem. First, we will have to plan menus wisely, including items that are good sources of nutrients at a reasonable cost. Second, we will have to shop wisely for the items we need to make up the menus we have planned.

Making a Menu Plan

The first step in smart menu planning is to plan ahead. Begin by making a list of menus for the days ahead. The list may be put down on paper, or it may just be a mental note. A menu plan can only be a general guideline and must be flexible. Changes may be necessary because of unexpected guests or family activities. Changes may also be necessary because items included in the plan are not available. The plan should be flexible so that special bargains can be substituted for more costly items. A good menu plan will take good nutrition, cost, and family preferences into account.

Using Seasonal Bargains and Plentiful Foods

Prices of fresh food change throughout the year, depending on the season. Many fresh fruits and vegetables are available throughout the year but are especially expensive in the off season. During the off season and when the first of the new crop comes in, prices are high. As supplies increase, prices become more reasonable. Prices are at their lowest when the produce from nearby areas becomes available. These supply cycles follow a similar pattern each year and can be charted to help consumers plan their purchases (see Table 9-2). Apples, for example, are available all year round but are most plentiful in the fall and winter just after the new crop is picked.

One way to keep track of which foods are in plentiful supply and attractively priced is to watch the food pages of the newspapers. Home economists and marketing specialists in the Cooperative Extension Service provide newspapers with new information about plentiful foods every week.

Using the Food Ads to Find Specials

Grocers know that meat quality and prices have an important effect on where consumers decide to shop. They use advertised weekend meat

TABLE 9-2
Availability of Fresh Fruit

G = Good Supply, F = Fair Supply, S = Small Supply

	January	February	March	April	May	June	July	August	September	October	November	December
Apples	G	G	G	G	F	S	S	S	G	G	G	G
Bananas	G	G	G	G	G	G	G	G	G	G	G	G
Blueberries					S	G	G	G	S			
Cantaloupes		S	S	S	F	G	G	G	G	S	S	
Cherries					S	G	G	S	S			
Grapefruit	G	G	G	G	G	F	S	S	S	G	G	G
Grapes	S	S	S	S	S	F	G	G	G	G	G	F
Oranges	G	G	G	G	G	F	S	S	S	F	G	G
Peaches					S	G	G	G	G	S		
Strawberries	S	S	F	G	G	G	G	S	S	S	S	S

Source: U.S. Department of Agriculture

specials to win new customers and hold their present ones. Meat specials and other specials offer smart shoppers a chance both to fill out the week's menu at lower cost and stock up for the future.

Supermarket meat specials can provide substantial savings over the same cuts at regular price, at no loss of quality. Savings of 20 to 30 per cent are possible. It is difficult to make price comparisons among stores because trimming practices differ a good deal. Higher-priced specials may be the better buy if they provide more edible meat. Quality also differs among stores. Some stores consistently offer better-quality meat than others. Experience with eating quality and trimming practices has to be considered in judging a store's meat specials.

Shoppers need to remember that not everything in a store's ad is a special. Some items are advertised because the store wants to emphasize their everyday low prices. Other items are advertised because the processor has paid part of the advertising cost.

Economizing Wisely

Menu planners can cut food costs and still serve well-balanced meals if they follow some tips.

- Meat accounts for about one-third of the food budget. Economize by using less expensive substitutes for meat as a source of animal protein. Some economical sources of protein are cheese, canned fish, and eggs. It also is possible to substitute vegetable protein sources such as dried peas and beans and peanut butter.
- Combine meat, fish, or other high-protein foods with extenders such as noodles, spaghetti, macaroni, rice, or potatoes.
- Cut down on snack items. Soft drinks, potato chips, and candy are high in calories but provide few needed vitamins and minerals.
- Think twice and then think again before cutting down on fruits and vegetables or on dairy products. Many people's diets already are too low in these foods. If it is necessary to cut costs, find substitutes; for example, use canned instead of frozen fruit.

Deciding What You Really Need

An important step in smart menu planning is deciding what you really need—the quality that is right for the use you have in mind and the right quantity. It is not always necessary to buy the best quality. Less expensive grades and cuts of beef are fine for making stews. Lower-quality fruits and vegetables can be used when appearance is not important. For example, slightly blemished tomatoes can always be cut up and used in stews.

The smart shopper will learn to judge the quantity of food that is needed for a serving. The number of servings in a pound of meat differs depending on the amount of bone, fat, and inedible waste. For example, if we want 3-ounce servings of cooked lean meat, poultry, or fish then:

- Cuts with little or no fat provide three to four serving per pound—ground meat, lean stew meat, liver, center slice of ham, fish steaks, and fillets.
- Cuts with a medium amount of bone provide two to three servings per pound—most roasts, some chops and steaks, ham, and poultry.
- Cuts with much bone, gristle, or fat provide one to two servings per pound—spare ribs, short ribs, porterhouse and T-bone steaks, and chicken wings and backs.

We can see from the first column of Table 9-3 that 1 pound of ground beef provides 4 servings, while 1 pound of sirloin steak with

TABLE 9-3
Cost of a 3-Ounce Serving of Cooked Lean Meat

Retail Cut	Approx. Number Servings Per Pound	Price Per Pound of Retail Cuts															
		40¢	50¢	60¢	70¢	80¢	90¢	100¢	110¢	120¢	130¢	140¢	150¢	160¢	170¢	180¢	190¢
		Cost of a 3-Ounce Serving (cents)															
Beef																	
Sirloin steak–bone in	2½	17	21	26	30	34	38	43	47	51	55	60	64	68	72	77	81
Ground beef–lean	4	10	13	16	18	21	23	26	29	31	34	36	39	42	44	47	49
Chuck roast–bone in	2	18	22	27	31	36	40	45	49	54	58	62	67	71	76	80	85
Short ribs	1½	23	29	35	41	47	53	58	64	70	76	82	88	94	99	105	111
Pork																	
Loin roast–bone in	2	20	25	30	36	41	46	51	56	61	66	71	76	81	86	91	96
Loin chops	2	18	22	27	31	36	40	45	49	54	58	62	67	71	76	80	85
Ham slices	3	12	16	19	22	25	28	31	34	38	41	44	47	50	53	56	59
Ham roast–bone in	3	14	17	21	24	28	31	35	38	42	45	49	52	56	59	62	66
Lamb																	
Leg roast–bone in	2½	17	21	25	29	33	38	42	46	50	54	58	62	67	71	75	79
Loin chops	2	18	23	27	32	37	41	46	50	55	59	64	68	73	78	82	87
Poultry																	
Chicken–whole, ready-to-cook	2	19	23	28	32	37	42	46	51	56	60	65	70	74	79	84	88
Turkey–whole, ready-to-cook	2	19	23	28	33	38	42	47	52	56	61	66	70	75	80	84	89

Source: U.S. Department of Agriculture

Shoppers need to know the number of servings in a pound of meat before they can determine the right amount to buy. *(Courtesy E.I. du Pont de Nemours)*

the bone in provides only 2½ servings. We can also use this table to determine the cost per serving of different meat items. For example, if ground beef costs 90 cents a pound, a single serving costs 23 cents, while sirloin steak at $1.80 a pound costs 77 cents a serving.

Deciding How Much to Pay for Convenience

A wide variety of food products that save preparation time is available, and dozens of new convenience foods appear on the market each year. Some of these foods save both preparation time and money. Others save preparation time but are more expensive than the same items prepared from "scratch."

Convenience foods that are cheaper than the fresh forms of the products usually are the result of processing that reduces the cost of moving them to the market. This is the case for frozen orange juice concentrate. The frozen concentrate eliminates the cost of shipping the rinds and water content of fresh oranges and reduces spoilage. Savings are also possible on other vegetables that include inedible parts, such as pods, or that are highly perishable. Many cake mixes are cheaper than buying the separate ingredients, and save time as well.

Many convenience foods provide important savings in preparation time but do cost extra. The extra cost may range from a few cents for every hour of preparation time saved, to several dollars per hour saved, as in the case of frozen baked goods and frozen main dishes.

SMART FOOD SHOPPING

When we finish our menu plan, we still have the problem of purchasing needed items at the lowest possible cost. Smart food shopping, like smart menu planning, depends on good information and workable plans. Making and using a shopping list, choosing a place to shop, and using label information all are important skills for smart food shoppers.

Before you go shopping for food, plan out your menus and prepare a shopping list of items you will need. Using a list helps you buy everything in one trip and avoid impulse purchases. *(Sepp Seitz, Magnum Photos)*

Using a Shopping List

The first step in smart food shopping is to prepare a shopping list of the items we need to complete the meals we have planned. This shopping list should also include staple items we need such as salt, sugar, and paper towels.

With a shopping list, we can avoid several costly mistakes. We can make certain we get everything we need and avoid extra trips to the store. Extra trips can be costly in both time and car-operating expenses. A shopping list also will help us avoid impulse purchases that will run up our grocery bill. A shopping list also can help us avoid overbuying perishables so that we can eliminate wasteful spoilage.

Choosing a Place to Shop

An important part of smart shopping is the choice of a place to shop. Prices and quality do differ among stores.

Price competition among supermarkets tends to keep prices from differing too much among different stores. Price differences are larger between supermarkets and small neighborhood and convenience stores. These smaller stores are open long hours, and their average sales are small. This raises their operating costs. Since the stores' total sales are small, their extra operating costs result in higher prices. Smart shoppers will try to hold their purchases from these higher-priced stores to a minimum. Many city and country dwellers do not have supermarket-type stores nearby. The extra savings from supermarket shopping may make some extra effort worthwhile, especially for large orders.

Choosing a supermarket may be difficult. Some stores try to draw in shoppers with attractive specials. These stores usually make up for these specials by charging higher prices for other items. Other stores advertise "everyday low prices" or "discount prices." To make up for their lower average prices, these stores may not offer good specials.

Understanding the Information on the Label

Information included on the labels of food products is strictly controlled by law. Food shoppers will find labels to be one of their most useful and reliable sources of information. Labels provide such important facts as the ingredients and the relative amounts of each that were used, the net weight of the package contents, the name of the processor or distributor, and federal inspection information.

Name of the Product   The idea of reading the product name on a package label seems so obvious that the casual shopper may ignore the information that the name can provide. This information is important for mixtures, especially those that include meat. For these products the wording of the name can be an important indication of the contents. For example, a product called "Turkey with Noodles" contains more turkey than one labeled "Noodles with Turkey."

Along with the name of the product, other useful information about the product may be indicated on the label. Here are some examples:

- *Meat.* "All Beef"—the product contains beef only, no other types of meat. "All Meat"—the product may include various types of meats, including beef, pork, and mutton, but no cereal or other extenders have been added. "Cereal Added"—indicates that cereal has been added to extend the meat.
- *Fruit.* The packing liquid, either syrup, juice, or water, is indicated. Syrups used may be light, heavy, or extra-heavy. Fruit packed in light syrup is the least expensive.
- *Vegetables.* Maturity of the product often is indicated. Younger varieties, baby beets and early peas, for example—suggest tenderness. Style of cut also may be indicated—sliced, diced, or fancy cuts such as French-style green beans or julienne carrots (both of which are cut lengthwise).

For many products there is a *standard of identity* that sets down the characteristics and ingredients that the food product must have before it can be labeled with a specific product name, such as "macaroni." Over 250 foods have standards of identity developed by the federal government. These standards cover many everyday food products, including bread, jam, peanut butter, and margarine.

A standard of identity is something like a recipe. It specifies the key ingredients and the minimum amount of each that must be included in a product. Strawberry jam, for example, must include 45 percent strawberries by weight. A strawberry jam that fails to meet this standard would have to be labeled "Imitation Strawberry Jam" even though it did contain some strawberries. Standards of identity also specify optional ingredients, which processors may include in their products if they choose. These optional ingredients are chiefly preservatives, colors, spices, and flavorings.

Products for which standards of identity have been set do not have to indicate required ingredients on their labels. The optional ingredients used, such as preservatives and artificial flavorings and colors, do have to be included on the label. Processors who use ingredients of special quality sometimes choose to list those ingredients even though this is not required.

Standards of identity for most processed foods are administered by the Food and Drug Administration in the U.S. Department of Health, Education, and Welfare. Standards for meat products are administered by the U.S. Department of Agriculture.

List of Ingredients   Foods that are not covered by a federal standard of identity must have their ingredients listed on the label. Some foods covered by a standard also have their ingredients listed, as we have seen. Ingredients are listed beginning with the one that weighs the most. If we saw two different brands of beef stew, and one label read "water, beef, potatoes" while the other read "water, potatoes, beef," we would know that the first brand contained more beef. Of course, we also would know that both contained more water than either beef, or potatoes. Spices, flavoring, and coloring do not have to be listed individually, but the label must indicate if they have been used. The use of preservatives must be indicated.

Net Weight of the Contents   The label, by federal law, must indicate the actual weight of the contents of the package, not including the weight of the package itself. The net weight stated on the container represents the combined weight of the food and the packing liquids or syrups used, except in a very few cases. In a few special cases, such as mushrooms and olives, the weight reported is a weight for the drained product only. Some consumer advocates have urged drained weight labeling for all food products.

Name of the Packer or Distributor   The label will include the name of the food processor who packages the item or the name of the firm that distributes it. Store brands typically list the retailer's name. The address and zip code is listed to assist customers who wish to send comments or complaints.

Inspection Information   Assurance that meat, poultry, and fish and their processed products are produced under sanitary conditions is provided by federal inspection stamps and seals. Federal inspectors go to processing plants and keep a careful watch to ensure that processed meat, poultry, and fish are wholesome and that they are produced under sanitary conditions. All meat and poultry and processed products must conform to federal standards, regardless of whether the products are moving within or between states. However, only a small fraction of the fish and fish products consumed in this country is covered by federal inspection. New legislation is badly needed to extend inspection coverage to all domestically processed and imported fish.

Open-Date Information A number of perishable foods have calendar dates on the package indicating when the product should be sold or used to assure quality and freshness. This date information is called *open-dating*. Four different kinds of open-dating are used. Many consumers do not understand the differences in what they mean, but each has its own meaning.

- *Pack Date.* the date of final processing or packaging. An example is "packed January 25." Pack dates are frequently used on fresh meat and poultry. The pack date does not provide shoppers any information on how long they can expect a product to be good.
- *Pull Date.* the last day a product should be sold at retail, still allowing time for home storage and use. An example is "Sell by August 25," indicating the date the product should be removed from the shelf. The pull date is the most widely used type of open date.
- *Quality Assurance Date.* the date after which the product is not likely to be at peak quality. Examples are "for maximum enjoyment use by August 14," and "better when used by December 23."
- *Expiration Date.* the last date the product should be used for assured quality. An example is "do not use after February 1979."

Consumers should be aware that the handling of a product has an important effect on quality, regardless of the date on it. If a product has been exposed to high temperatures, quality is likely to suffer.

Nutrition Labels Many foods now carry nutrition labels. These labels provide information on vitamin and mineral content, and on calorie content along with other nutrition information. This information can help us in understanding the nutrients in a particular food and in comparing different foods.

Labeling is voluntary for many foods, but it is required when any nutrient is added to a food. For example, breakfast cereal must be labeled when vitamins A or D have been added to it. Labeling also is required when a manufacturer makes nutritional claims about the product. If it is claimed to be a good source of vitamin C, it must be labeled.

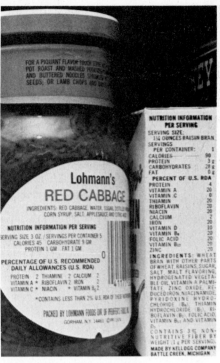

The label on the left is an example of open-dating; July 7 is the date of final packaging for these wieners. The label on the right shows nutritional information. This includes serving size; calories per serving; and the amount of protein, carbohydrates, fat, and vitamins per serving. *(Left, Oscar Mayer & Co.; right, Susan Berkowitz)*

When products are labeled, the information must be provided in a standard format to make comparisons between products easier. Certain information is required on all labels:

- Serving size (in standard household units such as cups or ounces) and the number of servings in the can or package.
- Calories per serving
- The amount of protein, carbohydrate, and fat (measured in grams) per serving
- The amount of protein and of 2 minerals and 5 vitamins provided, measured as a percent of the U.S. Recommended Daily Allowance (USRDA)

Certain other optional information also may be included if the manufacturer wishes.

Understanding USRDAs is essential for understanding nutrition labels, because vitamin and mineral content is expressed as a percent of the USRDA. The USRDAs are the amounts of each vitamin and mineral adequate to meet the needs of nearly all healthy people. They are more than adequate for most people except pregnant women and nursing mothers.

Nutrition labels can tell us a variety of things. They can tell us that pizza is a good source of calcium (because of the cheese used). They can tell us that there are 75 calories in a slice of white bread. They also can help us compare the nutritional value of different foods, such as different brands of breakfast cereal.

Nutrition labels also remind us that every food has calories along with vitamins and minerals. Most of us need more vitamins and minerals. Few of us need more calories—and the weight problems which go with them. What we need to do is get the most vitamins and minerals we can for every calorie we consume. Foods which are high in calories (usually because they are high in fat and sugar) but have few vitamins and minerals do not do their share. This is why they are often labeled "empty calorie foods" and "junk foods."

Nutritional labels can help us locate good sources of the nutrients which are often in short supply in young people's diets. Because they have big appetites, most boys usually end up with better nutrition intakes than girls. Girls should give some attention to getting adequate amounts of protein and iron. Both boys and girls, like the rest of our population, would benefit from adding foods which are good sources of calcium, vitamin A, riboflavin, and iron to their diets.

Since nutrition labeling is voluntary, manufacturers of "empty calorie foods" are unlikely to label their products. Consumers should recognize that many nutritious foods are not labeled either. This includes fresh fruit and vegetables, which often are sold unpackaged, and fresh meat.

Other Label Information   Other useful information may be included on the label, such as cooking directions or recipes. Information on the number and size of servings may be included.

Understanding the Use of Grades as Guides to Quality

Standards of quality have been developed to provide a basis for assigning grades to food products. These standards of quality are something like the grading system for a report card. They set down the characteristics on which a product will be judged and how well it must do to be placed in a particular grade category. Each grade category has a name attached to it in just the same way different levels of school performance are classified A, B, C, D, or F.

U.S. Grade Names   The food grades used by the federal government are generally letters or adjectives. The system for naming grades unfortunately differs among products, and thus confuses many consumers. The top grade of beef is USDA Prime; the top grade of butter is U.S. Grade AA; and the top grade of poultry is U.S. Grade A. To make the best use of grades, the shopper will have to learn the meanings of the grades commonly seen in the supermarket. Some states and some processors also use grading systems and assign grade names to their products. These should not be confused with the U.S. grades. U.S. grade labels always include a shield and the letters U.S. or USDA.

Most of the federal grading program, including grading for beef, chicken, eggs, dairy products, fruits, and vegetables, is administered by the U.S. Department of Agriculture. Fish grading is administered by the U.S. Department of the Interior. Participation in grading programs is voluntary. Many of the processors who choose to participate have high-quality products and wish to use the U.S. grade as a selling point to emphasize the quality of their products. All plants producing U.S.-graded products are inspected for sanitation, so a U.S. grade provides assurance both of quality and wholesomeness.

Beef Grades   Of the eight U.S. grades for beef, only the three top grades are usually seen in grocery stores. These three grades in order of quality are Prime, Choice, and Good. "Choice" is the grade seen most frequently. Beef of "Prime" grade goes chiefly to exclusive restaurants and fancy grocery stores in larger cities. Meat of a quality that would be graded "Good" typically is sold ungraded or may be marked with a store's or meat packer's own brand.

While grades are not perfect predictors of the tenderness and flavor of beef, they are one of the best guides consumers have. Key factors used in the grading of beef are as follows:

- *The Age of the Animal.* Prime, Choice, and Good beef all must be from young animals.
- *The Color and Texture of the Lean Meat.* A fine, velvety-looking texture and a bright red color are considered most desirable. In general, the older the animal the darker the meat.
- *The Amount, Color, and Texture of the Fat.* Higher-grade cuts

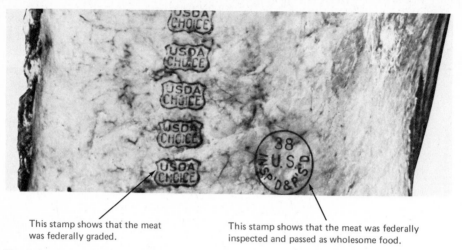

This stamp shows that the meat was federally graded.

This stamp shows that the meat was federally inspected and passed as wholesome food.

The federal government grades many products, including meat, for both quality and wholesomeness. However, processors must choose to have their products graded.

include more marbling (the small flecks of fat scattered through the lean portion of the cut) and a good covering of firm, white fat around the edge of the cut.

From this discussion, it should be clear that beef is judged by its appearance rather than by mechanical or chemical tests. While grades are fairly good predictors of eating quality, they have no relation to nutritional value because vitamin and mineral content differs little among grades.

Choosing Manufacturers' Brands or Store Brands

Grocers offer shoppers a variety of items in the hope that at least one item will suit them. They do this by offering several brands of each product at different prices and quality levels. For example, a store may offer three choices of canned peaches, including both manufacturers' brands and store brands (see the discussion in Chapter 4 of manufacturers' brands and store brands). The top-priced item usually is a widely advertised and well-known manufacturer's brand of high quality. Next in price will be a store brand of perhaps equal or slightly lower quality. Often this brand carries the store name. The lowest-priced item usually will be another store brand of somewhat lower quality; the fruit may be broken or blemished and the syrup lighter.

One reason store brands are cheaper than manufacturers' brands of similar quality is that their price does not have to cover any separate advertising costs. Advertising and sales promotion costs are a substantial part of the cost of some foods. Producers of peanut butter, crackers, and cookies spend about 4 percent of their sales revenue on advertising and sales promotion; cake mix producers spend about 7 percent; and producers of ready-to-eat cereals spend about 20 percent.

Checking the Appearance of the Package

Before an individual package is selected, it should be examined carefully. Do not buy or use cans that are bulging or leaking. The contents are likely to be spoiled and may be dangerous. The contents of a dented can are safe as long as the can has not been pierced.

In buying frozen foods, choose only firm, solidly frozen packages. Wet, limp, or sweating packages are signs that the contents have thawed or are in the process of thawing. Stained and frost-covered packages also should be avoided. They may have thawed and been refrozen. When packages are partly thawed or have thawed and then been refrozen, there is danger of spoilage. The quality of the contents is certain to have suffered. When buying food in jars, avoid jars that show evidence of having been opened.

Checking Your Reading

1. Why is a good supply of nutrients essential?
2. What four food groups make up the Basic Four? What nutrients does each group provide? How many servings from each group should someone your age eat each day?
3. Name four ways in which we can improve our eating habits.
4. When are the prices of fresh fruits and vegetables highest and when are they lowest?
5. Is everything listed in a grocery store ad a special?
6. How can families reduce their spending on meat and still obtain needed protein?
7. Why should most families think carefully before cutting their spending on fruits, vegetables, and dairy products?
8. Why do some cuts of meat provide more servings per pound than others? What kind of cuts provide the most servings per pound? The least?

9. What are convenience foods? Are all convenience foods more expensive than the same items prepared from "scratch"? Why?
10. Why is a shopping list useful?
11. Why are prices usually higher in small neighborhood grocery stores and convenience stores than supermarkets?
12. What is a standard of identity?
13. What can the consumers learn from the order in which ingredients are listed on a food package?
14. What do federal inspection seals on meat, poultry, and fish products indicate?
15. What is a "pull date"? What does it indicate?
16. What information must be provided on a nutrition label? How is the amount of vitamins and minerals in a food measured? What is a USRDA?

Consumer Problems and Projects

1. Using the table on page 144 in this chapter, determine the months when prices are likely to be highest and lowest for the following fresh fruits: apples, cantaloupes, strawberries, oranges.
2. How good was your diet yesterday? Write down everything you ate yesterday. Make a chart like Table 9-4, and place each item you ate in the correct category of the Basic Four. Did you get the recommended number of servings in each category?

TABLE 9-4
Basic Four

Your Meals	Vegetables and Fruits	Meat	Milk	Bread and Cereals

3. How can you improve your diet? Review the categories in the exercise above in which your diet fell short. What food items are needed to meet the Basic Four recommendations? Are there any foods you ate yesterday that you might have been better off without?

4. Make a list of 10 menu items a family could use to reduce spending on meat.
5. Using the table on page 146 answer the following questions:
   a. If lean ground beef is $1.10 per pound, what is the cost per serving?
   b. How many 3-ounce cooked servings could we expect to get from a 1-pound slice of ham?
   c. Which cut of meat is cheaper per serving—ground beef at $1 per pound or short ribs at 50 cents per pound?
6. Make a list of five processed food items that your family frequently uses and that provide a list of ingredients on their labels. Choose as wide a variety of products as possible; for example, canned soup, frozen dinners or chicken pot pie, canned spaghetti and meat balls, and frozen or canned fruit drinks. What are the three leading ingredients in each product?
7. Check the food pages of your local newspapers for information on foods that currently are in plentiful supply and are good buys.
   a. Make a list of the products suggested.
   b. Prepare a menu plan for one day that includes as many of these items as possible. Be sure your plan meets the Basic Four requirements.
8. How economical is the "large economy size"? Identify five grocery items that are offered in several sizes; for example, laundry detergent, breakfast cereal, toothpaste, and soft drinks. Select a particular brand of each item and record the various sizes offered and the price of each size. Calculate the price per ounce (or per unit) for each size. Which size is the most economical buy?
9. Collect nutrition labels from three different food products.
   a. When we compare a serving of each, which is the best source of each of five vitamins and two minerals listed?
   b. How many calories are there in a serving of each item?
   c. Which product provides the most protein per calorie? (Divide the number of calories in a serving into the percent of the USRDA of protein provided.) Which provides the most calcium per calorie? The most vitamin A?

10

Buying Cars

Getting from one place to another takes a good part of our incomes. If you own a car, perhaps you have a fairly good idea of how much you spend each week for such things as gasoline, oil, and repairs. Did you know that for most families, transportation is the third biggest item in their budgets? (Only housing and food rank higher.) In fact, the average moderate-income family in our country spends 14 cents to 15 cents out of every dollar for transportation. Most of that money goes for cars—buying the cars and then paying for such necessary things as insurance, parking, fuel, maintenance, and repairs.

In the late 1970s more than two out of five families owned two or more cars. Why are cars so popular? As you well know, in many cases there is no choice. If you need to travel from one place to another in your community, such as to and from work, you simply must have a car.

BUYING USED CARS

Used-car sales people are sometimes looked upon as persons who cannot be trusted. Perhaps they have this reputation because they have a need to make a profit, and they make their profits by *bargaining* with their customers. For many of the things we buy, a price is listed on the package or article, and we and the salesperson know that this is the price that will be paid for the item. Not so with cars. The seller may quote a price, but he is willing to sell for less. Because the customer in most cases knows the price quoted is high, he tells the salesperson that he won't buy the car at the price. The customer may offer to buy at a lower price than the seller suggests, or the customer may just ask that the price be reduced to a more reasonable amount. Arriving at a price in this way is known as bargaining, and it is common in the used-car business.

Do you think you are a good match for the used-car salesperson in the business of bargaining? Think about this fact: The salesperson may sell two or three hundred (or more) cars in a year. How many cars does a customer buy each year? The point is, if you are going to buy a used car, you need to arm yourself with as much information as possible about how to go about buying a car wisely. Obviously, not all used-car dealers are the same. Some use sales schemes that border on fraud. Others are honest business people who have built excellent reputations for giving good service.

The Starting Point

Before searching for a used car in the want ads or on used-car lots, check some of the guides available for consumers. For example, *Consumer Reports*, the magazine published by Consumers Union, regularly gives information about used cars, such as the frequency-of-repair record for various models. *Motor Trend* magazine's annual issue on used-car buying also is a valuable source of information for a person ready to buy a used car.

Price information about used cars is in the price guides that exist for dealers and banks, but they usually disagree somewhat on prices. Some of these guides include the National Automobile Dealers Association's *Official Used Car Guide*, *The Kelly Auto Market Report (Blue Book)*, and the *Red Book Official Used Car Valuations*. Loan officers at banks or other lending institutions will usually permit customers to look at whichever price guide they have. These guides show the wholesale or dealer price and the retail price of each model, as well as the prices for various options. With this price information, you can do a much more intelligent job of bargaining for the used car you have in mind.

Newspaper want ads list some of the available used cars in the local market, but these ads can be very misleading. For example, a bait-and-switch scheme would advertise a low price on a popular model that purportedly is in excellent shape. When you arrive at the used-car lot, you are told that the car has already been sold, but many other fantastic buys are still available. The ad may have been just a come-on to induce you to visit the lot. An ad may read, "Repossessions—take over payments." Most readers of the ad would conclude that the offer means a buyer can take over the payments left by a former owner who could not keep them up. In fact, this ad, too, may be simply a way to induce people to visit the lot. Some of the cars may have been repossessed at one time, but they are now selling at the regular price.

A New-Car Dealer or a Used-Car Dealer?

Probably in most cases the best source for a used car is the used-car lot of an established new-car dealer. Most new-car dealers operate a used-car lot to sell the best of their customers' trade-ins. The dealer has the shop facilities and the mechanics to put a used car in saleable shape, and will more likely stand behind the warranty. Trade-ins that have been in accidents or are in poor shape for some other reason are sold to the wholesalers who sell to used-car dealers. Buying a used car from a new-car dealer may mean paying a few dollars more for the car, but it may well be worth the money.

Many car lots sell only used cars, and they differ considerably. Some are small, one-person operations. Others are huge, glittering layouts with row after row of used cars. Some deal in good, solid cars and do a profitable business through sound, honest business practices. Others engage in practices that are deceptive and dangerous. For example, a dealer may hire a mechanic who is good at making a car bought cheaply at an auction operate well enough to attract a buyer. These lemons are known in the trade as "dogs" or "iron." Some of the tricks used to hide defects include putting heavier oil in the engine to mask worn rings and bearings; placing fiber packing in the transmission, differential, and drive train to muffle noise; and using a wedge of wood or a tie-back cable to correct alignment.

Checkpoints for Buying a Used Car

Following are a few pointers that a prospective used-car buyer should bear in mind.

The used-car lot of an established new-car dealer is often the best place to buy a used car because most new-car dealers use these lots to sell the best of their customers' trade-ins. (*Kip Peticolas*)

- Decide how much money you are willing to pay before you visit a car lot. Unless you are sure of your limits and your needs, you may end up with a car you had no intention of buying.
- Have an impartial mechanic check the car over thoroughly to determine whether or not it will be a reasonably reliable car. A mechanic can, for example, look under the car for indications of frame straightening that show that the car has been in a major accident. Some localities now have diagnostic clinics (see page 175) where mechanics specialize in applying elaborate tests to determine the condition of a car. The cost of a checkup might be as high as $30, but that could be money well spent if it reveals that a car is in poor condition.
- Take the car for a road test. Over a rough stretch of road, check for any looseness in the steering mechanism. Check for bounce that may reveal worn shock absorbers. Listen for odd noises. Accelerate rapidly to 60 miles per hour to determine whether the car gains speed smoothly without sputtering. Check the brakes. Brakes should hold equally on all four wheels without causing

the car to veer to one side. While the car is stopped, race the engine and check the exhaust. Blue smoke means the engine is burning oil.

- Do not take a salesperson's word for the fact that the car is in good condition. In most cases, he or she does not know that much about the car. Especially in large lots, used cars are cleaned thoroughly (even the engines) and often painted.
- Check the frequency-of-repair record of the make and model you are interested in buying. *Consumer Reports*, for example, features such information in certain issues. In addition, automotive magazines available in libraries can be a good source of information about the dependability of various models.
- Always offer less than the displayed price. Your chances of saving money are good if you stick to your guns, and the amount of your saving may be substantial.

BUYING NEW CARS

Unless the prospective buyer is buying a first car, he or she usually faces the problem of deciding when an old car should be traded in for a new one. Should it be traded in in the fall just before the new models come out? Should the buyer wait until the new models are available and then trade in the old car for one of the previous year's models (a leftover)? Should the buyer trade in a present car for a new model when the new models first come out? Or would it be better to wait until, say, December or January? How many years should a car be driven before it is traded in for a new model?

To begin with, the consumer should know that the biggest single cost in owning and operating a car is *depreciation*. As the car grows older, its market value decreases. Age, in fact, is usually more important than mileage in determining a car's worth.

How much does depreciation cost? Some authorities estimate depreciation for the first year alone to be as high as one-third of the original cost of the car. In each succeeding year, the car depreciates 25 percent of its current value. More typical of depreciation estimates, however, are the ones given in the chart on page 165.

Thus, a car costing $4500 would depreciate about $1350 the first year (30 percent of $4500). During the second year, the car would decline in market value another $800 (18 percent of $4500). By the end of the third year, the market value of the car could be expected to be about $1750, or less than half the original cost of the car.

Some people say that the most expensive drive you will ever take is when you drive that new car home from the dealer's showroom. The

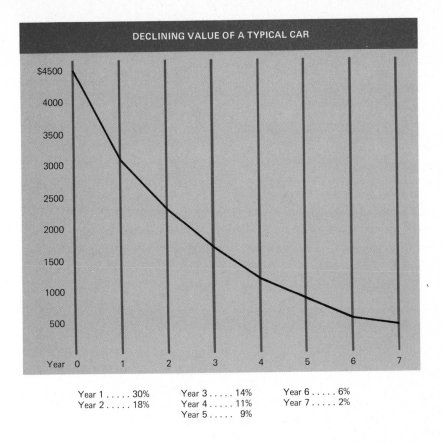

DECLINING VALUE OF A TYPICAL CAR

Year 1 . . . . . 30%	Year 3 . . . . . 14%	Year 6 . . . . . 6%
Year 2 . . . . . 18%	Year 4 . . . . . 11%	Year 7 . . . . . 2%
	Year 5 . . . . . 9%	

statement is true, at least on the basis of cost per mile. Once it is sold by the dealer to the customer, the car is "used," and its market value has decreased several hundred dollars.

You have noticed that depreciation costs become less each succeeding year, so that by the end of the sixth year depreciation is very little Why, then, does it not make sense to keep a car for many years so that depreciation costs will be minimized? One catch to this line of thinking is that while depreciation costs decrease as a car grows older, maintenance costs tend to increase.

A study by the U.S. Department of Transportation indicates that repairs and maintenance costs begin to exceed depreciation costs during the car's fourth year. Many other reasons could be given for wanting to trade in a car for a new one after two, three, or four years. For example, an older car generally requires more repair work, and most of us do not like the inconvenience of being without a car while it is being repaired. Furthermore, a newer car may be safer. Then, of course, many of us suffer from something known as "new-car fever." We have many personal reasons for wanting a new car—some logical, some not so logical—and we sometimes succeed in convincing ourselves that we should make the purchase.

Changing Times magazine asked Runzheimer and Co., Inc., a management consultant firm specializing in business travel expenses for major corporations, to study the problems of the individual car owner and indicate the best time to trade in an old car for a new one. The consulting firm considered three principal costs: depreciation, maintenance and repairs, and tires. The figuring was done for a fully equipped, standard-size car, and it was assumed that the car would be driven for 12,000 miles a year. On this basis, the conclusion reached is that the best time to trade is early in the fourth year of ownership.

Another study done by the U.S. Department of Transportation looked at the actual costs of such things as depreciation, insurance, repair bills, and maintenance for a full-size, four-door sedan equipped with V-8 engine and automatic transmission. In a comparison of the costs of buying such a car every 2 years with keeping the car for 10 years, the conclusion reached is that it is cheaper to keep the car 10 years. The study showed that buying a new car every other year would cost the owner $4000 more over a 10-year period than keeping one for 10 years.

What is the best time to trade for a new car? The best time for us to trade in a car depends upon so many variables (for example, how many miles it is driven per month, whether the driving is on rural roads or modern freeways, and the climate in which the owner lives) that it is very difficult to say at exactly what time an old car should be traded in for a new one.

Where Should You Begin?

The place to start shopping for a new car is at home. Prepare a careful buying plan by gathering facts from as many sources as possible. Among the best sources are the annual auto issue of *Consumer Reports*, published in April, and the yearly *Buying Guide Issue of Consumer Reports*, published in December. Also, such auto and motor journals as *Car and Driver*, *Road & Track*, *Motor Trend*, and *Road Test* compare performance and other aspects of each new model. *Changing Times* magazine also gives performance data on new cars.

Before starting on a tour of dealers, the new car buyer should know a great deal about what kind of car he or she needs, how much he or she can afford to pay, how much will need to be financed, where to get financing, and where to get insurance.

More specifically, the car buyer should decide as rationally as possible whether to buy a big luxury car with a big engine, an intermediate-size car with a medium-size engine, or a compact or subcompact car with a small engine. A luxury car not only costs more to buy but also uses more fuel. Should the family buy a station wagon? Why? If hauling things a few times a year is the reason for wanting a station wagon, would it be cheaper to rent a trailer or pay someone to haul the items?

When a business firm buys equipment that costs, say, $4000, do you think they simply approach one supplier and make the purchase? Not unless they have such a good trade relationship with the supplier that they are assured that they are getting the best deal possible. Ordinarily, a company purchasing agent would ask many suppliers to make bids. Some consumers approach buying a new car in this same way. They duplicate a bid that spells out in detail exactly the car they want to buy. The letter on page 168 is a bid form. A letter such as this one could be sent to all dealers in the area selling the kind of car wanted.

Another technique used by some consumers is to make the dealer an offer in writing for a specific car with the provision that the dealer must accept the offer within a certain period, say 24 or 48 hours. In this case, the letter would be sent to just one dealer, of course. If the dealer refused to respond during the time shown, then a similar letter could be sent to another dealer. A letter making a firm offer is shown on page 169.

How Much Should You Pay?

Fortunately, the consumer can get some approximate information on how much a car should cost. By federal law, all cars sold must have price information posted on them. The *sticker*, as it is called, includes the manufacturer's suggested retail price for the car with standard equipment, the price of each item of optional equipment, transportation charges, and taxes. Few cars, however, are sold at the sticker price. In fact, according to the Federal Trade Commission, less than 2 percent of domestic cars and about 19 percent of foreign cars are sold at the price indicated on the sticker. Discounts of at least $200 off the sticker price are given in nearly nine out of ten cases. Persons willing to pay the sticker price are known as "barefoot pilgrims" by car dealers.

312 Golden Valley Road
Hastings, Minnesota 55033
July 2, 19—

Golden Valley Motors, Inc.
1234 Main Street
Hastings, Minnesota 55033

Gentlemen:

Please make to the undersigned a firm offer to sell one Chevrolet Malibu,
4-door Colonade sedan, 100-hp, turbo thrift 250, six-cylinder engine,
harbor blue, 19— model. This automobile is to have the standard equipment
plus the following accessories:

J50	Power Brakes
N40	Power Steering
C60	Four-Season Air Conditioning
C50	Rear Window Defogger
A01	Soft-Ray Tinted Glass: All Windows
ZJ9	Auxiliary Lighting
D33	LH Remote-Control Mirrors
B93	Door Edge Guard
U63	Push-button AM Radio

To be considered, your offer must be received by me personally by July 24, 19—,
at the address shown above.

Yours truly,

Raymond F. Miller

Raymond F. Miller

To estimate how much the dealer paid for the car, take the sticker price and deduct the freight charges. Then deduct from 17 to 25 percent, depending upon the size of the car. For a compact car without accessories, for example, deduct about 17 percent; for an intermediate-size car, deduct 20 percent; for a full-size car, deduct 25 percent.

Let us say the sticker price on a full-size car is $5285 and the freight charge is $125. Subtracting the freight charge leaves $5160. The cost to the dealer is $5160 minus 25 percent, or about $3870. To determine about how much you should be charged, add to the dealer's cost the freight charge plus from $200 to $250 to cover the dealer's expenses and profit. Thus, you would expect to pay between $4195 and $4245.

More exact information on the dealer's cost is available in one of the paperback books containing wholesale and retail prices of cars. For example, one source is *Edmund's New Car Prices* (American makes) or *Foreign Car Prices*, from Davis Publications, Inc., 229 Park Avenue South, New York, NY 10003.

312 Golden Valley Road
Hastings, Minnesota 55033
July 2, 19—

Golden Valley Motors, Inc.
1234 Main Street
Hastings, Minnesota 55033

Gentlemen:

The undersigned hereby makes to you a firm offer to purchase one Chevrolet
Malibu, 4-door Colonade sedan, 100-hp, turbo thrift 250, six-cylinder
engine, harbor blue, 19— model, for the cash price of $4380.00 with delivery
thereof within 60 days after acceptance. This automobile is to have standard
equipment plus the following accessories:

J50	Power Brakes
N40	Power Steering
C60	Four-Season Air Conditioning
C50	Rear Window Defogger
A01	Soft-Ray Tinted Glass: All Windows
ZJ9	Auxiliary Lighting
D33	LH Remote-Control Mirrors
B93	Door Edge Guard
U63	Push-button AM Radio

This offer will remain open until 5 p.m. on July 24, 19—. It must be accepted
in writing within that time by delivery of acceptance to the undersigned personally
at the address shown above.

Yours truly,

Raymond F. Miller

Raymond F. Miller

You can get a computer printout showing the dealer's cost and the
suggested retail price of any car from Car/Puter International Corporation, 1603 Bushwick Avenue, Brooklyn, NY 11207. For $10 the com-
pany sends a form on which you list the car you want and the accessories you would like. You send the form to the company and they
send by return mail a printout showing the price the dealer pays for
the car and for each of the accessories. The printout also shows the
suggested retail price of the car and the accessories.

If you cannot buy a car from a regular dealer at what you believe is a
fair price, a subsidiary of Car/Puter, United Auto Brokers, will order
most domestic cars for you for $125 over dealer's cost. The cars are
delivered from participating dealers with full service and with the
manufacturer's warranty.

Complicating the matter of determining a fair price is the trade-in
that most persons have. The car dealer may offer an extremely attractive price on the new car and then make up the difference by knocking
down the trade-in offer on the old car. Or, the dealer may begin by

All cars sold are required by law to have a sticker that shows the manufacturer's suggested retail price for the car and for each piece of optional equipment. However, the sticker price is rarely the actual sale price; discounts of at least $200 are given in most cases. (*Michael Wheatcroft*)

making a high trade-in offer on the old car and then not give as big a discount on the new car.

Knowing how much the old car is worth is, then, just as important as knowing what is a fair price for the new car. It is possible for consumers to get information on the approximate value of used cars. A banker or a credit union can give information on the values of various makes, models, and years of cars. The banker consults the *National Automobile Dealers Association Official Used Car Guide*. The guide is an up-to-date book with figures showing the average prices paid for all types of used cars sold at wholesale auctions. With information about the true wholesale value of your used car, and with an idea of the cost of the new car to the dealer, it is possible to estimate the amount of cash needed to make the transaction (the difference between the price of the new car and the trade-in value of the old car).

Should You Buy a Leftover Car?

Some people save money on new-car purchases by waiting until the new models appear and then buying an old model that the dealer still has on hand. The dealer may be given factory rebates on leftovers, so it is possible to pass this saving on to the customer. Then, too, the dealer has his capital invested in these cars, and he should want to clear his inventory of old-model cars as rapidly as possible after the new models come out. Some reports have indicated that discounts offered range from $500 on compact cars to $800 on full-size medium-priced models. One must remember, however, that discounts are also common on current models, so the entire amount of the discount on a leftover car is not due to the fact that it is a leftover car.

Whether or not buying a leftover car is a wise choice depends upon many factors. Remember that a leftover is a year-old car (even though it is brand new), and the first year's depreciation is from 25 to 30 percent. So if the buyer intends to sell the car within a year or two, buying a leftover may not be wise, unless the unlikely situation exists where the dealer's discount is large enough to cover the first year's depreciation. If the car will be kept for a number of years, and if the consumer is not especially concerned about the model year, then buying a leftover may make sense.

HOW SHOULD YOU DEAL WITH DEALERS?

Some car dealers use reprehensible tricks to induce people to buy cars. One popular technique, known as "low-balling," is to suggest that the car can be bought for a certain price that the prospective customer recognizes as a rather low one and that is therefore attractive. The price is so attractive that the customer often stops shopping at other dealers. Furthermore, the prospective buyer becomes more and more eager to get the car and get it soon. He has made the decision to buy. Now he wants to enjoy the car. When he finds out that the car cannot be bought for the first price, he is disappointed, but often he will buy anyway because he has his mind set on owning the car.

Even careful shoppers are often taken in by low-balling. A family may shop carefully at many different places for a particular type of car. A price is agreed on at one of the dealers, and the family then waits for several weeks while the car is being obtained by the dealer. When the car arrives, the dealer "discovers" that the price quoted originally is in error. Not only has the family wasted time, it has also stopped shopping around. Often the car is bought at a much higher price.

What can be done about low-balling? For one thing, be certain that the price quoted is approved in writing by an authorized representative of the firm, and be certain that the deal is binding. Also, if you are the victim of a low-ball scheme, do not buy from the dealer. The better business bureaus and the automobile industry consider low-balling reprehensible and suggest that dealers using such a tactic be avoided. Most new-car transactions involve trading in an old car, and a technique known as "high-balling" is sometimes used by unscrupulous dealers. The scheme in this case is to offer more for the old car than it is really worth.

Consider the case of a woman who owns a 5-year-old car that sold for about $4400 when it was new. She knows that the car depreciates each year, and using the percentages given on page 165, she calculates that the total depreciation on the car to date may be about $3212. She hopes, however, that the car will bring much more than $1188 ($4400 less $3212) because it has been well taken care of and is a fairly popular model. Actually, she is hoping to get about $1500 on a trade-in. The salesperson might say something like, "How would you like to get $1800 for that old station wagon of yours? I think that I may have a buyer for it."

The prospective customer might be so overwhelmed at this unexpected generosity that she wants to close the deal quickly before the salesperson has a change of mind or discovers that a mistake has been made. Later the buyer discovers that the high price is subject to reappraisal when the new car is picked up and the old car is turned over to the dealer. By this time, the buyer wants the new car and may accept the deal, even though the cash now necessary (the difference between the price of the new car and the trade-in value of the old car) may represent an increase of $200 or $300.

Other schemes are used by some car dealers to get people to pay more money for cars. For example, in a prearranged setup, a salesperson may say some rather harsh words to a customer who has turned down a proposal. The sales manager just "happens" to hear the insult and rushes out to stop the customer, who will be in the process of leaving the premises in anger by that time. After begging the customer to wait a few moments so an apology can be made, the sales manager scolds the salesperson for his or her conduct. The sales manager may even threaten to fire the salesperson. All this is done, of course, in the presence of the customer. Then the customer is invited to the sales manager's office, offered a soft drink or coffee, and given a profuse apology. To make up for the unkind words of the salesperson, the sales manager then offers to make a "special" deal on the car under consideration. The price may be just a few dollars ($25 to $75) under that offered by the salesperson and refused previously by the customer.

Although the scheme seems rather far-fetched, it is used and often works.

Some dealers have even gone so far as to bug their small sales offices. The salesperson uses some pretense to leave the husband and wife for a few moments. While the husband and wife discuss privately what they think of the latest offer that has been made, the salesperson listens through an intercom and thus has the advantage of knowing the private thoughts of the buyer.

Choosing a dealer is considered especially important by some people who place high value on service. In fact, some dealers in certain cities are now advertising the fact that they charge slightly more for their cars because they expect their customers to want good service, and the dealers expect to give good service. A dealer in or near your neighborhood may give you the full benefit of a new-car warranty. A dealer farther from your home may offer a bargain price, but the cost and inconvenience of taking the car to this dealer for service may offset the savings in the price of the car. Of course, the dealer can claim to give good service and thus charge more, but in fact the buyer has no real assurance that the service will be any better.

FINANCING A CAR

Many car purchases, especially new-car purchases, involve borrowing money for part of the cost. Typically, a customer hands over the old car as the down payment on a new car and then signs an installment agreement with the dealer. No cash changes hands.

Often the customer can save money by arranging the financing through a credit union or a bank. The car dealer in most instances has an arrangement with a finance company for an installment contract. The dealer customarily gets a rebate from the finance company recommended.

A dealer may offer financing on a 3-year $3500 loan, for a total interest charge of $725. In contrast, a bank might offer a 3-year $3500 loan, for a total interest charge of $630. The difference between finance charges in this case may not seem especially large, but consider how important $95 seems when the salesperson and the customer are trying to agree on the price of the car. Furthermore, the difference in finance charges between the dealer's arrangement and a bank or credit union may be much larger than the illustration given here. For used cars, particularly, finance companies operating through dealers often charge considerably more than the customer would have to pay if he or she shopped around for lower interest rates.

In summary, the wise consumer shops around carefully not only for a car but also for credit.

CAR REPAIRS

Mr. Hanks drove his car to a meeting in a city about 150 miles from his home. On his return home, Mr. Hanks stopped at a service station for gasoline. One of the attendants lifted the car's hood to make the usual service checks. After several minutes, he explained to Mr. Hanks that the car's oil level was fine, but he had spotted a bad alternator—a very serious situation. The attendant showed him the problem and explained that the alternator was about to stop working. He suggested that Mr. Hanks not try to drive any great distance before having the part replaced. Where can an alternator be bought? Well, the attendant checked his stock of supplies and discovered he did happen to have one on hand. Mr. Hanks bought a new alternator.

The service station attendant had sprayed oil on the car's alternator, causing it to appear to be malfunctioning. Thus, a new alternator seemed necessary. Another dirty trick used by some swindlers is to bend wires on the alternator to make the red warning light glow. Some service stations have drained the acid from a battery cell, replaced it with plain water, and then used a hydrometer check to "prove" that the battery is dead. Others have dropped baking soda or antacid tablets in battery cells to cause them to foam and appear to be damaged or dead. You have no doubt heard of many such despicable tricks as not pushing the dipstick all the way in to make it appear that oil needs to be added to the engine. Pouring "oil" from an empty can is an old trick that still is used to take money from people. These dishonest practices are not resorted to by the majority of service stations, of course, but schemes such as these are used.

Modern cars have so many different parts with overlapping functions that most owners find it difficult, if not impossible, to have a good understanding of their cars. Dishonest shops have many ways of getting money from car owners. A mechanic can show the customer metal filings taken from the bottom of the automatic transmission case. Such particles may come from the normal meshing of gears, but because the car owner does not know this, he can easily be convinced that he needs a several-hundred-dollar transmission overhaul. What the customer may get is a single change of transmission fluid. The better business bureaus report that they receive many complaints from travelers far from home who fall prey to unscrupulous mechanics and service station attendants who have found "something wrong" under the hood.

Locate a Good Mechanic

The time to start looking for a good repair shop is before you need repairs. The choices might include the car dealer from whom you bought your car; independent general mechanics; gasoline service stations that employ mechanics; and shops specializing in certain kinds of repair work, such as brake relining, wheel alignment, and muffler replacement. In states which license car repair shops, sticking to licensed businesses certainly makes good sense.

Some new car dealers may be eager to give good service and reasonable prices because they want you to buy your next car from them. Also, such a dealer should be familiar with your type of car and have an ample stock of the parts the car is most likely to need. If the dealer is not interested in giving good service, however, you should obviously go elsewhere.

Unless you know something about the mechanical nature of cars, you can be in for some trouble when you have your car repaired. An unusual noise might mean a 5-minute adjustment, or it might mean that you need major work that will cost hundreds of dollars. How do you know? To some extent, at least, many of us must rely on the mechanic. This mechanic might be honest and competent. On the other hand, he or she might be dishonest or incompetent, or both.

In 1974 the diagnostic clinic of the Automobile Club of Missouri surveyed cars after they had been repaired by auto mechanics. They found that 37.7 percent of the repairs were done badly or not at all, and the average repair bill for this fraudulent or incompetent work was $148.

Diagnostic centers could be helpful to consumers, and such centers do exist in certain parts of the country. They range from relatively small slots in service stations to long lanes in special buildings that can handle a dozen cars at the same time. The expensive electronic equipment in these larger centers probably offers the best means now available to discover defective, worn-out, and maladjusted items on a car.

A diagnostic center with complete equipment and trained diagnosticians can check the performance of an amazingly large number of

An independent auto diagnostic center, with its sophisticated equipment and skilled technicians, can help the consumer determine a car's condition. (*Courtesy Ford Customer Service Division*)

items. Such things as the horns, lights, and windshield wipers are examined as part of a general inspection. Then the car is lifted for an examination of such things as the steering mechanism, wheel bearings, tires, springs, exhaust system, and the front suspension. Leaks from the engine, transmission, and differential are investigated.

An oscilloscope and related electronic gear are used to test the engine. The car may be put on a dynamometer and given a simulated road test as the wheels turn against huge rollers in the floor. Break testing can also be an integral function of the dynamometer.

Most diagnostic centers, unfortunately, are connected with repair shops. If the diagnosis shows a need for repairs, the firm stands to benefit. For this reason, some consumers have not placed a great deal of trust in the diagnosis. When a diagnostic center is a part of a new-car dealer's operation, the possibility exists that in some cases the repair estimates could be inflated enough to make buying a new car seem like a good idea.

A few diagnostic clinics that operate independently of repair shops do exist. The centers use skilled technicians and modern diagnostic equipment. Furthermore, they will not recommend a mechanic.

Saving Money on Upkeep

Many experts believe that preventive maintenance avoids large repair bills. Thus, one should pay attention to proper maintenance in order to keep the costs of operating the car as low as possible. The cost of certain preventive maintenance procedures can, however, add up to quite a sum of money over a period of time. In the long run, then, is it really cheaper to keep the car in good condition with regular maintenance checks? Or could you save money by just letting parts wear out and then replacing them when necessary (with the exception of safety-related things such as brakes and tires)? The answer probably depends on such things as how long you expect to keep the car and the extent to which you value dependability.

The owner's manual should be studied carefully because, in addition to the maintenance schedule the owner is required to follow to keep his warranty in effect, it has many tips that can help keep the car in good shape for years.

Checking Your Reading

1. About how much does the average moderate-income family in our country spend for transportation? Where does transportation rank as an expenditure in most family budgets?
2. In which magazines can consumers find information about used cars, such as frequency-of-repair records?
3. List five pointers that a prospective buyer of a used car should follow.
4. What is the biggest single cost in owning and operating a car? Give an indication of this cost during the car's first year.
5. Discuss how a consumer should begin shopping for a new car before actually visiting new-car dealers.
6. When should a family car be traded in for a new car?

7. What is meant by the "sticker price"?

8. Although, because of federal law, new cars must have price information posted on them, few cars are sold at their sticker price. How can one determine about how much is a reasonable price to pay for the car?

9. How can one get an estimate of the value of an old car that is to be traded in for a new car?

10. Explain when buying a "leftover" car (one that is a year-old model, even though it is brand new) may be a good buy and when it may not be a good buy.

11. Explain what is meant by the car-selling techniques known as "low-balling" and "high-balling."

12. Explain two schemes (in addition to low-balling and high-balling) used by unscrupulous dealers to sell cars.

13. Cite two examples of fraudulent schemes used by some service station attendants to sell products to consumers who do not need the products.

14. What is an automobile diagnostic center?

15. In what ways can an owner's manual be valuable to the car owner?

Consumer Problems and Projects

1. Visit (or write to) an office of the American Automobile Association to get pointers on how to conserve gasoline. In addition, use library indexes to locate articles in periodicals on gasoline conservation methods. Summarize the information you obtain.

2. Because so many car owners complain about the high price of repairs, manufacturers have made available manuals and kits to help car owners do some of their own repair work. From car dealers in your community, or from the manufacturers, collect two or three of these do-it-yourself manuals. Make a list of the jobs for which each manual gives directions.

3. From as many sources as possible, gather information on car repairs. (For example, the Council of Better Business Bureaus publishes *Tips on Car Repair*, a pamphlet available at most better business bureau offices.) With the information you have collected, prepare a skit that dramatizes some of the things a consumer should not do when his or her car needs repair work. For

example, before you take your car to a repair shop, you should make a list and take it along with you. You should state all trouble precisely, and then include your name and a telephone number where you can be reached. Part of your dramatization could show a consumer flagrantly violating this advice.

4. Assume that a tune-up for a car will require the following parts: spark plugs, points, condenser, distributor cap, rotor, spark plug wire set, and coil. Compare the cost of a tune-up done at home by the car owner and the cost of one done at a garage. Obtain prices for the parts at auto supply stores. Get estimates for a tune-up requiring these parts at as many garages as possible. Estimate as realistically as possible the amount of time an average car owner would spend on the tune-up job. Draw conclusions as to the desirability of doing one's own tune-up work.

5. As a buying project, assume that you will buy a new car. Follow the advice in this chapter by beginning your shopping "at home." First, decide what type of car you should buy (consider such things as size, price range, and style). Write a brief justification of your decisions. Then, arm yourself with as many facts as you can find in consumer magazines and automotive magazines. Finally, visit new-car dealers and get as much price information as you can.

6. Investigate the kinds of car tires being sold. For example, cord materials in general use are nylon, rayon, polyester, fiber glass, and steel wire. Three common types of construction in use are bias ply, belted bias ply, and radial ply. How important are the cord materials? Is one type of construction superior to other types? What are the differences in price? Is it possible for consumers to know what type of tire they are buying? Can one compare the quality of tires of different manufacturers? Are guarantees of any value?

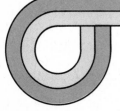

11

Buying Other Vehicles and Insurance

During the late 1970's, the National Highway Traffic Safety Administration asked car makers to report on what cars would be like in the 1980s as a result of fuel economy laws. One manufacturer thinks that by 1985 "large" cars will weigh 300 pounds less than 1977 compacts. Every fourth car will have a diesel engine, which has better fuel economy than regular gasoline engines. Furthermore, V-8 engines will not be used, according to this car manufacturer. These are just guesses, of course. What is sold depends in large part on what consumers will buy.

Some observers think that because of the fuel shortage, motorized bikes and motorcycles will become more popular in the years ahead. Two other kinds of vehicles are now selling quite well because of the practical purposes they serve: pickup trucks and vans. After examining these kinds of vehicles, this chapter will consider safety and car insurance.

MOTORIZED BIKES

Crowded streets, the clean-air movement, and high-priced gasoline have made bicycling more popular in our country. But steady pedaling requires a great deal of effort, of course, so motorized bikes look attractive to more and more people. These bikes are called *mopeds*, short for motor/pedal bicycles.

Mopeds do not go very fast. Maximum speeds range from 18 to 30 miles per hour. But owners can travel as far as 200 miles on 1 gallon of gas! Mopeds weigh from 60 to 100 pounds, and their engines are far smaller than the engines on most lawn mowers. The cost of mopeds in the late 1970s ranged from about $300 to $500.

Most mopeds have been made in Europe. In fact, they are an everyday means of transportation in many parts of Europe. They are also popular in the Orient.

Several states have passed legislation to govern motorized bikes. This legislation usually specifies a maximum speed and places a restriction on the power of the vehicle (such as 1.5 horsepower or less).

Mopeds, or motorized bicycles, have maximum speeds of 18 to 30 mph and can go up to 200 miles on one gallon of gas. Accident statistics from Europe, where they are an everyday means of transportation, show that mopeds are safer than cars. (*Martin Adler Levick, Black Star*)

In states without such legislation, mopeds usually fall under the laws governing motorcycles. Mopeds cannot meet the strict equipment requirements for motorcycles, but there is no reason that they should. Because of this, sales of mopeds in our country have been restricted largely to states that have laws relating to them. The Motorized Bicycle Association, which represents European manufacturers, is working to get other states to pass reasonable moped laws.

How safe are mopeds? The National Highway Traffic Safety Administration set specific equipment standards in 1974. Thus, all mopeds sold in this country since that time meet or exceed federal standards on headlights, taillights, reflectors, brakes, tire strength, and design of controls. According to European accident statistics, mopeds are safer than cars.

MOTORCYCLES

Motorcycles offer transportation with low initial cost and good gasoline mileage. They are also easy to maneuver in traffic and need only a small parking space. But they can also be dangerous for inexperienced drivers. About 20 percent of the persons involved in motorcycle accidents are riding for the first or second time, according to the Motorcycle Safety Foundation. More than half of the accidents involve persons between the ages of 16 and 20. The foundation says that the major cause of motorcycle accidents is human error, rather than weather, road, or vehicle conditions.

Most states require motorcycle riders to pass a test in order to be licensed, and in some states the test is more difficult than the test given for car drivers. Insurance is essential, of course, and it is bought in much the same way as car insurance (see pages 188 to 190).

Motorcycles are usually known by engine size. The engines are described in cubic centimeters of piston displacement rather than in cubic inches, as is the case with cars. Engines are one, two, three, or four cylinders, and they come in two types: the four-cycle engine (similar to car engines) and the two-stroke engine (similar to most outboard motors). The advice given by most experienced riders is to buy a motorcycle that best fits your travel needs. A beginner would probably buy a motorcycle with an engine from 100 to 250 cc. For trips to and from work, the minimum size should be about 250 cc. Proficient riders often want larger, more powerful motorcycles that are more comfortable for riding long distances. These larger motorcycles have heavier frames and have engines in the 500 to 1200 cc range.

PICKUP TRUCKS AND VANS

During the past several years, pickup trucks have become more numerous. People have discovered that pickups can be a handy second vehicle. A pickup truck can be used for going to and from work; it can also be used to haul such things as garden equipment, antiques, appliances, and lumber. It may also be used to carry a camper.

Pickup trucks may cost less than cars of the same wheelbase. If roads are bad, pickup trucks have an advantage over cars because they are sturdier. In recent years, certain luxury extras have been added to many pickups. For example, pickup trucks now offer such things as AM/FM stereo radios, air conditioning, power steering, carpeting, luxury upholstering, wide tires and wheels, and custom wheel covers.

Although pickup trucks may have an abundance of comfort features, it is well to remember that they are trucks. Unless a pickup is carrying a payload, it is light in its rear end, and this can affect steering and braking. Because of the greater weight capacity of its springs, a pickup will usually give a harsher ride than a car. The question the consumer should ask before buying a pickup truck is "Do I really need it?"

You can get a van with a finished interior, or you can furnish the van yourself or have a customizing shop install the items you want. (*Kip Peticolas*)

Vans have been around for quite some time (the Volkswagen bus has been a familiar vehicle for many years). But they became quite popular in the mid-1970s. Now some people in the car industry say it is only a matter of time before vans take the place of station wagons. Most vans offer more room than station wagons. The manufacturers now make available for vans just about every option available for cars. In addition, they offer such extras as dark tinted glass for side and rear windows. Many now are made with high-backed chairs that swivel.

Some vans are available with finished interiors. Others come with just a single seat. For buyers who want to do their own furnishing, it is possible to buy a set of blueprints from one of the shops that sell van supplies. For example, a few things that can be bought for a van are a couch that converts to a bed, an icebox, wall- or ceiling-mounted lights, and tables. Another way to furnish a van is to choose a customizing shop and pay to have their experts install what you want.

THE IMPORTANCE OF SAFETY

About 50,000 people are killed every year in vehicle accidents in the United States, and another 2 million are injured. Probably half of the highway deaths are in one way or another related to drinking. An easy way to reduce accidents, it would seem, would be to reduce the number of drunk drivers. But we are quite lenient with drunk drivers in the United States. People with several drunk-driving arrests on their records are still driving—and still causing accidents. Many persons concerned about the problem advocate much stiffer penalties for people caught driving while intoxicated.

Many highway deaths could have been avoided over the years if additional safety features had been required on cars. Not until Ralph Nader's book *Unsafe at Any Speed* did Congress become concerned enough about safety to really take action. In 1966 the Motor Vehicle Safety Act was passed, and it forms the basis for most of the current safety requirements. Included in these requirements are such things as dual braking systems, nonprotruding interior appliances, safety belts, and impact-absorbing instrument panels.

Safety-Belt Laws

One safety device that didn't last long was the ignition interlock. This device kept the engine of cars from starting until the front-seat occupants fastened their safety belts. The law took effect with the 1974 cars. Unfortunately, about 40 percent of the drivers disliked the system and disconnected it. So Congress ordered the National Highway Traffic Safety Administration (NHTSA) to allow car manufacturers to build cars without the interlock. Cars built after February 24, 1975, needed only warning lights and buzzers. The buzzers could be limited in duration rather than continuous like those in the 1973 models.

The NHTSA estimates that if everyone wore a safety belt, auto deaths would decline by at least 40 percent and injuries would be reduced 28 percent. Thus, it is unfortunate that so many people do not want to wear safety belts. One thing that could be done to increase the use of safety belts, according to Consumers Union, would be to make them more comfortable and convenient. A survey of owners of 1974 cars conducted by Consumers Union and NHTSA revealed that almost half of the people complained that belts were difficult to buckle and that many shoulder straps chafed the wearer's neck.

Many people who dislike safety belts say that their decision not to use them affects no one but themselves. They say a law to require them to wear belts is an infringement of their right to risk their own lives. Do you agree? When injuries are more serious and when deaths increase, all of us who drive cars will have to pay more for insurance premiums because insurance companies must pay out more money in claims. The increased burden on hospitals and ambulances is a social cost that affects all of us. A more direct way in which not using a safety belt affects others is that belts help keep a driver behind the wheel and in control of a vehicle after an abrupt maneuver or a collision. Innocent people may be hurt when a car goes out of control.

Passive Restraints

A *passive restraint* is a device that protects motorists in a crash but does not require them to do anything. Persons concerned with car safety think that the most promising *passive restraint* developed so far is the air bag. After a front-end crash, an air bag opens in a split second and becomes a giant pillow. The air bag restrains the person before he or she slams into the windshield or instrument panel. Then the bag quickly deflates. The NHTSA had announced that beginning in 1977 all new cars were to be equipped with air bags or some other passive restraint. But Congress intervened and told the NHTSA that the 1977 deadline would not be met and that NHTSA must hold a public hearing before issuing any such requirement again.

Although in the late 1970s passive restraints are not mandatory,

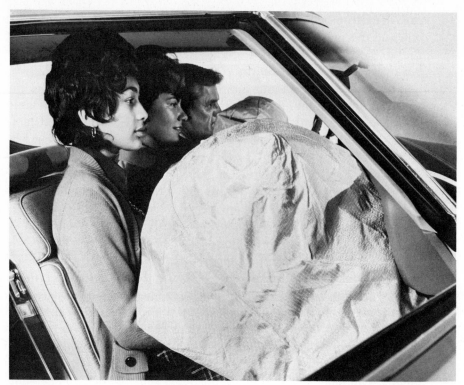

Slow motion demonstrations show how air bags protect riders. After a front-end crash, the air bag opens to become a giant pillow that keeps the rider from hitting the windshield or instrument panel. It is considered the most promising passive restraint so far developed. (*General Motors, Inc.*)

auto manufacturers are making them optional in certain cars. Crash tests have shown that today's air bags are effective.

The Safety of Small Cars

The emphasis in cars changed in the mid-1970s. For decades gasoline was relatively cheap, and automobile manufacturers provided big, luxurious cars with V-8 engines. But in 1974 came the Arab oil embargo. Gasoline became scarce, and its price rocketed. Consumers began to demand small cars with good gas mileage. Manufacturers responded, of course, with smaller cars with better gas mileage.

Because so many people want small cars in order to conserve energy and cut costs, the question now is whether or not small cars can be made relatively safe. Studies of auto safety have indicated that big cars are much safer than small cars. A New York State study covered

712,000 cars involved in accidents. In that study the occupants of small cars suffered more than 3 times as many serious and fatal injuries per 100,000 miles driven as did the occupants of the most expensive full-size cars. Other studies have shown that the chance of a fatality in small cars is just about twice that in large cars.

Research is now being conducted on ways to make small cars safer. Why are small cars less safe? In any crash, much of the force's energy is absorbed by the car's sheet metal as it crumples. Small cars have less area of sheet metal. Since the force of a crash can push the engine and fire wall into the passenger compartment, the amount of interior room in a car is important. Small cars have less interior room. Some ways being experimented with to make small cars safer include the use of plastic foam (to absorb energy in a crash) in open sections under the hood and in the doors. A foam plastic knee restraint and a steering column that gives way in whatever direction the driver hits it are other possibilities for making these cars safer.

THE BASIC PRINCIPLE OF INSURANCE

Let us assume that exactly 1000 students in your school have formed a camera club and have each purchased a camera costing $100. The students recognize that their cameras could be lost or stolen.

Although there is no way of knowing how many cameras will be missing at the end of the school year, assume that the students estimate that during the first year five will disappear. If they are right, five students will suffer $100 losses. So the students decide that if each of them (1000 students) contributes 50 cents to a fund, they would have $500 that they could give to the unlucky persons whose cameras were stolen. The students are spreading the loss—insurance people would say that they are "sharing the risk." The club might have collected $1 from each student, in case the losses are closer to $1000 a year.

Risk sharing is the basic principle of insurance. An insurance company collects money (called a *premium*) from each person who wishes to be a part of the plan. Because insurance companies insure so many people, they can rely on past experience to estimate quite accurately how much they will pay out in claims each year. They set premium rates by estimating how much they will pay out in claims and then adding to that their administrative expenses and the profit they must earn. The discussion here pertains to automobile insurance. When you read about life insurance and health insurance in later chapters, you will recognize that these are also based on risk sharing.

Car Insurance

A major expense resulting from owning a car is insurance. Although the cost of car insurance has been increasing considerably during recent years, the need for such insurance is so great that you should not operate a car unless you are adequately covered by insurance. An automobile insurance reform plan known as "no-fault" insurance is being instituted in the United States, and its backers hope it will eliminate long court fights and give motorists a greater return for their insurance dollar. The plan provides that insurance companies promptly pay their clients' claims for actual losses regardless of who was at fault in the accident. Before examining no-fault insurance more completely, we will look at the traditional five types of protection that offer car owners complete insurance coverage: (1) liability insurance, (2) collision coverage, (3) medical payments coverage, (4) uninsured motorist coverage, and (5) fire, theft, and comprehensive insurance.

Liability Insurance. Liability insurance protects the insured against claims for personal injuries or claims for property damage when the insured is driving his or her car or someone else's car. The insured gets nothing for his or her own losses; the payments go to others for their injuries, property damages, lost wages, or similar losses. Most states require all car owners to carry both personal and property liability insurance. This is by far the most important insurance a car owner buys because at today's high speeds cars can cause fantastic damage.

Liability is referred to in a three-part series describing its coverage. For example, a policy referred to as "100/300/10" means that the insurance company's liability is limited to $100,000 for injury to one person, $300,000 for two or more persons injured in one accident, and $10,000 for property damage. A policy as large as 100/300/10 is becoming more common, but less coverage is possible, of course. The premium for liability insurance does not increase in proportion to the coverage. One company, for example, charges a driver over age twenty-five an annual premium of $117 for personal liability coverage of $5,000 for injury to one person and $10,000 for injury to two or more in a single accident. Increasing the protection to $100,000 for one injury and $300,000 for multiple injuries increases the premium to $189.54. Thus, protection is increased 30 times at less than twice the cost. Liability policies are important, and it does not make sense to try to skimp on the coverage. Some people with considerable assets carry million-dollar liability policies to protect them from damage suits.

Collision Coverage. Collision insurance covers the repair or replacement of the insured's own car after an accident, unless the accident was caused by another car in which case he or she collects from the negligent driver (or the negligent driver's insurance company). Money can be saved on collision coverage by agreeing to pay more of the repair bill out of your own pocket. Most collision coverage plans include a deductible clause. On a $50-deductible policy, for example, the car owner pays the first $50 of repair, and the insurance company pays the remainder. By agreeing to a $100-deductible clause, you can save a good deal of money on the premium. The insurance company obviously does not pay out as much money, nor do they pay out as often (thus saving on paperwork). Drivers who believe they can absorb a loss as high as $250 without undue financial strain can save money on premiums by purchasing $250-deductible policies.

As a car gets older, of course, the need for collision insurance decreases. When a car's value decreases to about $500, the need for collision insurance should probably be questioned seriously.

Medical Payments Coverage. Medical payments coverage takes care of medical, hospital, and funeral costs for the insured, his or her family, and his or her passengers, whether or not the insured is at fault, and for the insured and his or her family, no matter whose car the victim was in. This type of coverage also compensates the insured and his or her family for certain medical expenses that result from being hit while a pedestrian.

Uninsured Motorist Coverage. The purpose of uninsured motorist coverage is to protect the car owner who is unable to collect from a negligent driver who does not have liability insurance. The car owner's own insurance company makes liability payments, but usually up to a limit such as $10,000 per person or $20,000 per accident. The policy also pays off if the negligent driver's insurance company is insolvent or if the guilty person cannot be found (a hit-and-run driver).

Fire, Theft, and Comprehensive Insurance. Fire insurance compensates for fire or lightning damage to the car, but it does not cover damage to the owner's clothes or to other articles that happen to be in the car. Theft insurance compensates the owner for a stolen car, but it does not cover the contents of the car. (Special fire or theft policies may be taken out on the contents.) Fire insurance alone may be obtained, but theft insurance is never written without fire insurance.

Most people now buy what is known as comprehensive coverage. Comprehensive automobile insurance combines fire and theft coverage with coverage for many other kinds of damage to the car, including damage resulting from tornadoes, windstorms, hail, water, riots, falling objects, and many other causes listed in the policy. This type of policy costs slightly more than the standard fire and theft policy.

Group Plans for Car Insurance. Although group life and health insurance has been available for quite some time, group car insurance has just recently become available through employers. The insurance company sells the insurance to the employees of a firm. Each employee who participates in the plan decides on the extent of coverage he wants and pays rates tailored to the coverage. The employer withholds each employee's premium from his paycheck and periodically sends a single check to the insurance company.

Fewer agents are needed to bring in customers, and the insurance company has fewer expenses because the employer takes on the burden of collecting the premiums from the insured persons. Therefore, the insurance company can usually afford to offer a discount. This type of insurance may become increasingly popular in the years ahead.

NO-FAULT CAR INSURANCE

Our auto insurance system has operated on the principle that people must pay for the results of their negligence. So we buy personal injury and property damage liability insurance that protects us against the claims of other people for our negligence. Liability insurance works fairly well in paying for vehicle and property damage; those costs are easy to define and simple to predict. But determining the cost of personal injury can be a very difficult problem.

How is negligence established in most accidents? Some experts say that even prudent motorists commit driving errors every time they operate an automobile. Some cases are clear-cut, of course. When a driver shoots through a stoplight and rams another car, or when a drunken driver weaves into the wrong lane and crashes into someone else, fault is relatively easy to determine. But in all other accidents, establishing guilt can become a maze of confusion, claims, and counterclaims. For this reason, much of the premium dollar paid to insurance companies goes for investigation and legal fees.

In addition to placing a claim for medical bills and lost wages, people who have suffered because of the negligence of someone else can submit a claim for what the law calls "pain and suffering." How much money can be collected for pain and suffering? How much money should a person collect when he or she has lost a limb? Or how much money will adequately compensate a young person for a permanently disfigured face? Juries are unpredictable. Under prevailing law, the answer is most likely whatever a skilled lawyer can talk a jury into providing. Or the answer might be whatever a worried insurance company is willing to settle for out of court. In either case, reimbursement to most accident victims seldom matches the amount of their claims. Further, lawyers often charge one-third of any final amount awarded in court; thus, claims must exceed actual loss so that the victim has a chance of being fully reimbursed.

Auto Liability Insurance Has Not Worked Well

Curiously, people who are the victims of accidents involving large losses fare less well than persons involved with accidents involving small amounts of money. For example, national statistics show that accident victims are usually reimbursed for less than half their losses when the losses exceed $5000. When losses exceed $25,000, victims are lucky to get a third of their money. In contrast, when the accident is relatively minor and the damages are under $500, settlements often exceed the amount of damages because the insurance company wants to avoid expensive legal bickering. One other fact needs to be mentioned here. About one-fourth of all accident victims collect nothing.

Another reason auto liability insurance has not worked well is the fact that no one has to pay until blame is established. So the accident victim has to cover the cost of medical bills and find a way to make up for lost wages until the insurance companies establish the blame. This is often an expensive process. The system has also created what some people call the "injury industry." The cost of this industry, which includes many highly paid expert witnesses, is passed on to consumers through higher premiums for liability insurance.

The No-Fault Idea

The idea of no-fault insurance is to eliminate the need to establish who is at fault in accidents. That is, a driver is paid for accident expenses by his or her own insurance company—regardless of who was at fault. A no-fault policy covers the driver, the driver's family, any occupants of the car, and pedestrians. Medical bills and income losses are paid immediately. People in other cars involved in an accident are taken care of by each driver's policy. Thus, no-fault insurance displaces automobile liability insurance as the primary source of compensation for the injured. Under no-fault plans, injured persons collect medical and other payments much more quickly. Payments tend to be based more on need and less on courtroom skill.

The direct indemnity for injury offered by the no-fault idea is better than the auto insurance that has been traditionally offered. Under no-fault insurance, bills for medical care of those injured are paid without waiting—and without expensive lawsuits. Medical bills and lost income resulting from inability to work are paid at once.

In states that have had experience with no-fault plans, such as Massachusetts and Florida, premium rates have been reduced.

Opposition to No-Fault Insurance

The American Trial Lawyers Association argues that no-fault is unconstitutional because it denies a motorist the right to sue and thus deprives the motorist of due process of law. This point troubles even some strong backers of no-fault insurance. Auto insurance in no-fault states still includes liability coverage, and victims can still sue for losses not covered by no-fault. Under a proposed Senate bill, a negligent driver could be sued only if the victim of the accident died, was totally disabled for three months, or was seriously injured or disfigured for life. The prediction is that the vast majority of pre-no-fault liability claims will be barred.

Arguments against no-fault auto insurance come mostly from lawyers (through the American Bar Association and the American Trial Lawyers Association) and some insurance companies. Lawyers argue that insurance regulation is the total responsibility of each individual state, and by passing federal legislation, Congress is overstepping its boundaries. Some insurance companies, however, favor a federally enacted, uniform no-fault plan.

An Effective No-Fault Insurance Plan

To be effective, a no-fault plan should include these key elements:

- A driver is paid for accident expenses by his or her own insurance company. This eliminates the need for costly litigation to determine the blame and to decide whose insurance company is financially liable.

- A higher barrier to liability claims should exist. Thus, the right to sue for additional compensation should be restricted severely.
- All drivers should be required to buy no-fault automobile insurance. This spreads the cost of accidents among the entire driving population and it assures economic benefits for all injured passengers and pedestrians. Making the insurance compulsory also ensures that victims can recover losses without going to court. In addition, some safeguards must exist against cancellation or nonrenewal by insurance companies.

The present automobile insurance system worked well when the auto was more of a luxury than a necessity. In recent years, however, the increased frequency and severity of auto losses combined with long, drawn out legal actions have made the system function poorly. Many believe that no-fault automobile insurance is an idea whose time has come.

Checking Your Reading

1. What evidence is there that motorcycles can be dangerous for inexperienced drivers?
2. Give reasons why pickup trucks have become popular in recent years.
3. About how many highway deaths are related in some way to drinking alcoholic beverages?
4. According to the National Highway Traffic Safety Administration, to what extent would auto deaths be reduced if everyone wore a safety belt?
5. "When I don't wear a safety belt, I hurt only myself." Why is that statement wrong?
6. Under our traditional form of auto insurance, why does much of the premium dollar paid to insurance companies go for investigation and legal fees?
7. Discuss how much money can be collected for "pain and suffering" resulting from an automobile accident.
8. What do national statistics show about the recovery of money for people involved in car accidents as related to the size of the loss?
9. Explain what is meant by the idea of no-fault insurance.
10. For what reason does the American Trial Lawyers Association think that no-fault insurance may be unconstitutional?
11. What key elements should a no-fault insurance plan include if it is to be effective?

Consumer Problems and Projects

1. Write to the Motorized Bicycle Association, 1001 Connecticut Avenue, N.W., Washington, D.C. 20036, for information about legislation for motorized bikes. Make a list of the states with motorized bike legislation and indicate for each state the restrictions, if any, on engine size, power, maximum speed, minimum age of driver, and whether a license and insurance is needed by the driver.

2. Check with at least three insurance agencies to get information about insurance for motorcycles. Be sure to find out whether the policies issued by the companies cover drivers if they lend their motorcycles to others. If your state has a no-fault insurance law, does it include motorcycles?

3. By consulting library indexes, such as the *Reader's Guide to Periodical Literature*, locate articles about highway safety. The National Safety Council has been active in publicizing statistics pertaining to car accidents and fatalities, and popular magazines have featured articles about traffic accidents and what is being done about the problem. Note particularly the trend in the statistics. (Have fatalities been increasing or decreasing?) Also, note predictions for future years. To what extent are solutions being sought by improving the cars? To what extent are drivers considered the problem? Report your findings to the class.

4. Construct a bulletin board display with the heading "What Consumers Should Know About No-Fault Auto Insurance." Include the latest statistics about the cost savings for auto insurers in Massachusetts since the passage of the state's no-fault insurance plan. If your state now has a no-fault plan, include information about it. Daily newspapers and news magazines often feature stories about no-fault plans. From these sources, and from the information in this chapter, indicate the advantages of no-fault plans and the questions raised by those opposed to them.

5. A news story indicated that a new model of a certain American car had a list price of $3500. If all the parts of the car were bought individually, their total cost would be $7500. Labor to assemble the parts would cost another $7500. Thus, the total cost of this car would be $15,000 if one bought the parts separately and paid to have the car assembled. Discuss the implications of this fact for car insurance premium rates. What recommendations can you make to car manufacturers?

PART THREE
Finding and Equipping a Place to Live

12

Deciding on a Place to Live

Almost everyone wants to have an attractive and comfortable home. For some people, this means finding a suitable apartment or house to rent. For others, it means owning a home. When we consider that housing is the largest item in most family budgets, we get a better understanding of the importance of making a good choice when we are deciding on a place to live.

HOUSING NEEDS DIFFER

An important factor influencing our housing needs is our stage in the family life cycle. The *family life cycle* is the stages of development through which a family moves, beginning with the new household formed by young singles. This stage is followed by the formation of a new family at marriage. Most people move through all the stages of the family life cycle:

1. *Young singles.*
2. *Newlyweds.*
3. *Young Family.*   Made up of parents and young children. (Ex-

perts on family life sometimes call this the "nest-building stage.")
4. *Older Family.* Parents and older children, sometimes called "the full-nest stage."
5. *Older Couples with No Children at Home.* Sometimes called "the empty-nest stage."
6. *Single Adult.* The surviving husband or wife living alone.

Most single people prefer living in a rented apartment. Apartment living usually enables a single person to enjoy the maximum in convenience and comfort with a minimum of effort and investment. The majority of young couples begin their life together in a rented apartment or house. Because income and savings at this stage of life are usually not adequate to make a down payment on a home, their housing needs can usually best be met by renting. Renting gives new families a chance to decide what type of home they want and where they want it before they invest in a home of their own.

Families with growing children or with youngsters in school often find that their housing needs can best be met by buying rather than renting. Income is usually higher at this stage of life than it is in earlier years, and the family may be ready to make a long-term investment. Owning a house usually offers the advantage of additional space. This can be an important consideration for families with growing children.

An older couple whose children no longer live at home may find it convenient to sell their house and rent or buy a smaller house or an apartment. Their need for space has decreased, and their income is sometimes lower. They often find that smaller and more convenient living quarters are more practical and desirable.

DETERMINING YOUR RESOURCES

Many families find that they cannot obtain the kind of housing they need and want because of the limits that their resources place on them. These resources include their financial resources, the spare time and energy they have available for home care, and their special home-care skills.

Two kinds of financial resources affect housing decisions. Monthly or weekly income influences how much a family can afford to commit to rental or mortgage payments and other housing costs. The amount of savings available determines whether the family is in a position to consider purchasing a home. If the family has enough money for a down payment, plus the extra money required for moving and for the

People who are skilled in home repair and decorating may choose to buy or rent a home that is in poor condition but costs less, then use their skills to make the home more livable. (*Armstrong Floors, Inc.*)

other costs involved in purchasing a home, it is in a position to consider buying a home. Young families and young single people usually have few savings; as a result, they have little choice but to rent.

The spare time and energy that family members have available for home care also influences housing choices. Young single people usually do not want to spend their spare time mowing grass and raking leaves. An apartment is better suited to their wants. Individuals' special skills in home repair and care also may affect their choice. Those who are skilled at painting, repairs, and decorating may choose to rent an apartment or buy a house that is in poor condition but costs less. They know they can use their special skills to make the place more livable.

EVALUATING THE ALTERNATIVES

Our choices as housing shoppers fall into several categories. These are the most familiar:

- Buying a house
- Renting a house or apartment

Another possibility has become more familiar in recent years:

- Buying an apartment or unit in a condominium or cooperative development

Finally, a fourth possibility:

- Buying a mobile home and renting or buying a site to locate it on

The advantages of each of these four alternatives will be examined in the sections that follow.

First let us define exactly what we are talking about when we mention some of the less familiar types of housing.

- *Condominium.* An ownership arrangement under which an owner has legal title to a particular unit in a development and a share in the ownership of the common areas such as lobbies, halls, lawns, and swimming pool. The common areas are maintained by an owners' association, and the expenses are divided among the owners. Developments owned in this way include attached town houses, garden apartments, and high-rise apartment buildings.
- *Cooperative.* An ownership arrangement under which each member owns a percentage share of a nonprofit corporation which has legal title to a building. Each member has a long-term lease on a specific apartment. Operating expenses are divided among the members on the basis of their percentage share in the ownership. Most of the buildings owned as cooperatives are apartments.
- *Mobile Homes.* A factory-built dwelling which is constructed on a permanent chassis. It is towed from the factory to a site where it can be set up on either a permanent or temporary foundation. Mobile homes are designed for permanent, year-round housing. They should not be confused with smaller recreational trailers. Most mobile home owners rent a site in a park especially for mobile homes. Some buy both the home and land to locate it on.

The advantages of each of these five choices will be discussed in the sections that follow.

Advantages of Buying a Home

Most young people, studies show, hope to someday own a home of their own. For most of them, buying a home will mean undertaking a long-term mortgage with payments spread out over many years. Because buying a home is the largest investment that most people ever make, it deserves careful consideration. Some of the advantages of owning a home are listed below. All of the advantages listed apply to condominiums and cooperative apartments as well as to houses.

- Making payments on a home is one method of saving automatically. As you pay for a home, you build up an equity, that is, ownership, in real estate. Also, owning a home can provide you some protection against inflation. House prices rise along with the price level.
- A homeowner has a feeling of security and independence. As long as you continue your payments, you need not worry about where you are going to live. Renters, on the other hand, cannot always be sure how long they can remain in their homes.
- There are some tax advantages in owning a home. Property taxes and interest charges on a mortgage are allowed as income tax deductions. Renters may pay rent of $1800 a year, and none of it will count as an income tax deduction. As a homeowner, on the other hand, you may pay out the same $1800 a year, but $340 may represent property taxes and $660 may represent interest on the mortgage. As a homeowner, you would have a $1000 income tax deduction that you would not have as a renter.
- The homeowner is often given a better credit rating. In addition, the equity in the home investment can be used as security to borrow money in emergencies.
- As a homeowner, you can arrange your home to suit yourself. You can remodel and decorate any way you like.

The Advantages of Renting a Home

Renting a home has many advantages. It gives you a chance to study a neighborhood or a community and decide whether or not you want to live their permanently. Those who prefer to rent offer the following arguments in favor of their position.

- There is a definite limit to the financial risks involved in renting. If your income decreases, you can leave a rented apartment or house with little loss of savings or investment.
- When you rent, you are not tied down to one spot. You are free to move to bigger or smaller quarters, to leave a neighborhood you do not like, or to accept a better position in another city. Over a lifetime there are many reasons for moving.
- You usually are not responsible for maintaining property. You will not be faced with unexpected repair bills that may upset your budget. Paying for repairs is the landlord's problem.
- If you have a lease, you can easily plan a budget for housing, since rent payments are the same each month. Rising property taxes and utility costs will, of course, eventually raise your rent.
- Renting is frequently cheaper than buying, at least on a short-term basis. This is because you avoid the real estate commissions, property transfer taxes, and closing costs that home buyers must pay.

A mobile home can be moved if necessary; this is one of its advantages. (*Salt River Project*)

The Advantages of Buying a Mobile Home

Most mobile-home buyers are both buyers and renters. They buy the mobile home and rent the space on which it is located. New mobile homes provide clean, newly built quarters for a relatively low monthly cost. They can be purchased complete with furniture if desired. Mobile homes have several advantages.

- Financing is easy to arrange. Most mobile homes are bought with credit arrangements similar to those for automobiles. Although interest rates usually are higher than for house purchases, there are no large closing costs at the time of purchase.
- Because of their compact size, the low-upkeep materials used, and small lots, mobile homes are easy to maintain.
- Although most mobile homes are not moved after they are placed in a park, they can be moved if this becomes necessary.
- Mobile-home owners, like house owners, are free to make interior changes and redecorate to suit themselves. Mobile home park rules may, however, limit what they can do outside.

FACTORS TO CONSIDER IN SELECTING A PLACE TO LIVE

Once we have some general idea of our housing needs, our resources, and the kinds of alternatives available, we are in a position to begin making a more detailed study of the housing choices that are open to us. In judging each particular choice, a number of factors have to be taken into account. These include not only the space provided and the equipment, but also the neighborhood and community in which it is located.

Distance to Work

A key factor that influences housing choices is the distance to be traveled to work. Most people would like to live close to work because of the savings in time and transportation costs. Rents and house prices reflect this preference. Good housing close to urban centers is more expensive than similar places in outlying areas. Some people are attracted by the lower prices in outlying areas but fail to consider the extra transportation costs that are involved. These extra costs may not become clear until they discover that their auto operating and repair expenses are a good deal higher than they had expected.

Community and Government Services

To inexperienced home shoppers, the choice of a community may not seem very important. They may focus all their attention on the house or apartment they are interested in and not pay much attention to the community in which it is located. The community we choose can, in fact, be quite important. It determines the community services we have available, such as stores, shopping facilities, and medical facilities. It also determines the amount of taxes we will have to pay and the kind and quality of government services we will get for our money.

Personal Relationships

The opportunity to live near our family and friends is important to many of us. If this is not possible, we would like to live near the kind of people whom we would like to have as friends. Some people feel more comfortable living in a neighborhood with people of similar interests and life-styles. Some young single people, for example, prefer to live near others the same age rather than in a neighborhood made up mostly of families. Others find a neighborhood with many different kinds of people more interesting. Families with children usually feel it is important to have playmates for their children nearby.

Recreation Facilities

Opportunities to develop our special interests and enjoy leisure time play an important part in how we judge different communities. Larger communities have a wide range of recreational, cultural, and entertainment facilities. Smaller ones may have only a few.

Recreational facilities are important to most of us. These include outdoor facilities such as parks, swimming pools, tennis courts, bike and hiking trails, and golf courses. Indoor facilities include those which youth clubs sometimes provide, basketball courts, gyms, bowling alleys, and dance floors. Entertainment facilities, such as movie theaters and cultural activities, also contribute to the quality of life in a community. Special interest clubs, hobby groups, and service clubs also play an important role in personal development and can add enjoyment to life. Think about the areas you would regard as pleasant places to live. Why do you feel this way? An important factor in your rating is almost certain to be the recreational, entertainment, and cultural activities they have available.

With the increasing emphasis on leisure time in our way of life, recreational facilities such as community tennis courts can be an important factor in choosing a place to live. (*Kip Peticolas*)

Physical Environment

Along with the things we have discussed above, most of us would like to have a pleasant physical environment in which to live. We would like to live in a neighborhood which is attractive, safe, and free from pollution.

When people across the country were asked recently about problems in their neighborhoods which bothered them (see Table 12-1), the problem which they named most often was "too much noise." Traffic noise, aircraft noise, and construction noise all were part of the problem. This suggests that one of the questions we need to ask about a neighborhood is how quiet it is. Do the streets carry only local traffic? Is the area away from airports, fire stations, and other sources of noise?

Safety factors were also important in people's ratings of neighborhoods. Are the streets in good repair, well-lighted, and well-patrolled?

In addition to a pollution-free neighborhood and a safe one, most of us would also like one which is attractive to look at. We need to look

TABLE 12-1
How People Rate Conditions in Their Neighborhoods

	Percent Reporting	
	Owners	Renters
No undesirable conditions	24%	22%
One or more undesirable conditions*	76%	78%
Street noise	32	39
Heavy traffic	28	35
Poor street lighting	28	19
Streets need repair	19	14
Airplane noise	17	16
Crime	16	22
Commercial or industrial business	13	25
Litter	14	15
Odors	9	9
Total	100%	100%

*Reported undesirable conditions will not add to this total because more than one problem could be reported by the same household.
Source: U.S. Department of Commerce/U.S. Department of Housing and Urban Development.

carefully at the neighborhoods we are considering. Are the buildings in good condition, or does the area show signs of becoming run-down? Is there an interesting variety of architecture, or do all the buildings look like they were cut out with the same cookie cutter? Is there attractive landscaping and street trees?

Communities differ in control of air pollution, noise, and heavy traffic. They also differ in zoning laws and practices. In some communities, zoning laws are weak or subject to change because of pressure from big developers and business interests. Home buyers in such communities may find the value of their houses and their privacy destroyed when a seven-story apartment house goes up in the vacant lot next door.

Interior and Exterior Space

When you look at an empty apartment or house, it often is difficult to imagine how usable the space will be. One thing you will want to consider is how well the usual furniture pieces will fit. Is the space laid out so that large pieces such as sofas and beds can be arranged

When you are looking at an empty apartment or house, you should consider whether furniture will fit easily into the available space, taking into account the placement of windows and doors. (*Susan Berkowitz*)

easily? Or are the wall spaces so cut up with doors and windows that there is little room for furniture along the walls?

Another thing you will want to consider is how well the plan and the room sizes fit your life-style and your usual activities. In a study of housing preferences, researchers found four different types of families. The preferences of these four types reflect basic differences in their values. Where would you place yourself among these groups?

- *"Economy" Value Group.* Concerned about good practical housing that gives good value for the money spent. This group puts more emphasis on space and durability than on special features or other extras. Family life is informal. Meals are usually eaten in the kitchen, and a separate dining area is not felt to be very important. Watching television is a favorite recreation. This needs to be taken into account in living-room planning.
- *"Family" Value Group.* Concerned about the well-being and development of family members. This group puts much emphasis on shared family activities and interests. They want space for joint family activities and children's play. A separate dining area in the living room or a family room big enough to entertain large numbers of relatives at meals is considered desirable.
- *"Personal" Value Group.* Concerned about self-expression and space for family members to work on their individual interests. This group wants bedrooms for individual activities such as reading and listening to records. Yard space should provide privacy.
- *"Prestige" Value Group.* Concerned about using their home to gain others' approval. These families are trying to move ahead economically and socially and are concerned about good taste and current styles. They like to entertain formally and want a separate dining area. They are willing to give up some things in order to have impressive features such as a fireplace in the living room.

Ideas about housing design have changed over the years. Knowing something about these ideas will help you to judge housing plans and to think about your own design preferences. Recent designs have aimed for a feeling of openness and spaciousness. Walls and doors have been eliminated wherever possible. Separate dining rooms have been replaced by dining alcoves or els in the living room or family room. Large windows and sliding glass doors with views to the outside also have been used to give the feeling of spaciousness. Modern plans also emphasize easy indoor-outdoor movement. Outdoor living areas are regarded as extensions of interior spaces and are connected to them with sliding glass doors. To really be useful for family activities, outdoor spaces should provide both shade and privacy.

The emphasis on openness has made the problem of *zoning*, the separation of different family activities, more difficult. This kind of separation is needed when one activity can interfere with another. For example, a plan with good zoning will provide separate, quiet areas for family members who need to study while the rest of the family watches television.

Equipment

Although space and the way it is arranged are important in determining how livable a home will be, housing is not just a series of rooms. The equipment in a home also affects how livable it will be.

How satisfied we are with the place we live in depends to a great extent on how well we can control the amount of light, heat, and air. These factors are key parts of our environment and are essential to our comfort. Even if we like everything else about a place, it can make us miserable if we can never get the heat above 60°F [15.4°C] in the winter, or if it is always too hot in the summer.

Landlords and builders often use "extras" to attract customers. You will want to check to be certain that these extras are really worth having. Too often the appliances installed are stripped-down models without the desirable features or durability of middle-of-the-line models. Eye-catching features such as large mirrors, fancy light fixtures, and fake ceiling beams are often used to give a feeling of luxury and comfort. The careful shopper will look behind these extras to check the basic quality of the construction and the equipment provided.

HOW MUCH CAN YOU AFFORD TO PAY?

Because housing is such an important commitment, it is important to determine all the costs involved in a particular choice. Deciding how much we can afford to pay for a place to live is not just a matter of deciding how much we can pay for rent or for a mortgage payment. We also have to take the other costs which are closely linked with each alternative into account. A careful comparison of the costs of different alternatives will take these other factors into account. They include:

- Commuting costs
- Utilities costs
- Property taxes
- Upkeep and yard-care costs

Family finance experts do not completely agree on how much a family can afford to spend on housing. One rule of thumb is the one suggested by Sylvia Porter. It is that a family can expect to spend 1 to 1½ weeks' take-home pay for each month's *total* housing expenses. In this total she includes rent (or mortgage payment), taxes and insurance, utilities and heat, repairs and upkeep, and the costs of commuting to work. Using this rule of thumb, someone with monthly take-home pay of $480 could afford to spend up to $180 a month.

THE HOUSING CRISIS

In recent years the shortage of reasonably priced housing has become an increasing problem. Many people have not been able to find or afford the kind of housing they want and need. Young people interested in buying their first home and lower-income people have been the most seriously affected.

Just how did this situation come about? Two factors are involved—both the demand side of the market and the supply side. The demand for housing has been high in recent years. Many new households are being formed as the large numbers of young people born in the late 1940s and the 1950s set up on their own.

Although there is strong demand for moderately priced housing, the supply is inadequate. Housing costs have risen so rapidly in recent years and have gotten so high that many people cannot afford decent housing. We all know about the rapid increases in the prices of consumer goods in recent years. The prices of building materials, labor, and land have risen in the same way. Other costs which are also part of the total housing bill also have risen sharply. These include property taxes and utility costs.

High interest rates also have affected the supply and the price of housing. The high interest rates of the late 1960s and the 1970s have discouraged both home builders and home buyers. Home builders have found it expensive to borrow to finance their operations. People interested in buying homes have found mortgage loan rates expensive. These high rates were a result of government economic policies designed to slow the rate of inflation. By raising interest rates for loans of all types, the government hoped to discourage borrowing and hold down the supply of money. High interest rates have affected apartment building in much the same way single-family home building was affected.

What Can Be Done to Cut the Cost of Housing?

Rising building costs have put new houses beyond the reach of many families. In the mid-1970s the price of a typical new house was over $40,000 and was rising by several thousand dollars each year. To meet the mortgage payments on such a house, along with taxes and utilities, would take an income of $25,000 a year or more. It is clear that such houses are too expensive for most families. Only a few new houses are available at prices which families in the $10,000- to 15,000-a-year range could afford.

The rising prices of new houses have helped raise the prices of older houses. Because of the rapid increases in the prices of new and old houses, many families who hoped to move up to bigger or better houses have been unable to do so. This has slowed down the usual process in which older houses sold by middle-income families become available to lower-income families.

Most of the efforts to hold down the cost of housing have been aimed at two key parts of the problem: building costs and land costs. One of the things which is being done is to scale down the typical new house being built. Over the last 25 years the typical new house has increased in size and in the amount of equipment provided. Recently builders have begun to build somewhat smaller houses with less equipment in order to cut prices.

New attention has been given to building housing more efficiently as a way to cut costs. A number of attempts have been made to use mass-production techniques. Parts and entire sections of houses are being built in factories with assembly-line techniques. The parts may include wall, floor, and roof panels that are erected at the building site, where wiring, plumbing, and heating are installed. Larger sections, or *modules*, completely assembled with walls, floors, ceilings, and roofs and including utilities also are being factory-built. At the building site, two or more of these modules are joined together on a permanent foundation to form a completed house.

Modular-home construction and the use of other new construction materials and techniques have been restricted by local building codes. New efforts are being made by federal and state governments to encourage the modernization of these codes and, at the same time, provide adequate protection for home buyers.

In the past, housing codes were written in terms of descriptive standards. *Descriptive standards* describe, in detail, the kinds of lumber, electric wire, and other materials to be used. Newer codes set performance standards. Instead of requiring the use of a particular material, *performance standards* set the level of performance that must be provided. Any material that can provide this level of performance is considered acceptable. This makes the use of new, less expensive laborsaving materials possible.

Rising construction costs have increased the interest in mobile homes. Mobile homes are available in a variety of sizes, in widths from 8 to 14 ft [2.4 to 4 meters (m)] and in lengths up to 70 ft [20.9 m], with 14 by 65 ft [4 by 19.5 m] currently the most popular size. Since mobile homes are factory-built, savings due to mass production are possible. In addition, mobile homes do not require a permanent foundation, and this further reduces costs.

A variety of approaches to reducing the cost of land used for housing have been used. One new idea that has attracted wide attention is the idea of *new towns;* these new towns, which offer a full range of services, are built on cheap, vacant land away from existing urban centers. Other attempts to reduce land costs have focused on ways of placing more housing units on each acre of land. Some developers have economized on land by constructing houses side by side in town house or row house style, rather than separately. Other developers have employed the *cluster development* concept. Housing units are grouped together closely to leave as much open space as possible for recreation.

What Is the Government Doing to Help?

The government has been involved in improving the quality and supply of housing since the 1930s. It has provided three types of help:

- Mortgage insurance provided by the Federal Housing Administration (FHA), which has helped home buyers get long-term mortgages with small down payments and lower interest rates.
- Money for low-rent *public housing,* which is run by local housing authorities.
- Various subsidy programs, including rent-supplement payments to local nonprofit groups which provide housing to low-income families at reduced rents.

It is clear that both new approaches to cutting housing costs and government help are needed if we are to provide safe, durable, and comfortable housing for people in all walks of life—for the rich and the poor, and for both city and country dwellers.

Checking Your Reading

1. How does each stage in the family life cycle affect people's housing preferences?
2. How do a family's financial resources affect its housing decisions?
3. List five advantages of buying a home. Do these advantages apply to cooperative apartments and condominiums?
4. List five advantages of renting a home.
5. List four advantages of buying a mobile home.
6. Is a low-priced house out in the country a better buy than a similar house in town? What factors would you need to consider in deciding between these two choices?
7. What have researchers learned about differences in family lifestyles and the way families use their homes?
8. What factors have affected the demand for housing in recent years? The supply?
9. What is meant by modular-home construction?
10. What is the difference between building codes with descriptive standards and those with performance standards?
11. What approaches have been used to reduce land costs in building housing?
12. What three types of help in improving the supply and quality of housing has the federal government provided?

Consumer Problems and Projects

1. When you think about the kind of home you would like to have someday, which characteristics are most important to you? How would you weight these characteristics if you were thinking only of a home for yourself? If you were thinking of a home for yourself and a future family? (Use a scale of 10 for your weights, with 10 as the highest.)
2. There are many important programs and proposals aimed at solving the housing problems discussed in this chapter. Prepare a report on one of these programs or proposals. Your report should describe the program or proposal and consider its successes and failures. Some possible topics are: New towns; building codes;

zoning and urban planning; building techniques developed to reduce construction costs; approaches to reducing land costs (town houses, cluster developments, etc.); urban renewal; open housing; public housing; government rent subsidy programs; government home mortgage insurance programs.

3. How adequate is the supply of housing at different price levels in your community? Check the listings in the classified ad section of your local newspaper. Prepare a report on the number of listings at different price levels for *either* rental housing or houses for sale. For example, how many apartments are available for less than $100 per month? Does this include utilities?

4. What do you think would be the best housing choice in the following situations? Give the reasons for your answers.
   a. A young woman who is just starting out on her first job in a town 150 miles from her parents' home.
   b. A young couple with two children who have $6500 in savings.
   c. An older couple whose children have left home and have jobs in other cities.

5. Sue and Jack Whitestone and their two children are planning to move to a different town and are looking for a house there. They have found two similar three-bedroom houses in the same neighborhood. One rents for $250 a month; the other is for sale. If the Whitestones bought the house, they would have to make a down payment of $6000. Their monthly mortgage payments on a 20-year loan at 8½ percent would be $250. Jack Whitestone says that because the monthly payments are the same, common sense dictates that they buy the house that is for sale. He reasons that $250 paid for rent would simply be "money down the drain," while the $250 mortgage payments eventually would enable them to own their own home. Is Jack's reasoning sound or are there other considerations to take into account? What are they?

6. Are there differences in the cost of similar apartments or houses located in different parts of your community? Why do you think these differences exist? Discuss this question with your parents. They will be able to suggest examples of differences and the reasons for them.

7. Jodie Jackson has just finished technical school and started work in a medical laboratory. Her monthly take-home pay is $600 a month. Using the rule of thumb for housing costs discussed on p. 208, how much could she afford to pay out for *all* her house expenses?

13

Choosing an Apartment or Mobile Home

Most young people make their first home in a rented apartment. In recent years mobile homes also have provided first homes for many new families. Both apartments and mobile homes give young people with limited funds an opportunity to set up housekeeping on their own. Renting an apartment or purchasing a mobile home involves such legal complexities as rental agreements, leases, and purchase contracts. Although these commitments may seem a good deal less complicated than buying a house, they still deserve careful attention. Apartment leases and mobile home purchases involve promises to pay out hundreds and thousands of dollars. Wise consumers need to consider such a step carefully.

Once they set up their own homes, young people begin to accumulate many new possessions, such as sofas, rugs, stereo equipment, and television sets. They need to know how to protect themselves from financial loss if these items are destroyed in a fire or are stolen. The use of property insurance to protect against such losses will be discussed in the final portion of this chapter. Having your own home also makes you responsible for injuries to others who are visiting you or making deliveries. The use of personal liability insurance to provide protection against such risks also will be discussed.

FACTORS TO CONSIDER IN SELECTING AN APARTMENT

A wide variety of rental quarters is available, ranging from rented rooms to one-room efficiency apartments on up to apartments with two or three bedrooms. The prices for these different types of apartments also vary a good deal, but the factors to consider in selecting an apartment are the same regardless of the size of the apartment.

In the previous chapter, we discussed the factors that need to be considered in any choice of housing. In this section, we will look at some additional factors that are important when you are shopping for an apartment.

Management

Renters have to depend on their building's management for many important services. For this reason, it's important to find out just how they view their role. Are they concerned about providing a pleasant place for people to live? Or are they mostly concerned about collecting rent and spending as little on upkeep as possible? One good indication of their attitude is how well the building is kept up. Are the halls littered and dirty? Are there burned-out light bulbs which need to be replaced? If so, the apartment shopper can expect difficulty in getting problems corrected and repairs made.

It is important to have some representative of the management available at all times. Is there a resident manager in the building? If not, whom can you contact if you have problems? You may want to ask one or two of the building's tenants about the management. Are they fair and honest? Are repairs made quickly? Are they concerned about safety and security in the building?

Safety

Poor management and upkeep can result in many safety problems. Damaged hand rails and stair treads can make stairways dangerous. Littered hallways can create a fire hazard. Failure to keep fire extinguishers in place and properly maintained may mean that any fire that starts will be hard to control.

Fire is a particular danger in apartment buildings because of the large number of housing units located close together in one building. A fire in one unit can quickly create dangers for others. To provide fire safety, the best apartment designs are those which provide *com-*

partmentalization. In apartment buildings with compartmentalized design, fires can be contained in one unit. Concrete floors and ceilings and cinder block walls do the best job of compartmentalizing fires. Fires spread more rapidly in buildings in which the apartments are divided only by walls of plasterboard on wood studding.

Security

Since most apartments are in urban areas where crime and theft are a problem, security is important to consider when looking for an apartment. Lobbies which are well lighted and designed so that the entire lobby can be seen before you enter help discourage crime. Well-lighted and uncluttered hallways and locked outside entrances also help.

Apartment doors should be of sturdy construction. They should be strong enough so that they cannot be kicked in and should have strong locks. Metal doors set in metal frames are best. If wood doors are used,

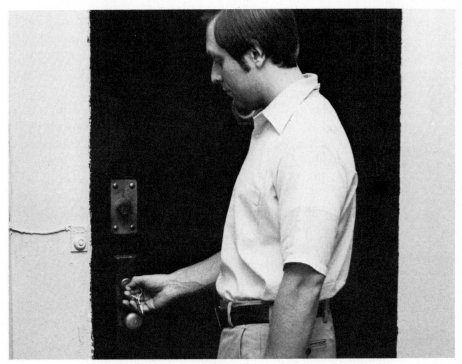

The most secure apartment door is one constructed of metal and set in a metal frame. A mortise lock, in which the keyhole is above the doorknob, is more secure than the best key-in-knob lock. (*Susan Berkowitz*)

they should have solid cores and be tightly fitted in the frame to prevent prying.

Many apartment doors are equipped with only cheap key-in-the knob locks that can be opened easily with a strip of plastic. Key-in-the-knob locks with an extra trigger bolt separate from the main latch provide security against this means of entry. Even the best key-in-the-knob locks can be opened easily if the knob is broken off or damaged. Mortise locks, ones in which the keyhole is above the doorknob, provide more security, especially when the dead bolt as well as the latch is engaged. Locks should be changed by the landlord each time a new tenant moves into an apartment.

Another factor that affects security is the location of the apartment in the building. Basement and first-floor apartments can be entered easily unless special window grilles and locks are provided.

Space

Since apartment dwellers live close together, privacy may be a problem. Buildings should be soundproof enough to muffle the sounds of talking, plumbing, and music between apartments and between hallways and apartments. Apartment dwellers usually are bothered more by sounds from the floor above than the floor below. Upper-floor apartments usually are quieter for this reason, and also because they are further away from street and parking lot noises.

Storage may be a particular problem in small-size apartments, so attention should be given to the amount of closet space provided. Some apartment buildings provide storage lockers in the basement. This space usually is not secure enough to provide safe storage for valuable items, but it can be useful for storing empty packing boxes and crates.

Control of air movement and the temperature should be checked carefully. Will the apartment be cool in summer and warm enough in the winter? Although top-floor apartments have advantages, they may be uncomfortably hot in the summer because of the heat absorbed by the building's roof, unless special attention has been given to insulation.

Equipment and Utilities

The appliances and equipment furnished should be checked to ensure that they are in good working order. If they are not, repairs should be agreed on. Prospective renters should also be certain that they understand which utilities are included in the rent and which will be billed separately by the utility company. If heating and cooling costs are not included in the rent, get an estimate of typical costs from the landlord or tenants. Comparisons of rents among different buildings should take differences in the utilities provided into account.

Rental Arrangements

Although many rooms and apartments are rented without formal signed leases, most landlords want the protection that a lease gives them. Rentals may be arranged with only an oral agreement on such details as the amount of the rent and when it is to be paid. This type of agreement is called *tenancy-at-will*. It can be terminated or ended at any time by giving notice one rent period in advance—a month in advance if rent is paid monthly or a week in advance if rent is paid weekly.

Most rentals, especially those in larger buildings, require a lease. The lease is a written contract between the landlord and the tenant setting the terms under which a particular piece of property is rented. Prospective renters should be aware that a lease is a legal contract that commits them to paying hundreds of dollars. In return, they are provided with the use of an apartment.

Lease Terms

Because of the amount of money involved and the difficulty of getting released from a lease contract, leases should be signed with caution. The following items in the lease should be given special attention:

- *Identification of Unit Rented.* The apartment rented should be clearly identified by address and number. You should insist on seeing the unit you will be renting, rather than just a "model" apartment.
- *Term of the Lease.* The beginning and ending dates of use should be specified.
- *Rent.* The amount of rent and where and when it is to be paid should be indicated. Attention should be given to any provisions that permit increases in the rent during the term of the lease. Some leases provide for rent increases if property taxes are increased.
- *Number and Kinds of Occupants.* Limits on the number, kinds, and ages of occupants, such as rules against children, should be spelled out clearly. Restrictions on pets, if any, should be made clear.

- *Security Deposit.*   Most leases require a security deposit to protect the landlord against damages or nonpayment of rent. Renters should be certain that they get a separate receipt that specifically states that the amount paid is for the security deposit. Landlords' practices in returning security deposits have been a continuing source of problems for tenants. Some landlords refuse to return deposits. They claim unusual wear and tear or extra cleaning costs regardless of the condition in which an apartment is left. Others are fairer and adjust their charges to the situation.

   Renters have little protection against unfair withholding of security deposits short of legal action. One way of protecting yourself is to avoid buildings where the landlords are known to be unfair. Present tenants often can tell you what the landlord's practices are. Another way to protect yourself is to insist that the landlord go through the apartment with you before you leave and point out specific reasons for the deductions from your security deposit.
- *Repairs.*   The lease should clearly state who is responsible for arranging and paying for repairs. Some leases make the renter responsible for repairs. It would seem more reasonable to make the landlord responsible for repairs, except for damage caused by the renter.
- *Furnishings.*   If an apartment is rented furnished, it is a good idea to get a detailed inventory of the contents and notes on the condition of each item attached to the lease.
- *Right to Sublet.*   The lease should permit you to sublet the apartment to others, in case you need to move before the period of the lease is up. Most leases provide that the landlord has the right to approve or disapprove prospective tenants who wish to sublease.
- *Utilities and Services.*   The lease should specify what utilities are provided as part of the rent and those for which the tenant is personally responsible.
- *Landlord's Right of Entry.*   The conditions under which the landlord can enter the apartment should be spelled out. The landlord will, of course, need to enter in case of emergencies and to show the apartment to prospective renters after being notified that the lease is to be terminated. Some leases give the landlord the right to enter at "any reasonable time," while others let the tenant insist on advance notice.
- *Termination Procedure.*   The lease should indicate the procedure to be followed when the tenant wishes to end the lease. Some leases contain *automatic renewal clauses* that set a date before which the landlord must be notified if the lease is to be terminated. If the landlord is not notified by this date, the lease is renewed automatically.

   Some annual leases require that the landlord be notified as much as 90 days before the lease expires. Wise tenants will keep careful track of these notification dates. Letters notifying the landlord about plans to terminate a lease should be sent by registered or certified mail so that there will be official records that they were received.

Some leases include a *holding over* provision. This states that occupancy of the apartment after the end of the lease term can be regarded by the landlord as a renewal of the lease. The sample lease on pages 220–221 contains holding over provisions which permit the landlord to double the rent.

Signing a Lease

Lease forms are usually long, with lots of small print. Rental agents usually try to rush renters into signing by telling them that the form they have been given is "the standard form." The fact is, there is no single standard form. Landlords can and often do put whatever they want into a lease form. In general, lease forms are written to conform to state and local laws. They may, however, have sections which will not hold up in court. A lease, for example, may say that the landlord can enter the apartment any time he feels it necessary. If this issue went to court, the court might decide that this was unreasonable. Landlords also can make whatever rules they please. They can allow cats and not dogs, or vice versa, as it suits them. Leases are written mostly for the protection of landlords. For this reason it is important for you to know exactly what is in the lease you are asked to sign. If you do not understand a section, ask to have it explained.

Just because something is printed on a lease form does not mean it cannot be changed. If you object to particular sections, you can ask to have them changed. Your luck in getting such changes will be better if apartments are in plentiful supply in your area and the rental agent is eager to make a deal. Changes in lease forms should be initialed by the rental agent to indicate acceptance. Any special arrangements you make with the rental agent should be written into the lease. Oral promises will not be binding if the lease indicates some other arrangements. Once a lease is signed, the renter should get a signed copy at once or a written promise setting the date when it will be delivered.

Protecting Tenants' Rights

On close examination, most leases are rather one-sided. They are made up mostly of rules about what renters must do and sections

APARTMENT LEASE

Unfurnished

Lessee

Name *Marilyn and Joseph Holtzer*

Apt. No. *3-C Northbrook Terrace*

Address of *750 W. 8th Street*

Premises *Northbrook*

Lessor

Name *Diablo Enterprises Inc.*

Business *201 Central Ave.*

Address *Northbrook*

Lessor hereby leases to Lessee and Lessee hereby leases from Lessor for residential purposes the demised premises designated above. The Lessor and Lessee hereby make the following mutual covenants and agreements:

TERM

1. The term of this agreement shall be for *one year*, beginning *July 1, 197-* and ending *June 30, 197-*.

RENT

2. Lessee shall pay Lessor or Lessor's agent $ *195.00* a month, payable in advance, on the first day of the month, until termination of this lease.

SECURITY DEPOSIT

3. Lessee has deposited with the Lessor, a security deposit of $ *195.00* for the performance of all agreements herein. Said deposit may be applied by Lessor toward payment of any amounts due from Lessee. Upon termination of the lease, that portion of the Security Deposit which remains unapplied shall be returned to Lessee. This deposit does not bear interest except as required by law. When any portion of the Security Deposit is applied by the Lessor toward repair of property damage, Lessor shall provide to Lessee an itemized statement of such damage and of the actual or estimated cost of repairs.

UTILITIES

4. Lessor will supply hot and cold water to the premises for the use of the Lessee. Lessor also will supply heat in reasonable amounts and as necessary from October 1st to May 31st. In addition the landlord will supply the following other utilities to the demised premises: (indicate as appropriate)

Electricity *yes*   Gas   *no*

Garbage removal *yes*   Trash removal *yes*

Other (specify) *Master TV antenna - yes*   *J.D.P.*

CONDITION OF THE PREMISES

5. Lessee has examined and knows the condition of the premises. Lessee has received the premises in good order and repair except as may be otherwise specified below. No other agreements concerning the condition or repair of the premises have been made except as expressed herein.

TENANT'S DUTY TO MAINTAIN PREMISES	6. Lessee will take good care of the apartment demised. No cat, dog, bird or other animal will be kept in or about the premises. Cooking shall be done only in the kitchen and under no circumstances on porches, balconies or in other exterior areas. Upon termination of this lease the lessee will vacate the premises, return all keys and leave the premises in as good condition as it was received (with allowance for normal wear-and tear). Lessee agrees to repair all damage resulting from misuse or neglect. Upon Lesee's failure to make such repairs, after reasonable notice by Lessor, Lessor may make such repairs and Lessee shall be liable for any reasonable expense incurred.
SUBLET	7. The Lessee will not assign this lease or sublet the premises without the written consent of the Lessor.
INSPECTION BY LESSOR	8. Lessee will allow Lessor free access to premises at all reasonable hours for the purposes of inspecting the premises, exhibiting the unit to prospective purchasers or tenants or making repairs.
HOLDING OVER	9. If the Lessee shall continue to occupy the premises after the expiration date, then the Lessor may at Lessor's option serve written notice on the Lessee within 30 days indicating that such holding over constitutes a renewal of this lease for one year at double the rental specified in section 2.
DEFAULT BY LESSEE	10. If the Lessee defaults in payments, as set forth above, or in any agreement contained herein, it shall be lawful for Lessor or his representative to declare the term of this agreement ended, to re-enter the premises and to expel or put out the Lessee and any other persons occupying the premises, using such force as he may deem necessary and again repossess the premises. The Lessee expressly waives all right to any notice from the Lessor of his election to declare this lease at an end; the fact of non-performance of any agreements of this lease shall constitute a forfeiture of this lease.

11. Additional convenants and agreements (indicate if any)

a. Lessor will repair or replace air-conditioner and change entry door lock to mortise-type lock prior to beginning of lease term.

J.D.P.

b. In connection with Section 3, Lessor agrees to inspect premises not later than one week before end of lease term and to notify Lessees of any damage charges to be made. Lessor agrees to return balance of Security Deposit not later than two weeks after ending date of this lease.

J.D.P.

In witness whereof, the parties hereto have executed this lease agreement:

Marilyn Holtzer

Lessee: *Joseph Holtzer*   Lessor: *Thomas D. Pappas*
     (Signature)   (Signature)

June 15, 197—   *June 15, 197—*
  (date of signature)   (date of signature)

which protect the management if renters fail to do something. Under the terms of most leases, renters are obligated to pay their rent on time and to not cause disturbances. They are obligated to keep their apartments clean, place refuse in the proper containers, and obey regulations set forth in the lease. It would seem fair, in turn, if landlords were obligated to keep apartments in good repair, provide the utilities promised, and maintain adequate supervision over the behavior of other tenants in the building.

The fact is, however, that many leases do not include promises that the landlord will do any of these things. Even those leases which include promises about repairs or heat usually do not indicate what rights a tenant has if the landlord does not provide these services.

There is, however, some protection available to tenants when landlords do not live up to their obligations. One is direct legal pressure and the threat of a lawsuit—this could be expensive unless legal aid or a small claims court is available.

If local safety and health regulations are being violated, complaints can be made to your local health department. In some areas, tenants' associations have been formed to negotiate with landlords; they use the threat of a rent strike to force attention to their demands. A number of city and state governments recently have given more attention to the problems of tenants and have passed laws that permit tenants to withhold rent when they feel the landlord is not meeting his obligations. These laws usually provide for the payment of rents into a special account that is held until needed repairs are made or promised utilities are supplied.

CHOOSING A MOBILE HOME

Mobile homes make up an important share of the new housing units being built each year. This relatively new form of housing has helped fill the need of large numbers of families for a moderately priced place to live. Mobile homes have been especially popular with those who need only a limited amount of living space—single people, young married couples, and retired people.

Factors to Consider in Selecting a Mobile Home

There are several different types of mobile homes. The most familiar is the single-wide type. The most common width for single-wide homes is 14 ft [4.2 m]. Most single-wide mobile homes are from 60 to

In some areas tenants have formed associations within buildings to negotiate with landlords. One weapon these associations can use in upholding tenants' rights is a rent strike, or withholding of rents until the landlord makes needed repairs or meets some other obligation. (*Art Zollo*)

75 ft [18 to 22.5 m] long. The length measurements quoted for mobile homes usually include the 4-ft [1.2-m] towing hitch. As a result, the popular 14 by 75 ft [4.2 by 22.5 m] model provides usable living space 14 by 71 ft (994 sq ft) [4.2 by 21.3 m (89.5 m²)]. Prices for single-wide homes range from $6000 to $17,000; the average price in recent years has been around $10,000. The popular 14 by 75 ft single-wide model can provide three bedrooms, two baths, and a living room with adjoining kitchen.

A second type of mobile home, the double-wide, consists of two separate units that are moved separately and joined together at their final destination to make a single living unit. The average price of double-wide models in recent years has been $17,000. The floor plan of a typical double-wide home includes three bedrooms, two baths, a kitchen, a living room, and a separate dining room.

Most mobile homes are sold completely equipped and fur-

Most mobile homes are sold completely equipped with furniture, carpeting, draperies, and kitchen appliances. (*Kip Peticolas*)

nished—with furniture, carpeting, draperies, and kitchen appliances. Equipment such as central air conditioning, laundry appliances, and dishwashers is optional.

There are other extras usually needed that add to the cost of a mobile home. These include:

- *Entry Steps.* These will be needed for each door. They should be well built, and for safety reasons, they should be equipped with handrails.
- *Skirting.* Panels are placed around the bottom of the mobile home to conceal the wheels. Skirting is required in many mobile home parks.
- *Supports or Piers.* These are required to provide a temporary foundation.
- *Over-the-roof Ties or Anchors.* These are needed in many areas to provide protection against high winds.
- *Other Extras.* Many owners equip their homes with patio awnings to provide additional outdoor living space and a sheltered front-door entry. Storage sheds also are often added to provide a place for tools, lawn furniture, and auto equipment.

Complaints about poor-quality construction and fire dangers in mobile homes led to the passage of the National Mobile Home Construction and Safety Standards Act in 1974. Since 1976 all mobile home manufacturers have been required to meet federal standards for design, construction, and performance set by the U.S. Department of Housing and Urban Development. The designs used by mobile home manufacturers and the units built are checked by private and state inspection organizations to see that they meet the federal standards. The standards require use of fire-resistant materials, the installation of smoke detectors in each bedroom area, and provision of two outside doors to ensure greater fire safety. They also set requirements for structural strength to ensure durability and protect against damage by heavy snows and high winds. The unit must be insulated and must have a certificate indicating the lowest outside temperature at which the heating unit can maintain a 70°F [20.9°C] inside temperature. The act requires manufacturers to provide other kinds of information about the unit, its equipment, and the area of the country for which it was designed. The act also sets up a recall procedure much like that used for automobiles if the manufacturer discovers safety hazards or defects.

Factors to Consider in Selecting a Site

Before buying a mobile home, it is important to check carefully where you will be able to put it. The available locations usually are limited to mobile home parks, except in small towns and rural areas which allow mobile homes to be placed on separate lots.

Mobile home parks vary a great deal in design and in the facilities provided. Newer parks typically are less crowded and provide larger lots that are better suited to the larger-size mobile homes now being built. Many parks have provided recreation facilities, and some even have swimming pools. The utilities provided also differ among parks. In some cases, water, sewer facilities, and garbage collection are provided as part of the lot rent.

Monthly rents for spaces differ with the services provided and the area of the country. They range from as low as $45 to over $125 in parks with luxury features and choice locations. Rentals ranging from $60 to $90 a month are more typical. In comparing rents among parks, it is important to take account of differences in the utilities provided. Many parks require leases. These should be studied and read carefully before signing.

Parks cater to different groups of people. Many welcome families with children—and people of all ages. Others cater chiefly to older

Many of the newer mobile home parks are less crowded and provide recreational facilities as well. This Florida park takes advantage of its waterfront location by providing docking for pleasure boats; other mobile home parks in other areas of the country may take advantage of special facilities in that area. (*Wide World Photos*)

adults and retired persons. Some parks are open only to those who have bought their mobile home from a particular dealer or particular group of dealers. Dealers with such arrangements use their ability to place the homes they sell in attractive parks as one of their major sales appeals.

It is clear that the basic quality of the construction of a mobile home, its floor plan, and the park in which it is located all play an important part in determining consumer satisfaction. Each of these product characteristics is important in the choice of a mobile home and deserves careful attention.

PROPERTY AND LIABILITY INSURANCE

Many renters believe that they do not need any insurance protection against property losses from fire. They think that since they do not own the apartment in which they live, they have little to lose in a fire. Those who think this way completely forget the value of the clothing, books, stereo equipment, appliances, and furniture that they own. The value of these things is likely to total hundreds and even thousands of dollars. Few of us would want to run the risk of a loss of this size. Renters also tend to forget their financial liability for injuries suffered by visitors to their apartment or by delivery or service people. Renters, mobile home owners, and house owners all need both property insurance and personal liability insurance to protect against these losses and risks.

Property Insurance

A variety of property insurance policies are available. They vary in the kinds of property they cover and in the kinds of losses they insure against. Some policies cover only a dwelling; others cover only its contents; some cover both. Some kinds of property insurance cover only a few kinds of losses or *perils*; others provide more extensive coverage. Property insurance policies are classified into three types depending on the number of perils they include.

- *Basic Form.* Provides protection against losses by fire or lightning and such other perils as windstorm or hail, explosion, aircraft or vehicles, smoke, theft, vandalism, and riot.
- *Broad Form.* Provides coverage against all the perils covered by the basic form and, in addition, covers such other perils as the weight of ice, snow, and sleet; collapse of the building; leakage or overflow of water from plumbing; and freezing of the plumbing or heating system.
- *Comprehensive Form.* Covers all the perils included in the broad form and all other perils except flood, earthquake, war, and others specifically listed in the policy. This type is sometimes referred to as an "all-risks" policy, even though some types of damage are not covered.

Flood and earthquake coverage are available in many areas and can be added to a property insurance policy.

The cost of property insurance increases with the value of the property covered and the number of perils covered. The comprehensive form includes a large number of perils and all kinds of accidental damage. Suppose, for example, you accidentally spilled a can of paint and badly stained the floor. Such damage is covered by a comprehensive form policy. As a result, the cost of comprehensive coverage is several times the cost of broad form coverage.

Home insurance policies are usually written for terms of one, three, or five years. The longer the term of insurance, the less the annual cost, so it is usually wise to get at least a three-year policy. If for any reason you want to cancel the policy, you may do so at any time. Part of the premium you paid for the insurance will be returned.

About one-third of all property losses are under $100. Because paper work on these losses is costly, many companies include a *deductible* in their policies. These deductibles usually are $100 or a larger amount and work the same way deductibles for auto insurance do.

Real estate values have increased rapidly in recent years. Property owners who have not increased their fire insurance coverage are likely to be underinsured. The value of your property should be carefully reviewed each time a policy is renewed. To help keep coverage up-to-date during the life of a policy, many companies now offer an *inflation guard endorsement*. This addition to a policy increases the coverage provided by 1 percent every 3 months.

Personal Liability Insurance

A painter may slip while painting your house and break a leg; the milk deliverer may fall on your icy walk; a neighbor's little boy may trip over your garden tools and injure himself; your dog may bite someone, either on or away from your premises; or you may hit a ball on the golf course and injure another golfer. All these instances—and many others—might result in a lawsuit and cost you a great deal of money. Liability insurance covers both the legal costs of a lawsuit brought against you and the payment of any damages for which you, your family, or your pets are responsible.

Most policies which cover public liability also contain *medical payments coverage* under which medical expenses will be paid to anyone injured while on the insured person's premises. This provides protection for your guests or for others who may not have a legal claim against you.

Homeowners' Policies

Most insurance companies offer a *homeowner's policy* that covers in one package all the usual property and liability insurance needs of the homeowner. Similar package policies tailored to the needs of renters, mobile home owners, and condominium owners are also available. A homeowners policy is, of course, more expensive than an individual fire insurance policy or a separate personal liability policy. But it may be considerably less expensive than purchasing this coverage in separate policies.

The provisions of a particular type of homeowner's policy are usually the same regardless of which company is offering it. For example, in a particular state the provisions of a homeowner's policy with broad form property coverage are likely to be identical. This make it easy to compare the rates of different companies. Studies show that the rates charged by different companies for the same coverage vary widely. Shopping to find a reliable company with low rates can produce real savings.

Checking Your Reading

1. If you are concerned about fire safety in an apartment building, what things should you check?
2. Why do key-in-the-knob type locks provide little security? What types are better?
3. List two reasons why upper-floor apartments may be more desirable than those on the ground floor.
4. What is meant by a tenancy-at-will agreement?
5. How do automatic renewal clauses work?
6. How should changes or additions to a lease be made?
7. What can tenants do if landlords fail to live up to their obligations?
8. With what types of people are mobile homes especially popular?
9. How does the way a double-wide mobile home is constructed differ from that for a single-wide?
10. How do the federal standards for mobile homes help increase fire safety?
11. How does broad form property insurance coverage differ from basic form coverage?
12. Why is comprehensive form property insurance so expensive?
13. What costs are covered by personal liability insurance?
14. How does a homeowner's policy differ from a property insurance policy?

Consumer Problems and Projects

1. Study the lease form on pages 220–221 and answer the following questions:
   a. After Marilyn and Joe moved in, the landlord told them they would have to pay $15 a month to rent a parking space. They

felt this was not fair, since they had never been told they would have to pay extra for parking. Under the terms of the lease, are they entitled to parking?

b. Joe was cold one night in September and complained about the lack of heat. Under the lease, are Marilyn and Joe entitled to heat?

c. Marilyn broke the ceiling fixture in the living room while practicing her golf swing. The landlord notified Marilyn and Joe to replace the fixture but they did nothing about it. After 3 months it was replaced by the landlord and they got a bill for $45 for the fixture and installation costs. They felt this was unfair because they had planned to make the repair the next week. Under the lease, what are the rules about the repair of damages?

d. Joe is being transferred to another town. Marilyn and Joe have decided to sublet the apartment and have located a renter. Under the lease, what are they required to do before subletting?

e. When Marilyn and Joe's lease ended, the landlord deducted $75 from their security deposit and said it was for "clean-up." Under the lease, are Marilyn and Joe entitled to a better explanation of the reasons for this charge?

f. If Marilyn and Joe decided to stay in the apartment for an extra week after the end of the lease, what rights would the landlord have under the terms of the lease?

2. How do you feel the lease form on pages 220–221 could be changed to provide more protection to tenants and still be fair to landlords? Rewrite the sections you feel should be changed. If you were a landlord, would you be willing to sign a lease which included the changes you have suggested?

3. Study the ads for apartments in your community and make a list of some of the abbreviations used. What do these abbreviations mean? Try to figure out as many as you can.

4. What characteristics do you feel are most important in an apartment? How would you weight these characteristics (use a scale of 10 for your weights, with 10 as the highest). You may want to include housing characteristics discussed in the last chapter, as well as characteristics discussed in this chapter.

5. Susan and Jack McGuire have a homeowner's policy with basic form property damage coverage. Does their policy cover the fol-

lowing types of damage (state what coverage applies in each case):

   a. The television repairperson stumbles over the dog and breaks an arm.
   b. The toilet overflows and ruins a new rug.
   c. An earthquake knocks an expensive wedding present off a shelf.
   d. A tree in the parking lot at Susan's office falls on their car.
   e. Their stereo equipment is stolen.

6. Al Williams intends to buy a house in the near future. He says that he has just examined statistics regarding the number of fires in homes in his community, and he has decided that the chances of suffering a loss due to fire are so low that he doubts that he will buy fire insurance. Discuss Al's reasoning. Do you agree with him? Why?

7. Does your family have a homeowner's policy or a property insurance policy? If so, ask your parents to let you examine the policy. What type of policy is it? What kinds of perils are covered? Does it include public liability insurance? Medical payments? Do you feel the amount of coverage is adequate? What is the term of the policy? Are savings possible by going to a longer term? If your family does not have any household insurance, what kind of policy do you feel would be appropriate? What kind of coverage should it include?

8. What are the recent trends in the apartment and mobile home markets? Prepare a report on either apartments or mobile homes discussing such topics as (a) trends in number and types being constructed, (b) factors influencing consumers' demand for this type of housing, (c) the effects of government programs on the supply and demand for this type of housing, (d) design features which are currently popular or sought after, and (e) trends in prices. Can you observe any of these trends in your own community? Consult the Readers' Guide to Periodical Literature for useful references.

14

Buying a House

Most young people hope to own their own home someday. In recent years rapid increases in the prices of houses have made this goal more and more difficult to reach. In the late 1970s the typical new one-family house was a one-story ranch style with three bedrooms which cost around $50,000.

Because house prices are so high, few families who buy either new or older homes are able to pay cash for them. Most families instead make a cash down payment and borrow the rest of the money needed. Their mortgage loans require monthly payments for a period of many years.

The process of buying a house is a complicated one. It involves a lot of decisions, complex legal arrangements, and financial commitments which will go on for years. In this chapter, we will look at each of the different steps in buying a house in the order they arise in a typical purchase.

DECIDING WHAT YOU CAN AFFORD

The first step in buying a house is deciding how much you can afford to pay. In the past many real estate salespeople and lenders have used

232

rules of thumb to advise families on how much they safely could spend. One frequently used rule of thumb was that a family could afford a house which cost 2½ times its annual income. They said, for example, a family with an annual income of $14,000 could afford a $35,000 house.

Rules of thumb such as this one are out-of-date and probably should be disregarded. They were developed years ago when such operating costs as property taxes and fuel costs were low. A safer and more up-do-date approach is to look at your total budget and then decide how much you can devote to housing, including operating costs. This is the approach we discussed in Chapter 12. Using this approach, you can calculate what monthly payments you can afford. Based on this you can estimate how big a mortgage you could handle and an appropriate price range to look at.

SHOPPING FOR A HOUSE

In Chapter 12 we discussed some of the things which you might want to take into account in judging a neighborhood and a community as a place to live. We also considered some of the things you should look for in the layout and equipping of a place to live.

In buying a house, there are some additional concerns. These include the site of the house, the quality of the construction, the facilities provided, and the general condition of the house.

Few houses will get top marks in all these categories. Some sort of compromise is always necessary. One house you like may be more expensive but in good condition, while another house may need paint and a new roof but costs a good deal less. In situations like this, you will need to decide whether the condition of the first house justifies its extra cost. It may be that the second house, even with the expense of extra repairs, is a better bargain.

Site

One of the first things about a house you will want to check is its site. Is the site well drained and safe from flooding? Many homes are built in valleys or low-lying areas where there is danger of flooding in rainy weather. Although such areas are poorly suited for houses, developers have built homes on them because the land was cheap.

Only recently have communities begun to develop zoning plans that prohibit building in areas that are likely to be flooded or are poorly drained. A check for watermarks on basement walls will provide some clues about past flooding problems.

You should also check to see if the ground on which the house is built is firm and stable. When homes are built on filled land or in swampy areas, foundations and walls may crack as the house settles. Serious settling problems may eventually break water lines and damage the basic structure of the house. Special attention also needs to be given to the stability of houses built on steep hillsides. You can check for excessive settling by placing a marble on an uncarpeted floor and watching to see if it rolls.

The position of the house on the lot also deserves attention. How is the house placed in relation to the movement of the sun? Will hot afternoon sun pour into picture windows and make the house uncomfortably hot? How will the movement of the summer sun affect the use of porches and patios? Patios and porches on the west side of the house are likely to be too warm in the afternoon unless there is shade.

Another question is the placement of the house in relation to typical

Trees that shade a house from the sun are not only aesthetic but also can affect cost by reducing the need for air conditioning in hot weather. (*Kip Peticolas*)

wind patterns. The house should be positioned to take advantage of summer breezes. It should also have entries sheltered from driving rain and blowing snow.

The landscaping provided also deserves some attention. Are there trees that will shade the house from the heat of the summer sun? This will make the house more comfortable and reduce the need for air conditioning.

Construction

The foundation of the house is its basic underpinning. It is essential that it be strong and well constructed. Signs of settling and cracks are evidence of possible problems. Hairline cracks are generally no cause for concern, but larger cracks are.

Basements should be dry. Wet walls may be the result of condensation—this can be cured with better ventilation or a dehumidifier. Wet walls can also be the result of seepage from the outside—a more serious problem. Seepage sometimes can be controlled with better rain gutters and drains. If the problem is serious, it may be necessary to dig out the earth around foundation walls, apply waterproofing, and drainage tile. If the house is in a wet, low-lying area, even these steps may not solve the problem.

Floors and Walls. To prevent squeaking and swaying, floors should be built with *cross bridging*. These are cross braces nailed in an X shape between the beams supporting the floor. These braces can be seen when you look up at the floor from the basement. You can judge the sturdiness of a wooden floor by jumping up and down in the middle of a large room. The floor should not give or sway noticeably.

The interior walls of most newer homes are plasterboard rather than plaster. Using plasterboard, or dry wall as it is often called, can cause several problems. It is relatively thin and weak, and holes can easily be punched through it by accident. When green lumber is used for the studding inside the wall, the nails used to install the dry wall tend to pop out, creating bumps. The joints between dry wall panels will show if the installation has been poorly finished.

Insulation and Moisture Control. Rising heating and cooling costs make insulation more important then ever. Attic floors should have at least 6 inches (in) [15 centimeters (cm)] of insulation, but more is better. A quick check of the attic will tell you how much insulation there

The insulation of a house will affect heating and cooling costs. An attic floor, which is easily checked, should have at least six inches of insulation. (*Owens/Corning*)

is and whether it was applied carefully. Was it applied evenly and pushed into corners and cracks? Wall insulation is important too. Many older homes were built without insulation in the walls and its installation would be expensive. In colder weather you can check wall insulation by touching the outside wall of a room and comparing its temperature to an inside wall.

Peeling paint on outside walls can be a sign of a serious construction problem. It often is a result of moisture condensing inside exterior walls in cold weather. This occurs when warm, moist air from the interior of the house hits the cold surface of the outside wall. Condensation inside exterior walls can be controlled by the installation of *vapor barriers.* These are materials that prevent the movement of water vapor and should be installed when a house is built. Vapor barriers may be a layer of vapor-proof paper or foil on one side of the insulation, or they may be a separate sheet of plastic.

If vapor barriers have not been used or the ones used are inadequate, it may be necessary to install vents to the outside of the roof and walls. This installation can be expensive and complicated. When condensation is not controlled, it will be necessary to repaint every year or two and damage from wood rot and decay may occur.

Construction Standards.   It is difficult for the average home buyer to judge the quality of the construction in a house. Local building codes provide buyers with some protection. *Building codes* are local regulations which set standards covering the construction, remodeling, and upkeep of buildings. They set down specific requirements covering such things as design and installation of the wiring and plumbing and the strength of construction. Not all local governments have building codes, and many communities do not enforce their codes strictly. Strict codes which are strictly enforced ensure that minimum strength, safety, and health requirements are met.

Many of the houses built in recent years have been constructed to meet the standards of the Federal Housing Administration (FHA). FHA standards are requirements which must be met for a house to be eligible for an FHA-insured mortgage loan. Like building codes, FHA standards are minimum requirements.

Another type of protection is provided by the guarantees which are available with some new and older houses. One plan for new homes is the Home Owners Warranty (HOW) developed by the National Association of Home Builders. This guarantee provides 10-year protection against construction defects and other problems. The cost of this protection is paid by the builder and included in the price of the house. Several different companies offer similar protection to buyers of older houses. Like all guarantees, these should be checked carefully so that you know exactly what is being promised.

Facilities

The cost of heat is a major operating expense for households in most parts of the country. Operating costs are affected both by the efficiency of the heating system and by the soundness of a house's construction and insulation. In older homes you can get some idea of costs by asking about the previous year's fuel bills. You may want to double-check them with the fuel company's records.

Heating Systems. Gas and oil are the two most widely used heating fuels. In recent years, electric heat has been installed in many new homes. Builders like electric heat because installation costs are lower than for gas or oil heat. Operating costs for electric heat may be high unless houses are specially insulated and local electricity rates are low.

Electrical Systems. In the chapter on appliances, we noted the substantial increase in recent years in the number of appliances we own and use. The wiring of many houses, both old and new, is not adequate to handle this load. Both the total amount of current available and the number of circuits available to distribute are important.

The total current available is determined by the electrical service entrance. Today minimum service is considered 100 A (amperes) with both 120-V (volt) circuits (for lighting and small appliances) and 240-V circuits (for electric ranges, water heaters, large air conditioners, and electric heat). An entrance of 150 or 200 A is needed for houses with an electric range and electric heating or air conditioning. Some older houses have only 60-A entrances. The electrical-entrance capacity is usually indicated on the fuse box.

Most houses have only six separate electric circuits but need at least eight to ten. The number of separate circuits can be determined by counting the number of fuses (or circuit breakers) in the fuse box. There will be one fuse for each 120-V circuit and two for each 240-V circuit. If the total number of circuits is inadequate, individual circuits will become overloaded, fuses will blow frequently, and appliances

The electrical system of a house can be checked by examining the circuit breaker or fuse box. Electrical-entrance capacity is usually marked on the box, and the number of separate circuits is shown by the number of circuit breakers or fuses in the box. (Edison Electric Institute)

may not work properly. In extreme cases wiring may become danger-ously overheated.

Plumbing. Inadequate water pressure is a frequent and annoying problem. When water pressure is low, shower temperatures can sud-denly become too hot or too cold when faucets are turned on or toilets flushed in another part of the house. To check for low water pressure, turn all the tub and sink faucets on fully and then flush the toilet. If the water pressure is good, the flow of water will not vary too much.

Condition

Houses in good condition, with fresh paint and attractive lawns and shrubs, usually command top prices and are in short supply. Home buyers are likely to find that the available choices need some repairs or redecoration. The costs of needed work should be considered care-fully. Interior and exterior painting can be done on a do-it-yourself basis for a few hundred dollars. Refinishing floors may require expert help and will be more expensive. Replacing carpeting and vinyl floor-ing is a major expense. Estimates of the costs involved are a good idea.

In looking over the condition of the interior, you should check for signs of paint stained and plaster damaged by water leakage. Such damage may be a result of a leaky roof or leaky plumbing. In either case, it is a sign of a serious problem.

Before agreement is reached on a purchase, the house should be inspected to ensure that it is termite-free. Termites are a particular problem in the Southeast and in California. They also are a serious concern in the Middle Atlantic states, the Middle West, and South-west. The inspection should be made by experts (many mortgage lenders require this). Termites can move through cracks in concrete foundations and slabs and can be a problem in all types of houses.

MAKING A SALES AGREEMENT

When you have found a house you would like to buy, the next step is reaching an agreement on price with the owner. This will involve some bargaining. Few sellers expect to get what they ask. Typical home buyers may be uncertain about how well they have judged the condition of the house and whether the price is a fair one. They can get expert help with these questions by hiring their own appraiser to inspect the house and report on its condition and a fair price for it.

After the seller and buyer have agreed on the terms of the sale, a

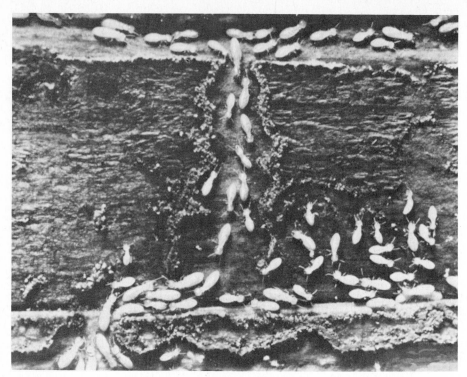

Termites can be a problem in all types of houses. Many mortgage lenders require professional termite inspection before they agree to finance a house. (*Wide World Photos*)

written contract setting down these terms is prepared. This contract or *sales agreement* covers the following items:

- The purchase price.
- The legal description of the property and any fixtures, appliances, and equipment which are included.
- The date the buyer may take possession.
- A promise by the seller to provide the deed and a marketable title (i.e., a title to the property clear of claims by others).
- An agreement about how taxes, water bills, and other charges will be divided.
- Other agreements in connection with the sale. This may include an agreement that completion of the sale will depend on the buyer's ability to get a mortgage loan, or on the results of the termite inspection.

Experts feel that the sales agreement is the most risky step in buying a house and that is the step at which a lawyer's help is needed the most. There are many possible pitfalls which should be covered by the sales agreement. For example, what happens if the house burns down after you have agreed to buy it, but before the sale is completed?

ARRANGING A MORTGAGE

The next step in home buying is to shop for a mortgage. A *mortgage* is a loan contract in which the lender agrees to lend a specified amount of money at a specified interest rate. The borrower agrees to repay according to the terms of the contract and pledges the property purchased as security for the loan. If the borrower fails to repay the loan, the lender has the legal right to *foreclose*, that is, to obtain possession of the property.

Ordinary mortgages have only two parties involved, the borrower and the lender. In some states a *deed of trust* (also called a *trust deed* or *trust indenture*) is used instead of a mortgage. If a deed of trust is used, the borrower gives control of the property to a third party, a trustee, as security for the mortgage loan. When the debt is paid, control of the property is returned to the borrower. If the borrower fails to keep up payments, the trustee has power to sell the property so as to repay the lender. This arrangement is used in California, Illinois, and Virginia and in several other states.

Mortgage loans are usually repaid on the *amortization plan*. This type of arrangement provides for repayment in uniform monthly installments covering both interest and principal. As the loan is paid off, the amount charged for interest decreases and the amount used to pay off the principal increases. The size of the monthly payments is determined by the amount borrowed, length of the loan, and interest rate.

The amount of money you can borrow will depend on your credit rating and income and on the value of the home you are mortgaging. Before you can obtain a mortgage loan of any size, the lender will want to be sure that title to the property is clear, that you will keep the property covered by insurance and in good condition, and that you will pay the taxes promptly.

Types of Home Mortgage Loans

There are four basic types of home mortgage loans available: conventional loans, Federal Housing Administration (FHA) loans, Veterans Administration (VA) loans, and Farmers Home Administration (FmHA) loans. The four types vary in the amount of down payment required, length of the repayment period, and interest charges.

Conventional Loans.   Conventional loans are the most common type of home mortgage loans. Such loans involve only two parties, the lender and the borrower. They are made on the basis of the borrower's credit rating and the value of the house pledged as security. Because of the risks involved to the lender, the down payments required for conventional loans are larger (20 to 25 percent) than those required for FHA, VA, and FmHA loans. The repayment periods for conventional loans usually are shorter than those for FHA, VA, and FmHA loans. The usual repayment period is 20 to 25 years.

Conventional loans with low down payments (5 to 10 percent of the sales price) are available to some borrowers if the risk to lenders is insured by a private mortgage insurer. The Mortgage Guaranty Insurance Corp. (MGIC) is the best-known company offering this insurance. Borrowers pay a small monthly fee for this protection.

FHA-insured Loans.   FHA-insured loans currently make up a relatively small percent of all home mortgages. FHA insurance protects lenders against bad-debt losses. FHA loan insurance was developed to make it possible for people to purchase homes with only a small down payment and low monthly payments. Because lenders are protected against loss by the FHA, they are willing to accept low down payments, charge a lower interest rate, and permit long repayment periods (up to 30 to 35 years). A small monthly fee is charged borrowers to insure their loan.

VA-guaranteed Loans.   Loans guaranteed by the Veterans Administration make up a small proportion of all home mortgage loans. These loans, often called *GI loans*, were developed to make it possible for veterans to purchase homes for little or no down payment and low monthly payments. By protecting private lenders against loss, VA loans permit low interest rates, long repayment periods (up to 30 years), and lower down payments. Borrowers are not charged for this guarantee.

Farmers Home Administration.   In recent years the Farmers Home Administration (FmHA) has helped arrange almost as many loans as the FHA or the VA. FmHA, which is an agency of the U.S. Department of Agriculture, makes loans only in rural areas and in small towns. Its loans are available to low and moderate-income families who are unable to obtain mortgages from other sources, but would be able to meet monthly mortgage payments and operating expenses.

Loans are available, without down payment, for terms up to 33 years at interest rates somewhat below those for conventional mortgages. Information on these loans is available from FmHA offices located in most county seat towns.

Terms of Home Mortgage Loans

Home buyers need to shop for mortgage loans for the same reasons other borrowers need to shop for credit. Shopping for mortgage loans is, however, somewhat more complicated. Different lenders offer different interest rates, have different down payment requirements, and lend for different lengths of time.

Interest Rates. Because mortgage loans are made for long periods of time, small differences in interest rates can have a major effect on the total interest paid over the life of a loan. In Table 14-1 you can see, for example, that a difference of one-half of 1 percent results in a difference of several thousand dollars in the total interest paid on a typical mortgage loan.

The interest rates charged for conventional mortgage loans are influenced by the state of the loan market. If funds for long-term loans such as home mortgage loans are in short supply, interest rates will be high. This was the case in the 1970s when interest rates of 8 and 9 percent were common, in contrast to rates of 5 and 6 percent just a few years before.

TABLE 14-1
Effect of Different Interest Rates on the Cost of a $30,000 Loan Over a 25-Year Period

Interest Rate (percent)	Monthly Payment (including principal and interest)	Total Interest Paid Over 25-Year Loan Period
7	$212.04	$33,612
7½	221.70	36,510
8	231.55	39,465
8½	241.57	42,471
9	251.76	45,528
9½	262.11	48,633
10	272.62	51,786
10½	283.26	54,978
11	294.04	58,212

The maximum interest rates on conventional mortgage loans are set by law in most states. The VA and FHA also set maximum interest rates on the mortgage loans they guarantee. When money is scarce, lenders may consider these rates too low and charge a premium or "points" to make a loan. This increases their return on the loan without violating the law. A *point* is a one-time charge made at the time a loan is arranged. It is equal to 1 percent of the total mortgage loan. A two-point charge on a $20,000 mortgage loan would be $400.

Points affect the lender's return from the loan in much the same way charging a higher interest rate would. To avoid violating the law, the lenders require the seller to pay the extra charge for points. Even though sellers pay the extra charge, buyers are affected because sellers will probably increase the price that they ask.

Length of Loan Period.   Longer loan periods reduce the size of the monthly payments required. At first glance, they may seem desirable. Borrowers need to keep in mind that the total interest paid on a loan increases rapidly as the loan period is lengthened. As you can see in the table below, lengthening the period of a loan from 20 to 25 years increases the total interest paid by about 30 percent. You should also note that the total interest paid over 20 years on this loan is greater than the principal borrowed.

Increasing the monthly payment by just a few dollars can cut the length of a mortgage a good deal. As you can see in Table 14-2, by increasing the monthly payments from $220.13 to $250.94, the length of this mortgage is cut by 10 years.

Down Payment.   The larger the down payment made, the less a home buyer needs to borrow. When the amount borrowed is smaller, total interest costs will be less. A larger down payment may also be useful in obtaining a more favorable interest rate, since the risk to the lender is reduced. Although large down payments have important advantages, home buyers need to keep back enough money to cover closing costs. In addition, they also should have a reserve for emergencies.

Sources of Home Mortgage Loans

There are several sources of home mortgage loans. Although all lending institutions make the same types of loans, they do have different lending practices and policies. You should be familiar with a few basic

TABLE 14-2

Effect of Different Loan Periods on the Cost of a $30,000 Loan at 8 Percent

Length of Loan Period (years)	Monthly Payment (including principal and interest)	Total Interest Paid Over Loan Period
5	$608.30	$ 6,498.00
10	363.99	13,678.80
15	286.70	21,606.00
20	250.94	30,225.60
25	231.55	39,465.00
30	220.13	49,246.80

characteristics of each lender. The lending institutions that offer home mortgage loans include the following:

- *Savings and Loan Associations.* Savings and loan associations are permitted to lend a relatively large proportion of the appraised value of a property. The repayment periods usually are a maximum of 30 years. They handle FHA and VA loans as well as conventional loans.
- *Mortgage Bankers.* Mortgage bankers are a relatively new source for mortgage loans. They have connections with many other sources of credit, including banks, insurance companies, and pension funds. They lend the money initially but usually sell their interest within a month or so to another lender.
- *Commercial Banks.* For conventional loans, commercial banks generally require relatively large down payments and limit the repayment period to 20 to 25 years. When banks make FHA-insured loans, they will lend a higher percentage of the property value.
- *Savings Banks.* Savings banks are licensed to operate in a number of states, chiefly in the Northeast, and are an important source of credit for home mortgage loans. State laws vary, but usually savings banks can lend from 60 to 90 percent of the purchase price of the property and can offer the borrower up to 30 years to repay. They handle conventional, FHA, and VA loans.
- *Life Insurance Companies.* For conventional loans, life insurance companies require relatively large down payments but permit long repayment periods. They also make FHA and VA loans.
- *Mortgage Brokers.* Mortgage brokers are firms or individuals who, like mortgage bankers, assist the prospective borrower in locating a lender. But unlike mortgage bankers, they lend no money. They merely act as a go-between to help a prospective borrower and a lender get together.

SETTLEMENT ARRANGEMENTS

The final step in buying a house is the completion of the sale. This step is called the *settlement* or *closing*. At this step, the seller is paid and title to the property passes to the buyer. If a mortgage loan is involved, the lender and buyer together pay the seller and the mortgage goes into effect.

Settlement Costs

At settlement there are a number of charges which the home buyer must pay. These charges are often substantial, ranging from a few hundred dollars to a thousand dollars or more, and often catch home buyers by surprise. Recent federal legislation has made it easier for home buyers to know what to expect. It requires lenders to provide an estimate of the *settlement costs* (also called *closing costs*) within 3 days after a mortgage application is made and to provide all the information which is available just before the final settlement day.

Settlement costs will include some or all of the following items:

- *Charges in Connection with the Loan.* These charges may include an appraiser's fee for checking the property to make certain it is good security for the mortgage loan and a fee for a credit report on the buyer. They also may include payments into an *escrow account*, an account from which the lender pays property taxes and insurance. There also may be origination fees to cover the lender's costs in processing the loan. "Points" charged on the mortgage also are collected at this time.
- *Payments to the Seller.* Under most sales agreements, buyers are expected to pay sellers for any taxes or utility bills which have been paid in advance and will cover part of the period they will occupy the property.
- *Title Charges.* These charges include the cost of an *abstract* or *title search*, which is a check of official property records to make certain that the seller has an acceptable title to the property. Some lenders require *title insurance* to protect themselves against loss in case of errors in property records or title search. Buyers who want to be protected against such problems will have to get a separate policy to protect themselves.
- *Government Charges.* These include government fees for recording the deed and the mortgage in official property records. Local governments, counties, and states also charge taxes on the transfer of property.
- *Other Charges.* Additional charges include the costs of a survey and fees for inspections, such as termite inspection. Attorneys' fees for preparing and checking the legal documents covering the sale and mortgage also are paid at settlement.

Houses are one of the most complicated purchases we make. In this chapter we have touched on some of the key things you should know when buying a house. There are many other important and useful things to know. When the time comes for you to buy a house, you will need to do some careful reading, studying, and questioning to get ready for the decisions you will have to make.

Checking Your Reading

1. Why are rules of thumb about how expensive a house a family can afford based only on its income now considered out-of-date?
2. Discuss four things about the site of a house that should be considered when judging it.
3. What should you look for when examining the basement or foundation of a house? Why?
4. What is meant by cross bridging? Why is it important?
5. Discuss the problems that can occur when plasterboard is used in a house.
6. Why are vapor barriers installed in houses? If vapor barriers have not been installed, what problems can occur?
7. What is considered to be minimum electrical service in homes today? When a house has an electric range and electric heat or air conditioning, what entrance is needed?
8. Describe an easy way to check for low water pressure in a house.
9. What items should be included in a sales agreement?
10. How do a regular mortgage and a deed of trust differ?
11. Under most amortization plans, the amount of money that goes to pay off the mortgage loan increases and the amount paid for interest decreases as payments are made. Why is this true?
12. How do FHA and VA loans differ from conventional loans?
13. Explain why FHA loans can be made with lower down payments, lower interest rates, and longer repayment periods.
14. Who is eligible for FmHA loans?
15. Some lenders charge points to make a loan. What are they? Explain how they work.
16. What is the difference between mortgage bankers and mortgage brokers?
17. What happens at settlement, or closing?

Consumer Problems and Projects

1. Tony and Terry DiRinaldo have been renting an apartment for which they are paying $250 a month with all utilities except phone included. They would like to buy a house and feel that this amount is about the most they could afford to spend for housing. They have seen a house they could buy with a $30,000 mortgage loan at 9 percent for 25 years. How much would the monthly payment on this loan be (use Table 14-1)? Do you feel this house would be a wise choice for Tony and Terry? State your reasons.

2. Janie and Jack Hampton have found a house they would like to buy for $35,000. An FHA mortgage will require only $1,750 down. Jack wants to use all their $5000 in savings as a down payment to reduce interest costs. Janie wants to put down only the required minimum. What would you recommend and why?

3. Joan and Vic Weaver are trying to decide whether to apply for a 20-year or a 30-year mortgage loan. If they were considering a $30,000 loan at 8 percent, what would the difference in interest cost be (use Table 14-2)? Which choice would you recommend and why?

4. Prepare a table comparing conventional loans, FHA loans, VA loans, and FmHA loans. How do they compare in terms of down payment requirements, interest rates, and length of loan period? Also indicate if there are any special requirements a borrower must meet to be eligible for a loan.

5. How does your family's house or the place you live rate on the tests discussed in this chapter? Make a test report on the following: watermarks and cracks in basement walls, the marble test, floor jump test, wall insulation test, fuse box check, and toilet flush test.

6. Prepare a report on one of the following topics:
   Condominiums
   Deception in the sale of leisure home property
   Federal Housing Administration
   U.S. Department of Housing and Urban Development
   Open housing laws—Laws to ensure equal housing opportunity
   Federal government activities affecting housing from 1934 to the present
   Local housing laws—building codes, housing codes, and zoning

15

Choosing Furniture

When we set out to buy furnishings, we need to consider what we want our home to be like and what we want it to do for us. Is it to be a center of family life with a place for the hobbies and activities of everyone in the family? Do we prefer a casual life-style or a more formal one? How important is impressing others?

Sometimes the opinions of family members conflict. Recently one girl complained that after her mother got all-white furniture for the living room, the family was never permitted to enter the room except when there was company. According to the girl, her mother even went so far as to keep a rope across the door and take it down only when the doorbell rang. The girl summed up her views: "It was like living in a museum." Do you think it was worth it?

In judging furniture, we need to consider how well it meets our goals and values, and we also need to judge it on three other criteria:

1. Does each piece look attractive by itself and do the pieces go well together?
2. Are they appropriate for the place we live?
3. Will they give good service and value for the price paid?

In this chapter, we will consider how to judge furniture on all of these counts.

TURNING GOALS INTO A PLAN

In Chapter 12 we introduced the idea of the *family life cycle*, the stages in the development of a family beginning with the forming of a new household by young singles followed by the beginning of a family at marriage. The same changes in the size and makeup of the family that affect housing needs also affect furniture needs. Because of the differences in the makeup of families at different life cycle stages, there are important differences in what they need and want.

In the first two family life cycle stages, young singles and newlyweds need to assemble basic furniture for their new home. Because they usually have time and money available for leisure activities, they often buy televisions, stereo sets, and equipment for entertaining guests. With the birth of children the family moves to the third life cycle stage. Families with young children need to provide furniture and play space for them. Because they want increased play space, many families buy houses at this stage and need additional furnishings for them. The needs of young families often outrun incomes, and families at this stage usually are heavy users of consumer credit.

Older families with children often are concerned about making their home an attractive place for their children to bring friends and entertain. They may find they need to replace furniture that they bought earlier. Special family interests often lead to the purchase of pianos, Ping-Pong and billiard tables, and sports equipment that all need a place in the home.

Setting Up Housekeeping

Just how much does it cost for a young person or a young couple to set up housekeeping on their own? A rough estimate is that the basic furniture for a one-bedroom apartment would cost about $2000. For this amount it would be possible to buy new, good-quality items that would be both durable and attractive. The $2000 estimate does not include many items most young people might want. The living room furnishings include a sofa, one chair, two end tables, two lamps, a 9 by 12 ft rug [2.7 by 3.6 m], and draperies. For another $1000 other desirable items could be added. For the living room this would include a portable color TV set, a second upholstered chair, a coffee table, and a floor lamp. Dishes, cooking equipment, bed linens, and towels are not included in the estimate. We can see from this estimate that furnishing even a small apartment can be expensive. Many people, of course, spend less. To cut costs they have to rely on second-hand purchases, gifts, and things they make themselves.

Few young people are likely to be able to afford all the furniture they want right away. This makes it especially important for them to decide what they need first and plan a program of purchases. Such a plan has several advantages. It will help them move toward their goals more easily and quickly. It may also help them decide that they do not need to buy everything right away on credit and run the risk of building up large installment debts. A plan will also help in judging whether the overall goal is realistic.

In recent years the furniture industry has begun to think more about the special needs of young adults and has begun to design more furniture suited to their limited budgets and small living spaces. Multipurpose furniture, fold-up and nesting tables, and tall, vertical storage pieces all have been designed to save floor space.

Some young people save money by buying used furniture. Pieces that are still sturdy can be made usable with new slipcovers or a coat or two of paint. Unfinished furniture also may provide an opportunity for savings. Other young people may prefer to make their own furniture from low-cost materials. Some examples are bookcases made with bricks and boards, desks made from a door placed on top of a pair of

In recent years stores have begun to stock more multipurpose furniture designed to meet the needs of young adults with limited floor space. (*Kip Peticolas*)

two-drawer file cabinets, and coffee tables and end tables made with electric cable spools. In estimating the real cost of used and unfinished pieces, we need to include the cost of finishing materials and the value of our time along with the prices of the pieces themselves.

Learning About Good Design

Understanding good design can help us choose furnishings that are attractive and look good when combined. Two general goals guide the best designs, whether they are of individual furniture pieces or entire rooms.

The first goal is that the form or shape of an item should follow or grow out of its purpose or uses. In judging furniture against this goal, we must realize that most items have several uses or functions. Chairs are not just for sitting; they should also be pleasing to look at and should provide durable, economical service. There are many different ways these different functions can be provided. Good design provides them all.

The second goal of good design is providing variety within a unified whole. This means that a total design should include interesting and varied features, such as varied colors, textures, and shapes. These varied features should be chosen so that they all make up a unified, total design. Drawer pulls on chests and dressers, for example, should be related to the design of the piece and should not look as if they were stuck on as an afterthought.

Choosing a Furniture Style. One of the first things furniture shoppers are likely to think about is choosing a furniture style. The choice is complicated by the wide variety of styles available. They range from copies of furniture dating back hundreds of years to the newest modern styles. Furniture styles fall into two broad groups: traditional and modern. Traditional styles copy or are based on the designs of the past. This group includes such styles as Early American and Spanish-Mediterranean. Modern styles are simple, straightforward designs without carving or other decorations.

There are formal and informal styles in both these groups. The informal styles look heavier and sturdier. Their finishes are duller and sometimes are antiqued or distressed to look like they are worn with age. The upholstery fabrics used are rough or nubby. Oak, pine, and maple are among the woods often used for informal styles.

The formal styles are lighter and more delicate-looking. Their

There are two broad groups of furniture styles. Traditional styles, such as the bed on the left, are based on the designs of the past. Modern styles, like the bed on the right, are simple designs without carving or other decorations. (*Left, The Lane Co.; right, Aquabed, New York, NY*)

finishes are smooth and polished. Upholstery fabrics include delicate-looking velvets and silks. Mahogany, walnut, and highly polished metal are often used in formal styles.

Early American is one of the more informal traditional styles. Most Spanish-Mediterranean and French Provincial furniture is informal, but some designs with refined lines and polished finishes are more formal. Traditional English styles such as Queen Anne and Chippendale are rather formal. Among the modern styles, Danish Modern is informal, while designs using highly polished chrome and glass tend to be formal.

When we are choosing a furniture style, we should keep the life-style we prefer in mind. People that like a more casual, relaxed life-style probably will feel more comfortable with furniture in an informal style. The sturdier lines and fabrics of informal styles are also well-suited for active families and families with young children.

Applying the Rules of Design. The rules of design apply both to choosing individual pieces of furniture and to combining them to furnish a room. Furniture should serve its intended use well. Upholstered furniture should be comfortable. Dressers and other storage pieces should have designs that emphasize useful storage space, not fancy carvings.

Furnishings should "go together" well. A room can be unified by repeating colors, upholstery fabrics, and furniture styles. Most designers think the typical home interior is too varied with too many different and unrelated colors, patterns, and textures.

Furniture must also be chosen with the size of room in which it will be used in mind. Most young poeple live in a few small rooms. They also move frequently. This makes smaller-size pieces especially useful. Triple dressers, king-size beds, large stereo-television consoles, and extra-long sofas are likely to be hard to get through doorways and up stairs. They may be even more of a problem when we have to find a place for them in a small room.

There are a number of places furniture shoppers can get design help. In deciding on a furniture style and color choices, the interior design books available in most libraries and the home furnishings magazines are helpful. Many larger stores have interior designers who will give free advice on simple problems. They also will develop designs for entire rooms when all the purchases are made through their store. Furniture manufacturers have tried to help by developing color-coordinated upholstery fabrics that look attractive in combination.

FURNITURE CONSTRUCTION

In judging any piece of furniture, we should first begin with a general inspection of the piece. Does it stand evenly on the floor without wobbling? When moved or lifted, does it feel rigid and well-made, or does it sag or sway? Is the finish of the exposed wood parts smooth and evenly applied? Are the seams of the upholstery neatly sewed and even? Are the patterns of the upholstery matched well at the seams? Exterior appearance provides important clues to the overall quality of the piece. However, to fully judge furniture quality, we need to learn how to look beneath the surface.

Case Goods

In the furniture trade, furniture pieces are classed in two groups: case goods and upholstered pieces. *Case goods* are all-wood pieces such as chests, dressers, and desks, while the upholstered group includes sofas and upholstered chairs.

Construction—Frames and Joints. We can get a better look at the way case goods are built by removing a drawer and looking at the interior. Case goods, we can see from the interior, are made of flat sheets, or panels, that are fastened together and to a supporting frame. The frame is the skeleton of a piece and gives it strength and support. Books and articles on furniture buying often suggest that hardwood is a better choice for frames than softwoods, such as pine. Either is acceptable as long as the frame is strong enough to support the piece. Wood used in the frame should be free of knots. It also should be kiln-dried to help prevent warping and shrinking.

Strongly made joints are important for holding the frame together firmly. Interlocking joints should be used to join the pieces of the frame, since they are stronger than butt joints. Butt joints are made by placing or butting the end of one piece of wood against the end of another. There are several kinds of interlocking joints. Mortise and tenon joints and double-dowel joints are two of the strongest.

The pieces of the frame should be glued neatly together at the joint. Nails should not be used because they cannot hold frame pieces together as rigidly as glue can. Important joints should be reinforced with corner blocks. These are wedge-shaped pieces of wood glued into the angle formed by the two frame pieces which are being joined. Large corner blocks should be held in place by screws as well as glued. Without a strong frame and strong joints, a piece can break apart quickly. When a joint or the frame breaks and is not repaired, other joints and parts of the frame are strained. They are likely to break too. Soon all that is left is a pile of high-priced splinters.

Panel Materials. The sides and top of case goods are fastened to the frame. Years ago these pieces, which are called panels, were made of solid wood. These days very little furniture is made of solid wood. Instead, most panels are veneered. Veneer panels are built up of thin plies of wood glued together over a core material. Panels with four plies plus a core are used for tabletops or other important surfaces. Drawer bottoms and the back panels on pieces are usually two plies plus a core. Veneer panels have advantages over solid wood. They are less likely to swell, crack, or warp. They also are less expensive.

The Federal Trade Commission has a number of rules covering the way panel materials can be described. Terms such as "solid maple" should be used only when all the exposed surfaces are made of solid pieces of the wood named. When veneer has been used in making a piece, this should be made clear. For example, a piece made with solid walnut legs and walnut veneer panels, should be described as "walnut veneered construction," or as "walnut solids and veneers."

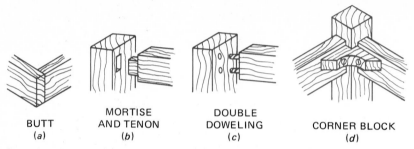

| BUTT
(a) | MORTISE
AND TENON
(b) | DOUBLE
DOWELING
(c) | CORNER BLOCK
(d) |

Strongly made joints are an important factor determining the quality of a piece of furniture. Interlocking joints (mortise and tenon or double-dowel) are stronger than butt joints. Important joints should be reinforced with corner blocks.

The FTC rules also require that when one wood is finished to look like another, this must be made clear. For example, birch stained to look like maple should be described as "maple color" or "maple stain finish." The use of plastic finished to look like wood also must be indicated. Plastic is widely used for table tops and the tops of other case goods. Plastic, particularly polystyrene, also is used to imitate wood carvings and door panels. Well-made plastic parts look so much like wood they often are hard to detect. The chief problems with plastic parts are that they are difficult to repair when cracked or scratched and that the color match with real wood may not be quite perfect. The use of plastic parts should not be regarded as an attempt to trick the consumer. Good-quality plastic tops are durable and can provide more protection against spills than wood. Plastic imitation wood carvings help cut costs. What is important is to make sure plastic parts are well made and clearly labeled.

Drawer Construction.   The construction of drawers often provides useful indications of quality. Drawers should pull out smoothly and close easily. They should fit closely without being either too loose or too tight. High-quality furniture has glued dovetail joints joining all four drawer sides. The bottom panel of the drawer should be fitted tightly in grooves and held firmly in place with small glued corner blocks. Some lower-quality furniture is made without interlocking joints on the drawer sides. In such pieces, rabbet joints are used along with nails or staples instead of glue. Drawers made in this way are not as rigid as those with glued dovetail joints. They are more likely to jam or pull out less smoothly and evenly. Drawers should have center or side guides of hardwood; softwood is too likely to wear over time.

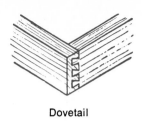
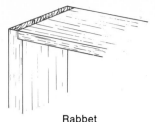

Dovetail   Rabbet

High-quality furniture has glued dovetail joints at all four corners
of the drawers, while some lower-quality furniture has rabbet
joints secured with nails or staples.

Durable drawer guides can also be made of metal or plastic. The
interior surfaces of drawers should be smoothly finished. In better-
quality furniture they are waxed or lacquered. In better-quality case
goods the spaces between drawers are separated by dust panels.

Finish. The final finish on wood surfaces should be smooth and
evenly applied with no runs or drips. The wood tones should be uniform over the entire piece rather than spotty or uneven. Most interior
designers prefer finishes through which the grain is clearly visible
rather than finishes that hide the grain. High-quality pieces have a
smooth, almost silky finish, while low-quality pieces have rougher
surfaces. One of the indications of a top-quality piece is that the back
and other less visible parts are neatly stained and smoothly finished.

Upholstered Pieces

Judging quality in upholstered furniture is more difficult than in case
goods because the outer covering hides the basic construction of the
piece. A strong frame and joints is just as important for upholstered
goods as it is for case goods. The basic frame of an upholstered piece
should be made of knot-free, kiln-dried wood. Interlocking glued
joints, either mortise and tenon or doweled, should be used in the
frame, reinforced with glued corner blocks or metal plates.

Seat and Back Construction. Several different types of springs are
used in chair seats and backs to allow them to "give" comfortably.
Years ago, only coil springs were used. Now S-shaped (or zigzag)
springs and flat springs are also used. These two types of springs have
less give than coil springs. Chairs and sofas in which they are used
will not provide the comfortable "sink-in" feeling that coil springs

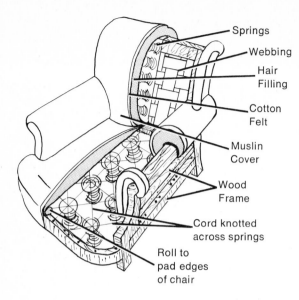

Springs

Webbing

Hair
Filling

Cotton
Felt

Muslin
Cover

Wood
Frame

Cord knotted
across springs

Roll to
pad edges
of chair

Essentially, upholstered furniture is made by building a frame, attaching seat and back bases, and adding springs and various padding materials.

give. The springs are fastened to the frame and to each other. This holds them in place and allows them to move together more smoothly and evenly. Better furniture uses more springs, placed closer together.

Once the springs are in place, a sheet of burlap or some other insulation material is placed over them to keep the padding material in place and separated from the springs. Padding is then added on. Cellulose and cotton are used for padding in relatively inexpensive furniture, while urethane foam and polyester fiberfill are used in somewhat higher-priced furniture. Some furniture is made with combinations of these materials, such as a thick sheet of urethane foam over cotton padding. Padding should be applied evenly and smoothly over the entire piece. It should be thick enough on chair arms so that the sharp edges of the frame cannot be felt. In high-quality pieces, muslin is applied over the padding before the piece is upholstered. This holds the padding in place and gives the upholstery a smoother appearance.

Loose cushions often are stuffed with a block of polyurethane foam. Wrapped foam cushions also are used and have the advantage of a softer "feel" and a plump, comfortable appearance. They have a polyurethane core wrapped in polyester fibers. Some other types of cushion materials, such as cotton and down, also are used. Down filling for cushions is very expensive and now is found only in high-priced pieces. Most pieces with foam cushions have a zipper closing on the back side. You can open this zipper and examine the foam used.

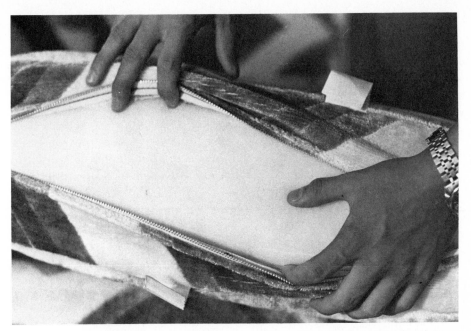

You can examine the foam used to stuff loose cushions. A heavier weight, better-quality foam will have smaller, more widely spaced holes, and the cushion will weigh more than a lower-quality cushion. (*Kip Peticolas*)

A heavier weight foam will be longer lasting and will provide better support. You will be able to tell the heavier foam because the holes in it will be smaller and farther apart and the cushion itself will weigh more. Shredded foam is used in some lower-quality furniture. It has the disadvantage that it tends to pack down with use and lose its springy feel.

By law, in most states, the material used in cushioning and padding furniture must be stated in a label attached to the piece. These labels can provide some useful information for judging the quality of upholstered pieces and should be read carefully. They may be removed after the piece is purchased.

Size and Comfort. No one piece of upholstered furniture is likely to be comfortable for you and everyone else in your family. If you are tall, you will be more comfortable in a seat that is higher from the floor and has a deep cushion from front to back. If you are shorter, you probably will prefer a lower seat and a shallower cushion. The seat back should be high enough to provide comfortable support for the upper portion of your shoulders. It should be set so that you can lean back at a comfortable angle. The only way to be certain that a piece will be comfortable is to try it out for a few minutes. The sofa and chairs for the living room or family room should be chosen so that every family member can have a place to sit comfortably.

Upholstery Fabrics. In contrast to the label information provided about padding and cushioning, most furniture makers provide little information on the upholstery fabrics used. The shopper is left without clues about a fabric's durability, its resistance to fading from sunlight, and its ease of care.

A fabric's basic content does, however, give some indications of the kind of performance that can be expected. Each textile fiber (such as cotton, wool, or polyester) has certain characteristics that usually carry over after these fibers are woven into fabrics. Often several fibers are combined to take advantage of the best characteristics of each. Textile experts say that a fabric must have at least 15 to 20 percent content of a fiber for it to increase durability.

Cotton, rayon, and acetate are used often as upholstery fabrics because they are inexpensive and are easily dyed. They are, however, less durable than other popular upholstery fabrics and stain easily. Wool is more durable, but it is more expensive and also stains easily. The newer synthetics offer important improvements in durability and stain resistance. Nylon and olefin have become especially popular because they have a number of good characteristics. They are strong and resistant to the effects of *abrasion*, or rubbing. They also are resistant to stains and have good *resilience*, the ability to spring back when crushed. The characteristics of the fibers most commonly used in upholstery fabrics are listed in Table 15-1.

Another factor that affects a fabric's performance is its *construction*, that is, how the fibers are joined together to form a fabric. Woven fabrics are the kind we know best. The closeness of the weave gives some indication of how durable a fabric will be. Fabrics with more threads per square inch are more resistant to abrasion, stretching, wrinkling, and raveling. Loosely woven fabrics of heavy yarns are popular because of their interesting rough texture. Such fabrics are more durable when acrylic or rubberized backing is used to help hold fibers in place. Pile fabrics, including velvets and fake furs, have an interesting "feel" but are more likely to stain because of the amount of fiber surface exposed.

Knit fabrics are being used on some modern-style pieces because they conform well to curved lines and rounded shapes. Knit fabrics are wrinkle-resistant but may snag and run. Some knit fabrics are laminated to foam backing to help control stretching and sagging.

Nonwoven fabrics, such as the vinyl plastics, are popular because they are durable and easy to care for. Vinyls are nonabsorbent but can pick up some stains. They also tend to feel hot in the summer and cold in the winter. Vinyl fabrics with woven or knitted backs are more flexible and less likely to tear or rip than those without backing. Expanded vinyl has a thin layer of foam betwen the vinyl face and the backing; this layer helps give it a softer, more comfortable feel. Leather is another nonwoven material used in upholstery. It is soft, flexible, and long wearing but expensive.

There are several special fabric finishes that help to control staining. These finishes reduce the rate at which a fabric absorbs moisture so that spills bead up on the surface rather than soaking in. Fluorocarbon finishes (such as Scotchgard and Zepel) protect against both watery and oily stains.

A variety of upholstery fabrics are available for most pieces of furniture. These fabrics come in different "grades" at different price levels. The same sofa upholstered with different fabrics may differ in price by as much as several hundred dollars. Upholstery grades indicate price level and do not necessarily indicate quality or durability. Some of the least expensive fabrics, such as cotton and rayon, probably will be less durable than more expensive ones such as nylon, olefin, and wool. The most expensive grades generally are fancy velvets and elaborately patterned fabrics that do not necessarily provide good wearing quality. Many inexperienced furniture buyers make the mistake of trying to save money by sacrificing upholstery quality. Since both the fabric and labor costs involved in reupholstering are high, it is cheaper in the long run to buy good-quality upholstery.

CARE AND USE

Furniture which is well cared for will last longer and stay looking better. Most furniture is not built to stand up to unusual strains some people put on it without thinking. Sitting on the arm of a chair or standing on the seat can crack the frame. Standing on a sofa can break a spring. The cost of repairing damage like this is likely to be so high that it might be cheaper to replace the piece than to repair it.

Upholstery should be vacuumed regularly and spots should be removed promptly. Spot removal will be more successful if you know

TABLE 15-1
Characteristics of Textile Fibers Used in Home Furnishings

Fibers and Selected Trade Names	Resistance to Fading from Sunlight	Strength	Resistance to Abrasion	Resistance to Stains	Resilience
Cotton	Good to excellent	Good to excellent	Medium	Fair to poor	Fair to poor
Rayon *Avisco* *Bemberg* *Celanese* New Rayons *Avril* *Avron* *Zantrel*	Good to excellent	Fair to poor; improved in new rayons	Fair to poor; improved in new rayons	Fair to poor; improved in new rayons	Fair to poor
Acetate *Avisco* *Celanese* *Chromspun*	Good to excellent for fibers dyed in solution or in spinning; others fair to poor	Fair to poor	Fair to poor	Medium	Fair to poor
Acrylic *Acrilan* *Creslan* *Orlon* *Zefran*	Good to excellent	Fair to poor	Fair to poor; may pill	Good to excellent	Good to excellent

Nylon *Antron* *Cantrece* *Caprolan* *Cumuloft*	Good to excellent	Good to excellent	Good to excellent	Good to excellent	Good to excellent
Olefin *DLP* *Herculon* *Vectra*	Good to excellent	Good to excellent	Good to excellent	Good to excellent	Good to excellent
Polyester *Dacron* *Fortrel* *Kodel* *Vycron*	Good to excellent	Good to excellent; spun yarns may pill	Good to excellent	Good to excellent, but has low resistance to oily stains	Good to excellent
Wool	Good to excellent	Fair to poor	Medium	Fair to poor; should have mothproof finish	Good to excellent

Reference: Josephine M. Blandford and Lois M. Gurel, *Fibers and Fabrics*, U.S. National Bureau of Standards Consumer Information Series No. 1.

what the fabric is and use recommended procedures. Some manufacturers suggest stain removal procedures. Unfortunately only a few put permanent labels on their upholstered furniture to indicate the cleaning procedures they recommend. If no procedures are recommended, use a stain-removal guide such as the one we discussed in the chapter on clothing. Many furniture makers provide or sell arm caps and back covers to protect arms and backs from heavy wear and staining. Many furniture cushions now have zippers. Furniture makers point out that they are installed so that cushion seams can be straightened more easily. They warn that the cushion filling should never be removed.

Even fabrics which are resistant to fading from sunlight do not stand up well to long periods in the sun. You can protect upholstery from direct sun by drawing shades or drapes or by placing furniture away from windows.

Only a few furniture makers provide written guarantees. For this reason, it would be wise to ask retailers about their own and the maker's policy on after-sale service before you buy. A group of furniture makers called the Furniture Industry Consumer Advisory Panel (FICAP) has organized to help consumers with their complaints. When the consumer finds that the retailer and maker either cannot or will not resolve a complaint, the FICAP will try to help resolve it. The group's address is FICAP, 209 South Main Street, High Point, North Carolina 27260.

After reading this chapter, you can see how we can ensure satisfaction from our furniture choices: by considering carefully the characteristics which are important to us; by shopping carefully for furniture which has these characteristics; and by knowing the care and use which will protect the investment we have made.

Checking Your Reading

1. How does the stage of the family life cycle influence a family's furniture needs?
2. What two general goals guide the best furniture designs?
3. What are the two broad groups of furniture styles? What is an example of an informal style in each of these groups?
4. In judging the quality of a piece of furniture, what is a useful first step?
5. What are case goods?

6. Why do case goods have frames?
7. Why are interlocking joints and corner blocks used in making case goods?
8. Why is veneer so often used in making furniture?
9. How does the wood used in making pieces labeled "solid walnut," and "walnut stain finish on solid hardwoods" differ?
10. Why are dovetail joints used in making drawers?
11. How can the shopper find out the cushioning and padding materials used in making a piece of upholstered furniture?
12. What characteristics does an upholstered piece need if it is to be comfortable for a tall person? A short person?
13. What are the good and bad features of cotton, rayon, and acetate when used in upholstery fabrics?
14. What is meant by fabric construction?
15. Are upholstery grades a useful guide to wearing quality?

Consumer Problems and Projects

1. What style of furniture do you prefer? Why do you feel it is a good choice for you?
2. Collect some pictures of furniture pieces from newspapers and magazines that you feel represent good and bad design. In what ways do the good designs meet the two goals of good design discussed in this chapter? In what ways have the bad designs ignored these goals?
3. If you had an apartment of your own, what furniture pieces (not including appliances) would you like to have? Make a list of these. Visit a local furniture store or use a mail-order catalog to obtain prices for the items you would like to have. List these prices along with your choice of furniture. In what order would you buy these pieces if you could not afford them all at once? Why?
4. Check around your house for examples of furniture defects such as cracked joints and worn or stained upholstery. What construction and design features should you and your family look for to avoid these problems in the future?
5. Sally and Jack Bogen are considering buying a new living room sofa. They especially like a 10-ft [3-m] sofa upholstered in white velvet. When they asked the salesclerk about how durable the

fabric would be, he said he was not sure but that the fabric was the finest quality cotton. Sally and Jack are expecting their first child in 3 months and are hoping to buy a home of their own soon. What are the possible disadvantages of the sofa they are considering?

6. Select an item of furniture in which you are interested, for example, a desk. Check the price levels of this item at a local furniture store or in a mail-order catalog. How do the features offered, the construction, and overall quality differ among price levels? If you were to buy, which particular piece would you select? Why?

7. Joe Dvorchak was offered the choice of either rayon or nylon upholstery in the new car he is buying. Which would you advise him to choose? Why?

8. Terry Johnson is about to get her own apartment and needs to buy some furniture. Terry likes outdoor sports, casual clothes, and informal parties. She does not want to have to spend a lot of time cleaning or caring for her apartment. She likes both formal traditional furniture styles and modern informal styles, but is not sure which suits her best. What do you think would be the best choice of style and fabrics for Terry?

16

Appliances and Utility Costs

Some people believe that they could cut their electrical bills and help solve the nation's energy problems just by throwing away their electric toothbrushes and electric corn poppers. Actually the solution to high utility bills and America's energy problems is a little more complicated than that.

We all have gotten used to the convenience of appliances and rely on them. Some of the appliances we might be most willing to give up are ones we do not use very often. They also are ones that do not use very much electricity when we do use them. It is the appliances we probably would be least willing to give up which are the big energy users. This includes televisions, stoves, refrigerators, and air conditioners.

It is important for us, as citizens, to learn more about appliances and energy costs. Wise choice and wise use of appliances can help contribute to the solution of America's energy problems. Careful use of energy also helps in reducing pollution. It also is important for individual consumers to learn more about appliances and utility costs. Appliance purchases are a major investment. Their operation, care, and maintenance are a major expense. Clearly, buying appliances carefully and using them intelligently are important.

In this chapter we will first look at how our individual needs affect our choice of appliances. Next we will look at the factors that should be taken into account in shopping for appliances, in arranging their purchase, and in using them. In the final section, we will look at utility costs and some ways of reducing them.

EVALUATING YOUR NEEDS AND SITUATION

What electric appliances do you own and use? A radio? A stereo? A tape player? An alarm clock? A study lamp? Perhaps a typewriter? A hair dryer? An electric shaver? Your own TV set? Hobby equipment? Maybe a sewing machine?

Most people have at least a few of these appliances and want to add more. When young people start out on their own, their first appliance

The amount shown on the price tag is not the total cost of a new appliance. You must also consider how long the appliance can be expected to last, how much it will cost to operate, and how often it will need repair and what that will cost. (*Kip Peticolas*)

purchases are likely to be television sets and stereo equipment. As they move into later stages of the family life cycle, they begin adding other pieces of major equipment.

When you begin to think about any appliances that you would like to have, you need to balance the benefits and the costs involved. The benefits are usually easy to think of.

- *Time Saving.* Slow, time-consuming, hand work or a long trip out to the coin-operated laundry is eliminated.
- *Cost Savings.* The job gets done better or less wastefully; or perhaps the need to pay someone else for the use of their equipment is eliminated.
- *Convenience and Pleasure.* For some appliances, especially entertainment equipment, the most important thing may be having them available to enjoy whenever you want.

The costs in adding a new appliance also need to be considered.

- *Cost of the Item and Its Expected Life.* Even though an item is an expensive one, its cost per use or per year may not be very high if it lasts a long time. As you can see from Table 16-1, many major appliances are used a long time. For example, a color television typically is used 12 years by its first owners before it is replaced. A small-screen set purchased for $400 would cost $33.33 a year.
- *Operating Costs.* Appliances for heating, cooking, or cooling are heavy users of electricity. You can see from Table 16-2 that adding a room air conditioner might increase a family's electric bill $25 a year or more. Other appliances use less electricity and

TABLE 16-1
Service Life of Appliances

Appliance	Expected Years of use by First Owner
Electric Refrigerator	15
Electric Clothes Dryer	14
Gas Range	13
Electric Range	12
Television Set—Color	12
Television Set—Black and White	11
Automatic Washer	11
Dishwasher	11

Source: Consumer and Food Economics Institute, U.S. Department of Agriculture.

TABLE 16-2
Operating Costs of Electrical Appliances

Appliance	Average Wattage	Estimated Kilowatt Hours Used Annually	Estimated Annual Operating Cost*
Refrigerator (automatic defrost, 16-18 cubic feet)[4.8-5.4 m³]	–	1,795	$57.62
Range—with oven	12,200	1,175	37.72
Air conditioner—room (operated 1000 hours)	860	860	27.61
Television—color (solid state)	145	320	10.27
Radio	71	86	2.76
Hair dryer	381	14	.45
Toothbrush	1	1.0	.03

*Based on 1975 national average cost of 3.21 cents per kilowatt hour for home users.
 Source: Edison Electric Institute.

are less costly to operate. A color TV set, for example, costs around $10 a year to operate.

- *Repairs.* Repair costs are hard to estimate; some types of appliances run for years without needing any repairs. For others, such as color television sets, repairs are needed more frequently and must be taken into account. Even in the first year, most color TV sets need some repairs. When repairs are needed, they are not cheap; bills of $30 to $50 are not unusual.

Once we have the costs and the benefits of appliance ownership more clearly in mind, we are in a better position to decide how badly we really need a particular appliance. Maybe it would be cheaper and just about as convenient to rent an item we would seldom use. Maybe we can get along awhile longer using a coin-operated laundry. Or perhaps we may decide that we can get along without our own TV set for awhile and use the money for something that's more pressing. On the other hand, the benefits of ownership may so clearly outweigh the costs that it makes sense to buy.

SHOPPING FOR APPLIANCES

Once we have our needs more clearly in mind, we are ready to actually begin gathering information on the different brands and models

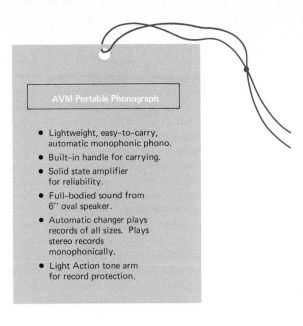

Labels that provide basic information on important product features help consumers make intelligent comparisons between products.

available. One of the biggest problems in shopping for appliances is finding out the features and characteristics of different models and how important they are. Just how should we judge an appliance? What are the important evaluation criteria?

Salespeople are not always as well-informed or helpful as they could be. Descriptive sales brochures often are hard to locate. One of the most helpful sources of information on the criteria which should be used in judging different models is *Consumer Reports* and *Consumers' Research Magazine*.

Some manufacturers are providing labels on their products with rating information on key evaluation criteria. Such information can be a real help. It would be even more helpful and comparisons would be even easier if all manufacturers provided their information in the same standard form. The phonograph label illustrated here represents one company's efforts to supply consumers with product information in an easy-to-read form.

Safety

Because the energy sources used—gas and electricity—can have deadly effects, safety is a key consideration in choosing appliances. Shock hazards are a risk with all electric equipment. These hazards can be controlled by good design and good manufacturing practices.

Because safety is an important consideration in choosing appliances, consumers should always look for the UL and AGA seals. (*UL seal courtesy of Underwriters Laboratories Inc. AGA seal copyright American Gas Association. Used by permission.*)

Because of the work of Underwriters Laboratories (UL) in these areas, shoppers should look for the UL seal on electric appliances (see above). They should also look for the star seal of the American Gas Association on gas appliances (see above). These seals, however, cannot fully guarantee safety, since production-line errors, wear, and misuse all can make an individual appliance dangerous. All electricity

Using equipment with a ground wire and a properly grounded outlet box protects against electric shock.

follows the shortest and least resistant path to the earth. Shock hazards from electric appliances with short circuits are eliminated when the appliance is grounded—that is, when the appliance is linked to the earth by an electric conductor such as a cold-water pipe, a drainpipe, or a grounding wire. When an ungrounded appliance contains a short circuit and users are in contact with the ground, electricity can pass through their bodies on its path to the earth. In such cases, a shock hazard exists. Shock hazard is even greater should the user have wet hands or be standing on a damp or wet surface. This is because water is a pretty fair conductor of electricity. Using ungrounded appliances around sinks and bathtubs, on damp basement and garage floors, and on the bare earth itself is so dangerous because *you* become the shortest and least resistant path for the electricity to pass through.

Shock hazards can be controlled by insulating electric equipment to prevent current leakage and by building in a grounding wire or grounding conductor. If there is a short circuit in a piece of equipment, the grounding conductor allows the current to travel safely to the earth rather than through the user's body. Equipment with a built-in grounding conductor can be recognized because it has three wires in the appliance cord instead of the usual two and has a special three-prong plug or a regular two-prong plus a "pigtail."

Everyone should remember that appliances with a grounding conductor are grounded *only* when they are plugged into a grounded outlet box. Individuals can help protect themselves by plugging appliances with grounding conductors into grounded outlet boxes and by taking special care in using appliances near grounds. Consumers Union has paid particular attention to shock hazards when testing appliances, and an appliance with a design that creates a shock hazard is rated "Not Acceptable."

Performance

After we are sure they are safe, our chief concern with appliances is how well they do what they are supposed to do. We want answers to such questions as how good a TV set's picture is compared with other models. How good is its tone? The evaluation criteria we need to take into account differ with the purpose of the appliance. We want a tape player which reproduces sound accurately and a washer which gets clothes clean. *Consumer Reports* and *Consumers' Research Magazine* identify the criteria we should use in judging models of a particular type of appliance. They also tell us how well each model rates on these criteria.

Extra features offered on top-of-the-line models need to be evaluated carefully. Are they really worth the extra cost? Or would a less expensive model with fewer features do the job almost as well? In choosing a model, it's useful to remember that while most of the features on the most expensive models would be desirable, not all are really necessary. In fact, many home economists advise avoiding models with complicated extra features because of the extra repair problems involved.

Durability

Reliable service is another thing consumers want from appliances. Breakdowns and repairs are both inconvenient and expensive. Consumers can protect themselves by choosing brands and models that have good frequency-of-repair records. *Consumer Reports* collects information from a large number of its readers on the repairs their appliances have needed. This information can be a guide to models which are most likely to be trouble-free. Many brands seem to have the same kind of record year after year. Those with good records continue to keep them. Those with poor records continue to need an above-average number of repairs.

Operating Costs

Different appliance models may use quite different amounts of electricity to do the same amount of work. Some use electricity efficiently. Others do not. These differences in efficiency may be especially important in appliances for heating and cooling which use large amounts of electricity. Differences in operating costs also may be important in areas where electrical costs are high.

The federal government recently began a program that requires manufacturers to label major appliances with information on how efficiently they use energy. These labels will show estimated annual operating costs or other energy efficiency information that will help consumers to compare models. The estimates will be based on average use patterns and average energy costs. These energy efficiency labels eventually will appear on all products which are heavy energy users. This includes refrigerators, freezers, air conditioners, kitchen

Cold King Air Conditioner

Model 1750 B

Estimated yearly energy cost $50.75

This model has a 10,000 BTU capacity.
Models with 9,500–10,500 BTU capacity
will provide about the same cooling
performance. The yearly energy cost
of models in this range varies from
$40.25 to $75.60.

Energy efficiency labels on major appliances show estimated annual operating costs or other information that will help consumers compare models.

ranges, TV sets, home heaters and furnaces, and water heaters. The difference in operating costs probably will surprise most of us.

Because of the need to cut energy use and operating costs, some manufacturers are beginning to offer new high-efficiency models. These new models use less energy, in some cases as much as a quarter or a third less, to produce the same output. The high-efficiency models do, however, usually cost more because of extra insulation, more efficient motors, and other special features. To figure out whether such models offer real savings, we will have to figure out how the savings in operating costs over the product's life compare with the model's extra cost.

Convenience

Although convenience is not the first consideration in choosing an appliance, it should be given some thought. We do need to consider whether the item is easy to use. Are the control dials easy to read? If the item is going to be used in a dark room, are the dials lighted? Are they easy to reach and set? Is the item easy to carry? What kinds of maintenance or special care is it going to need? These questions need to be answered along with the ones asked earlier about performance and durability. An appliance can work well and last a long time and still not be very handy to use.

We also need to remember that convenience features may add to operating costs. For example, the automatic defrosting feature for refrigerators may require several dollars worth of electricity a year to operate.

Service and Warranties

Unsatisfactory repair service and disagreements over the terms of guarantees are major headaches for consumers. Consumers can protect themselves, to some extent, by studying the warranties of different models before they buy. Guarantees offered by different companies for a particular type of appliance often differ. There may be differences both in the length of time labor charges are covered and in the length of time parts are covered. Do the guarantees make clear what is covered and what is not? How well do they conform to the requirements for a good guarantee that we discussed in Chapter 4 (pages 64–66).

The availability of appliance parts for repairs is often a serious problem. It will pay to check the arrangements that have been made to keep parts available for the appliance in which you are interested. Where is the nearest parts supply center? How long does it take to obtain parts? How long will parts be kept available?

Used Appliances

Many consumers have learned how to get good value for their money by buying used appliances. Most of the shopping techniques we have discussed can be used in purchasing used appliances as well as new ones. For example, suppose you were considering buying a used television set. After checking the picture on different channels, you could check the age of the set by looking at the nameplate on the back or inside. All major appliances have such plates, and all carry a serial number, part of which is a code number for the year the appliance was made. Once you know the serial number, you can check the age of the set by making a phone call to an authorized repair shop for that brand. At the same time, you could also ask what problems that year's models tend to have and how serious they are. Once you know the model number and year, you also can check back in *Consumer Reports* and *Consumers' Research Magazine* to see how it was rated when new.

PURCHASE, DELIVERY, AND USE

Few appliances are sold only at list price nowadays, so it pays to shop around. Even the first price quoted may be subject to bargaining. It pays to find out. Discount stores frequently quote the lowest prices but often make up for this by charging more for installment credit. If you plan to buy from a discount house and plan to use credit, you may want to borrow elsewhere.

When a final price is quoted, it should be clear whether delivery and installation are included. Does delivery mean delivery to your front door or delivery to the desired place inside your home? What is or is not included in installation also should be clear. This is particularly important for items such as clothes dryers that require venting and also for clothes washers and dishwashers, which require both electrical and plumbing hookups. The sales receipt should clearly show the brand and model number purchased and any qualifications or limitations on the guarantee. There sometimes are limitations in the case of "floor models." The receipt should be saved along with the guarantee as evidence of the date of purchase in case any work covered by the guarantee is needed.

When a new appliance is delivered, it is desirable to check it out fully before the installation workers leave. It is also desirable to get a demonstration on how to operate a complex new piece of equipment such as a color television set or an automatic washer. When it is not possible to check an appliance in the store or on delivery, it should be checked as soon as possible afterward so that complaints and adjustments can be made promptly.

Use and Repair

Instruction books should be read carefully. They contain directions on operating appliances and information on what to do when particular operating problems arise. A careful review of the operating instructions may eliminate the need for an expensive service call. It has been estimated that nearly one-fourth of all appliance service calls are unnecessary. Typical problems are as follows:

- Failure to check to be sure the appliance is plugged in
- Failure to check fuses
- Failure to check control settings
- Failure to ensure that doors that must be fully latched before equipment will operate are tightly shut.

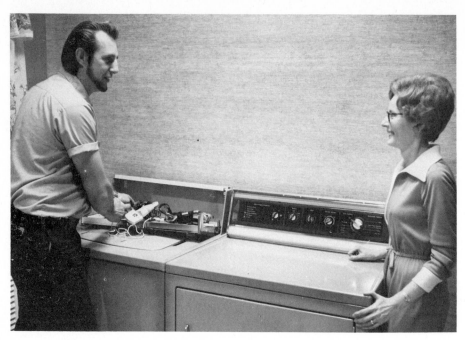

You should always check out a new appliance before the installation workers leave, and you should also have its operation demonstrated. (*JC Penney Company Inc.*)

When service is needed, call the dealer from whom you purchased the appliance, the service agency the dealer recommends, or an organization franchised by the manufacturer to repair your brand. Repairs covered by the guarantee should be made without charge. In arranging for service, you will want to check the method used in calculating service charges. Many shops charge a set fee for home service calls plus labor charges for the time needed to make the necessary repairs. They may also charge a "bench fee" for diagnosing problems of appliances brought into the shop in addition to a labor charge for the actual repairs.

Appliance manufacturers have set up a special consumer committee to help consumers who have problems with major appliances. Consumers who are unable to get satisfactory solutions to their problems with major appliances (home laundry equipment, refrigerators, ranges, freezers, room air conditioners, garbage disposals, dishwashers, dehumidifiers, and water heaters) may send their complaints to the Major Appliance Consumer Action Panel (MACAP). MACAP is a group of independent consumer experts who communicate consumer problems and concerns to appliance industry executives. Complaints may be sent to the Major Appliance Consumer Action Panel, 20 North Wacker Drive, Chicago, Illinois 60606.

Planning for Replacement

When buying appliances, consumers should be aware of how much useful life they can expect from a new piece of equipment. Studies of the average number of years appliances typically are used before they are replaced provide some clues. As you can see from Table 16-1, the useful life of different appliances varies. With information on the life of individual appliances, you can begin to plan ahead for their replacement in the same way businesses plan the replacement of worn-out machinery. Some family financial experts advise building up a replacement fund as appliances become worn out. The fund then can provide cash to pay for a replacement when it is needed. With a replacement fund for appliances, families can avoid costly borrowing on credit when a new appliance is needed.

UTILITY COSTS

Only about 25 per cent of the energy used in American homes is used in operating appliances. The major part is used in heating space and heating water. About 60 per cent is used in heating or cooling homes, and 15 per cent is used for hot water heaters.

If we want to cut utility bills, help save energy, and reduce pollution associated with energy production and use, we should give some attention to these two major uses. Use of energy for home heating and cooling and water heating can be reduced in four ways: (1) by choosing efficient water heaters and equipment for heating and cooling; (2) by keeping equipment in good working order; (3) by finding ways to reduce waste and leakage; and (4) by reducing unnecessary uses.

How can we put these ways of saving energy into actual practice? There are several ways.

- Use energy efficiency information in choosing new or replacement equipment.
- Keep furnaces, air conditioners, air filters, and radiators clean and follow suggested maintenance procedures.
- Reduce waste and leakage by improving insulation, adding storm windows and weather-stripping, closing shades or draperies, and repairing leaky hot water faucets.

Adding storm windows and weather stripping to your home reduces leakage and waste of heat. The energy and utility cost saving can be substantial, since 60 percent of the energy used in American homes is used for heating and cooling. (*Daniel S. Brody, Editorial Photocolor Archives*)

- Reduce unnecessary heating and cooling by setting household thermostats lower in the winter and higher in the summer, reducing heating and cooling in unused areas, using lower temperature settings on water heaters, and running only full loads in washers, dryers, and dishwashers.

These are only a few very general suggestions for saving energy. Can you think of others you and your family could also use?

Checking Your Reading

1. What costs should be considered when deciding whether you need a particular appliance? What benefits should you consider?
2. Is purchasing an appliance that you need and use always a good idea?
3. Where can you get information on the features that are available on a particular appliance model?
4. What useful information do appliance labels sometimes give?
5. Do the UL and star seals on electric and gas appliances fully guarantee their safety? Why?
6. In what situations can an electrical shock hazard exist?

7. What kinds of information about product performance do *Consumer Reports* and *Consumers' Research Magazine* give?
8. Why do many home economists suggest avoiding appliance models with costly extra features?
9. How can frequency-of-repair records be useful to appliance shoppers?
10. For what particular kinds of appliances are differences in operating costs likely to be especially important?
11. Why is it important to know what services are included in the sale price of an appliance?
12. Why is the promise that repair parts will be kept available an important addition to appliance guarantees?
13. What kinds of problems often result in unnecessary service calls?
14. Whom should you call for appliance repairs?
15. How can families use a replacement fund to help them avoid credit costs?
16. Why is it important for families to check their use of energy for heating and cooling and for heating water?

Consumer Problems and Projects

1. If you had an apartment of your own, what appliances would you want to have? Make a list of these items. Visit a local appliance store or use a mail-order catalog to obtain prices of the appliances you would like to have. What is the total cost? If you could not obtain all these items at once, which ones would you want first? Why?
2. Check some recent issues of *Consumer Reports* and *Consumers' Research Magazine* for reports of tests of electric and gas appliances. Select an appliance in which you are interested or would like to own. What product characteristics were tested in rating it? What brands and models were given top ratings? If you bought the item, which brand and model would you buy? What are the reasons for your choice?
3. Visit local stores to check the availability of the two or three brands and models that you rated highest in problem 2 above. How do the prices in these different stores compare? Using the information you have gathered on product features, on availability, and on prices, which brand and model would you choose? Where would you buy it? Why?

4. Select an appliance in which you are interested that is available at several different price levels. Some examples are radios, electric typewriters, electric shavers, and electric drills. Visit local stores or use a mail-order catalog to gather information on differences in construction and features among these price levels. What are the basic differences among the various price levels? If you were to buy the item, at which price level would you buy? Why?

5. Josie and Bob Hamilton are trying to decide between two different air conditioner models. Both have the same cooling capacity. One is a high-efficiency model which costs $275; its estimated annual operating cost is $30. The other model is less efficient but also costs less. It costs $195 and its estimated annual operating cost is $50. Josie and Bob believe they would get about 12 years use out of either model. Which do you feel would be the best choice? Why?

6. Joe Dorfman has just washed his car and is standing on the wet grass polishing it with a buffer pad attached to an electric drill. What safety precautions should he have taken?

7. Lynda Barrios has a chance to buy a three-year-old refrigerator for $75 from a friend who is moving out of town. After checking the classified ads and used-appliance stores, she is convinced the price is fair. She wonders, however, if she is likely to have a lot of problems with the refrigerator since it is used. If she asked you for advice, what would you tell her?

8. What steps have you and your family taken at home to cut energy use and utility costs? Are there other steps you could take? List the steps you have taken and those you could take.

PART FOUR
Financial Security

17

Savings Programs

If you set aside $4 a week from your income for the next 10 weeks so that you will have $40 available for a tennis racket, you have begun a savings program. If an engaged couple agree to spend less money while on dates and instead build up a sum of money to buy furniture, they, too, have started a savings program. Again and again during our lifetimes, we must decide whether to spend money for something that seems important at the moment or save with the purpose of spending it later.

What methods do people use to save money? Why do people save money? How is interest figured on savings? These questions are answered in this chapter. In Chapter 18 information is given about investment programs.

METHODS OF SAVING MONEY

When we think of saving, we usually think of putting some of our income aside in a safe place, such as in a bank, savings and loan, or a credit union. We do, however, save in some other ways. For example, when income is used to buy fairly expensive goods that last for some time, a form of saving takes place. Let's say a family buys a $700 color television set and pays for it over a one-year period. The television set will give service for more than one year, of course. Let's say it is worth $500 at the end of the first year. In that case, the family has so far really "consumed" just $200. They have savings (in the form of a television set) of $500.

Some saving is done as part of a formal agreement; this type of saving is often called *forced saving*. A common example of forced saving is the repayment of money borrowed to buy a house. Part of the monthly payment is for interest (the cost of borrowing the money), and part of it is for paying back the amount borrowed. The part of the payment used to repay the loan represents a form of saving for the house buyer. Part of the premiums paid on certain life insurance policies also represent saving because a cash value is being built.

Pension plans, too, represent forced saving. The term "forced" may be a little misleading. The consumer enters into such an agreement voluntarily and can usually quit the plan without any loss of money. The plans are called forced saving because people enter into the agreements in order to force themselves to save money.

When we commonly think of saving, however, we think of putting some of our income aside in a safe place, such as in a bank or a credit union. It is this type of regular, voluntary saving that you will read about in this chapter.

WHY PEOPLE SAVE MONEY

The key to successful saving is to save with a goal in mind. Saving just because of a desire to have lots of money is pointless. In fact, pointless saving is just the kind most likely to be abandoned at the first excuse. When we have a reason for saving, we find saving much easier. Saving can be fun if you look forward to using the money in the future for some purpose that will give you more happiness than present spending will give. Instead of setting aside $4 each week for a tennis racket, you could, no doubt, find many ways to spend the extra money each week. The question is whether or not spending the extra money each week on perhaps the foolish or unnecessary things will bring you as much happiness as the tennis racket will bring you.

The first point about saving that should be remembered, then, is that when you save a dollar, you are not forever surrendering your right to spend it. The second point is that as soon as you have savings, you have a silent partner working for you. You work for your money;

Your savings plan has a better chance of success if you save with a goal in mind.

then you put your money to work for you. But before looking into how your money will work for you, we will check some of the more specific reasons for saving money.

Emergency Fund

For most individuals and families, the most important savings is an emergency fund. In fact, creating an emergency fund that can be drawn upon when necessary should be the starting point for any savings plan. Once the fund is established, it should be maintained within certain dollar limits. When money is withdrawn from the fund, the amount taken should be replaced as soon as possible.

People use money saved in an emergency fund for many different reasons. Unexpected repair bills on a car, for example, might be an important reason for having money on hand. A friend or relative living in another state might die, and the cost of traveling to the funeral is an expense that would have to be met.

Unfortunately, no family can predict accurately how much money is needed to take care of emergencies. A traditional rule of thumb that had been followed through the years was to have available in a savings account an emergency fund equal to from six months' to a year's income. The savings was to be used only in extreme emergencies; for example, to pay a major medical bill or to pay living expenses during a period of unemployment. The amount of money needed for emergencies has probably changed somewhat in recent years. For example, families can more easily protect themselves against heavy medical bills through medical insurance plans. Government unemployment compensation may help when one loses a job, and there are other financial cushions that breadwinners can fall back on in times of crises. In our present society, many bills can be paid 30 days or even later after a debt is incurred.

So, how much money is now needed in an emergency fund? Probably the best answer to this question is that it depends on the individual or the family. It depends on the security of one's job, the financial needs of the family, the life-style of the family, the extent of insurance protection, and many other variable factors. A self-employed worker probably needs a larger emergency fund than a salaried employee. An unskilled worker might need a larger fund than a skilled worker, because an unskilled worker might be more likely to hit job slumps for longer periods of time.

Changing Times magazine reported in the 1970s that a poll of money management authorities produced guideline figures about the size of a family's emergency fund. The figures ranged from two months' to a year's income. The consensus was that an emergency fund equal to three months' income is a realistic goal for many people. Sylvia Porter, an economist and syndicated columnist on money matters, has recommended that the emergency fund should equal at least two months' income. But she adds that the fund should be for protection against unexpected financial emergencies. The size of the fund should be no more nor less than needed for that purpose.

Large Recurring Expenses

Some people save money regularly so that when large recurring expenses such as income taxes, annual insurance premiums, and real estate taxes are due, money will be available for payment. In this case, the amounts needed are predictable and the money that must be saved each week or each month can be quite exact. Chapter 3 discusses in greater detail the need for planning for these relatively large expenses.

Material Wants and Needs

Many times during everyone's lifetime expensive items must be purchased. Buying such items out of current income is usually not possible, so the consumer must decide whether to borrow money for these purchases (or buy the goods on the installment plan, which is a way of borrowing money) or to save in advance so that enough cash is available when the purchase is made. Most consumers, of course, do both. Borrowing money means paying an interest charge, of course. Money saved earns interest, so the consumer who saves money in advance to pay for expensive items gains in two ways: by paying less because there is no interest charge, and by earning interest on the money being saved.

Our ability to save during our early years is a good indication of the life we will build later on. A good education, fine books, travel, and other things that enrich our lives can more often be purchased by us if we look ahead and plan our spending carefully. Other material wants and needs, such as a good car and a fine home with convenient appliances, will also be available to the person who plans wisely.

All families experience times when large funds are required. For example, there may be a time when a down payment of several thousand dollars is needed for the purchase of a home. There may be a time when money is needed to help pay for a child's education. These and many other needs must be recognized and planned for with a savings program.

Retirement

Some retirement income is provided for most workers through the compulsory old-age, survivors, and disability insurance program (often called the social security program) administered by the federal government. Many workers are also covered by pension plans or retirement-income savings plans provided by their employers. Many people, however, want to supplement the income received from these sources with savings accumulated during their working years. The typical American works for 40 years. If a person is to be financially independent after retirement from active work, he or she must look ahead to the years of retirement and plan to save money during productive working years.

Money put away over many years in a savings account will grow into a sizeable amount, but such a plan does not take into account inflation. *Inflation* is a rise in prices—or to look at it in another way, it

In order to be financially independent and enjoy life after retirement, you should plan to save money during your working years. (*Timothy Eagan, Woodfin Camp & Associates*)

is a decrease in the purchasing value of the dollar. For example, the monthly cost of providing food for a family of four might now be $300. Forty years from now, if inflation continues at its present rate, the cost might be double, or $600. Thus, money put away for retirement purposes might better be invested in some way that closely follows the basic changes in the economy. Inflation and investments will be discussed in Chapter 18.

HOW MONEY GROWS

In the last few pages, you have learned that the first point about savings is that when you save a dollar, you are not forever surrendering your right to spend it. The second point is that as soon as you have savings, you have a silent partner working for you. The money works for you by earning interest. A hundred dollars in a savings account that pays 5½ percent interest compounded annually will become $170.81 in 10 years. At 6 percent the money will double itself in 12 years. And it is possible to get more than a 6 percent return on certain savings plans.

Money deposited in a savings institution grows rapidly because of compound interest. During the first interest period, interest is paid only on the amount deposited, but during the second period, interest is paid also on the interest earned during the first period. Thus, in every succeeding period the amount of money in the bank—called the *principal*—will be greater, growing slowly at first but more rapidly later.

To see how money grows when interest is compounded, let us consider Table 17-1, which shows the growth of savings of $100 on which interest is compounded annually at 5 percent. During the first year, the principal is $100. The interest earned the first year is $100 multiplied by 0.05 (5 percent), or $5. The $5 is added to the principal, so the principal during the second year is $105. The interest earned the second year is $105 multiplied by 0.05, or $5.25. Thus the principal during the third year is $5.25 plus $105, or $110.25. Notice that by the twentieth year, the interest earned exceeds $12, which is more than twice the interest earned the first year. And by the end of the twentieth year, the principal has grown from $100 to $265.33.

A convenient way to estimate the number of years it takes to double any amount of money at any rate of interest is to use the "rule of 72." Simply divide 72 by the effective rate of interest. Thus, if the interest rate is 6 percent, the money will double in about 12 years (72 divided by 6 equals 12). At 8 percent, money will double in about 9 years. The same formula can be used, of course, to determine the approximate interest rate needed to double money in any given number of years.

TABLE 17-1

Year	Principal During Year	Interest Earned (5% of principal)	Principal at End of Year
1	$100.00	$ 5.00	$105.00
2	105.00	5.25	110.25
3	110.25	5.51	115.76
4	115.76	5.79	121.55
5	121.55	6.08	127.63
6	127.63	6.38	134.01
7	134.01	6.70	140.71
8	140.71	7.04	147.75
9	147.75	7.38	155.13
10	155.13	7.76	162.89
15	197.99	9.90	207.89
20	252.70	12.63	265.33

Just divide 72 by the number of years. If you want to double your money in 15 years, the interest rate that needs to be earned is about 4.8 percent (72 divided by 15 is 4.8).

The Frequency of Compounding Interest

In the illustration of compound interest given in Table 17-1, the interest was compounded annually. Interest is often figured now at more frequent time intervals. The true annual rates depend on the frequency with which the interest is compounded. Take our $100 principal earning 5 percent interest as an example. If the interest were figured semiannually (twice a year), then at the end of six months $100 would be multiplied times 0.05 and then that figure would be multiplied by ½ (because the time is one-half of a year). Thus, the interest at the end of six months would be $2.50 ($100 times .05 times ½). The new principal at the end of the first half-year would be $102.50. During the second half of the year, the interest would be figured as follows: $102.50 × 0.05 × ½ = $2.56. So, during the first year (first two 6-month periods) the interest earned would be $105.06. The new principal at the end of the first year would be $105.06. By compounding semiannually rather than annually, the account earned an additional 6 cents. That may not seem like much, but on larger amounts of money it may add up to a tidy sum.

Some savings institutions compute interest quarterly, monthly, and even daily. Computing interest so frequently is possible now, of course, because the institutions have the use of computers. The interest rate stated is usually called the "nominal annual rate." If interest is figured annually, this is the rate of return received on the savings. If interest is compounded more frequently, however, the true annual rate is higher. Table 17-2 shows the true annual rate for certain nomi-

TABLE 17-2

Nominal Annual Rate	True Annual Rate When Compounded . . .				
	Semiannually	Quarterly	Monthly	Weekly	Daily
5.5	5.5756	5.6144	5.6407	5.6509	5.6536
6.0	6.0900	6.1363	6.1677	6.1799	6.1831
6.5	6.6056	6.6601	6.6971	6.7115	6.7152
7.0	7.1225	7.1859	7.2290	7.2457	7.2500
7.5	7.6406	7.7135	7.7632	7.7825	7.7875
8.0	8.1600	8.2432	8.2999	8.3220	8.3277

nal rates when interest is compounded semiannually, quarterly, monthly, weekly, and daily.

Shopping for Savings Accounts

A consumer should shop carefully for savings accounts because the interest paid by savings institutions varies considerably. Obviously, the more often the interest is compounded, the better. But you should also check how often the interest is credited. An institution may compound frequently but credit or pay the earnings less often. Interest can earn interest only after it has been credited (added to the balance in your account).

The American Bankers' Association says there are more than 100 ways to compute interest on savings. Senator Vance Hartke of Indiana, a proponent of truth-in-savings legislation, has stated that money earned can vary as much as 150 percent over a 6-month period with the same interest rate applied. In addition to knowing the interest rate and how often it is compounded and credited, consumers need to check some other important facts about savings accounts. Here are some additional points on which savings accounts should be compared.

Grace days. Some savings institutions give a certain number of grace days within the interest period so that deposits or withdrawals can be made without losing interest. Some institutions do not give grace days. The more grace days given, the more flexibility the saver has.

Minimum balance. A savings institution may require the saver to maintain a specified balance in order to earn interest.

Method of figuring interest. The various methods used to figure interest can be difficult to understand, and so many different methods are used that often getting a clear-cut answer is a problem. In fact, often the people in the lending institution with whom consumers talk do not have ready answers. Some institutions pay interest on the lowest balance in the account during an interest period. Thus you may deposit money every month for three months, but your interest is figured on the lowest balance during that period.

A savings institution may use a FIFO method. The acronym FIFO comes from the phrase *first in, first out.* One FIFO method applies to the first deposit of the interest period. Withdrawals are deducted from your first deposit. Let's say you made your first deposit of $2000 on January 15. On March 10 you withdraw $1000. You would lose interest on the $1000 from January 15 until the end of the interest period.

The "day of deposit to day of withdrawal" method is generally best for consumers. Under this method, the institution pays interest for the actual number of days that money is in the account. If you have $1000 in an account from January 12 to March 16, you will collect interest for all of those days.

How Deposits Will Grow

Now let's see how regularly invested savings will grow. Table 17-3 below illustrates how much money will be accumulated if, at the end of each half year, $100 is invested at various annual rates of interest compounded semiannually. If you invest $100 at the end of each 6-month period, and if the annual interest of 6 percent is compounded semiannually, you will have $1146.39 at the end of 5 years. At the end of 6 years, you will have $1419.20. At the end of 20 years, your fund will have grown to $7540.13

If you wanted to save $5000 in 15 years, and if you could earn 6 percent interest compounded monthly, how much do you think you would have to save each month? The answer may surprise you. You would have to deposit $17.19 each month in the savings institution. Now do some figuring. If you deposited $17.19 in your savings account every month for 15 years, you would make 180 monthly deposits

TABLE 17-3

| Period (Years) | Principal | | |
	At 4 Percent	At 6 Percent	At 8 Percent
5	$1094.97	$1146.39	$1200.61
6	1341.21	1419.20	1502.58
7	1597.39	1708.63	1829.19
8	1863.93	2015.69	2182.45
9	2141.23	2341.44	2564.54
10	2429.74	2687.04	2977.81
12	3042.17	3442.65	3908.26
14	3705.12	4293.09	4996.76
16	4422.70	5250.28	6270.15
18	5199.44	6327.59	7759.83
20	6040.20	7540.13	9502.55

(12 months times 15 years). You would deposit, over the 15 years, a total of $3094.20 ($17.19 times 180). How much would your money earn for you?

THE DISCIPLINE TO SAVE

Deciding where to put savings is a problem that consumers must face, of course. But a far bigger problem for most of us is the act of disciplining ourselves enough so that we do in fact begin to save money regularly. We would like to save money each week or each month, but we so easily find other uses for our money. Think back about our earlier illustration about buying a tennis racket. Even though you know you need about $40 for that racket, putting aside $4 every week may be hard to do. One week you may want to spend the $4 for a theater

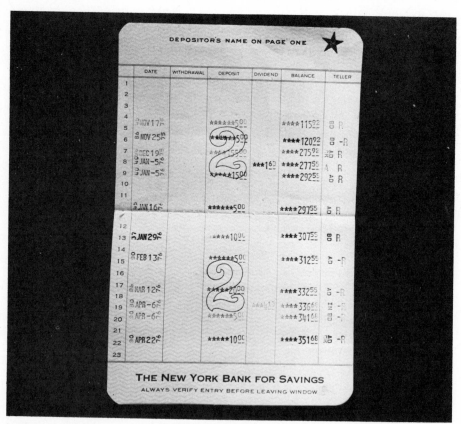

In order to succeed at saving money, you should make a habit of saving regularly, even if you can only save a small amount. (*Kip Peticolas*)

ticket. If you save the $4, you must forgo attending a play that many of your friends are going to see. At another time it might be tempting to use the $4 to help buy an article of clothing that you really would like to have.

Families, too, find saving money difficult because there are so many uses for their money. The high cost of raising a family discourages many young married couples from saving at the very time that many of them should be starting a savings program.

Savings must be started early in life. If you do not form a habit of setting aside some of the money you earn, you will find that money has a way of sliding through your fingers. People who have been success- ful at saving money often say that they owe their success to their resolve to set aside part of their income for savings first and then live on what is left. As money experts often put it, if you think you will pay all your living expenses and all your bills first each month and then save whatever money remains, you are fooling yourself.

A good way to build savings is to set aside a sizable portion of all pay raises or other increases in income. Some young families split all pay increases: half of the increase goes into a savings account, and the remaining half is added to the funds available for immediate spend- ing. In any case, to be successful at saving, most persons have to divert the money at its source. If you do not have the money, you cannot spend it. Two ways in which money can be saved by making certain that it is not easily available for immediate spending are discussed in the following paragraphs.

Payroll Deductions

Many business firms encourage employees to save by offering plans that permit payroll deductions. The employer is authorized to transfer a set amount from each paycheck to a savings fund, just as is done for income tax and social security deductions. The deduction may be put in a savings account in a bank or in a savings and loan association. Or the money may be used to buy United States savings bonds. If the company has a credit union, the money may be placed in this type of savings account.

Automatic Deductions from Checking Accounts

Another way to save regularly is to have your bank transfer each month a certain amount from your checking account to a savings ac- count. Some employers will send payroll checks directly to the worker's bank for deposit in his checking account. When this is done, it is easy to take the second step. The only action this step entails is to ask the bank to transfer part of the money to a savings account.

SAVINGS INSTITUTIONS

Savings should be placed in an institution where the money will produce financial returns for the saver and economic growth for society. But how does a person go about choosing such an institution? In making a choice, he should consider four important factors.

1. *Safety.* The money should be as secure as possible against loss through economic trouble or criminal action. The degree of safety depends on how the savings institutions are regulated and insured and in some cases on how they invest their assets.
2. *Liquidity.* *Liquidity* is a business term that refers to the ease and speed with which an investor can get his or her cash when it is wanted. In some cases, invested money can be readily liquidated—that is, turned into cash. In other cases, it might be necessary to wait a number of days, or even months, to obtain cash for the amount invested.
3. *Earnings.* Earnings must be satisfactory. One of the major reasons for placing money in a savings institution is to earn interest. If you want safety and liquidity, however, you have to sacrifice some earnings. Generally, the higher the rate of interest promised, the greater the risk.
4. *Purpose.* The purpose for which a person is saving money should affect the choice of a savings institution. If you were saving to buy a $500 television set in two or three months, there would not be enough time for the savings to earn much interest. All you would really need would be a safe place to keep the money. On the other hand, if you were saving money to buy a house in three or four years, your money could be earning valuable interest as it accumulated.

When sizable amounts of money are involved, the wise investor will not want to keep all savings in the same place or in the same form, for there would always be the danger that the failure of any one person or institution would wreck him financially. Fortunately there is a variety of safe and convenient savings institutions, and the investor can put various funds in various suitable places.

Commercial Banks

Most consumers deal regularly with commercial banks. Commercial banks provide checking facilities for individuals and businesses; they grant loans; they offer safe-deposit facilities, student-aid programs, and various types of financial advisory services. Most commercial banks offer savings account facilities as well.

Many consumers find it helpful to maintain a checking account. They find it convenient to pay bills by mail, and their canceled checks are a valuable record of payments made. A checking account also provides a safe place for small funds to accumulate—either for spending or investing. But large sums of money should not be left in a checking account for a long period of time, for the money will earn no interest.

In selecting a bank in which to open a savings account, the safety of your money is, of course, of prime importance. But since all banks are closely supervised by state or federal governments, and since individual deposits are insured up to $40,000 in banks that are members of the Federal Deposit Insurance Corporation (FDIC), one bank is frequently as safe as another. Nearly all commercial banks in the United States (97 percent) are insured by the FDIC. You can choose a bank so insured by looking for a displayed metal plaque that announces the bank's membership in the FDIC. If the bank is not covered by federal insurance, it probably is covered by state insurance. If you do not see the FDIC plaque, ask. There is no point in taking a chance.

In the late 1970s, 5 percent was the typical interest rate on regular passbook accounts—those accounts that you can add to or withdraw from at will. On special time-deposit accounts, commercial banks offer slightly higher interest rates. A time deposit, for which a certificate of deposit is issued, is usually made for six months, one year, or longer. The higher interest rate on time deposits is payable only if the funds are left untouched in the account for the full period. Thus, these accounts are not as liquid as regular ones. If you need money in a hurry, liquidity may cost you part of the return expected. Some of the time accounts require withdrawal notice, so you cannot get your money immediately.

Commercial banks offer a great deal of convenience, especially for consumers who want their savings in the same institution as their checking account. Also, persons who want such services as automatic transfer of funds from checking accounts to savings accounts or automatic payroll savings plans will find commercial banks convenient. You may want the services of a large commercial bank that carries huge business accounts, or you may feel more at home in the friendly atmosphere of a small neighborhood bank that handles chiefly personal accounts (possibly a branch of the larger one).

Mutual Savings Banks

Mutual savings banks specialize in savings accounts and use the deposits mostly to make home mortgage loans and home improvement loans. These institutions are chartered in only 18 states, mostly in the northeastern part of the United States. They are nonprofit savings institutions that are organized and operated for their depositors on a mutual basis.

The interest paid on savings in mutual savings banks is slightly higher than in most commercial banks, making them an attractive place for setting aside savings to be used for emergency funds.

Almost all mutual savings banks have the same type of FDIC insurance as commercial banks, so the principal considerations in choosing one are generally its convenience and suitability to your purposes. Ordinarily, funds may be withdrawn from mutual savings banks without notice, but in times of crises an advance notice of one to three months could be required. The period varies from state to state.

Savings and Loan Associations

Savings and loan associations are sometimes known as building and loan associations or as savings associations. These institutions are associations of people who pool funds and lend money to people who wish to buy or build a home. They do not perform the usual banking functions.

Most savings and loan associations operate as mutual associations, and in this respect they are much like mutual savings banks. The money entrusted to these associations earns dividends. The rate of dividend payment tends to be stable in large communities, and competition among savings and loan associations has resulted in fairly uniform dividend payments. A few associations are organized as business corporations, with the owners sharing profits in the form of dividends and the savers receiving their interest at a specified rate. The interest rates depend on overall earnings and vary from one association to another and from time to time. In the late 1970s the general range of association rates on regular passbook accounts was about 5.25 percent.

Most savings and loan association accounts are insured up to $40,000 by the Federal Savings and Loan Insurance Corporation (FSLIC) in the same manner in which FDIC insures banks. In fact, about 4100 of the nation's 5200 savings and loan associations are covered by FSLIC. Those not insured by FSLIC may have state agency or private insurance.

As in the case of banks, savings and loan associations can require depositors to give advance notice before withdrawing savings, but there is usually no delay in withdrawing money. For saving money, these institutions are nearly as convenient as commercial banks, although there are not as many of them and they lack commercial bank services. For example, they do not offer checking accounts, so it is not possible to have automatic transfer of funds to savings accounts.

Credit Unions

Credit unions are one of the fastest-growing savings institutions in the nation. The original purpose of credit unions was to help wage earners whose money needs (saving and borrowing money) were not being met by other financial institutions. A credit union is a nonprofit organization owned by its members. The membership is limited to people with some common bond or interest, such as employment in the same business firm. Other common bonds might be membership in a church, a club, a fraternal association, or a labor union. The eligibility rules for joining a credit union are being liberalized, and credit unions have been adding members in large numbers during the 1960s and 1970s. In 1976 there were 23,000 credit unions with more than 31 million members.

The appeal of credit unions is good returns on savings, low-cost loans, and sympathetic service. They range in size from small ones with fewer than 100 members to large ones with thousands of members and millions of dollars in assets. Just over half of all credit unions are chartered and regulated by the federal government's National Credit Union Administration. The others are governed by state agencies.

Federally chartered credit unions cannot pay more than 7 percent interest on savings. Actually, the savings are known as "shares," and the interest paid is referred to as a "dividend." In the late 1970s the typical dividend rate on credit union shares was 6 percent. Bonus dividends may be declared at the end of the year, but the total annual dividend rate on any account cannot top the percentage set by law. Some state-chartered credit unions have paid interest rates higher than 7 percent.

For some time, credit unions were the only savings institutions that did not have insurance on accounts through the federal government.

As you read earlier in this chapter, banks have insurance through FDIC, and savings and loan associations have insurance through FSLIC. In 1970 Congress enacted a mandatory share (members' savings) insurance law for credit unions with federal charters. Members' savings are now insured up to $40,000. Some states have enacted laws either making it possible for state-chartered credit unions to get federal insurance or requiring that they have insurance from a state-operated program.

CHECKING ACCOUNTS

Another service offered by banks is checking accounts. These accounts are both safe and convenient. With a checking account, you do not need to keep large amounts of cash on hand and risk losing it. Then, too, bills can be paid by mail when checks are used.

At the present time, money kept in checking accounts does not earn interest. In fact, the law prohibits banks from paying interest on checking accounts. During the past few years, however, proposals have been made to change this law so that the money in these accounts will earn interest. In most banks, if a certain minimum amount of money is kept in a checking account, the only charge made to the customer is for printing the checks.

Banks usually have different types of checking accounts in order to meet the needs of the many people they serve. For example, if you have a small amount of money to place in the account and do not write many checks, you may be charged a small fee (such as 10 cents) for each check written. If you maintain a certain minimum balance in your account, such as $200, most banks will charge you nothing for your check-writing privileges.

The illustration on page 301 shows a check properly written. Checks are numbered consecutively. Numbers are usually printed on all checks. If they are not, they should be written in by the check writer. The date is entered in the proper space. The person to whom payment is to be made is written after the words "Pay to the order of." A line should be drawn from the name to the end of the line so that all the space is used. Checks may also be made out to "Cash." Checks made out in this manner, however, can be cashed by anyone. So a check should not be made payable to "Cash" unless it is to be cashed immediately.

The amount of a check is written twice. First, it is written in figures after the printed dollar sign. Writing the amount close to the dollar sign is important because it prevents a dishonest person from increas-

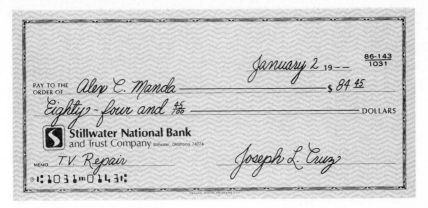

ing the amount of the check by inserting another figure between the amount and the dollar sign. Second, the amount in dollars is written in words on the next line. After the amount in dollars is written in words, the amount in cents is written as a fraction of a dollar. The writing should begin at the far left of the line so that the amount cannot be changed by adding a word at the beginning. A line should be drawn from the fraction to the printed word "Dollars" so that all space is used.

Some check forms include a space to record the purpose for which the check was written. In the illustration shown, the purpose is written at the lower left corner after the word "Memo."

Finally, the check is signed by the person who is paying out the money. The signature should be the same as that written on the signature card that the bank asked the checking account depositor to sign when he or she started the account.

Checks are seldom written for less than one dollar. When it is necessary, however, it should be done as follows. Assume the amount is for 65 cents. In the space following the dollar sign, write as follows:

(65¢)

On the next line, write the amount in words as follows:

Only sixty-five cents ————————

UNITED STATES SAVINGS BONDS

Many families in the nation buy United States savings bonds. At the beginning of the 1970s, more than $50 billion worth of these securities were outstanding. Some persons are attracted to government savings bonds because of appeals to patriotism, but there are other sound reasons for investing money in this way. Some of these reasons are listed below.

1. Savings bonds are considered to be an extremely safe investment because they are backed by the credit of the United States government.
2. Savings bonds can be quickly and easily converted into cash when cash is needed. They can always be redeemed at a stated value on demand two months from the date they are issued. When these bonds are cashed in early, however, the interest earned is less than when they are held to maturity.
3. The interest on savings bonds is not subject to state or local income tax or to personal property taxes. They are subject to federal income tax, however.
4. If savings bonds are lost, stolen, or destroyed, they can be replaced without cost.
5. Savings bonds are easy and convenient to buy. Neighborhood banks sell them, post offices sell them, and many employers make it possible for workers to buy savings bonds through payroll savings plans.

Federal projects such as national parks require a great deal of money to maintain. One way in which the government raises this money is by selling savings bonds. (*American Airlines*)

The federal government is an extremely complex organization with complex activities. The money used to finance these activities comes, of course, from various taxes collected from individuals and business institutions. Sometimes, however, the tax receipts are insufficient to finance the programs of the government. When this happens, the government must borrow money. Much of this money is borrowed from commercial banks and other financial institutions, but a sizable amount is also borrowed directly from individuals by issuing savings bonds. When consumers save money by investing in United States savings bonds, they are also lending money to the federal government.

Currently, only two types of savings bonds are being sold: Series E and Series H.

Series E Bonds

Series E bonds are known as "discount bonds." The financial return to the holder is the difference between what is paid for the bond and what is received when the bond is cashed. The bonds may be redeemed for cash at any time after they are two months old, but unless they are held for more than six months, the holder gets only the amount paid for the bond. The period of time the bonds must be held before they mature has changed over the years. In the late 1970s they had to be held five years from their date of issue. The following table shows the amount the buyer pays and the amount received at maturity (after five years) for various denominations of Series E bonds.

Cost	Maturity Value
$ 18.75	25
37.50	50
75.00	100
150.00	200
375.00	500
750.00	1,000

The difference between the amount paid for the bond and the amount received for it at maturity is, of course, the interest earned. The interest rate for bonds held to maturity is now 6 percent. Thus, if you purchased a bond for $75 now and held it for five years, you would receive $100 upon redeeming the bond. If you should redeem the bond before the five years have elapsed, you would receive less than 6 percent interest. The yield is 4.5 percent the first year, and it increases gradually until it reaches 6 percent after five years.

No Series E or Series H bonds have yet been retired because of age. The old bonds still being held have had their original maturity extended, and their current interest rate is 6 percent.

Series H Bonds

The other type of United States savings bond now being sold is known as the Series H bond. This series is sold in denominations of $500, $1000, $5000, and $10,000. The main difference between the Series H bond and the Series E bond is that the interest on the purchase price of a Series H bond is paid every six months by check, while the interest on a Series E bond accrues and is paid to the purchaser when the bond is redeemed. If you purchase a $500 Series E bond, you would pay $375 and then redeem it for $500 after five years. If you purchased a $500 Series H bond, you would pay $500 and then receive a check for the interest from the government every six months. The maturity date on Series H bonds is 10 years from the date of purchase. The interest is 5 percent the first year, 5.8 percent for next four years, and 6.5 percent for the second five years. These rates produce an average rate of 6 percent for the 10-year period. The Series H bond may be redeemed at any time after six months from the issue date.

Checking Your Reading

1. When income is used to buy an expensive item, such as a refrigerator, a kind of saving takes place. Explain why this is a kind of saving.
2. Explain what is meant by "forced saving."
3. What is meant by these two statements?
   a. When you save a dollar, you do not forever surrender your right to spend it.
   b. As soon as you have savings, you have a silent partner working for you.
4. Why should an individual or a family establish an emergency fund? How much should be in the emergency fund?
5. Explain how compound interest works.

6. If the nominal annual rate of interest is 6 percent, will the true annual rate be more or less if interest is compounded quarterly? Why?
7. List five things consumers should look for when shopping for the best place to put their savings.
8. What is meant by the business term "liquidity"?
9. How are deposits in most commercial banks insured and for how much?
10. What is the name of the federal organization that insures most savings and loan associations? For how much are accounts insured by this organization?
11. Who may join a credit union? For what purposes do people join credit unions?
12. Give five reasons for investing money in United States savings bonds.

Consumer Problems and Projects

1. Assume that you spend $5.75 each week for between-meal snacks. You have decided to reduce this amount to $2 a week and save the difference.
   a. How much will you save in a half year? A whole year?
   b. Discuss whether or not this decision is a wise one.
2. Assume that you have deposited $1500 in a savings institution that pays interest at the rate of 5 percent compounded annually.
   a. What amount of interest will be earned the first year? The second year? The third year?
   b. What will be the value of the principal at the end of the first year? The second year? The third year?
   c. What is the total amount of interest earned during the 3-year period?
3. If $3200 is invested at 5 percent compounded annually, how much will the principal be at the end of 20 years? (You may use table 17-1.)
4. If you invest $1200 at the end of every six months during a 10-year period, and if the interest is compounded semiannually at 4 percent a year, how much will your fund be worth at the end of 10 years? (You may use Table 17-3.)

5. Assume you have $5500 to invest for one year. What would be your return if you received interest at the following rates?
   a. 7 percent compounded annually
   b. 7½ percent compounded annually
   c. 7 percent compounded monthly
   d. 7½ percent compounded monthly
   (You may use Table 17-2.)
6. Make a comparison chart listing the advantages and disadvantages of the various kinds of institutions in which you can invest your savings. This chart can guide you in making your savings plans for the future.
7. List as many services as you can that banks offer to their depositors. Find out how many in your class make use of each of these services.
8. Visit your local bank. Plan in advance the things you are going to look for and the questions you would like to have answered, such as: Is the bank safe? How can you tell? What facilities and services are offered to depositors? If there are several types of banks in your community, you may wish to send a committee to each and compare the reports.

18

Investment Programs

Any consumer who is saving money for future use must recognize the fact that the dollars being saved now probably will not buy as much in the future. They will not buy as much because of *inflation*, the word used to describe the increase in the cost of living. Newspaper and magazine articles continually remind us that today's dollar is worth only a fraction of what dollars were worth 10 or 20 years ago. Our dollars are worth less, of course, because the prices we must pay for the things we buy keep going up. In fact, the cost of living in 1975 was 6 times what it was in 1900.

THE EFFECT OF INFLATION

What will future inflation be? No one can predict the rate of future inflation, of course, but some increase is almost certain. What happened to prices between 1900 and 1975? They remained the same in only 6 years, and they decreased in only 13 years. In the other 56 years, prices increased. Nearly every advanced, industrial nation of the world experiences some inflation. It is the price paid for continual growth and prosperity. But because of inflation, special care needs to be exercised to protect the purchasing power of long-term saving.

In 1975 a meal like this one cost more than six times what it cost in 1900. (*Jack & Betty Cheetham, Magnum*)

Let's say that in a recent year, prices rose about 6 percent. In that case, interest on savings during that year would have to be high enough to give a return after taxes of 6 percent. If interest payments received were not that high, the investors lost that year. Can you see why inflation needs to be considered by any consumer who is saving money? Special importance must be placed on protecting long-term savings from shrinkage due to future inflation.

Some savings methods are highly vulnerable to inflation, while others are less so. Savings methods discussed in Chapter 17 are best suited for money set aside for emergency funds, for large recurring expenses, and for purchases of such expensive items as automobiles and household goods. Money is always needed for these purposes, and it should be placed where it is easily available. When saving money for long-term purposes, such as retirement, the money should be invested with the thought of protecting it from inflation.

The ideal investment would have four characteristics:

1. It would be completely safe from loss.
2. It would be readily convertible into cash.
3. It would return a high rate of interest.
4. It would grow in value at least as fast as the increase in the cost of living.

Unfortunately, such an ideal investment does not exist. The problem is to find a combination of these characteristics that best meets our needs.

INVESTING IN SECURITIES

Buying securities is one way in which some persons invest the cash reserves they have accumulated. An adequate amount of money should be available in an emergency fund, and such important expenses as life insurance premiums should be planned for before considering investing in securities.

When you are ready to invest, you should investigate the two major kinds of securities: bonds and stocks. Let us consider some of the differences between these types of securities.

Bonds

When you buy bonds issued by a corporation or by a government, you are lending money to that corporation or government. Thus, by buying bonds, you become a creditor. The organization that issues bonds acknowledges that it owes the holders a certain sum of money and pledges to repay the sum on a certain date and under certain conditions; it also pledges to pay a certain amount of interest on specified dates.

Bonds are issued by many different types of corporations. By buying bonds, you are simply lending your money to the issuer of the bonds; but the many different types of bonds, or lending agreements, and the vast difference in the financial soundness of the organizations offering bonds for sale make the wise buying of bonds difficult.

Bonds are also issued by various political subdivisions, such as states, cities, counties, local public-housing authorities, and school districts. These types of bonds are often called *municipals,* and they offer a special advantage: tax exemption. The interest received from municipals is free from federal income tax. Because of this tax exemption, they can be sold at less interest than other bonds. To decide whether a tax-exempt bond is worth buying, you must compare the interest received with the interest on other investments after taking into account the tax you would have to pay.

Let's say a person has a taxable income of $16,000. This person's federal income tax is $3260 plus 28 percent of any amount earned over $16,000. Such a person is said to be in the 28 percent tax bracket because on each additional dollar of income he or she pays 28 percent in taxes (until taxable income reaches $20,000—then the person moves into the 32 percent tax bracket). Which would give a person in the 28 percent tax bracket a better return: A $5000 municipal bond paying 5½ percent? Or a $5000 corporation bond paying 7½ percent? On the corporation bond, the annual interest would be $375 (7½ percent of $5000). The municipal bond would pay just $275. But the interest on the corporation bond would be taxed at 28 percent. Thus, the investor would pay $105 in federal income tax (28 percent of $375), leaving a net return of just $270.

The higher the income tax bracket you are in, the more attractive municipal bonds are because of their tax-exempt feature. Since the bond market is quite competitive, their price is bid up so that only people in the higher tax brackets get any special benefit.

Corporation Stock

A stock certificate represents a share in the ownership of a corporation. If you purchase stock issued by XYZ Corporation, you become a part owner of that corporation. By contrast, if you purchase bonds issued by the XYZ Corporation, you are lending money to the corporation and you become its creditor. Unlike bonds, stocks are not sold by governmental bodies. They are sold only by business firms that are organized as corporations. The corporation issuing stocks may be a huge firm with millions of dollars in assets, or it may be a small firm with only a few hundred dollars in assets.

Since stockholders are the owners of the corporation, they share in its profits and losses. Their stock may rise or fall in value from day to day as the corporation's assets or potentiality for profit increases or decreases. Stockholders share in the profits of the business by receiving dividends.

There are so many different kinds of stocks in existence that it is often difficult to distinguish between the various grades. An investor should always carefully study the provisions governing a stock in order to determine the rights and obligations of the stockholders.

Common Stock

When just one kind of stock is issued by a corporation, it is usually known as *common stock*. The owners of common stock elect the directors of the corporation, who are responsible for making company policy and for appointing the officers who will administer the affairs of the firm. Common stock does not carry a fixed dividend; that is, the amount paid periodically to each stockholder is not set in advance. If corporate profits are small, dividend rates go down or dividends stop being paid. If profits go up, the dividend rates usually go up also. However, even though the directors of a corporation usually declare a dividend for holders of common stock when profits are high, they do not have to do so. They may decide instead to hold the money for future use or to invest it in research or equipment. You can see then that investing in common stocks can be risky. A bondholder can usually count on a fixed interest rate, but a holder of common stock is promised no specific return on an investment. If a company's financial situation becomes poor and dividends are not paid, the value of the stock (the amount that buyers are willing to pay for it) will go down. In extreme cases, a company can go bankrupt and its common stock become worthless.

Preferred Stock

In addition to common stock, many corporations also issue *preferred stock*. The holders of preferred stock do not ordinarily have a right to vote in the election of directors of the corporation, but holding this type of stock has some advantages. The dividend on preferred stock is usually set at a definite amount per share per year, and the owners of preferred stock receive their agreed upon and fixed share of the profits before the holders of common stock receive their dividends. In the event that the corporation goes out of business and the assets of the corporation are sold, the holders of preferred stock will be paid before the holders of common stock.

There are several types of preferred stock, and a buyer should always understand the provisions of the particular stock he or she buys. For example, some preferred stock dividends are *cumulative;* that is, any dividends for previous years that have not been paid must be paid in full before the corporation can pay dividends on its common stock. On the other hand, the preferred stock dividends can be *noncumulative.* In this case, if the corporation fails to earn a profit for a few years, dividends may not be paid. When dividends are again paid, the holders of preferred stock are paid first, but they do not receive dividends for the years during which no dividends were declared.

Some preferred stocks are *participating;* that is, holders of this type of stock share in any earnings that the company makes in excess of the stated rate of dividend. If a corporation still has surplus earnings available to distribute as dividends after paying the holders of preferred stock the regular dividend and the holders of common stock a certain agreed upon dividend, these earnings will be shared by the holders of common stock and participating preferred stock.

OPERATION OF THE STOCK MARKET

Knowing the differences between the various kinds of securities is the first step in understanding the securities market. An investor should also have an understanding of the methods by which stock values are determined and how buyers and sellers make sales transactions.

Companies issue stock in order to raise money for operations. The company sets a specific price on the stock when it is first offered for sale, but once the stock has been sold to the public, the price is no longer fixed by the company. It is then determined by the price the buyers are willing to pay and the price for which the stockholders are willing to sell.

If a particular stock is considered by many people to be too high at a certain time, many stockholders may want to sell the stock and invest in other securities. When this happens, the price of the stock usually drops. On the other hand, if a stock is considered to be a good buy (perhaps because it appears that the company will have an especially bright future), the price of the stock will probably rise, for the demand for the stock will enable the owners to ask and to receive higher prices. So the price of a security at any particular time reflects nothing more than the combined opinions of buyers and sellers about the value of that security.

Investors can follow the daily prices of their securities by consulting almost any major newspaper. On the financial pages, they will find listings of the current prices paid for all the more popular stocks traded. Sometimes stock prices vary only slightly, say, by an eighth or a quarter of a point, which means an eighth or a quarter of a dollar. At other times, the prices of certain stocks go up or down sharply during a day—by several points, or by many dollars.

Stock Exchanges

There are thousands of different stocks and bonds, but the ones that are bought and sold most frequently are those traded on the large exchanges. The largest organized exchange in the United States is the New York Stock Exchange. The American Stock Exchange, another

The stocks of large and small corporations are traded on stock exchanges, located in many major cities throughout the country. (*New York Convention and Visitors Bureau*)

large exchange, is also located in New York. In addition, regional exchanges are scattered throughout the country.

Buying and selling stocks on a security exchange is accomplished by means of the auction method. Someone may offer a stock for sale at a certain price; someone else may bid for the same stock at a different price. When a buyer and seller agree on a price, a sale is made. In financial circles, the agents who match up investors who want to buy or sell securities are called *brokers*. Brokers negotiate purchases and sales for their clients, and for this service they charge a commission that is based on the amount of the transaction. The actual buying and selling on the New York Stock Exchange is done by brokers who have bought memberships (commonly called *seats*). The members of the New York Stock Exchange represent brokerage firms located throughout the country.

A great deal can be learned about a stock by looking at the latest stock price quotation in a daily newspaper or in *The Wall Street Journal*. *The Wall Street Journal*, which is published weekdays in a number of regional editions, provides up-to-date financial and busi-

NYSE-Composite Transactions

Wednesday, July 21, 1976

Quotations include trades on the New York, Midwest, Pacific, Philadelphia, Boston and Cincinnati stock exchanges and reported by the National Association of Securities Dealers and Instinet.

–1976– High	Low	Stocks	Div.	P-E Ratio	Sales 100s	High	Low	Close	Net Chg.
60¾	37⅜	Data Genl		31	130	53½	52¼	53	+ ½
17⅜	10⅝	Dayco	.50b	5	8	16½	16¼	16¼	- ⅛
35½	26¼	DaytnHud	1	8	72	28⅝	28⅜	28⅜	– ½
19⅞	17	DaytPL	1.66	8	55	18¼	18	18	– ⅛
77	70	DPLpf	7.37	..	z100	76	76	76	+ 1
73¾	51¾	Deere	2	9	519	66⅜	65⅝	66¼	+ ¼
29⅜	22⅜	DelMon	1.40	7	106	28⅞	28⅝	28⅞	– ¼
13⅝	12¼	DelmaP	1.20	8	101	12⅞	12¾	12⅞	+ ⅛
45⅞	37	DeltaAir	.60	19	264	43¾	43	43½	+ ¼
7⅛	3¾	Deltec Intl		40	20	5⅝	5⅜	5⅝	+ ⅛
7⅝	3⅝	Deltona Crp		..	19	4⅜	4⅛	4⅛	......
23⅜	19⅛	DennisMfg	1	8	95	22⅞	22⅛	22⅝	+ ⅛
25¼	18⅛	Dennys	.44	14	49	23¾	23⅜	23⅝	+ ⅛
34¾	27½	Dentsply	.80	17	43	33	32⅝	33	+ ⅜
25⅜	15½	Deseret	.28	15	76	24	23¾	23¾	– ¼
11⅞	5¾	DeSotoIn	.40	10	21	10⅛	10	10⅛	– ⅛
15	13	DetEdis	1.45	10	469	14⅛	13⅞	14⅛	+ ⅛
62	55	DetE pf	5.50	..	5	59	57¾	59	+ ¾
93	82¼	DetE pf	9.32	..	z50	89¾	89¾	89¾	– ¼
76¾	66	DetE pf	7.68	..	z10	72	72	72	......

–1976– High	Low	Stocks	Div.	P-E Ratio	Sales 100s	High	Low	Close	Net Chg.
18½	11½	GoldWt Fin		6	70	15½	15¼	15¼	– ¼
19⅝	13⅛	GoldW pf	.78	..	13	16½	16⅜	16½	– ⅛
29¼	18	Goodrh	1.12	14	53	28½	28⅛	28½	+ ⅜
25¼	**20⅛**	**Goodyr**	**1.10**	**10**	**397**	**23½**	**23**	**23¼**	**+ ⅛**
16¼	11¾	GorJwlA	.32	6	15	12¾	12⅜	12⅜	– ⅜
39⅞	26¼	GouldIn	1.36	10	260	39⅝	39⅛	39⅜	– ⅛
29	19¼	Gould pf	1.35	..	25	28⅛	28	28⅛	+ ⅛
33⅞	24¼	Grace	1.70	6	151	27	26¾	27	+ ⅛
34⅛	24⅝	Grainger	.36	20	150	32½	32¼	32¼	......
15⅞	12⅝	GrandUn	1	8	6	14¾	14½	14¾	......
17⅜	12¼	Granitvl	.80	5	22	14½	14⅛	14½	+ ½
19⅞	13¼	GrayDrg	.60	5	4	15¾	15⅝	15¾	......
15⅝	10½	GtAtlPac		25	503	12⅝	12½	12⅝	......
24½	18⅝	GtLkD	1.20a	6	10	20⅞	20⅝	20⅞	+ ⅛
17⅛	14⅛	GtNoIr	1.25e	12	2	15⅞	15⅞	15⅞	– ⅛
34¼	28¼	GtNorNek	1	9	166	30	29⅜	29¾	– ¼
19⅜	13⅝	GtWnFin	.50	9	411	17¾	17½	17¾	+ ⅛
31⅞	21¾	GtWest Unit		2	4	25¼	25	25	– ⅜
20¼	17⅝	GtWn pf	1.88	..	4	18⅛	18⅛	18⅛	......
18¼	15¼	GrGiant	1.08	17	56	17¼	17	17⅛	– ⅜

ness news. A section of the New York Stock Exchange quotations of July 21, 1976, is shown here. Dollar signs are omitted, and the fractions shown represent parts of a dollar. Quotations and actual stock sales are made in eighths of a dollar, which is 12½ cents.

- The first two columns give the high and low sales price range per share for the current calendar year (in this case 1976). During the first few months of a year, the ranges from the previous year are included. For example, the price of Goodyear (abbreviated Goodyr) stock ranged from a low of 20⅛ ($20.125) to a high of 25¼ ($25.25).
- The figures immediately following the name of the stock show the amount of the current annual dividend paid per share. Goodyear is expected to pay $1.10 a share to its stockholders during the year.
- The column headed "P-E Ratio" gives the price-earnings ratio for the stock. This is probably the most widely used measurement for trying to arrive at a judgment on the worth of a stock. Starting in early 1973, newspapers added P-E ratios to the New York and American Stock Exchange tables. The P-E ratio is arrived at by dividing the current price of the stock by the earnings over the past 12 months. For example, a stock that is now selling for $40 and that earned $2 a share over the past 12 months has a P-E ratio of 20 ($40 divided by $2). The price-earnings ratio for Goodyear was 10 on July 21, 1976.
- The column headed "Sales 100s" shows the number of shares of that stock sold during the day. Amounts are listed in hundreds.

The number of shares of Goodyear sold on the day shown was 39,700.

- The next three columns show the highest price, the lowest price, and the closing price paid for a share of stock during the day. During the day, the price of a share of Goodyear stock fluctuated from a high of 23½ ($23.50) to a low of 23 ($23). The closing price (the amount paid by the last buyer of the day) was 23¼ ($23.25).
- The amount in the column at the extreme right shows the difference between the final price shown and the final price of the day before. A plus sign means the stock rose in price by that amount since the day before. A minus sign means a drop in price. Buyers paid one-eighth of a dollar more for a share of Goodyear stock on the day of the quotation than buyers had paid on the day before.

Unlisted Securities

Some securities are not listed on any exchange. These stocks and bonds, which are known as *unlisted securities*, may be bought and sold through individual brokers or, in some cases, may be traded on an exchange without having been accepted for formal listing. When securities are sold through brokers, the transactions are popularly called "over-the-counter" transactions. Government and municipal bonds are traded in this way, and so are the stocks of most banks and insurance companies. Generally, however, unlisted securities are those of small companies that are likely to be known better locally than nationally. Because unlisted securities are traded less frequently, it is sometimes difficult to determine the price at which they can be sold. Partly for this reason, over-the-counter stocks are considered a less conservative investment than listed stocks.

Investment Clubs

During the past couple of decades, investment clubs have become popular throughout the country. In the mid-1970s there were about 60,000 investment clubs across the nation with an estimated membership of more than a million. An investment club is simply a small group of people who band together to learn about the stock market and invest a small amount of money periodically. The main idea of an investment club is to have its members learn about stocks by taking an active part in their selection. Clubs usually have 10, 15, or 20 people who meet once a month to invest money regularly. The members each contribute $10, $15, $20, $25, or perhaps as much as $50 a month into a fund that is used to buy stocks.

Many brokers are glad to help organize investment clubs and to supply their members with regular reports on companies and market conditions in general. According to the National Association of Investment Clubs, a nonprofit organization, the majority of the clubs in operation for several years have profited.

Investment Companies

For persons who want to invest in the stock market but have neither the time nor the experience to keep informed about their holdings, investment companies might be the answer. An *investment company* sells its shares to investors and then uses the money received from the sale to buy the securities of other companies. An investment company obtains its income from the dividends paid on the securities it has purchased and from the profit it receives when it sells certain securities that have increased in value. The income thus earned by the investment company is then passed on to people who own shares in the investment company.

By now you realize that investing in the stock market involves many risks. Ideally, the investor guards against these risks by spreading investments among different kinds of industries and geographic areas. If an investor buys a dozen different securities and one proves to be bad, he or she will not lose the whole investment. The investor may even still make a profit. Spreading the risk in this way is known as *diversification.*

It is difficult, however, for persons with relatively small amounts of money to invest to achieve diversification on their own. The investment company offers this type of investor the advantage of diversification. If the securities selected by the investment company increase in value, the stockholders make money; if they decrease in value, the stockholders lose money. Buying shares in an investment company, then, does not eliminate risks. But because the investments are spread over a number of different stocks and bonds carefully selected by investment experts, the risks are greatly reduced. Furthermore, securities purchased by an investment company are reviewed constantly by a team of experts, who buy and sell as changing values and potentials present opportunities for profit. There are two kinds of investment companies: closed-end and open-end (or mutual funds).

Closed-end Investment Companies. A closed-end investment company is a corporation that invests in the securities of other companies.

Closed-end companies issue only a limited number of shares when they are formed and usually no more. It is for this reason that they are called "closed-end" companies. Furthermore, closed-end companies do not agree to buy back their shares. When you want to sell, you have to find a buyer, just as you do when selling shares of Continental Oil or Chrysler. The shares of the most active closed-end companies are traded on the stock exchanges, and you pay a commission computed in the same way that your commission would be figured in buying shares of any industrial corporation.

Mutual Funds. An investment company that is organized to issue and sell new shares at any time so that the number of outstanding shares is always changing is an *open-end* company. These companies are known popularly as "mutual funds." In addition to creating and selling new shares in itself whenever there is a market for them, the open-end company also buys back and retires shares whenever a shareholder wants to cash them in.

In the mid-1970s there were about 600 mutual funds in existence. They can be bought through brokerage offices or through selling organizations set up to handle one or more funds. Commission costs vary, from as high as 8½ to 9 percent of the total cost of the shares for small investments to half that rate or less for especially large purchases. This sales commission is known as a "load charge." The load charge varies with the mutual fund.

Mutual funds that charge commissions are known as "load funds." The mutual funds that do not charge a sales commission are known as "no-load funds." When a prospective investor is interested in a load fund, a salesperson is typically quite available and eager to explain the mutual fund with charts, figures, and other information to assist you in understanding the investment. This is not so with no-load funds. To acquire shares in a no-load fund you have to write to the fund for a *prospectus,* information that government regulations require the fund to supply before an investment can be made. Then, if you decide to buy, you mail your check. The managers of both load funds and no-load funds receive a management fee for handling the investors' money—the fee is commonly one-half of 1 percent a year or less.

In recent years, no-load funds have become increasingly popular. Of the 600 mutual funds in the mid-1970s, about 150 were no-load funds. People have become aware that they are around and that they provide a big savings in commissions. The long-term records of the no-load funds compare favorably with those of the load funds. Experience has shown that for both load funds and no-load funds, there has been a great deal of variation in performance. Certainly no one should pick a mutual fund simply because it does not have a sales commission. A well-managed load fund is a better buy for an investor than a no-load fund with consistently poor performance.

Over a long period of time, the records of mutual funds compare quite well with stock averages. Over the short term, however, the performances of mutual funds can be poor. During the early 1970s, for example, many of the mutual funds had bad records. After 1974, however, the records of mutual funds improved. One reason for the improvement, of course, was the fact that stock market prices began to go up. Perhaps, too, people were buying mutual funds because they believed that it was a sure way to make money in the stock market. They may have ignored the fact that all a mutual fund does is relieve the investor of the job of selecting individual securities. Mutual funds do not relieve one of the risks of owning securities. Some investment experts say that not more than 10 or 20 percent of the price change in diversified stock holdings are due to qualities of the securities for which the investment adviser is responsible. The other 80 or 90 percent reflects the overall movement of the stock market.

Mutual funds exist for every type of investment objective. Following are some main categories of funds.

- *Growth Funds.* The objective of growth funds is to achieve an increase in the value of the shares and the eventual growth in income. Growth fund assets are usually invested in common stock, especially that of fast-growing industries such as chemicals and electronics. For young people who are more interested in capital gains than immediate income, this type of mutual fund would be attractive.
- *Balanced Funds.* Investments are divided among common stock, preferred stock, and bonds when the purpose of the mutual fund is to provide a balance between growth and income. When prices in the market are rising, balanced funds will not show the increase in value of a growth fund.
- *Income Funds.* The investments of this type of mutual fund are mostly in securities that provide a high yield, such as utilities and rails. The main purpose of these mutual funds is to provide steady dividend income. For people who are approaching retirement and are interested in a steady source of income, this type of fund would be attractive.
- *Specialized Funds.* These funds may restrict themselves to certain types of securities, or they may be designed for a certain type of investor. Some of the specialized funds concentrate on a par-

ticular industry or type of security. One fund invests in the stock of companies that will benefit from scientific developments and technical advances. Others may concentrate on such things as life insurance, energy, or utilities.

- *Money Market Funds.* These mutual funds were introduced during the 1970s. Money market funds are backed not by stocks but by short-term (usually 30 days to a year) investments. The funds invest money in such things as United States government securities and bank certificates of deposit. In 1973 and 1974, short-term interest rates were unusually high. Certificates of deposit of $100,000 or more paid 11 percent and even higher. Small investors could not take advantage of these unusually high interest rates, of course, because they lacked large amounts of money. But money market funds made it possible for investors to buy shares in small amounts and thus get some advantages of the high rates on these short-term investments that big investors get.

Different systems of buying mutual funds also are available. Following are two general methods.

- *Open Account.* Under some of these plans, the investor can buy as many or as few shares as desired whenever he or she wishes. Other plans provide that the investor buy shares at regular intervals, but the number bought can vary. The dividends may be reinvested automatically, and the agreement to make regular purchases can be terminated at any time the investor wishes. No requirement exists that the investor make a fixed number of purchases.
- *Contractual Plan.* A contractual plan requires that the buyer sign a contract that binds him or her to make an investment regularly for a specified period of time. The investor is making a commitment to make regular payments that over time add up to an investment of a sizable amount of money. The investor can, of course, drop out of the plan at any time he or she wants; but if payments are stopped, money is lost because of the way in which the loading charge, or sales commission, is figured. The contractual plan may provide for a loading charge of 9 percent of the total investment, and as much as half of the loading charge may be deducted from the money the investor pays in during the first year of the plan. If the investor discontinues the plan during the first few years, he or she may receive less than had been paid in because of the heavy commission paid during the early part of the period.

Small investors looking for professional management of their money may decide to buy shares of a mutual fund or a closed-end investment company. Such an investment represents a good way to achieve the kind of diversified risk that might be difficult to reproduce in straight purchases of securities. Generally, an investor should look at the record of the fund during the past ten years. If it is above average, the management has probably done a good job. Some funds show spectacular profits over a period of a few years, but over a longer period of time they might not show up so well. Stockbrokers and many libraries have copies of *Investment Companies*, an annual compilation of comparative data published by Wiesenberger Services, Inc., One New York Plaza, New York, NY 10005. This publication gives information about the performances of mutual funds and closed-end investment companies.

INVESTING IN REAL ESTATE

The single largest investment most people make during their lives is their home. During the past decades the resale value of an average house has kept up with inflation, and in many cases, house values have gone up faster than inflation. If a house is selected carefully, the buyer can be money ahead in two ways. First, the house will increase in value as the years go by. Second, because of inflation, the house buyer will be paying off the loan in future years with cheaper dollars.

Buying a house is an investment; for most people, it is their largest single investment. (*Susan Berkowitz*)

How about investing in real estate other than your own house? According to investment experts, to make a higher than normal rate of return in any type of land investment you would have to have information that other people do not have. Will the land become valuable because the area's population will increase rapidly? Are certain industries going to build near the area? If you know such things, won't other people also have such knowledge?

Although on average, more money might be made on real estate, on average a greater risk is also taken. The value of land can fall, just like the value of anything else.

The purpose of investing, of course, is to earn a bigger return on your money than you could from a savings account. If that is not possible, then the investment is not worth the risk. Every investment should be looked at as a trade-off between risk and rate of return. Remember, the higher the potential rate of return, the higher the risk.

Checking Your Reading

1. By how much did the cost of living increase during the first 75 years of this century?
2. What four characteristics would an ideal investment have?
3. Why are persons who buy bonds considered to be creditors?
4. What are municipal bonds, and what special advantage do they offer the investor?
5. What does the term "participating" mean when it refers to preferred-stock dividends?
6. Once the stock of a corporation has been sold to the public, how is the price of the stock determined?
7. Where can you find a listing of the current prices paid for popular stocks?
8. What are over-the-counter securities transactions?
9. How do investment clubs operate?
10. What is the main purpose of an investment club?
11. What is meant by the term "diversification" as it is used in this chapter?
12. Explain the difference between closed-end and open-end investment companies.
13. What is the difference between mutual funds known as "load funds" and mutual funds known as "no-load funds"?

14. Explain how an investor can lose money by dropping out of a contractual plan for buying mutual funds.
15. State two ways in which a buyer of a house can be money ahead if the selection of the house is made carefully.

Consumer Problems and Projects

1. A person in the 32 percent tax bracket is considering buying a $10,000 municipal bond that pays an interest rate of 5½ percent. He can also buy a $10,000 corporation bond that pays 8 percent. Which bond will give him the best net rate of return?
2. Check a newspaper daily for the closing prices of six common stocks. Make a graph showing their closing prices for a four-week period.
3. Rex Lasorda is 26 years old. He has been married for four years and has one child. His income is about average for a man his age. Two years ago, he purchased a house, taking out a mortgage that will be paid up in 30 years. Mr. Lasorda's life is insured for $20,000. He has just made his last payment on his two-year-old car. The Lasordas' budget shows that they can now save $100 a month. Mr. Lasorda is considering investing the $100 in a mutual fund. Mrs. Lasorda thinks he should place the monthly savings in a savings account. What do you recommend? Why?
4. Imagine that you have $10,000 to invest and that after you investigate several good companies you select one with a very bright future whose earnings are expected to be high for several years. The return on the preferred stock is good, but before you buy this particular stock, your broker advises you to buy common stock in the same company instead. What reasons might your broker have for this position? If the preferred stock were participating, how would this influence his opinion?
5. A common saying in investment circles is "Don't put all your eggs in one basket." This, of course, means to diversify your holdings and thus avoid the risks involved in putting all your money into one investment. In what sense would you be ignoring this saying if you invested in the common stock of three companies: one a producer of fishing rods, another a producer of outboard motors, and the third a producer of lightweight aluminum boats?

19

Introduction
to Life Insurance

By the mid-1970s two out of every three people in the nation were insured by some type of life insurance policy. More than nine out of ten families now have at least one member who owns life insurance. But an insurance industry survey of widows showed that more than half of them got less than $5000 from their husbands' insurance. Other studies have revealed that many persons do not have enough life insurance coverage. Thus, although life insurance is popular in our nation, many people are seriously underinsured.

Why is life insurance so necessary? Mainly because most people now depend so completely on the money income earned by one or more members of the family. Let's take the case of a family in which one person earns most of the income. What would happen if that person—whether husband, wife, or another family member—should die suddenly? How would the family continue to buy the things it needs in the years ahead? The first few years would be difficult if the money supply were suddenly cut off. The problem has not always been so serious. In earlier times, ties among relatives were much stronger. In those days a family could look to grandparents, cousins, and other relatives for financial help in the event of the death of the breadwinner. But today most families cannot look much beyond their own household when money problems arise.

WHY ARE PEOPLE UNDERINSURED?

Perhaps some persons fail to buy enough life insurance because they underestimate how much they really need. A sum of $25,000 seems large to most of us, but do you realize that if a $25,000 policy were to be paid in monthly installments over ten years, the payments would be about $250 a month? For many families more money than that is needed from life insurance if the chief breadwinner should die. As a rough rule of thumb, for every $1000 of life insurance coverage, about $10 can be paid each month for 10 years. Thus a $10,000 policy would provide $100 a month for 10 years. If the money is to be stretched over 30 years, a $10,000 policy would provide just $48 a month.

Another reason so many Americans are underinsured is that they are sold policies that are not really appropriate for their needs. A young family may want to insure the life of the breadwinner for $75,000. But when the salesperson gives the size of the *annual premium* (the cost of the insurance each year), they might discover they just can't afford it. If the family had known something about the differences between the major kinds of policies, they might discover that they could afford a policy that would give them adequate coverage. Instead, they often settle for a smaller amount of insurance. Later in this chapter, you will learn about the difference between the two major types of life insurance.

If persons buying life insurance would compare costs accurately among the many companies selling life insurance, they would find a large cost difference for similar policies. Chapter 20 gives information on how consumers can compare costs among the various companies.

THE PURPOSES OF LIFE INSURANCE

In a nationwide survey conducted by the life insurance industry, families gave several reasons why they owned life insurance policies. The reasons given fell into one of two major categories. Life insurance is purchased (1) to provide financial security for dependents after the insured's death and (2) to build up savings.

There are many ways to save money, of course, and saving money through life insurance policies may be a poor way for most people to save. Nevertheless, the life insurance industry advertises savings as a main reason for buying life insurance. For some people, saving money by means of life insurance policies may not be a bad idea. In Chapter 20 we'll look at the cases where saving money with life insurance makes sense.

The main purpose of life insurance, however, is to provide money for persons who are financially dependent on the insured should he die early. Money should be available through life insurance to enable the family to fulfill reasonable financial goals. Looked at in this way, most families are underinsured.

Who is the breadwinner in a family? That depends on the family. In many cases, both husband and wife work, and thus both contribute to family income. In other cases, just one person brings in money. Today there are more than 35 million women in the United States work force. Some of these are homemakers who combine this work with an outside job. Others pursue full-time careers in the work force. Women as heads of households are growing in number. In fact, the insurance industry estimates that by 1980, one in four households will be headed by women.

Whether the head of a household is a man or a woman, a sobering thought must be faced: If that person should die, his or her dependents would be left without their chief source of income. This problem

The need for financial help if the breadwinner dies is greatest when children are small and expenses are large. (*United Nations*)

is usually greatest during the early years of married life, for at this time children are small and expenses are large. The head of a household, therefore, uses life insurance to create an estate for the family immediately and thereby provide money for them to take care of such things as those discussed in the paragraphs that follow.

Last Expenses

Most people want to leave at least enough money to pay for their funeral expenses and for any medical bills resulting from their last illness. Then, too, they should leave enough money to pay other current bills. Many people have sufficient money for this purpose in a savings account, and in that event they need not be concerned about covering this need with life insurance. In any case, needs for immediate cash might be covered by a policy for from $5000 to $10,000 payable as a lump sum. This amount is not large compared with the total insurance needs of an individual, but it may be an important item to keep in mind when considering life insurance needs.

Funds for Dependents

Most workers are now covered by social security. The benefits available to widows and children through this program provide a basic family insurance program that is a starting point in figuring life insurance needs. For more families, social security benefits are not enough. They do, however, provide basic protection that can be added to with life insurance.

If the head of a household dies before his or her dependents, they will need income during a period of readjustment in which they develop a new way of making a living. In some cases, this income is needed for a relatively long period of time. For example, while children are small, one of the parents should be able to stay at home or provide good care for the children in some other way and still be able to meet the regular expenses of maintaining a home.

For many persons, especially parents with small children, the long-term support of dependents is the most important purpose of life insurance. Obviously, this type of coverage requires a sizable amount of insurance. In addition to providing for the basic needs of a family, insurance may be wanted for the education of children. If the breadwinner dies prematurely, the remaining family members should expect to fend for themselves to some extent. But many parents want a fund of money available for the college education of their children.

The Home

Families repaying a mortgage on a home can use insurance to cover the amount of the mortgage. Some families may decide that in the event of the breadwinner's death they would move to a smaller house or to rented living quarters. But in the majority of cases, the family would want to continue living in the same house. In this event, an insurance policy large enough to enable the family to pay off the mortgage would be desirable.

LIFE INSURANCE NEEDS ARE DIFFICULT TO MEASURE

From what has been said up to this point, you should have concluded that life insurance is very important for consumers. Perhaps a few people are wealthy enough to have no real need for life insurance, but most of us who have financial responsibilities to others must figure our life insurance needs and decide what kind of life insurance to buy. Thus, the value of life insurance is not questioned. The important questions are how much and what kind.

When buying insurance to cover property, such as a house or a car, deciding how much to buy is not really very difficult. We can be guided by the replacement value of the house or the car. But life insurance presents a much more complex problem. We do not know how long we will live, so we do not know when our families will need the money from our life insurance. If a father or a mother dies at an early age, the period of time during which dependents will need money for living will be longer. So the total amount of money needed is larger. If we knew that we would live to the age of 80, we would probably conclude that we really did not need life insurance at all. Chapter 20 will examine ways to estimate life insurance needs.

The Role of Life Insurance Agents

Most life insurance is sold by sales representatives who are usually called *agents* or *field underwriters*. The task of these agents, according to the life insurance ads, is to help customers or prospective customers estimate the amount of insurance needed. An agent should be selected carefully because of the great importance of life insurance to the security of one's family.

The agent sells a variety of different life insurance packages with many different names and confusing provisions. The easy thing for a

Insurance agents sell a variety of types of insurance and will help consumers select the one they need. Wise consumers, however, will not rely entirely on the recommendations of the insurance agent. (*Metropolitan Life*)

consumer to do is to place implicit trust in the agent and buy what is recommended. Is this a wise thing for the consumer to do? Or should the consumer become as familiar as possible with the purpose of life insurance and the different forms available so that he or she is able to do a reasonably good job of judging the merits of agents' suggestions?

Most agents work for commissions, and the commissions vary considerably according to the type of policy. The payments made for insurance policies are called *premiums,* and agents receive as their commission a certain percentage of the premium payments. On some policies the agent may be paid a commission for as long as ten years. The percentage declines in the later years, however, and the first-year commission is far and away the largest that the agent receives. When a $10,000 policy that requires large premium payments is sold, the agent generally earns much more than when a $10,000 policy that requires small premium payments is sold. In fact, the difference in the agent's commission is often four- or fivefold.

Consumers Union reported on a study of life insurance that they conducted in the late 1960s. Consumers Union shoppers approached life insurance agents of five large companies in three different metropolitan areas: one on the East Coast, one on the West Coast, and one in the Midwest. The shoppers did not identify themselves as having a connection with Consumers Union. Thus, 15 agents were asked to recommend a policy for a 38-year-old man with a wife and two children (ages 16 and 8). The shopper (prospective policyholder) indicated that he had a $10,000-a-year income, a $10,000 group life insurance policy through his employer, $3000 in the bank, and $5000 ownership in a house; he also indicated that he had mortgage payments and taxes amounting to $1800 a year. Such a man would be underinsured.

One would think that given the information cited above, the agents would be reasonably uniform in their recommendations for life insurance coverage. The fact is that the agents suggested a variety of policies. According to the report issued by Consumers Union, some agents seemed to base their proposal on the shopper's paycheck rather than on a measurement of his need for protection. The recommendations for additional life insurance coverage given by the 15 agents ranged from $5000 to $24,145 at annual premiums from $210 to $1144. Just one of the 15 agents recommended on his own initiative a type of protection that gives the most coverage for the premium dollar.

Selecting just 15 agents at random from among the thousands of agents in the country may not give a completely fair picture of life insurance sales representatives. The experience does, however, show the importance of knowing something about life insurance coverage and choosing an agent with care. Considering the great importance of life insurance to the security of a family and the amount of money that will be paid for the insurance protection, consumers should be personally satisfied with the person who will be helping to make far-reaching recommendations. You could interview several agents from different companies and ask them to make suggestions for life insurance programs for you. Then you would be able to judge with more discernment both the programs suggested and the agents who present them.

As you probably are quite aware, there are many life insurance agents in most communities. Because the turnover rate among people who go into life insurance sales work is quite high, many life insurance companies are engaged in a continuous program of recruiting agents. Thus, many agents are beginners. Other agents, however, may have had years of successful experience. Most agents sell for a single company, but some are brokers for several companies. If an agent adds "C.L.U." after his or her name, you know this agent is a Chartered Life Underwriter who has met stringent requirements established by a professional organization known as the American College of Life Underwriters.

THE TWO TYPES OF LIFE INSURANCE

Life insurance is sold under many names. Most companies sell whole life, 20-payment life, paid up at 65, 20-year endowment, modified life, 10-year renewable term, mortgage protection, and many more. Some companies combine features of the common plans and then sell the "new" plan under their own brand name. There are, however, fundamentally only two types. The policies may be for certain purposes and contain certain complications, but they all fit into one of two categories: term insurance and cash value insurance.

Term Insurance Is Pure Protection

A term insurance policy insures your life for a set period of time, such as a year, five years, or ten years, or until you reach a certain age. A *term* insurance policy is pure protection—it has no savings account or cash value feature.

Suppose one thousand 25-year-old men decide to pool their financial resources and insure each life for $1000. Each man can name a *beneficiary,* the person to whom the $1000 will be paid if the insured man should die. The first problem facing the men is to decide how much money to collect so they will have enough to pay out the claims that might be made. If they knew exactly how many men would die during the next 12 months, their problem would not be so difficult, but of course they do not know this. They might guess that no more than six should die, so that in order to pay $1000 to each of the beneficiaries they would need a fund of $6000 available. By assessing each member of their group $6, they would collect the money they need for claims payments. But, of course, they do not know how many will die; so their calculations could be far off.

Actually, an insurance company begins its calculations of premiums by considering death rates for different age groups. Death rates, or *mortality rates*, are collected over periods of time and then presented in statistical form in mortality tables. Most insurers now use the Commissioners 1958 Standard Ordinary Mortality Table, a table constructed on the basis of mortality statistics in the United States for the years 1950 to 1954. The information given in Table 19-1 is taken from the Commissioners 1958 Standard Ordinary Mortality Table. The second column shows the number of deaths per 1000 persons, and the third column shows life expectancy for the various ages given.

If the one thousand 25-year-old men discussed earlier were insured by an insurance company, the starting point in computing the pre-

TABLE 19-1
Example of Mortality Rates

Age	Deaths per 1000	Expectation of Life
20	1.79	50.37
25	1.93	45.82
30	2.13	41.25
35	2.51	36.69
40	3.53	32.18
45	5.35	27.81
50	8.32	23.63
55	13.00	19.71
60	20.34	16.12

mium for the year would be to look at the mortality table. The number of deaths per 1000 persons at this age is 1.93, so the company would have to collect $1.93 from each man plus an amount to take care of expenses, profit, and the building of a reserve of money to cover contingencies—the possibility that more persons will die than the mortality table indicates. The premium needed in this case would then be considerably more than $1.93.

Persons known as *actuaries* compute premium rates for insurance companies, and their work involves more complicated mathematics than the average person can fully understand. The interest earned on the money insurance companies collect, for example, must enter their computations and as indicated earlier the premiums must reflect selling, collection, and administration expenses as well as reasonable margins for contingencies.

The type of insurance just described is term insurance. Term policies are written for various lengths of time, such as five or ten years. The actuaries come up with a *level premium*—a fixed sum of money that is paid for the number of years in the term agreement. In the case of a five-year term policy, for example, one company would charge a 25-year-old man $5.83 per thousand dollars of coverage for a policy guaranteed to be renewable at the end of the five-year term. So for a $10,000 policy, he would pay $58.30 each year for five years. At the end of five years, his insurance agreement would end. If he decided to insure himself for $10,000 for another period of five years, he could renew the contract with the company and pay this time the annual premium for a 30-year-old man: $5.91 per thousand dollars of coverage, or $59.10 for a $10,000 policy.

Cash Value Insurance Is Insurance Plus Savings

A cash value policy combines insurance protection with the gradual building up of a savings account. Such a policy is often called "permanent" because it protects the insured until he or she dies or discontinues the policy. A term policy, you remember, protects the insured for a set period of time.

Mortality rates increase with age. The mortality table mentioned earlier in this chapter shows the number of deaths per 1000 for 20-year-old persons to be 1.79. For 65-year-olds the death rate per thousand is 29.04. The rate increases to 101.19 per thousand at the age of 79, so for those persons the odds on not reaching the age of 80 are about 1 in 10. The mortality rates become larger at an increasing rate until the age of 99, when the rate is 1000 deaths per 1000 persons.

In the case of cash value policies, insurance companies enter into lifetime insurance contracts with policyholders. That is, the companies are willing to "insure" the person's life for as long as the person lives. How can an insurance company possibly continue to insure the lives of people when they reach older ages? The answer is that each year that the policy is in effect, the amount of insurance decreases and the amount of cash value in the savings account increases. Added together, the two sums of money at any time during the life of the policy equal the death benefit, or *cash value*, that will be paid to the beneficiary. The cash value that builds up steadily as premiums are paid is also called the cash surrender value of the policy because the policyholder can surrender his or her policy with the guarantee that the insurance company will give him or her this sum of money. The life insurance company asks the insured person to pay larger premiums than would be needed simply to insure his or her life. The extra amount that is paid builds up at a certain rate of interest.

To illustrate how the idea of decreasing life insurance and increasing cash surrender value works, let us assume a woman buys a popular type of cash value insurance when she is 25 years old. The face value of her insurance policy (the amount that will be paid her beneficiary when she dies) is $10,000, and she pays an annual premium of $138.50. At the end of 10 years, when the woman has reached the age of 35, the cash surrender value of her policy will be $940. If she should die at that time, her beneficiary would receive $10,000. But the $940 is part of that sum, so the "insurance" part of the death benefit is really $9060. The cash value builds up more rapidly with the passage of time, as illustrated in Table 19-2.

TABLE 19-2

	(1) Cash Surrender Value	(2) Death Protection	(3) Face Value of Policy
After 10 years	$ 940	$9060	$10,000
After 15 years	1700	8300	10,000
After 20 years	2560	7440	10,000
At age 60	4940	5060	10,000
At age 65	5730	4270	10,000

The formula, then, is simple. At any given year, column 1 plus column 2 equals column 3, which is the face value, or death benefit, of the policy. Thus, the insurance company is "on the risk" for the difference between the cash surrender value and the face amount of the policy. Actually, then, cash value (or permanent) insurance is really decreasing insurance. The premium payments remain the same throughout the life of the policy, and the death benefit stays the same. But the amount of actual "insurance" decreases. The premium payment is large enough to make possible the building up of a cash value that is used to help pay the death benefit.

Agents and others in the life insurance industry often extol the value of permanent or cash value life insurance by mentioning the fact that the insured person builds up a savings account while being insured. For example, a 25-year-old person might hear something like this: "By buying this $50,000 policy, you will have a cash value of about $30,000 at age 65—and all this while receiving $50,000 of protection for 40 years."

True, the cash value of $30,000 is available at age 65, but the amount of protection is $50,000 only at the beginning of the long period of time. As the years roll by, the cash value being built up provides some of the death benefit of the policy and during the later years provides most of the death benefit. The fact is that the policyholder can get the money only if he or she gives up the insurance policy. If a time comes when the policyholder needs the money, the insurance company can be notified and it will give the insured the money. But in return, the policyholder must surrender the policy. When this happens, the protection stops.

The policyholder can borrow from the cash surrender value, but interest must be paid on the money borrowed and the face value of the policy is decreased by the amount of the loan. The important thing for consumers to remember is that in order to get the cash surrender value of an insurance policy, they must discontinue the policy.

One additional point should be clear to consumers. Life insurance agents often urge prospective customers to buy cash value insurance because it is permanent, lifetime insurance. They also point out that the policy has a cash value and can be surrendered after a period of time, say 30 years, for cash. If insurance is to be permanent, if it is to be kept until the insured person dies, then the cash value is really meaningless. The insured person can get the cash only by surrendering the policy, and in that case the coverage is not permanent.

Although cash value insurance and term insurance are the fundamental types of life insurance protection, there are many variations of these two types. Some of these are discussed in the next chapter.

Checking Your Reading

1. Why is life insurance more essential now than it was in earlier times when ties among relatives were stronger?
2. Give two reasons for the failure of many persons to buy enough life insurance for their needs.
3. What is the main purpose of life insurance?
4. Explain why assessing our need for life insurance is more difficult and complex than assessing our need for other types of insurance, such as automobile insurance?
5. Why are funds for dependents so important for parents with small children?
6. What are the payments made for insurance policies called?
7. What does "C.L.U." after an insurance agent's name mean?
8. Explain what is meant by term insurance.
9. How does cash value insurance differ from term insurance?
10. What is a beneficiary?
11. How are mortality rates arrived at?
12. Explain what type of work is done by actuaries.
13. What is a cash value insurance policy?
14. What two elements added together make up the face value of a cash value insurance policy?
15. What must you do in order to get the cash surrender value of an insurance policy?

Consumer Problems and Projects

1. To what extent should life insurance be employed as a medium for savings and investment? Some people say that you should simply purchase the protection you need in the cheapest form— in term policies, for example—and put savings into other investments. Other people think of insurance as their major savings for old age. What is your opinion? Could you invest your spare funds to better advantage elsewhere? Will other investments be equally safe? Does the fact that insurance contracts force you to save systematically seem important to you? You might consult several persons who know about insurance and other savings and investment plans.

2. Locate in recent periodicals the cost ratings of specific life insurance policies offered by the major companies in our nation. (For example, in the January, February, and March 1974 issues of *Consumer Reports,* there appeared a special report that gave price data on policies offered by some 125 major companies. *Changing Times* and *Money* magazines have also published information on what life insurance really costs.) When you locate the information, examine the costs of policies of certain companies that you or the class choose. How does the annual premium charge compare with the interest-adjusted cost for each of the companies chosen? Which company has the lowest interest-adjusted cost? Which company has the highest interest-adjusted cost?

3. Obtain a copy of *The Consumers Union Report on Life Insurance*, 1972. A copy may be available in your school library. If it is not, it may be purchased for $2.00 plus 50 cents to help cover postage and handling, from Book Dept. A096, Consumers Union, Orangeburg, New York 10962. Find a family that will give you the information you need to fill in the "Life Insurance Planning Worksheet" presented at the rear of the booklet. (Or you may wish to make up financial information for a fictitious family for this purpose.) Arrive at answers to the following questions pertaining to the family.
   a. What are the requirements for a family income fund?
   b. What are the requirements for an education fund?
   c. What are the requirements for a widow's retirement fund and

for a widow's income fund for the years between child rearing and retirement?

4. Dorothy Turvana died at Municipal Hospital from injuries after an accident in which her car was struck by a hit-and-run driver. She was 20 years old. Surviving are her parents, two brothers, and a sister. Dorothy's family, which has an income of $270 a week, was faced with the following bills:

Hospital expenses	$ 650
Doctors' expenses	525
Ambulance	65
Undertaker	700
Miscellaneous	160
	$2100

Dorothy Turvana had been earning $175 a week. She had $470 in a savings account, $180 in a checking account, no life insurance, and no other assets. Generalize from this case history about the insurance needs of a young single person.

20

Life Insurance Programs

Life insurance is one of the most important purchases many consumers make. Although term insurance and cash value insurance are the only two basic types of life insurance protection available, insurance companies sell their plans in different kinds of policies designed to meet the needs of the people they serve. In this chapter, you will read about the kinds of policies offered to consumers. You will also find answers to such questions as these: Who should buy term insurance? Who should buy cash value insurance? Is there a reliable way to compare the real cost of similar policies sold by different companies? Who really needs life insurance protection? How much life insurance is needed?

THE CHIEF PROVIDER NEEDS COVERAGE

Many persons need some life insurance to take care of such expenses as medical bills resulting from their last illness and funeral costs. The amount needed for this purpose is not large—perhaps a $5000 or $10,000 policy is enough. The largest amount of money needed from life insurance is for dependents. If a young man, for example, has absolutely no one depending on him for money, he has no reason to buy life insurance for the purpose of providing funds for other people to live after he dies. But take the case of a young woman who provides money for a family consisting of three other people. If she should die, the money source for that family would be cut off. She needs to have enough life insurance on her life so that if she should die, the three people can have enough money to continue living at a reasonable level for at least a certain length of time.

The main purpose of life insurance is to provide financial protection for those who are dependent on the person whose life is insured. Life insurance companies have combined the chance for saving with many of their policies, but consumers should be concerned first and foremost with insurance when they look at their life insurance needs. Perhaps the term "death insurance" would be better than life insurance, since what is needed is financial security in case of death.

When does any person need life insurance? The answer is simple: when the person's death creates a need for more money than is left in his or her estate. When one or more persons must depend on a family member for money on which to live, the need for life insurance is most crucial. The breadwinner, then, is the key person whose life must be insured. What about other members of the family?

Insurance agents often stress the need for insuring the lives of children; they argue that the premium cost is low and that the death benefit will pay for the cost of a funeral. Usually, the death of a child reduces the financial responsibilities of the father by far more than the cost of a funeral. Another point mentioned in favor of insuring a child's life is the fact that the future insurance costs will be reduced if a person is first insured at a young age. The costs are lower, but the payments include money wasted for a number of years when insurance is not needed.

If a wife and mother works and her income is used to support or to help support others, it is important that her life be adequately insured. Her death would cause a reduction in the family income. If she is a homemaker, should her life be insured? A homemaker often provides many valuable services. She is often a dietician, cook, housecleaner, launderer, accountant, nurse, and perhaps many other things. If she should die, who would take over these duties? Hiring someone to do these tasks would be expensive. Thus, because the death of a homemaker creates a need for money, in most cases her life should be insured.

The conclusion is that life insurance is necessary when the death of the person means a need for income on the part of other persons. For most families, one person is the chief provider, or breadwinner, and this life is the one most important to insure. Certainly the largest life insurance coverage should be on the life of the breadwinner. The death of the breadwinner causes family income to stop, and in our society cutting off income for even a short period of time can be quite serious. Most breadwinners are considerably underinsured. If the father is the breadwinner, before spending money to buy life insurance on his children and his wife, he should make certain that his own life is adequately covered by life insurance. If other members of his family should die, the father (assuming he is the breadwinner) may suffer some economic loss, but his income continues, and he can no doubt weather the storm. If he should die, however, the family might well be in serious financial trouble if he is not adequately insured. If the mother is the breadwinner, before spending money to buy life insurance on her children and her husband, she should make certain that her own life is adequately insured.

HOW MUCH INSURANCE IS NEEDED?

After deciding whose lives should be insured, the next task is to decide how much insurance to buy. How does one know how much insurance is adequate? The answer to that question depends on so many things. It depends on the assets of the family. If a person is worth, say, a quarter of a million dollars, that person wouldn't need much life insurance to provide protection for the family. If, on the other hand, a person's assets were small but present income were large, that person's life insurance needs would probably be quite high.

As a rule of thumb, some experts have suggested that a person with a family to raise and educate probably should have insurance equal to at least 6 or 7 times his or her current annual salary. That means that a person with a salary of $18,000 a year would need more than $100,000 of life insurance coverage. But remember, rules of thumb must be used with discretion. Every family should determine its own insurance needs. The point is that many of us probably need more insurance protection than we think.

An adequate life insurance program need not cost a lot. The protection part of life insurance is relatively inexpensive. The thing that makes some policies so costly is the cash value, or savings, part of the plan.

The first step in figuring life insurance needs is to estimate social security benefits. The life insurance and disability plans of social security are not well known by people in the United States, but they do provide sizable benefits, and these benefits should be considered when beginning the task of deciding how much life insurance is needed.

The insurance needs of a family change as the family progresses from one stage of life to the next. Before children are born, life insurance needs are relatively low if both husband and wife are able to work. When children are small, the needs are quite high. A young mother who is widowed, for example, will need money to raise her family, and the number of years during which an income is needed is obviously greater when the children are young. As children grow to be teenagers, the need for insurance decreases because the length of dependency on the part of the children has now been decreased. Once the children have grown and left home, income protection needs have diminished even more. After the age of 65, there is really little if any need for insurance to cover the loss of earning power of the husband or wife.

TYPES OF TERM INSURANCE POLICIES

In Chapter 19 you learned that term insurance policies do not have a savings or investment feature. When an individual purchases term insurance coverage, he or she is simply providing financial protection for the beneficiary of the policy. Term insurance is often called *pure life insurance*. The word "term" is derived from the fact that the insured is covered by this type of insurance only if death occurs within a specified period of time, such as one year, ten years, or fifteen years. Thus, payment is made only if the insured dies within that period of time. If the individual lives to the end of the term, the policy expires and the contract is at an end.

Some term policies are renewable. *Renewable* policies guarantee the insured the right to renew the policy for another period of the same length when the original term has expired. A new medical examination is not needed. But if the policy is renewed, the premium is then increased to the rate applicable to the insured's age at the time of renewal. The renewability feature adds to the cost of the policy, but it is important.

Another provision often included in term policies is the *right of conversion*, which enables the policyholder, at any time within a period specified in the policy, to elect to surrender the term policy and receive in exchange a new policy on a permanent plan. The right of conversion is an important provision, for the insured can exercise this right without submitting to a medical examination or meeting other requirements that the company may have for a cash value (or permanent) plan of insurance at the time that the conversion is made. Most experts advise that any term policy bought should be renewable and convertible.

The basic kinds of term insurance policies are *level* and *decreasing*.

Level Term Insurance

Level term insurance has a fixed death benefit. The premium is also fixed for the duration of the term. Thus, in the case of a five-year nonrenewable term policy, the annual premium is the same each year for the five-year period. If the policy is a renewable term policy, the annual premium is the same for the five years but increases with each renewal. The new premium is based on the insured's age when the policy is renewed. The size of the death benefit can usually be decreased any year by the term insurance policyholder, but ordinarily the death benefit cannot be increased without a medical examination.

Decreasing Term Insurance

The death benefit of a decreasing term insurance policy decreases each year, falling to zero at the end of the term. Premiums usually stop a few years before the end of the term, when the policy expires. Because the face value declines as the risk of death rises with age, the premiums are relatively low.

Decreasing term policies have been popular with people who have relatively large mortgages on their homes. A young man with a $30,000 mortgage on his $40,000 home may not want his dependents to be burdened with mortgage payments if he should die. Thus, an insurance policy with a schedule of decreasing death benefits that roughly parallels the decreasing mortgage on his house would enable his beneficiaries to pay off the mortgage. Many insurance companies have designed decreasing term policies precisely for this purpose and call them *mortgage protection policies.*

As a matter of fact, decreasing term insurance has many uses in addition to providing mortgage protection. Once a family's living standard has stabilized somewhat, insurance needs typically go down each year. Furthermore, many families begin a program of systematic saving and investing. As their funds build up, the need for life insurance protection decreases.

Group Term Insurance

Group life insurance is a form of term insurance, and the premium rates are usually low. The insurance is written on a group of lives rather than on individual lives, and this helps to reduce administrative expenses. A master contract is issued instead of individual policies. Bookkeeping work on the part of the insurance company is simplified because payment for the premium is made in one check. This type of insurance is usually written on the employees of a particular business firm, but it may also be written on a group of people with some other common bond, such as members of a club. Many employers offer group insurance free or for a monthly charge.

Although premium rates in group plans are often quite low and represent an excellent insurance buy for consumers, they are rarely

Group insurance is written on the lives of a group of people, such as the employees of a company. (*General Motors, Inc.*)

guaranteed by the contract. Thus rates may be raised if more deaths occur than the actuaries anticipated or if the average age of the group increases to the point where an increased premium charge is necessary. Where membership is large and the group plan has a history of successful operation, the group life insurance plan should be a good buy. A comparison of the average annual net cost of a group plan for the past several years with the cost of other term policies should reveal whether or not the group plan is a good buy.

TYPES OF CASH VALUE POLICIES

The basic choice in life insurance is between term and cash value policies. Cash value plans are also called *whole life policies*. The three basic types of cash value policies sold by life insurance companies are ordinary life policies, limited-payment life policies, and endowment policies. In both ordinary life and limited-payment life policies, cash values are built up, and the policies are permanent in that they stay in force until the insured person dies. Endowment policies are primarily savings plans.

Ordinary Life Policies

The ordinary life policy, most popular of the cash value policies, is also called straight life insurance because it follows life expectancy to the very end. Premiums are payable for life, or until the age of 100 if that should come earlier. For persons who live much beyond retirement years there is no point in continuing the policy. It usually makes more sense to surrender the policy and take the savings or convert the policy to a lower face value, in which case no additional premiums need be paid. In ordinary life policies, the cash surrender value at the age of 65 is approximately 50 percent of the face amount of the policy, regardless of the age at which the policy was begun.

Premium rates for ordinary life policies are the lowest of any cash value policies. For a person who wants a policy that will provide a fixed sum of money for a beneficiary regardless of the age at which he or she dies, ordinary life will fit the bill. The person need not worry about the coverage stopping after a certain number of years or after he or she reaches a certain age. If the person lives to old age, however, he or she may find it difficult or even impossible to continue paying the premiums after he or she has stopped earning money. The person can, though, stop paying at any time on an ordinary life policy and take the choice of withdrawing its cash value, continuing the protection for a smaller amount, or continuing the full amount of protection, but for a limited period of time.

Limited-Payment Life Policies

The principal difference between a limited-payment life policy and an ordinary life policy is that you pay for the insurance faster. Premium payments are compressed into a shorter time so that eventually the policy is paid up. Still, the policy does not "mature" until the insured reaches the age of 100. Thus, even though the insured has completed premium payments, the face value of the policy is not paid until the person dies or reaches 100 years of age. Since premiums are paid for a shorter period of time, each premium is quite a bit larger than for an ordinary life policy. Cash surrender values build up much faster in limited-payment life policies, of course.

Many limited-payment plans are available. A 20-payment life policy, for example, is fully paid up after 20 years, but it stays in force as long as the insured lives, even though no further payments are made.

Some limited-payment plans are organized so that they will be paid up by retirement age. For example, a life-paid-up-at-65 policy pur-

Limited-payment life insurance plans may be attractive to such people as professional athletes, whose income is high for a relatively short period. (UPI)

chased by a 22-year-old man would require a lower annual premium than a 20-payment life policy, which would be paid up when the man reaches the age of 42. But a life-paid-up-at-65 policy would require a higher premium than that paid for a straight life policy.

The limited-payment plan should be chosen over an ordinary life plan only in special circumstances. People such as professional athletes whose earnings are high for a brief period of time may be interested in a policy that will be paid up when their high earnings cease. But such high-premium insurance for most young family men and women could mean that they might not be able to afford the protection their families need.

Endowment Policies

Most of the emphasis is on savings rather than on insurance protection in an endowment policy. It resembles a limited-payment policy in that it requires premium payments for a specified period only, say 20 or 30 years, or until a certain age, such as 60 or 65. You will recall that the face value of an ordinary or limited-payment life policy is payable only at the time of the insured's death or when the insured reaches the age of 100. An endowment policy provides for payment of the face value to the insured on a certain date called the *maturity date*. If he or she dies before this date, the face value is paid, of course, to the beneficiary named in the policy. The maturity date is usually at the end of the premium-paying period.

An endowment policy is used, then, mainly as a means of saving money. The cash value must build up much faster than in other types of cash value life insurance, so the "insurance" part of the policy decreases rapidly. In the case of a 20-year policy, the insurance falls to zero in 20 years. Actually, endowment policies represent the most "temporary" kind of insurance available. They are primarily savings plans. Premium payments on endowment policies are quite high for the insurance protection given.

COMBINATION POLICIES AND OPTIONAL EXTRAS

In addition to the principal types of term policies and cash value policies discussed in the preceding pages, life insurance companies also offer a number of combination plans and options. Most of these plans involve combining a cash value policy with term insurance.

Some of the more popular of these plans are discussed in the following paragraphs.

Modified Life

A cash value plan designed to appeal to a young person whose income is low but whose prospects for the future are good is called *modified life*. For the first few years, typically five years, the policyholder pays a lower premium than he or she would pay for an ordinary life insurance policy. Then, after the initial period of time, the premium becomes higher. The plan might appeal to a recent college graduate who thinks he needs a fairly large amount of permanent insurance but cannot afford the premium. If he thinks his income will increase during the next several years, he may be sold this type of policy. He could, of course, accomplish much the same thing by buying a 5-year convertible term insurance policy.

Family Plan

The family plan policy provides an insurance package that covers every member of the family. The policy might insure the father's life with $10,000 of permanent insurance. The same package might include $2000 of insurance on the mother until she is 65 years old and $1000 of insurance coverage on the lives of each dependent child, including those born after the contract is issued.

Family Income

A family income policy is usually an ordinary life policy to which a decreasing-term element is added so that if the policyholder dies within the term stated in the policy, the beneficiary receives a monthly income. The monthly income is often 1 or 2 percent of the death benefit, but it can be more. Let us say a woman bought a $20,000 family income policy on a 20-year plan that calls for a 2 percent monthly income. If she took out the policy on September 1, 1980, and died the month in which it was issued, her beneficiary would receive 240 payments (12 months times 20 years) of $400 (2 percent of $20,000). If she dies on September 1, 1991, her beneficiary will receive 120 payments. Should she die in August, 2001, the income payment would be made for only 1 month, since the expiration date is September 1 of that year. After the income-paying term expires, the face value of the policy, in this case $20,000, is collected.

Optional Extras

Insurance companies provide an assortment of benefits that can be added to almost any policy for extra payments. For example, by paying a small extra charge it is possible to guarantee the right to purchase additional insurance at standard rates regardless of insurability. Poor health in the future could make a person uninsurable, or insurable only at high rates. The guaranteed insurability option covers this risk.

The waiver of premium clause is another popular option. With this clause in effect, premiums throughout the remaining life of the policy are waived (need not be paid) if the policyholder becomes permanently and totally disabled, as defined in the policy.

PARTICIPATING AND NONPARTICIPATING POLICIES

Life insurance policies are either participating or nonparticipating, and in the life insurance industry they are often referred to as "par" or "nonpar." In a participating policy, the premium payments include what is in effect an overpayment, and at the end of the year the insurance company returns part of the payment as a "dividend."

Stock Companies and Mutual Companies

To understand the start of participating policies it is necessary to look at the types of life insurance organizations. In our country, state laws require that life insurance organizations be formed as corporations. Actually, there are two different types of life insurance corporations: stock companies and mutual companies. A stock company, like any other corporation, is owned and operated by its stockholders, and the stockholders share in any profits or losses that the company makes. A mutual company, on the other hand, has no stock and no stockholders. It is owned entirely by its policyholders. Each policyholder is a member of the company and has the right to vote in the election of the directors, who control and manage the company. Thus it can be seen that the policyholder's role in a mutual company corresponds in many ways to a stockholder's role in a stock company.

In actual practice, however, there is little difference in the management of stock companies and mutual companies. The average policyholder in a mutual company pays no particular attention to the management of the company. Mutual life insurance companies provided 51 percent of the life insurance in force in the mid-1970s. Stock life insurance companies accounted for the other 49 percent.

The Idea of Dividends

All United States mutual companies, but not all stock companies, pay dividends. Originally, dividends were issued by mutual companies only. The mutual companies reasoned that if the mortality rate among its policyholders was lower than expected during the year, and the company did not use all the money set aside for paying death benefits, the policyholders were entitled, as owners of the company, to receive a refund. A refund could also be made possible by higher returns on premium money invested or lower administrative costs than had been expected.

Now most stockholder-owned companies, too, sell participating policies. To meet the competition of mutual companies, it was easy enough for stock companies to issue policies that provided a refund at the end of each policy year. The premium payments are simply increased enough to make possible a dividend payment at the end of the year.

Some people have criticized the insurance industry for using the word, "dividend," stating that a more accurate word such as "refund" should be used. Indeed, the United States Internal Revenue Service says that insurance dividends are not taxed because they are not income but simply a refund of an overpayment.

Participating policies accounted for 59 percent of all life insurance in force with United States companies in the mid-1970s. Nonparticipating policies made up the remaining 41 percent. Unfortunately, it is not possible to say whether the net cost of insurance will be less for a participating or a nonparticipating policy.

THE COST OF LIFE INSURANCE POLICIES

The important thing to consider when buying life insurance is, of course, the amount of protection needed. A cash value policy is relatively expensive because it is a form of financial investment as well as insurance protection. Term insurance offers pure protection, and for this reason the cost is much less per dollar of protection.

Life insurance salespeople often say whole life is a bargain because you eventually get back most of your money, or even all of it. Some salespeople even argue that buying term insurance is like throwing money down the drain. After all, they say, if you don't die, you don't collect. The fact is, though, that you do receive something when you buy term insurance. You receive protection for dependents, and that is what insurance is all about. Part of the premium paid for cash value policies is also for protection (the other part is a savings plan). Nevertheless, a cash value plan might make sense for some consumers.

Cash Value Insurance as a Savings Plan

For many years experts have argued over whether it makes more sense to buy term insurance rather than a cash value policy such as ordinary life, and then invest the difference in premiums between the two plans. For example, let's say the premium for a term insurance policy is $165. The premium for an ordinary life policy of the same size is $410. Does it make sense to buy the term policy and invest the difference between the two each year? Consumers Union reported in 1974 on their research into this question. They concluded that investing in a whole life policy, such as ordinary life, can be a sensible long-term investment for those who could otherwise expect their investments to earn only 4 percent after taxes. If 5 percent after taxes can be earned on the money, then term appears preferable. If 6 percent after taxes can be earned, then term proves to be vastly superior.

One argument against buying term insurance and investing your own money is that some people will save only when forced to. Apparently, some persons think that paying insurance premiums regularly is a type of forced saving. This may be true, of course, but it need not be. Many people are able to save regularly. Automatic payroll deductions for United States savings bonds or for credit union savings accounts, for example, have helped people save systematically. Furthermore, the life insurance lapse rates testify to the fact that life insurance policies are limited in disciplining persons who would not otherwise save.

For some people, cash value insurance may be a good investment because of our current federal income tax laws. The money that accumulates in the savings part of a cash value policy is not subject to taxation (as are most other savings or investment plans) until the policy is turned in. Even then, if the owner turns in the policy for its cash value, he or she pays no taxes on it unless it exceeds the sum of all the premiums paid over the years. If the cash value is more than the sum of all premiums, then the policyholder pays taxes only on the difference. What this means is that in most cases, the cash value is tax-free. Thus, well-to-do people who want a safe, conservative, tax-sheltered investment often find cash value (or whole life) insurance useful.

Term Insurance Has Advantages

The fact is that only by buying term insurance can the average young breadwinner get enough insurance coverage to protect a family adequately during the years when it most needs protection. Savings plans should be considered separately by most consumers.

By keeping savings programs separate from life insurance, the family has the flexibility to change, stop, or withdraw funds without affecting the family's insurance protection. Then, too, by separating life insurance from savings plans, the family has the choice of where and how their savings are to be invested.

A Look at Premium Rates

Some persons have attempted to reduce life insurance buying to a formula based on the percentage of income that should be spent on premiums. A more sensible starting point is to figure your insurance needs and then attempt to fill those needs with the most sensible type of coverage. The amount of protection that can be brought for a given sum of money will be large or small according to the type of policy purchased. Table 20-1 gives costs of various policies for males at four different ages. Because women live longer, on the average, than men, rates for women are generally more favorable. Some companies simply use a three-year-lower age rating for women. The annual premium payments shown in Table 20-1 are for $1000 of protection. The rates are those charged in the 1970s by a large insurance company for nonparticipating policies.

The least expensive policy is the five-year renewable and convertible term policy. The policies with the largest "savings" plans require the largest premium payments.

One important thing should be noted when examining Table 20-1.

TABLE 20-1
Annual Premium Rates per $1000 for Selected Nonparticipating Policies, for Males

Type of Policy	Age 25	Age 30	Age 35	Age 40
5-Year Renewable and Convertible	$ 5.49	$ 5.73	$ 6.45	$ 8.19
Term to Age 65	8.80	9.97	12.10	14.50
Ordinary Life	13.64	16.01	19.09	23.31
20-Payment Life	22.48	25.40	28.83	32.75
Life Paid Up at Age 65	15.29	18.28	22.40	28.37
Endowment at Age 65	18.49	22.39	27.78	35.41

If a man buys the 5-year term policy at the age of 25, he will have to pay an increased premium at five-year steps as long as he wants the coverage. Let us assume he buys a $20,000 policy at the age of 25. His annual premium payments for the first five years will be $109.80 ($5.49 times 20), but they will increase to $163.80 should he still have the policy and want to renew it at the age of 40. In the case of the other policies, his premium payments would be based on his age at the time he took out the policy, and they would not increase over the years. The premium rates for term insurance policies increase as one gets older. At the age of 45, the annual premium rate for the 5-year term policy increases to $11.10 per thousand dollars of coverage. At the age of 50 the rate is $15.85, and at 55 it climbs to $23.40.

The fact is, though, that insurance needs typically decrease as one gets older, so in the case in the above paragraph, the man would no doubt reduce his term insurance coverage as he gets older. The argument against term insurance that points to the fact that it costs more as one gets older is misleading. All life insurance costs more as one gets older and mortality rates increase. Cash value policies have level premiums, but remember that the actual insurance element (the amount for which the company is "on the risk") decreases as the cash value of the policy increases.

As you get older and mortality rates increase, it costs more to buy life insurance. (*Sylvia Johnson, Woodfin Camp & Associates*)

The Interest-adjusted Method

Fortunately, consumers now can get cost information about the insurance policies issued by the many companies selling life insurance. One myth about life insurance is that insurance companies generally charge about the same rates. That is not true. Costs vary widely for the same kind of coverage. Herbert S. Denenberg, while he was Pennsylvania Insurance Commissioner, reported that the true cost of ordinary life insurance may vary by over 170 percent for the same coverage.

The interest-adjusted method of figuring costs of insurance plans was recommended several years ago by a group of insurance experts. The formula is considered a big improvement over previous methods of measuring costs. The Pennsylvania Insurance Department published in the early 1970s *A Shopper's Guide to Life Insurance*. The booklet gives cost data for ordinary life (or straight life) policies sold in Pennsylvania. *Consumer Reports*, the publication of Consumers Union, in the spring of 1974 gave quite extensive cost information on term insurance as well as cash value insurance policies issued by 125 companies, including all of the 20 largest companies. *Changing Times* magazine, too, has published cost information on policies issued by the largest companies. All these reports have used the interest-adjusted method of figuring costs. So consumers now can get valuable cost information to help them get the most for their money when buying life insurance.

Why is the interest-adjusted method of figuring costs a big improvement? Insurance salespeople have commonly used the "net-cost method" of showing consumers the cost of their policies. But this method can give misleading data. Let's say the annual premium on a $10,000 participating policy is $162.80. If the policy is surrendered after 20 years, the net cost method figures would look like this:

Total premiums ($162.80 for 20 years)	$3256.00
Less dividends for 20 years ($1046.00) and cash value at the end of 20 years ($2620.00)	3666.00
Cost of insurance for 20 years	− 410.00

Looked at in this way, the insurance has not cost money. In fact, the policyholder is ahead at the end of 20 years. The cash value is $2620, and the policyholder has received in dividends another $1046. The cost is negative. The cost per year per $1000 is a minus $2.05. The company loses money! However, we know that companies could not stay in business if they lost money.

The net-cost method omits something. The most important thing omitted is interest. When the company collects your money, it invests it, of course. If you did not have to pay premiums, you could invest the money and earn interest. The interest-adjusted formula takes interest into account. In our illustration above, if the premiums had been invested each year at 4 percent compound interest, the value of the money at the end of the 20 years would be $5,041.75. So the value of what the policyholder pays out over 20 years is $5041.75 rather than $3256. Likewise, the value of the dividends the policyholder receives from the company is more than $1046. If the policyholder invested the dividends received each year in an account earning 4 percent compounded annually, the sum would total $1421.45 at the end of 20 years. Using the interest-adjusted method, the cost of the $10,000 ordinary life policy for 20 years is $1000.30. The interest-adjusted cost per $1000 per year is $3.23.

Life insurance salespeople should be willing to give you interest-adjusted cost information on the policies they offer. By the late 1970s, certain states (Arkansas, California, Texas, West Virginia, and Wisconsin) required insurers to give interest-adjusted or similar figures to prospective buyers. Armed with such cost information, consumers should be able to do a better job of judging the cost of the policies of various companies.

Checking Your Reading

1. Describe the main purpose of life insurance and indicate why it is so important to have life insurance coverage for this purpose.
2. For which member (or members) of the family is life insurance coverage most important?
3. For what type of person might life insurance needs be especially high?
4. What makes some life insurance policies so costly? Why?
5. Why is term insurance sometimes referred to as "pure" insurance?
6. What is meant by a "renewable" term insurance policy?
7. What does the right of conversion enable the term insurance policyholder to do?
8. What are the two basic kinds of term insurance policies? Explain the difference between the two.
9. Discuss the uses for decreasing term insurance.

10. Explain what is meant by group life insurance.

11. What three types of cash value policies are sold by insurance companies?

12. For which of the cash value policies are premium rates the lowest?

13. Discuss the main difference between a limited-payment life policy and an ordinary life policy. How are they similar?

14. What kinds of persons might need a limited-payment plan of insurance?

15. Explain why endowment policies represent the most temporary kind of insurance.

16. What is the essential difference between the net-cost method of figuring life insurance costs and the interest-adjusted method?

Consumer Problems and Projects

1. Examine a life insurance policy. If you do not have one of your own, use the policy of some member of your family or ask a local insurance agent for a sample policy. Find answers in the policy to the following questions:

   a. Are the premiums to be paid annually, semiannually, or quarterly?

   b. What requirements are made for reinstatement?

   c. What additional charge is made for a premium waiver provision?

   d. What settlement options are available?

   e. What amount can be borrowed on the policy? At what rate?

   f. What provisions does the policy make for lapse of payment?

   g. Are provisions made to pay dividends? How often? In what form may the dividends be paid?

2. The following premium rates are charged by a certain company for each $1000 of either ordinary life insurance or 20-year endowment insurance. After examining the rates, answer the questions below.

Age at Nearest Birthday	Ordinary Life Premium	20-Year Endowment Premium
20 years	$14.71	$46.58
40 years	26.13	51.18

a. How do you account for the fact that the annual premium for ordinary life insurance at the age of 40 is almost twice the annual premium for the same plan at the age of 20, while the annual premium for a 20-year endowment policy at 40 years of age is just a few dollars more than it would be at 20?

b. What would be the annual premium for a $20,000 ordinary life policy issued at 20 years of age? at 40?

3. Janice Wells is 22 years old, is married, and has a child who is just a few weeks old. Mrs. Wells' life is currently insured for $5000 through a group life policy. The Wellses wanted to increase the amount of insurance on Mrs. Wells' life, and after examining their budget, they have decided that they can pay up to $180 a year.

The premium rates listed below are sample annual rates for a 22-year-old woman. The rates are for $1000 of insurance.

Insurance	Ordinary Life	20-Payment Life	20-Year Endowment
$5.40	$15.41	$27.65	$46.77

a. Using the rates above, estimate the amount of each kind of insurance Mrs. Wells can buy for $180.

b. Discuss the advantages and disadvantages of each of the four plans.

c. Do you think she should consider other plans of insurance? Which ones? Why?

4. Cash value insurance policies combine life insurance and savings. Following are two arguments for combining savings with insurance. Point out the fallacies, if any, in these two arguments.

a. The alternative to combining savings with insurance is to buy term insurance, in which case you lose all the money you paid in. If you buy a cash value policy, such as ordinary life, the cash value eventually will be more than all the money you pay in. You will have been insured those years free.

b. If you are like most people, you will not save money for old age unless the insurance company saves it for you.

21

Social Insurance

Social security is our country's basic method of providing a continuing income when family earnings are reduced or stop because of retirement, disability, or death. The social security program affects more people in our nation than any other government program. In fact, nine out of ten workers are now covered by the program.

How important is social security? Suppose that in the year 1977 a young father died. His two small children, both under five years of age, and his wife suddenly were cut off from their main source of financial support. What would have happened to this family?

Because of the social security program in the United States, the family would be receiving monthly benefit checks. In fact, if the father's average earnings covered by social security had been $700 a month, the widow and children would be receiving about $765 a month, or about $9180 each year. By the time the older child reaches 18, it is possible that the family will have received $119,000 or more. Probably the family would get larger monthly payments in future years, however, because the social security law provides for automatic increases in benefit checks as living costs go up. Then, when the widow reaches age 60, she could begin receiving monthly benefits.

The children could receive benefit payments until age 22 if they stay in school.

In Chapter 20 you read how important it is for a breadwinner to provide financial security for dependents in the event of his or her death. Fortunately, most persons in the United States are covered by social security and thus have a foundation on which to build a life insurance program.

The social insurance program in the United States covers old-age, survivors, and disability benefits, and sickness insurance. Why have we adopted such a program of social insurance? How does the social security system operate? The answers to these questions will be covered in this chapter.

OUR COMMITMENT TO SOCIAL INSURANCE

Over the years of our nation's development, both the state and federal governments have recognized that certain risks in an increasingly industrialized economy can best be met with programs of social insurance. Because we have so many successful private insurance companies in the United States, some people question the need for government social insurance programs. But the need for government social insurance plans in industrial nations is well established, and in the United States we have lagged behind other industrial nations in providing social insurance programs.

Social insurance has been shaped by changing economic and social conditions. Some of the main reasons for starting social insurance programs are given in the following paragraphs.

- At one time, we were mostly an agricultural society. Now we are mainly a highly mechanized society, and the conditions of life in such a society have increased our dependence on a money income. In the early history of our country, people did not depend so much on money as we do today. Families then produced for themselves much of the food, clothing, and other things they needed and wanted. Loss of earning power is much more serious now than it once was, because today we must buy with money just about everything we consume.
- In an earlier day, the family was an independent unit that took care of old people as well as young people. Many persons never left the home in which they were born and grew up, and few of them migrated to other cities or other states. But our industrialized society has become more complicated. Families now are not so closely knit as they once were. Family members are scattered—sometimes throughout the country or the world. Most

parents today want and expect to be financially independent when they retire. They do not want to be supported by their children.

- Many more people now live to older ages, as insurance mortality tables show us. At the same time, many employers force people to retire at relatively early ages, often at 65. The result is that the number of retired persons in the United States is greater than ever, and the length of time between retirement and death increases.

- The United States is certainly wealthy enough not to let individuals suffer extremes of misfortune and poverty, and many people believe that the federal government is the agency through which we can best provide a program of social insurance for the American people. Other Americans, however, believe that this program can be handled better through private agencies. For this reason, the United States has not developed social insurance to nearly so great an extent as the highly industrialized countries of Western Europe. For example, in the 1970s Sweden and the Netherlands spent 22 percent of their national income on social programs. Great Britain spent 12.5 percent. In the United States, we spent 10.8 percent of our national income on such programs. In the next few pages, we will look at the social security program provided in our country.

Beginning in colonial times, local towns recognized the need to help poor people when times were bad. Help was usually available from friends and neighbors, but when such assistance was not sufficient, local government was called upon. The aid was given grudgingly, however, and the repressive features of the public relief system were intended to discourage people from applying until their money problems were very serious. Progress in giving better relief came steadily, and by the mid-1920s a number of the states were experimenting with old-age pensions.

The nation had a severe depression in the 1930s, and it became apparent that certain economic risks—unemployment, disability, death, and old age—were not being met. The answer to the growing need among so many people had to be federal action. In 1932 the federal government made loans and then grants to the states to pay for relief. Congress then passed the Social Security Act, and it was signed into law on August 14, 1935.

THE BEGINNING OF SOCIAL SECURITY

The two social insurance programs started first by the Social Security Act were a federal system of old-age benefits for retired workers and a

The federal-state system of unemployment insurance was one of the first two programs started by the Social Security Act of 1935. (*Benyas-Kaufman, Black Star*)

federal-state system of unemployment insurance. Many changes and improvements were made in the program in the 1930s and 1940s, such as extending the old-age insurance program to provide monthly benefits for a worker's dependents and survivors (initially the program provided benefits for retired workers only).

Major changes in the social security program came during the decade of the 1950s, when it was broadened to cover many workers who were not covered at the beginning. Amendments during the 1950s extended social security coverage to farm operators, regularly employed farm and household employees, and most persons who work for themselves. Coverage was also made available on a voluntary group basis to employees of state and local governments. Today almost all jobs in the United States are covered by social security.

The social security program was expanded again in 1965 when Congress added hospital benefits. In addition, a voluntary system of insurance to pay doctors' bills was set up. Both programs are called *medicare*. At first, both of these programs were for persons 65 years old or older. But since 1973, medicare coverage has been available to people under 65 who have been entitled to disability checks for two or more consecutive years and to certain people with permanent kidney failure.

SOCIAL SECURITY TODAY

The social security program now includes a broader range of benefits than perhaps many people realize. In addition to pensions for workers and their dependents, the program includes such things as disability payments, aid to survivors of deceased workers, special minimum pensions for certain uninsured elderly people, and medicare. The program also includes supplemental security income for the needy aged, blind, and disabled.

By the end of 1976, 32 million persons were receiving social security checks. Of this number, 63 percent were retired workers and dependents, 23 percent were survivors of deceased workers, and 14 percent were disabled. More than 1300 social security offices are located conveniently throughout the country, and these offices send representatives regularly to 3500 other communities so that the public will be served. If you have worked, you no doubt already have a social security card. If you do not have a card, you need only visit a social security office in your community to apply for one. A social security number is a necessity for us all today. The social security number is used for income tax purposes, and many schools and colleges now use it as the student's identification number.

Social security offices answer questions about social security, supply pamphlets about the various programs and benefits, and help people apply for benefits. To find the address of the office nearest you, look in the telephone directory or ask at your post office.

How Is Social Security Financed?

Social security benefits are paid for by a tax, generally referred to as a "contribution," based on covered earnings. Each payday the employer must deduct the tax from the worker's pay, match it with an equal amount, and send the total monthly or quarterly to the Internal Revenue Service. Self-employed persons contribute at about three-fourths the combined employee-employer rate for retirement, survivors, and disability insurance. The hospital insurance contribution rate is identical for employers, employees, and self-employed persons. The self-employed person must pay the tax quarterly along with his or her income tax.

The tax rates also have been raised a number of times over the years. In 1937, for example, a worker paid a social security tax rate of just 1 percent on his or her first $3000 of income. So the social security tax for the year could not be more than $30. The employer paid an equal amount. In 1977 the maximum amount on which the social security tax was paid was $16,500. The tax rate in 1977 was 5.85 percent. Thus, in 1977 workers who earned $16,500 or more contributed $965.25 to the social security program. Their employers matched that amount.

Of course, benefits, too, have increased considerably over the years. Congress has voted many raises in benefits to keep up with inflation. In 1972 Congress acted to make benefits increase automatically in future years without any action by Congress when the cost of living goes up. The first such automatic increase took effect for the month of June 1975, with the increase in benefits paid in early July of that year.

Whenever social security cash benefits are raised because of increases in the cost of living, the law requires a review of wages covered by social security. If average wages have gone up, the earnings base (the maximum amount on which the tax can be figured) must be raised, too. Wages in 1975 increased by about 7.5 percent over 1974. That percentage was applied to the 1976 earnings base ($15,300) and rounded off to the nearest $300. Thus the 1977 base was set at $16,500.

Tables 21-1 and 21-2 show the present and future contribution rates as now scheduled in the law.

TABLE 21-1
Contribution Rate Schedule for Employees and
Employers (Each)

	Percent of Covered Earnings		
Years	For Retirement, Survivors, and Disability Insurance	For Hospital Insurance	Total
1976–77	4.95	.90	5.85
1978–80	4.95	1.10	6.05
1981–85	4.95	1.35	6.30

Source: *Social Security Information for Young Families.* HEW Publication No. SSA 76-10033. U.S. Government Printing Office, p. 7.

TABLE 21-2
Contribution Rate Schedule for Self-employed People

Years	Percent of Covered Earnings		
	For Retirement, Survivors and, Disability Insurance	For Hospital Insurance	Total
1976–77	7.0	.90	7.90
1978–80	7.0	1.10	8.10
1981–85	7.0	1.35	8.35

Source: *Social Security Information for Young Families.* HEW Publication No. SSA 76-10033. U.S. Government Printing Office, p. 7.

Under the present law, the maximum amount of annual earnings that can be taxed for social security (the base) will rise automatically in the future as earnings levels rise. Every year the increase in average wages will be determined, and if wage levels have increased since the base was last set, the base will be raised. However, the base is raised only if there is an automatic benefit increase the same year.

How Are Social Security Benefits Earned?

To be eligible for social security benefits, you must work for at least a certain minimum period of time in an occupation covered by social security.

Most workers get credit for one-fourth year of work (called a *quarter of coverage*) if they are paid $50 or more in one calendar quarter. In addition, any worker who earns the maximum wages creditable for social security for a year gets credit for a full year, even though he or she may work just part of the year.

Social security credit is given for work covered by the social security law no matter how young or how old the worker is. When the work is under social security, the social security tax must be paid regardless of the age of the worker.

What happens if you stop working on a covered job before you become insured? The credits you have built up and which have been reported for you will remain on your record. Later, if you should return to a job covered by social security, you can add to your credits.

The Social Security Administration classifies a worker as fully insured or currently insured, depending on the total amount of credit he or she has for work under social security. These types of insured status are explained in the following paragraphs.

Fully Insured. If you are fully insured when you reach retirement age, you and certain members of your family can receive monthly benefits. If you are fully insured at death, benefits can be paid to certain members of your family.

No one is fully insured with credit for less than 1½ years of work, and no one needs more than 10 years of work to be fully insured. Being fully insured merely means that certain kinds of cash benefits may be payable. The amount of the benefits depends on the worker's average earnings.

Currently Insured. Even if a worker is not fully insured, benefits may be paid to the widow or widower and their children if the worker is "currently insured" at death. The worker is currently insured if credit has been earned for at least 1½ years of work within 3 years before death.

Disability Benefits. To get disability benefits, a worker 31 or older must be fully insured and must have credit for 5 years of work in the 10-year period ending when the person becomes disabled. If the worker becomes disabled between 24 and 31, credit is needed for only one-half the time between age 21 and the time the person becomes unable to work. If disability starts before age 24, the worker needs credit for 1½ years of work in the 3 years before the worker becomes disabled. A worker disabled by blindness needs enough credit to be fully insured, but the requirement for recent work does not have to be met.

You are considered "disabled" if you cannot work because of a severe physical or mental condition that has lasted (or is expected to last) for at least 12 months or is expected to result in death. The Social Security Administration recommends that people who have questions about disability ask for more detailed information at a social security office. The people at the social security office will help a person request the appropriate medical reports from a doctor or from the hospital or clinic where he or she has been examined.

Family Payments.   Social security benefits are payable not only to a worker but also to certain members of a worker's family. Dependents and survivors eligible for benefits include the following:

- Unmarried children under 18 or between 18 and 22 if they are full-time students.
- Unmarried sons and daughters 18 or over who were disabled before they reached 22 and who continue to be disabled.
- A wife or a widow under 65 if she is caring for a child under 18 or is disabled, and the child.
- A wife 62 or widow 60 or older, or a disabled widow 50 or over, even if there are no children entitled to payments.
- A widowed father if he is caring for a child under 18 or if he is disabled, and the child.
- A dependent husband 62 or over or widower 60 or over, or a disabled dependent widower 50 or over.

In addition to monthly benefits, a lump-sum death benefit of $255 is paid at a worker's death.

Table 21-3 illustrates the principal types of family payments and the insured status needed for each.

How Are Benefits Estimated?

The exact amount of retirement, disability, and survivors benefits cannot, of course, be figured until there is an application for benefits. This is the case because all earnings up to the time of the application may be considered in figuring the benefit. The exact benefit available at the time of application will be figured by the Social Security Administration. Estimating the amount of retirement, disability, and survivors benefits, is, however, possible, and this information is valuable for consumers who are building an insurance program. Table 21-4 shows some examples of monthly benefit payments.

MEDICARE

Medicare is a popular name for the federal government's system of financing medical care for persons 65 years of age and over and those receiving social security disability benefits for at least two years regardless of their age. This government health insurance plan was started in 1965 when amendments to the Social Security Act added to the law a pair of related contributor health insurance plans for just about all people 65 years of age or older. The two plans are these: (1) a basic compulsory program of hospital insurance and (2) a voluntary program of supplementary medical insurance.

TABLE 21-3
Principal Types of Family Payments

Survivors

Monthly payments to your—	If you are—
*Widow 60 or over or disabled widow 50 or over	fully insured
*Widow or widower (regardless of age) if caring for your child who is under 18 (or disabled) and is entitled to benefits	either fully or currently insured
Dependent children (or, under certain conditions, grandchildren)	either fully or currently insured
Dependent widower 60 or over, or disabled dependent widower 50 or over	fully insured
Dependent parent 62 or over	fully insured
Lump-sum death payment	either fully or currently insured

Note: All types of widow's benefits may be paid to a surviving divorced wife under certain conditions.

Disability

Monthly payments to—	If—
You as a disabled worker and your family	you are fully insured and meet the special work requirements described above
Your child who became disabled before 22 and continues to be disabled	the parent receives retirement or disability benefits or the parent was fully or currently insured at death

Source: *Social Security Information for Young Families.* HEW Publication No. SSA 76-10033. U.S. Government Printing Office. p. 9.

Hospital Insurance

The first plan (sometimes called Part A) is the hospital insurance part of medicare. It helps pay for the care the person receives as a patient in a hospital and for certain follow-up care after the patient leaves the hospital. Most people 65 and older and those receiving social security benefits for at least two years are eligible for hospital insurance automatically. This protection is financed through contributions paid while the individual is working. Tables 21-1 and 21-2 show the contribution rate schedules.

TABLE 21-4
Examples of Monthly Social Security Payments (Effective June 1976)

Benefits Can Be Paid to a:	Average Yearly Earnings After 1950*						
	$923 or less	$3000	$4000	$5000	$6000	$8000	$10,000
Disabled Worker	107.90	223.20	262.60	304.50	344.10	427.80	474.00
Wife Under 65 and One Child in Her Care	54.00	118.00	186.20	257.40	287.20	321.00	355.60
Widow or Widower Caring for One Child	162.00	334.80	394.00	456.80	516.20	641.80	711.00
Widow or Widower Caring for Two Children	162.00	341.20	448.80	561.90	631.30	748.70	829.50
Child of Disabled Worker	54.00	111.60	131.30	152.30	172.10	213.20	237.00
Child of Deceased Worker	107.90	167.40	197.00	228.40	258.10	320.90	355.50
Maximum Family Payment	161.90	341.20	448.80	561.90	631.30	748.70	829.50

*Generally, average earnings are figured over the period from 1951 until the worker reaches retirement age, becomes disabled, or dies. Up to 5 years of low earnings or no earnings can be excluded. The maximum earnings creditable for social security are $3600 for 1951-1954; $4200 for 1955-1958; $4800 for 1959-1965; $6600 for 1966-1967; $7800 for 1968-1971; $9000 for 1972; $10,800 for 1973; $13,200 for 1974; $14,100 for 1975; and $15,300 for 1976. But average earnings cannot reach these latter amounts until later. Because of this, the benefits shown in the last two columns on the right generally will not be payable until future years.

Source: *Social Security Information for Young Families*. HEW Publication No. (SSA) 76-10033. U.S. Government Printing Office.

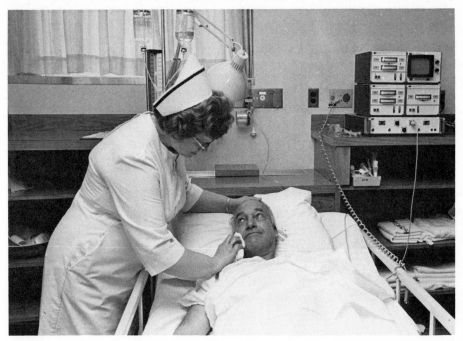

The hospital insurance part of medicare helps pay for the care a person receives as a patient in a hospital and for certain follow-up care the person receives after leaving the hospital. (*Authenticated News International*)

Medical Insurance

The second plan (sometimes called Part B) is the medical insurance part of medicare. It helps pay for doctor bills and the cost of many other medical items and services not covered under hospital insurance, including out-patient hospital services. Although coverage is voluntary, persons over 65 and those receiving disability benefits are automatically covered unless they decline. The basic premium paid by most persons was increased to $7.70 a month in July 1977. More than half the cost of medical insurance is paid from the general revenues of the federal government. The medical insurance part of medicare is kept on a pay-as-you-go basis, as required by law.

Additional information about medicare will be included in Chapter 22. The medicare program is far more complicated than the brief description given here suggests, but in broad outline, you can see that adequate hospital and medical care are now within the reach of most of America's citizens who are 65 years of age or older.

THE FUTURE OF THE SOCIAL SECURITY
PROGRAM

Critics of the social security system have been warning for some time
that the program faces a crisis in the years ahead. Some of these critics
have even suggested that the program be ended. What are the problems, according to these persons?

For one thing, some persons look with alarm at the fact that the trust
funds for both the disability and the old-age and survivors programs
began declining in 1974. In 1977 the board of trustees that examines
social security each year estimated that the disability fund would last
only until 1979. The trustees estimated that the old-age and survivors
fund would last only until 1984. But, of course, the trustees expect
Congress to do something about the funds. In 1977 the disability fund
was $5.9 billion and the old-age and survivors fund was $35 billion.
These are small funds when one considers the fact that $71 billion
dollars were paid out in benefits in 1976. But remember that social
security is really not an insurance program. Contributions do not go
into a trust fund, or reserve, that is used to pay you an annuity when
you retire. Instead, social security operates on a pay-as-you-go basis.
The taxes deducted each year from a worker's paycheck are used to
help pay the benefits that year for retired or disabled persons and their
dependents. Then why are trust funds set up at all? They are intended
only to even out temporary imbalances between income and expenditures.

Social security trust funds, therefore, are not like private insurance
company reserves. Insurance reserves are set up so that they can be
used to pay off policies if the company goes broke. To be fully funded
in that way, the social security system would need a fund now of
between $2.7 and $4.1 trillion, according to estimates. Establishing
such a huge fund would not be possible. Besides, it is not necessary
since the ability of the social security system to pay future benefits
depends upon the ability of the government to tax future workers.

Future Deficits

Unless some changes are made, in the years ahead the social security
program will be paying out more in benefits than it collects in taxes,
thus causing deficits. The deficits that are foreseen toward the end of
this century and the first half of the next century concern some people.
Deficits are expected because of a great age shift in our population. In
recent years, women have been bearing, on the average, 1.8 children.

Gradually raising the normal retirement age from 65 to 68 or even 70 could help hold down the costs of the social security system and increase its revenues. (*Arizona Public Service Company*)

A birth rate that small is not enough to replace the population. If a rate of 1.8 continues over the next 75 years (and social security officials think it will), the result will be a larger proportion of people of retirement age. In fact, by the year 2050, 51 people will be drawing benefits for every 100 paying social security taxes. Or, for every two persons working, one person will be paid social security benefits. In 1977 the ratio of those drawing benefits to workers was 31 to 100. By the middle of the next century, then, an additional burden will be put on workers.

Solutions to the Problem

Proposals for helping solve the money problems of the social security system have been numerous. In the late 1970s President Carter considered such ideas as raising the social security taxes paid by employers by requiring that they pay their share of social security taxes on all of an employee's income, rather than just on a portion. Some other solutions are presented here:

- Increase the tax base above the levels provided by the 1972 law. At present, someone earning $16,500 or less pays a larger proportion of income in social security taxes than someone earning more than $16,500. Remember, we pay social security taxes only on the first $16,500 of income. By contrast, our regular income tax rates go up with income.
- Finance part of the costs of social security with general tax revenues.
- Gradually raise the normal retirement age from 65 to 68 or even to 70. This would hold down the costs of the system and at the same time increase its revenues. Today, pressures are in the direction of *reducing* the retirement age. But in the next century, with only a small number of persons entering the work force, there may be pressures to keep people working longer. Perhaps we will have advancements in medical science that could result in a better health level, and therefore retirement at age 65 will be less attractive.
- Extend social security to all kinds of employment. Some important groups, such as federal employees, are still not included in the program.
- Tax married workers at a rate of 50 percent higher than that of single workers in order to pay for the nonworking spouse's benefits.

Does Social Security Offer Enough?

Some persons do not think the social security system delivers nearly enough in benefits. For many Americans, children are expected to help their aging parents, but these children are struggling themselves to make ends meet. According to social security statistics in the mid-1970s, the average benefit paid to individuals was $2256 a year. For couples, the average benefit was $3744. Unless the persons receiving the benefits had other resources, they had trouble buying the necessary things in life. As you might suspect, other people disagree with the view that social security does not provide enough in benefits. They point out that the original purpose of social security was to provide a basic floor of protection. This meant keeping the costs of the program low enough to encourage people to have private savings and investments. The social security benefits when combined with these private resources would then be high enough to enable most persons to maintain at least an acceptable standard of living during their retirement.

No doubt our social security system will undergo some changes in the years ahead. All proposals for change will probably stir up some controversy. But there does seem to be broad agreement that the system must be maintained.

Checking Your Reading

1. List the four principal reasons for establishment of social insurance programs.
2. Why is loss of earning power now much more serious than it was in the early days of our country?
3. How does the United States compare with Sweden, the Netherlands, and Great Britain in the proportion of national income spent on social programs?
4. As our economy became more industrialized, people faced certain risks that made social insurance desirable. What kind of social insurance was first made mandatory by state laws?
5. What is the broad range of benefits now provided by social security?
6. Where can one get questions about social security answered?
7. Explain how social security benefits are financed. How does the money reach the government?
8. What must a person do in order to be eligible for social security payments for him- or herself and family?
9. Explain the difference between "fully insured" and "currently insured."
10. When is a person considered to be disabled?
11. What are the two plans of medicare? How do these plans differ in the way they are financed?
12. Why are deficits expected in the social security system toward the end of this century?
13. List five solutions offered to the problem of deficits in the social security system.

Consumer Problems and Projects

1. Use Table 21-4 to answer the following questions about persons who are covered by social security.
   a. Linda Perez has just died, leaving as survivors her husband, who is 39 years old, and four children, ages 6, 9, 11, and 14. Mrs. Perez's average yearly earnings from 1951 were $6000. What will be the monthly payment to the family? What will be the lump-sum death payment?

b. Mr. Pinoak has just retired. He is 65 years old. His wife is 62 years old. Mr. Pinoak's average yearly earnings from 1951 were $6000. What social security benefits will Mr. and Mr. Pinoak receive each month?

c. Janice Menska is a widow. Her husband did not work on a job covered by social security. Mrs. Menska, however, has worked in a covered occupation. She is now 65 and will retire. Her average yearly earnings from 1951 were $5000. What will be Mrs. Menska's monthly payment?

2. Obtain display materials and pamphlets from a local office of the Social Security Administration, and make a bulletin board display of the provisions of the social security program. For example, you could get information about such things as how social security works for nonprofit organizations and their employees, how employees of state and local governments get social security credit, how the self-employed can obtain social security credit, and how social security benefits are financed.

3. Insurance companies report that it is generally easier to sell life insurance policies and annuity contracts to workers who are covered by old-age, survivors, and disability insurance. How do you account for this?

4. Report to the class on the changes that have been made in the social security program since 1935. Include in your report current proposals for new legislation that will affect the program. Some of the material for this report can be obtained from a Social Security Administration field office. Encyclopedias and current news magazines will also contain information that will be useful to you.

5. Prepare a debate—*Resolved:* That social insurance programs are detrimental to our economy.

22

Health Services and Insurance

Since the early 1960s medical costs in our country have risen rapidly. By the mid-1970s Americans were spending $118 billion a year for medical care, or about $540 for every man, woman, and child. Put another way, we are spending about $1 out of every $9 we earn for medical costs—and the costs appear likely to increase.

Prices for other things have increased too. But medical costs have been increasing 2 to 3 times faster than the cost of other goods and services we buy. One way to measure the increase in medical care is to express its cost each year as a percent of *gross national product* for that year. Gross national product (GNP) is the value of all the goods and services produced in a country. In 1960 medical care costs were 5.2 percent of GNP. In 1970 national spending for medical care was 7.2 percent of GNP. By 1975 medical care spending had climbed to 8.3 percent of GNP.

The Department of Health, Education, and Welfare reported in late 1976 that they believe medical costs will continue to go higher, reaching an estimated $224 billion a year by 1980. Many people believe that our nation faces a crisis in health care. What has caused the increase in costs?

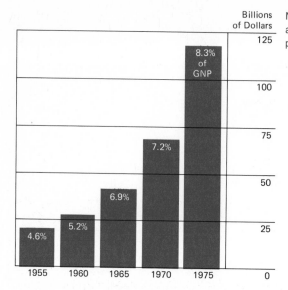

Billions of Dollars

125

8.3% of GNP

100

75

7.2%

50

6.9%

5.2%

25

4.6%

1955   1960   1965   1970   1975

0

National health expenditures and percent of gross national product.

WHY ARE MEDICAL COSTS SO HIGH?

Many reasons have been given for the increase in medical costs during the past two decades. The cost of new medical technology and the highly skilled personnel needed certainly has contributed to higher costs. For instance, in the last decade intensive-care units, where costs run several hundred dollars a day, have come into wide use. In just the past several years, hundreds of thousands of persons with heart disease have undergone the new coronary-bypass surgery. These persons can have hospital bills of $10,000 to $25,000 each.

Another reason for rising medical costs has been the high cost of training doctors. The increasing premiums many of them have to pay for malpractice insurance also adds to medical costs. The Health Insurance Association of America has estimated that malpractice lawsuits have added as much as $1.5 billion a year to the public's bill for health insurance. According to the Department of Health, Education, and Welfare, another $3 to $5 billion is added because of unnecessary "defensive medicine." To help guard against malpractice suits, doctors ask for x-rays, laboratory tests, and other procedures not medically indicated.

Still another reason given for increased costs of medical care is the fact that about 92 percent of all hospital bills are paid by some third party, either the government or a private insurance company. When patients do not have to open their pocketbooks to pay their bills, they

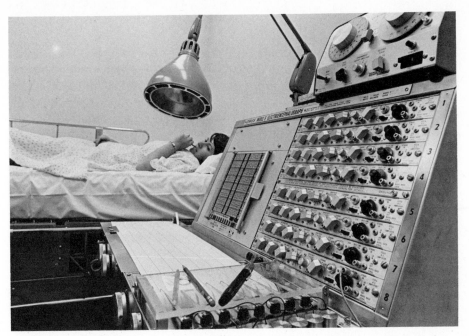

The increasing use of modern medical technology, such as this electroencephalograph, which must be operated and serviced by highly skilled personnel has contributed to today's higher medical costs. (*Burroughs Co.*)

do not have as much incentive to keep costs down, of course. Nor do doctors feel it so necessary to keep bills low when they know that the bills will be paid by insurance. Some economists believe that one solution would be to change the system so that patients pay a rather large portion of their bills. Patients might pay up to, say, 10 percent of their annual incomes; insurance would pay the rest. For example, someone earning $14,000 a year would have to pay the first $1400 of his or her medical bills each year. If bills totaled more than $1400 for a year, a person's insurance would pay the difference between the total bill and $1400. This plan, according to these economists, would provide an incentive to bring costs under control.

THE QUALITY OF MEDICAL CARE

We can be proud of the achievements of American medicine. Most of the antibiotics now in daily use in the world were developed by our medical researchers, and these medical researchers lead the world in Nobel prizes. Some of our medical centers, such as the Mayo Clinic in Minnesota, are world-renowned. But in the task of preventing and treating routine illness, our achievement is not quite so noteworthy.

The Shortage of Professionals

Some people believe the United States has a serious shortage of doctors and hospitals. Others argue that the nation has enough doctors and hospitals, but they are badly distributed. Many rural areas and some inner cities, for example, do not have enough doctors. At the same time, many suburban areas have more doctors than are really needed. In some locations, there is a serious shortage of general practitioners, internists, and pediatricians—the doctors we turn to when illness first strikes. The result of this is that many already overworked doctors must work even longer days.

The need for registered nurses is great. Hospital and clinics need trained workers in such areas as x-ray technology and respiratory therapy.

Paying for Health Services

In this age of increasing health costs and expensive new medical procedures, few people can afford a long illness or a serious injury. Many families would face serious financial problems if one member should suddenly need surgery and a long stay in a hospital. A severe heart attack requiring heart surgery and months of hospitalization, for example, would cost thousands of dollars. Furthermore, if the stricken member should be the breadwinner, family income might be shut off. How do American families pay for such medical care? Health insurance in its many different forms enables many people to protect themselves financially in the event of illness or accident.

Medicare, the federal government's program of health insurance for older people, has been helpful to many. A section of the medicare law popularly known as *medicaid* provides federal assistance to states to set up new medical care programs for the needy, regardless of age. Most people, however, have had to rely on private insurance plans to provide health insurance protection. Before looking at the national health insurance programs considered by Congress in recent years, we will examine the types of coverage offered by nonprofit plans such as Blue Cross-Blue Shield and by private insurance companies.

TYPES OF HEALTH INSURANCE

In a recent year, more than 178 million people in the United States, or more than 8 out of 10 persons, were protected by one or more forms of private health insurance. The number of persons with health insurance protection has increased markedly during the past few decades. Possibly the main reason for the increase in health insurance coverage has been the sharply escalating costs for medical care. Individuals and families have been forced to find a way to protect themselves against the expense. Employers and labor unions have recognized this need for health insurance, and offering group health insurance plans for employees as a fringe benefit has become an important part of labor's bargaining process.

Health insurance policies can be purchased in a variety of forms and combinations, but the available protection can be divided into six types of coverage. The first four types—hospital expense, surgical expense, regular medical expense, and major medical expense—are designed to help persons pay the costs of hospital care, surgery, and medical treatment. The fifth type of health insurance—loss-of-income protection—is designed to help replace income lost during periods of prolonged disability. The sixth type covers dental expense.

Hospital Expense Insurance

Hospital expense insurance provides benefits that cover all or part of hospital room-and-board charges as well as an allowance that may be applied toward such things as operating-room charges, laboratory fees, x-ray and fluoroscopic examinations, drugs and dressings, and occasionally, special nurses' fees. Hospitalization policies typically provide a specified number of dollars a day for a specified number of days—often 100 days or more for each accident or illness, although some plans pay for hospitalization for as many as 365 days. Because hospital charges have increased so sharply in recent years, the cost of hospital insurance has also been forced up. In a recent year, the nationwide average cost of a day in a hospital was $70, but at a growing number of hospitals the cost was $150 to $200 a day. Costs for luxury private rooms were even higher.

In a recent year, almost 178 million persons had hospital expense insurance coverage. More persons were protected by this type of insurance than by any of the other types of health insurance.

Surgical Expense Insurance

The next most popular type of health insurance coverage is surgical expense insurance. This type of insurance pays benefits according to a

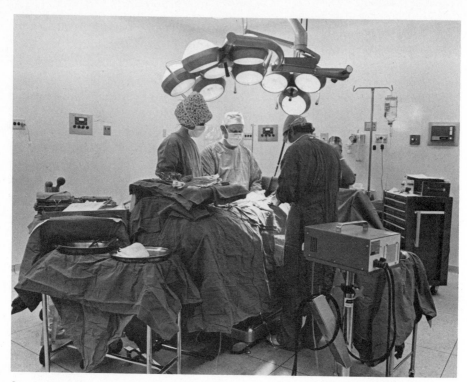

Surgical expense insurance will help pay for the actual cost of an operation, but hospital expense insurance is needed to cover such costs as operating room charges, room and board, and drugs and dressings. A comprehensive plan would cover both. (*Good Samaritan Health Service*)

schedule of surgical procedures, listing the maximum amount of benefits for each type of operation covered. Sometimes the benefit is stated as reimbursement up to the "usual and customary" charges in the region where the operation is performed. The number of persons with surgical expense insurance was nearly 169 million recently.

Regular Medical Expense Insurance

Regular medical expense insurance provides benefits toward a physician's fees for nonsurgical care given in the hospital or home or at the doctor's office. Some regular medical expense policies also provide benefits for diagnostic x-ray and laboratory expenses. Most companies usually provide a fixed sum of money for each visit, and the maximum number of calls for each illness or injury is usually specified.

Recently, almost 162 million persons were protected by regular medical expense insurance.

Major Medical Expense Insurance

Although few people can afford a medical bill of the size that would pile up should a serious and prolonged illness or injury occur, not even half the people in the nation are covered by the type of health insurance that protects against big bills. Major medical policies could more aptly be called "catastrophe insurance." None of the policies described earlier are designed to meet the needs of persons who require hospitalization for long periods of time and whose surgical bills are more than the maximum amounts set forth in the schedule of benefits paid by surgical expense insurance. Thus, major medical expense insurance serves a real need. A heart attack, a severe case of hepatitis, spinal meningitis, or an accident that might require extensive surgery and months of hospitalization are just a few examples of catastrophes that might hit any family at any time. The chances are not great that such misfortune will strike, but when it strikes a family without insurance coverage, the debt sometimes takes years to pay.

Major medical expense insurance is growing rapidly, but as indicated earlier, most persons in the nation do not have this important type of insurance. From 108,000 persons protected in 1951, when the coverage was first widely offered, the number grew to 92 million in 1975.

A variety of major medical policies is available, mainly from commercial insurance companies, but also from Blue Cross-Blue Shield and through independent health insurance plans, such as those operated by labor unions. About 94 percent of the people covered by major medical insurance have group policies, usually made available by their employers. The employer often pays part of or all the premiums.

Major medical expense policies have high maximum benefits. Maximum benefits range from $10,000 to $250,000 per person and higher, and in some cases they are unlimited. A 1975 survey by the Health Insurance Association of America showed that 67 percent of those with insurance company group major medical coverage had benefits of $50,000 or more available to them, and 39 percent had benefits of $250,000 or more. Costs of all types of medical treatment prescribed, in or out of the hospital, are covered, but most major medical policies have a deductible clause and a coinsurance clause.

The *deductible clause*, which is similar in nature to that found in most automobile collision policies, means that the insured must pay a certain amount before the insurer pays anything. For example, with a $100-deductible policy, the insured pays the first $100. If the expenses do not exceed $100, the insurance company pays nothing. The deductible clause, which is used to eliminate many small claims for expenses that the policyholder should be able to budget for, enables the insurance company to offer this type of insurance for a lower premium. Deductible amounts usually range from $100 to $1000.

The *coinsurance clause* requires the policyholder to pay part of the bill—usually about 20 or 25 percent—that remains after the deductible amount has been subtracted. This provision encourages the person insured to use only reasonable and necessary medical service.

Now let us see how a typical major medical policy with a $250 deductible clause and a 20 percent coinsurance clause works. Suppose a young man underwent surgery, and in addition to hospitalization, he needed a nurse at home for a few weeks. His total medical charges, including the cost of the home nurse, totaled $8320. In addition to his major medical expense policy, he was covered by a base plan of hospital expense and surgical expense insurance, which paid $2160. His insurance would be figured as follows:

Total charges	$8320
Less amount covered by base plan of hospital and surgical expense insurance	2160
Amount covered by major medical	6160
Less deductible of $250	−250
Balance subject to coinsurance	5910
Less coinsurance at 20%	−1182
Amount paid by major medical	4728

SUMMARY

Paid by base plan	$2160
Paid by major medical	4728
Paid by patient	1432
Total	$8320

As you can see, of the total bill of $8320, the young man paid only $1432. His major medical expense insurance paid $4728—or more than half the bill.

The major medical expense policy just described is known as a "supplementary" plan. A *supplementary* plan is designed to pick up where a separate basic hospitalization plan stops. Another major medical plan is known as a "comprehensive" plan. *Comprehensive* plans combine the basic and major medical protection in a single policy and typically cover all the hospital, surgical, and medical expenses incurred during an illness or because of an accident. Like the supplementary form of major medical coverage, comprehensive plans have both deductible and coinsurance features, although the deductible provisions do not call for quite so high an amount as those under a supplementary major medical plan.

Loss-of-Income Insurance

The oldest type of health insurance available is loss-of-income insurance, sometimes called *disability income protection*. This type of insurance pays benefits when the insured is unable to work because of illness or injury. At the beginning of this century, medical expenses were not high, and so the main financial problem when the wage earner became ill or suffered an accident that kept the person from working was the loss of income during the period he or she could not work. Loss-of-income insurance issued by insurance companies may pay as much as 75 percent of the wage earner's normal earnings for a specified period of disability. Usually the payments do not begin until after a certain waiting period has elapsed. There is a good reason for the waiting period and for the pay limit of three-fourths of the regular weekly or monthly income. If a person were able to buy a policy that paid as much or more than earned while working, he or she would have an incentive to fake an illness or contrive an accident. The companies would be kept busy trying to prevent fraud.

Loss-of-income policies usually also provide for payment of benefits to a beneficiary in case of the accidental death of the person insured. These policies often also provide for the payment of a certain amount to the person insured if he or she should lose an arm or a leg or some other part of the body.

Dental Expense Insurance

About 35 million people were protected by some form of dental insurance at the end of 1975. Dental expense insurance helps pay for normal dental care as well as damage caused by accidents. The insurance typically covers such things as examinations, fillings, extractions, inlays, bridgework, and dentures, as well as oral surgery and root canal therapy.

GROUP HEALTH INSURANCE

Many persons in the United States are included in health insurance plans because this is a benefit offered to them by their employers. Most group policies are written on the employees of business organizations, but they can also be issued to any group of people who have a common

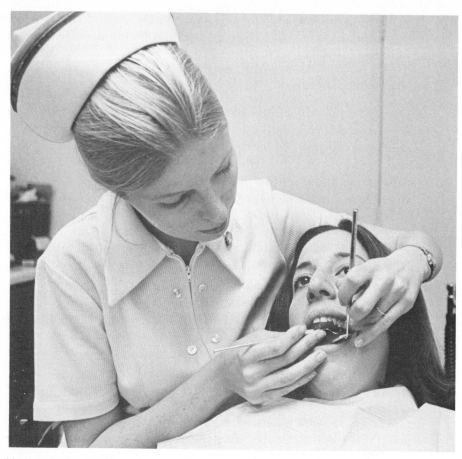

More and more people are protected by dental insurance which pays for normal dental care as well as damage caused by accidents. (*Ray Ellis, Photo Researchers*)

bond, such as labor unions, credit unions, churches, and professional associations. The members who make up the group are insured under one policy for an amount determined by a definite formula that applies to all members. Usually the contract requires that the insurance cover the whole group, or most of the group, without discrimination because of age, sex, or physical condition.

The group policy is usually the best health insurance available for the dollar. As is the case in group life insurance, the costs of insuring a number of people under a group plan can be much less than insuring the same people under individual plans. Furthermore, by insuring the whole group, the company eliminates the possibility of "adverse selection." This term is used to describe the situation in which people who believe they may collect benefits tend to buy insurance and people who believe they are healthy and will not collect do not buy.

The most common type of group plan is the one in which both employee and employer share costs. In some cases, the employer pays the entire premium. In that case all employees are automatically members of the group plan. Some group plans, on the other hand, require the employee to pay the entire cost. But even when the employee foots the entire premium bill, this kind of coverage is usually superior to an individual policy because of the low cost. A consumer should check the provisions of a group policy to determine whether there is a need for additional coverage with an individual policy.

NATIONAL HEALTH INSURANCE PROPOSALS

Most American families would have serious money problems if one of their members became seriously ill and needed extensive surgery followed by expensive treatments during a long hospital stay. In such countries as Sweden, England, and West Germany, the possibility of serious financial problems due to long and serious illness has been almost eliminated because of national health insurance programs. In the United States private medical insurance has expanded greatly during the past several decades, and the amount of money we spend for health purposes represents a large share of our resources. Yet dissatisfaction with what our system provides is widespread.

Although health insurance coverage has increased, the system has not tended to encourage efficiency in the use of hospitals. Most families have hospital expense insurance, for example, but no coverage for care outside the hospital. Health care outside the hospital is known as *ambulatory care*. The result of the lack of ambulatory care is that many patients occupy hospital beds for the purpose of gaining insurance benefits to cover the cost of tests and minor surgery that could just as well be done in doctors' offices or clinics at much less cost.

Several proposals for a form of national health insurance have been presented to Congress during the past decade, but in the late 1970s they had not been acted upon. These plans vary to quite some extent. Possibly the two most familiar plans proposed during the 1970s represent quite opposite points of view of what a national health plan should do for people. One proposal is the Kennedy-Griffiths plan, named after its original sponsors, Senator Edward Kennedy of Massachusetts, and Representative Martha Griffiths of Michigan. The other plan was proposed by the American Medical Association.

The Kennedy-Griffiths Plan

The Kennedy-Griffiths plan is an income-tax-financed plan that would require all people to participate. Just about all personal health-care expenses would be paid for by the plan. Some of the things that would not be covered would be some prescription drugs, some psychiatric care, and adult dental care. Unlike major medical plans, there would be no deductible clause and no coinsurance clause. An insured person would not have to pay any out-of-pocket costs. The Kennedy-Griffiths plan would not, of course, rely on private health insurance companies.

The American Medical Association Plan

The plan proposed by the American Medical Association is based on the voluntary purchase of health insurance from private companies. The federal government would be called upon to pay some premium costs for the poor. The plan would require a $50-deductible clause for each hospital stay. Also, the plan calls for a 20 percent coinsurance clause for the first $500 in hospital expenses. Private insurance companies would participate in the plan proposed by the American Medical Association, and these companies would be overseen by state insurance regulators (as they are now, of course).

Will We Have a National Health Plan?

What are the chances for passing a national health insurance program? Most observers believe that some form of national health insurance is coming, but some of them say it might take several years. However, it is probable that no proposal will survive the legislative process intact—compromises will be made.

HEALTH-MAINTENANCE ORGANIZATIONS

A new approach to offering health care to people has become increasingly popular in recent years. It is a plan by which people get all their medical care from the same source, and they pay in advance one fee for this service. The plans now in existence differ somewhat. Some own their own hospitals, clinics, and drugstores. Other plans make arrangements with existing independent facilities. The general term that has been applied to all these plans is "health maintenance organization" (HMO).

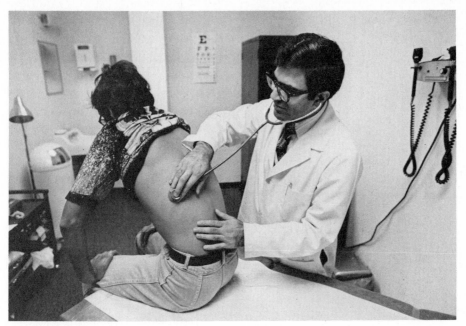

A real advantage of health-maintenance organizations is that they give doctors a strong financial incentive to be more efficient and to provide good preventive care. (*Jim Anderson, Woodfin Camp & Associates*)

In 1973 Congress passed the Health Maintenance Organization Act. It provides federal grants, contracts, and loan guarantees for the planning, development, and initial operating costs of HMOs. Amendments were enacted in 1976 to make the law more workable.

Many of the proposals for a national health insurance program place a strong emphasis on developing and enlarging HMOs as a means of providing health services. The two main features of the plan, remember, are these: (1) It brings together a comprehensive range of medical services in a single organization so that a patient has convenient access to these services. (2) It provides services for a fee paid in advance by all people who join the plan.

From 1971 to 1976 the number of HMOs increased from 33 to 176. The number of persons enrolled has risen from 3.6 to 6.0 million. By fall 1976, 21 HMOs were federally qualified under the Health Maintenance Organization Act as providing the required benefits.

One of the most important advantages of HMOs is that they provide a strong financial incentive for better preventive care and for greater efficiency. Under an HMO plan, most of a family's medical costs are paid for in advance under a single monthly fee, and the organization must operate with the money received from these fees. Under the traditional system, the more illnesses doctors and hospitals treat, the more their incomes rise. Thus there is no economic incentive for them to try to keep people healthy. In contrast, HMOs emphasize preventive medicine.

The patient who does not get good care the first time will return for more medical care. But since treatment has already been paid for, he or she will not be bringing in additional money. There is no profit in a sick member. Doctors are paid to keep people healthy.

A patient visiting an HMO doctor because of an injured shoulder would probably also be given a general examination if he or she had not had one recently. During the examination the doctor might discover that the patient has high blood pressure, so he or he is treated for that ailment as well as for the injured shoulder. Under our conventional system of medical care, the man might simply be treated for the injured shoulder, and health insurance might pay for the treatment. Later, the patient might suffer a heart attack because the presence of high blood pressure was overlooked. Of course, the value of preventive medicine to human life is very important. Of secondary importance in a case such as this is the high cost of the treatment for the heart attack. But the point being made here is that the insurance company would have to cover some extremely high bills, and such bills help to push up our nation's health costs.

Studies show that HMOs have saved money. The costs of health care are lower—as much as one-fourth to one-third lower than the costs of traditional care in some areas. Also, the members go to hospitals less often, and they do not stay as long. In fact, they spend from one-fourth to one-half less time in hospitals than do nonmembers. Thus HMO members receive high-quality care at lower cost.

Government-sponsored or government-supported health insurance is certainly not a new idea in the United States. In 1912 national health insurance was endorsed in the platform of Theodore Roosevelt's Progressive Party. This was followed by a campaign to enact a health program on a statewide basis. The campaign was dropped following the failure of key tests in California and New York. In 1935 a provision for national health insurance was considered for the social security bill, but it was not included.

During the 1940s and 1950s certain legislators worked to obtain health coverage for people in the nation. The first result of their efforts was the passage of Medicare in 1965, a program giving benefits to the aged. Most observers believe that some form of national health insurance for all people will be forthcoming in the near future. Consumers should know, of course, that one way or another they will continue to pay for medical care. The money may be paid in the form of premium payments. Or some of the money may be paid for by the government from general revenues. General revenues come from taxes, and those taxes will be paid for by people in the nation.

Checking Your Reading

1. Give three reasons for the increase in medical costs during the past two decades.
2. What is medicaid?
3. List the six types of coverage into which health insurance is divided.
4. Identify and define the two most popular types of health insurance coverage.
5. Explain what is meant by a deductible clause in a major medical policy.
6. Explain how a coinsurance clause works in a major medical expense policy.
7. How does a supplementary major medical plan differ from a comprehensive major medical plan?
8. Why do most loss-of-income insurance policies have a pay limit of three-fourths of a worker's regular weekly or monthly income?
9. Give two reasons why a group policy is usually the best health insurance available for the dollar.
10. Explain how the Kennedy-Griffiths plan for national health insurance would be financed.
11. How would the financing of the American Medical Association plan for national health insurance differ from the financing of the Kennedy-Griffiths plan?
12. What are the two essential features of a health maintenance organization (HMO)?
13. Explain one of the most important advantages claimed for HMOs.

Consumer Problems and Projects

1. Obtain a current copy of "Source Book of Health Insurance Data" from your library or from the Health Insurance Institute, 277 Park

Avenue, New York, NY 10017. In this book find the answers to the following questions:

    a. How many persons had hospital expense protection by the end of the most recent year reported? How many had surgical expense coverage? Regular medical expense coverage? Major medical expense coverage? Short-term disability income? Long-term disability income? Dental expense?

    b. Summarize the extent of the increase since 1960 in the seven types of coverage mentioned above.

    c. How much was spent by Americans for medical care in the most recent year reported? Does this represent an increase or a decrease over the amount spent in previous years?

    d. Summarize personal consumption expenditures for medical care. For example, how much is spent for hospital services? For physicians' services? For dentists' services?

    e. By examining consumer price indexes for medical care items, indicate which medical care items have increased and which have decreased in cost during the past several years.

2. Mrs. Fujita has just recovered from rather extensive surgery. Her total medical bill is $13,100. She is covered by a base plan of hospital and surgical expense insurance. In addition, she has a major medical plan that begins to pay only after the benefits of the basic plan have been exhausted. Other provisions of her major medical plan are these: a deductible clause of $250 and a coinsurance clause that specifies that the insured person pays 25 percent of the amount in excess of the deductible. Mrs. Fujita's base plan of hospital and surgical expense insurance paid $2,900. How much will the major medical insurance pay? How much will Mrs. Fujita have to pay?

3. Examine a group health insurance policy. Make a list of the chief provisions of the policy. Would some families need another health insurance policy to supplement this coverage?

4. Make arrangements to have a representative of an insurance company speak to the class about the risks we all face with regard to health and accidents. Prepare a list of questions to ask the speaker.

5. Prepare a debate—*Resolved:* Insurance should pay only those medical costs exceeding 10 percent of each consumer's annual income. (*Note:* Read again on page 375 the suggestion given by some economists that patients should be required to pay a rather large portion of their own bills.)

PART FIVE

Consumer Credit, Taxes, and Government Services

23

Consumer Credit

Buy now, pay later! A study in the mid-1970s showed that two-thirds of American families do just that for such day-to-day expenses as gasoline, clothing, household goods, and drugs. Some families even pay later for the vacations they take.

When consumers pay later for the goods or services they get, they are using consumer credit. In an earlier day, most consumer credit was for such relatively expensive items as home improvements, appliances, and cars. But now consumers use credit for just about any kind of purchase. Charge accounts and credit cards have made credit easy to use for many consumers.

In fact, credit is now a part of our way of life. Unfortunately, when credit is not used wisely, it can cause a great deal of grief. If credit is easily available, we may be tempted to buy more than our incomes will allow. Then, too, so many people ignore or just don't know what credit costs them. When we don't know the cost of credit and don't take the time to find out, we can waste many dollars. In this chapter you will learn that credit can be useful at times, provided the costs and benefits of consumer credit are understood.

Using credit is now as much a part of daily life as shopping, although at one time credit was available only for major purchases. (*Art Zollo*)

WHY CREDIT IS POPULAR TODAY

Widespread use of consumer credit is fairly recent. In 1945 the total amount of consumer credit was $5.6 billion. In the five-year period between 1945 and 1950, consumer credit increased to $21.5 billion—a fourfold increase. Since that time, the use of credit has continued to increase rapidly. By the mid-1970s total consumer credit had reached $190 billion.

More than half of all families in our country make installment payments of some kind other than mortgages. But "all" families includes older families—families that already own most home furnishings they want and who also tend to have higher incomes and thus have less need to borrow money. Some finance counselors estimate that about three-fourths of all young families make installment payments for goods they have bought.

Why Consumers Use Credit

Several things have made consumer credit popular. First, our economy is now based on the exchange of money. Most people depend on a cash income. A continuing flow of money has become as essential to our lives as a supply of oxygen is to an astronaut on the moon. If a person's supply of money is cut off for a short time, it may even become difficult to get food and shelter and the other necessities of life. When we have financial difficulties, as people sometimes do, we need what lenders call "remedial credit."

But present-day consumers need credit for other reasons too. A second thing that has influenced the growth of the use of credit is the fact that modern technology has made available to more people than ever before an abundance of "hard goods," such as automobiles, refrigerators, and television sets. These goods are too expensive to be paid for out of one paycheck. So many consumers, counting on future paychecks, borrow money one way or another in order to enjoy the many goods and services that are available.

Another reason consumers use credit is that it can be more convenient than paying cash. Consumers use gas and electricity in their homes and are billed later for what they use. This is a form of credit. Think of the inconvenience we would be caused if utility companies asked us to pay every day for the gas and electricity we consumed. Many consumers get credit from the dairy that delivers milk, the person who delivers newspapers, and the firm that collects garbage. Consumers often find it convenient to charge purchases at retail stores instead of carrying cash with them while they shop. So you can see that credit in some form is used by just about every consumer in the United States.

Why Merchants Offer Credit

Because competition is keen, merchants may give their customers the privilege of paying for goods at a later date. Many business firms help their customers arrange loans from banks so that expensive items can be bought immediately. The next chapter discusses the use of credit cards for buying merchandise.

Credit enables us to buy now and pay later. Why is the supplier of the product or service willing to wait for money? In some cases, of course, because it is convenient to do so. A dairy finds it easier and probably less costly to collect monthly for the milk left at a house. Some business firms may be willing to wait a reasonable time for

Not everyone who uses the family telephone is aware that he or she is using consumer credit by not paying for the service after each use. (*New York Telephone Company*)

payments because such a service to customers helps build goodwill. Most business firms give credit in return for a finance charge. The goods may be purchased with the agreement that payment must be made within a certain period of time, such as 25 days after the bill is mailed, or a finance charge will be added to the cost of the merchandise. Or a relatively expensive item, such as a sewing machine, may be sold under an agreement in which the consumer makes periodic payments (perhaps monthly) until the price is paid. A finance charge is, of course, added to such installment purchases.

IS CREDIT GOOD OR BAD?

Credit can be good news and bad news for consumers. Consumer credit provides the funds for the purchase of houses, cars, furniture, appliances, and many other goods and services that mark a high standard of living. On the other hand, credit has caused "responsible" families to get into financial trouble by overextending themselves.

Of course, some people save the money in advance and pay cash for the goods and services they buy. Such a practice may be cheaper, but for many persons, buying on credit seems to be easier. And if the payments are wisely budgeted and the cost of the credit is not too high, buying on credit may be perfectly sound. After all, business firms pay for new plants and expensive equipment over many years. It may be just as sound for a family to spread the cost of its expensive goods. At any rate, it is a fact that the possibility of buying on credit has brought people of average income into the market for things that were never before available to them. And bringing more consumers into the market has helped to make mass production and its economies possible.

Advantages of Buying on Credit

Many consumers describe the advantages of using credit in glowing terms. They cite as some of the advantages the convenience of buying, the ease of keeping records, and the satisfaction of using goods while paying for them. Still other consumers consider the use of credit as a form of forced savings. And even the most carefully managed family budget does not always allow for financial emergencies that can be met with the use of credit. These advantages of buying on credit are explained in the following paragraphs.

Buying on Credit Is a Convenience.   Merchants often allow their customers a certain period, such as a month after billing, in which to pay for their purchases. Consumers who have such credit do not have to carry large amounts of cash with them when they shop. Should they be short of cash during a certain month, they can nevertheless make the purchases they wish to make and pay for the purchases later. Then, too what happens when the item bought turns out to be bad in some way? Credit customers often find that making an adjustment is easier when the merchandise has not been paid for.

Credit Aids in Recordkeeping and Budgeting.   Especially in the case where many purchases are made during the month, recordkeeping is easier when one payment is made monthly. A family owning two cars, for example, may buy gasoline as often as 10 or 12 times a month. The monthly bill itemizes the purchases, and the family knows exactly how much they paid for gasoline for the period.

Goods May Be Used While Paying for Them. Expensive items, such as appliances and furniture, are often paid for in installments. The consumer has the use of the goods immediately. The alternative is to wait until enough money can be saved to pay cash for the item. In that case, the consumer must forgo having and using the product for a period of time. Also, the consumer must have the discipline to set money aside for the purchase.

Credit Is a Type of Forced Savings. A person may never be able to accumulate the money for a big-ticket or expensive item such as a freezer or refrigerator. Without the obligation of regular payments, some consumers might waste their incomes on less important things. If a refrigerator is needed, it can be bought on an installment plan, and the installment payments are, in a sense, a means of savings. For the privilege of buying on an installment plan, a credit charge is added to the cost of the product. But more will be said about that later in this chapter.

Credit Enables Consumers to Meet Financial Emergencies. Illness, accidents, or death can create unexpected expenses for which credit may be extremely useful to families. Unemployment may reduce or stop income for a period of time, and unless the family has built up sufficient reserves, credit may be necessary to have the basic necessities during the period.

Disadvantages of Buying on Credit

Credit can cause bad news. This bad news starts when credit is used unwisely by consumers. Financial disaster can result when people buy more than they can afford or when they pay no attention to finance charges, which can take a big portion of their incomes. There are also other disadvantages of buying on credit.

Credit Weakens Sales Resistance. The development of many new goods and services in our country has intensified selling efforts. In an earlier day, consumers were limited in what they could buy by the amount of cash they had available. One obstacle to high-pressure sales techniques was the inability of the consumer to meet the purchase price. The widespread availability of credit has broken down this defense. It is probably safe to say that in many cases providing money or credit with which to buy goods is as important in marketing goods as creating a desire for the goods.

Credit Can Get Out of Hand.   Credit can be bad for consumers when they use it to the point where they become so deeply in debt that they experience serious financial problems.

Credit Encourages Impulse Buying.   Credit can do harm when consumers buy goods or services on impulse because of the ease of paying for them. The possibility of getting a product for only $12 a week makes the purchase price seem unimportant to some persons, so the item is bought without any real analysis of need and without careful consideration of the other purposes for which the money could be used.

Credit Costs Money.   Finally, credit can be harmful to consumers when they cannot or will not consider the cost of credit. Many consumers will spend considerable time and effort shopping around to save $10 or $15 on the price of an appliance that sells for about $400. Then, having found their bargain, they will pay little attention to the finance charge required for the privilege of making installment payments. Yet the difference in finance charges between a two-year bank loan for $400 and a two-year installment loan for a $400 purchase offered by the dealer could be as much as $20 or more.

HOW MUCH DOES CREDIT COST?

The true cost of credit is the total of all the costs that the consumer must pay directly or indirectly for obtaining it. Since the Truth in Lending Act became effective, the total of all credit costs, except in certain cases, must be clearly stated in terms of dollars and cents. The total cost must also be expressed in terms of an annual percentage rate. More information on the scope of the act is given later in this chapter.

In order to arrive at the real cost of a product, the total credit cost must be added to the original purchase price. On some department store charge accounts a typical annual interest rate is 18 percent. That means that nearly $1 out of every $5 paid back on the account goes for interest. In most cases, the true cost of credit will depend on the time taken to repay the loan and the method used in calculating the annual percentage rate.

Almost $1 of every $5 paid on a department store charge account is interest if the store has an annual interest rate of 18 percent (a typical rate). (*Laima Druskis, Editorial Photocolor Archives*)

Time Element

Interest charges may seem to be low. For example, a rate of only 1½ percent a month seems rather low: on a $200 purchase it means an interest charge of just $3 a month. If, however, you take a year to pay for the purchase, the interest will amount to $36. In that event, the cost of the product is really $236. Thus, even a seemingly low interest rate becomes costly when you take a long time to repay the loan.

Table 23-1 illustrates how much money a bank loan for $2000 at 12 percent would cost for three different periods, assuming the loan will be repaid in equal monthly payments. Stretching out the repayment time of a loan makes the monthly payments smaller, but increases the total cost.

Although stretching out the repayment of a loan adds to the total interest cost, in times of high inflation the actual difference in cost on a

TABLE 23-1
Cost of a $2000 Loan at 12 Percent Annual Interest

Duration of Loan	Monthly Payment	Interest Cost
1 year	$177.50	$130
2 years	93.75	250
3 years	65.83	370

long loan when compared with a shorter loan may not be substantial. As Chapter 1 indicated, during times of inflation the purchasing power of dollars goes down. One way to look at a long-term loan during times of inflation is that the loan is being paid back with "smaller" dollars. Or look at it this way: The item you paid $2000 for would cost a lot more after three years with an inflation increase of, say, 6 percent a year.

Methods of Calculating Annual Percentage Rate

The next section of this chapter will discuss the Truth in Lending Act passed by Congress in 1969. The main purpose of the law is to help consumers understand just how much it costs to borrow money. (Money can be borrowed in the form of cash or in the form of goods and services.) The law requires lenders or merchants to give consumers complete information about credit costs. The fact is, though, that most borrowers still have problems understanding the ways interest charges are stated.

A study made several years after the Truth in Lending law was passed showed that only two out of three borrowers knew what interest rate they were paying on their used-car loans. Therefore, before looking at the Truth in Lending law, we will look at how interest rates are figured.

On a one-year loan for $100 to be paid back monthly, a creditor may ask you to pay a $7 finance charge. Does that mean the interest rate is 7 percent? The answer is no, and here are the reasons. You will pay back a twelfth of the $100 plus a twelfth of the $7 finance charge each month. Because you pay back some of the principal each month, you do not have the use of the $100 for the entire year. Actually, you have the use of only about half the money for the full length of time. Because you are paying $7 for the use of what averages out to about $50 over the full year, you are actually paying interest at an annual rate of nearly 14 percent (exactly 12.92 percent) on the money you use.

Two different ways are used to figure installment interest: the discount method and the add-on method. The *discount* method means that the lender subtracts the interest charge from the amount of the loan and gives you the remainder. For example, on a $1000 loan for one year at 6 percent interest, the lender would deduct 6 percent, or $60, from the principal and give you $940. You would pay back the $1000 in equally monthly installments. But you do not have the entire amount of money on which the interest charge is figured. The *add-on* method means that the interest is added to the principal, and then the principal plus the interest is repaid in installments. Thus, on a $1000 loan for one year at 6 percent, the lender would give you $1000 and then ask you to repay $1060 in equally monthly installments. The discount method of figuring interest is a little more expensive than the add-on method.

A rough rule for determining the actual rate of interest on installment loans is to double the apparent rate. Since the Truth in Lending Act became effective, comparing interest rates is not as difficult as it once was because lenders must now state in the contract the true annual interest rate charged. A simple formula can be used to compute the true interest rate:

$$r = \frac{2\,mi}{p\,(n\,+\,1)}$$

where r = the true annual rate of interest

           m = the number of payment periods in one year
                (usually 12 monthly or 52 weekly or 4 quarterly)
            i = the total cost of the loan in dollars and cents
            p = the amount, or principal, of the loan
            n = the total number of payments to be made

The figures 1 and 2 remain constant.

The formula shown should give the same true annual interest rate as shown in the contract the consumer is asked to sign before credit is extended. The formula can be used in all cases as long as the required payments are always the same amount.

Assume that you are offered a $400 television set for $60 down, with the balance to be repaid in six monthly installments of $58.65 each. You will pay a total of $351.90 (6 × $58.65), so the cost of borrowing $340 is $11.90 ($351.90—the total amount to be repaid—less the amount borrowed, $340).

$6 \times \$58.65 = \$351.90$ amount to be repaid
$\underline{-340.00}$ amount borrowed
$\$11.90$ cost of borrowing

To apply the formula, use the figures listed above.

r = true annual interest rate
m = 12 (used in all applications of the formula when monthly payments are made, regardless of the actual number of payments required)
i = \$11.90 (the cost of borrowing)
p = \$340 (the amount borrowed)
n = 6 (the number of monthly payments)

The formula using the above figures looks like this:

$$r = \frac{2 \times 12 \times 11.90}{340\,(6+1)} = \frac{285.60}{2380}$$

$$r = 2380\,\overline{)285.60}^{\,.12} \text{ or } 12\%$$

$$r = 12\%$$

TRUTH IN LENDING LEGISLATION

Since July 1, 1969, when the Truth in Lending Act, Title I of the Consumer Credit Protection Act, became effective, consumers have been able to do some comparison shopping for credit without a slide rule and an advanced degree in mathematics. The Consumer Credit Protection Act had much opposition in Congress but was finally signed into law by President Johnson on May 29, 1968.

Section 102 of the Consumer Credit Protection Act (Public Law 90-321) gives it purpose as follows:

It is the purpose of this title [law] to assure a meaningful disclosure of credit terms so that the consumer will be able to compare more readily the various credit terms available to him and avoid the uninformed use of credit.

This law does not limit the amount of money paid for credit. The intent is to give all borrowers and customers enough information so that they can compare costs and avoid the uninformed use of credit. Almost everyone who extends credit is required by the law to provide a complete and accurate explanation of all the charges and to express the interest rate in a standard, meaningful form.

JCPenney

CHARGE ACCOUNT STATEMENT

J. C. PENNEY COMPANY, INC.

NOTICE: SEE REVERSE SIDE AND ACCOMPANYING STATEMENTS FOR IMPORTANT INFORMATION.

WHEN PAYING IN PERSON, PRESENT ENTIRE STATEMENT AT YOUR PENNEY STORE.

PLEASE RETURN THIS PART WITH YOUR PAYMENT

ACCOUNT NUMBER	BILLING DATE
012-345-678-9-4	7/1/--

PREVIOUS BALANCE	PAYMENTS	CREDITS
450.00	340.00	10.00

FINANCE CHARGE IS COMPUTED ON THIS AMOUNT ▶ 100.00 (PREVIOUS BALANCE MINUS PAYMENTS AND CREDITS ▼)

	PURCHASES	INSURANCE PREMIUM
1.50	24.50	6.00

M=MINIMUM **FINANCE CHARGE**

PERIODIC RATES: 1.5% ON THE BALANCE UP TO $500 AND 1% ON THE EXCESS OVER $500.

ANNUAL PERCENTAGE RATE: 18% ON THE BALANCE UP TO $500 AND 12% ON THE EXCESS OVER $500. TO AVOID ADDITIONAL **FINANCE CHARGE** PAY THIS AMOUNT ▼ BEFORE THIS DATE ▼

NEW BALANCE	MINIMUM AMOUNT DUE	NEXT BILLING DATE
132.00	16.00	8/3/--

CHARGE ACCOUNT STATEMENT

Mary Smith
1234 Main Street
Hull, Illinois 62343

PAYMENTS, CHARGES OR MERCHANDISE RETURNED AFTER THE BILLING DATE WILL APPEAR ON NEXT MONTH'S STATEMENT.

132.00	16.00	8/3/--
NEW BALANCE	MINIMUM AMOUNT DUE	NEXT BILLING DATE

PAYMENTS MUST REACH US ON OR BEFORE ▲

The Truth in Lending Act requires the lender or merchant to disclose the finance charge and the annual percentage rate. This information helps the consumer compare the credit terms offered by different merchants. (*JC Penney Company Inc.*)

Some Provisions of the Act

Under the Truth in Lending Act, you must be told the total amount of the finance charge in dollars and cents and the true annual percentage rate. On a one-year loan for $100 to be paid back monthly you may be asked to pay $7 in finance charges. Many borrowers may think this amounts to a charge of 7 percent. But as you have learned, because the money is being paid back monthly in equal installments, the true annual interest rate in this case is really 12.92 percent. The lender must indicate the true annual interest rate. The percentage can be rounded to the nearest ¼ of 1 percent.

The lender is also required to include almost all fees you are required to pay as a condition for giving you credit. Before the Truth in Lending Act, the practice had been to separate the interest rate from certain fees and extra charges made as a condition for extending credit. The practice made the cost of credit appear low when the borrower looked solely at the interest rate. Also, certain unethical lenders could load up a loan with fees and make the loan appear to be reasonable by showing a lower interest rate. Not any longer. Now the finance charge or the annual percentage rate must include most fees. Some of these fees include such things as the following: appraisal and credit report fees (except in real estate transactions); any difference between the price of an item sold for cash and an item sold on credit; finder's fees; "points" (extra sums figured as a percentage of the loan amount and charged in a lump sum); service, transaction, and activity charges, and other carrying charges; any charge made because the lender is going to sell the obligation to another lender; the cost of credit; and life, accident, health, or loss-of-income insurance that the lender requires the borrower to buy.

Although most charges must be included in figuring the annual interest rate charged, a few items need not be included. For example, lenders need not include in the finance charge certain government-imposed expenses, such as taxes, or the fees charged for licenses, titles, and registrations.

The forms on pages 403 and 404 are samples distributed by the federal government that show the kinds of information that must be included on the forms used by lenders; that is, they illustrate the disclosures that must be made by the lender. The form on page 403 is for an installment sale, and the form on page 404 is for a revolving credit account. The list below summarizes some of the important disclosures shown on these forms that must be made by those who grant credit.

- Cash price
- Down payment
- Total amount financed
- Finance charge
- Annual percentage rate
- Late charges
- Total of payments
- Amounts of payments

Kinds of Consumer Loans Covered

Banks, savings and loan associations, department stores, credit card issuers, credit unions, car dealers, consumer finance companies, and many more lenders of money are covered by the Truth in Lending Act. In fact, the law exempts very few types of credit transactions involving consumers. Among the main loans that are not covered by the law are the following:

- Loans exceeding $25,000 that do not involve real property (All mortgages, regardless of amount, are covered by the act.)
- Business and commercial credit
- Loans from a registered broker for transactions in securities and commodities

The kinds of loans that are covered by the Truth in Lending Act include installment loans and sales, revolving charge accounts, and real estate mortgages.

Seller's Name: _____   **Contract #** _____

_____

RETAIL INSTALLMENT CONTRACT AND SECURITY AGREEMENT

The undersigned (herein called Purchaser, whether one or more) purchases from _____(seller) and grants to _____ a security interest in, subject to the terms and conditions hereof, the following described property.

QUANTITY	DESCRIPTION	AMOUNT	
Description of Trade-in:			
		Sales Tax	
		Total	

PURCHASER'S NAME _____

PURCHASER'S ADDRESS _____

CITY _____ **STATE** _____ **ZIP** _____

1. CASH PRICE $_____
2. LESS: CASH DOWN PAYMENT $_____
3.   TRADE-IN   _____
4.   TOTAL DOWN PAYMENT   _____$_____
5. UNPAID BALANCE OF CASH PRICE $_____
6. OTHER CHARGES:

   _____ $_____

   _____   _____

7. AMOUNT FINANCED $_____
8. FINANCE CHARGE $_____
9. TOTAL OF PAYMENTS $_____
10. DEFERRED PAYMENT PRICE (1+6+8) $_____
11. ANNUAL PERCENTAGE RATE   _____%

Insurance Agreement

The purchase of insurance coverage is voluntary and not required for credit.   (Type of Ins.) _____ insurance coverage is available at a cost of $_____ for the term of credit.

  I desire insurance coverage

Signed_____ Date_____

  I do not desire insurance coverage

Signed_____ Date_____

Purchaser hereby agrees to pay to_____ _____ at their offices shown above the "TOTAL OF PAYMENTS" shown above in _____ monthly installments of $_____(final payment to be $_____) the first installment being payable _____ 19_____, and all subsequent installments on the same day of each consecutive month until paid in full. The finance charge applies from ___(Date)___

Signed_____

Notice to Buyer: You are entitled to a copy of the contract you sign. You have the right to pay in advance the unpaid balance of this contract and obtain a partial refund of the finance charge based on the "Actuarial Method." [Any other method of computation may be so identified, for example, "Rule of 78's," "Sum of the Digits," etc.]

This form, distributed by the Federal Reserve System, shows how a creditor may comply with the disclosure requirements of the Truth in Lending Act for installment sales contracts.

Installment Loans and Sales.   The person extending the credit must furnish a full disclosure of loan conditions in writing, and this must be done before the credit is given. It can be done in the contract that is signed to complete the transaction, or it can be made in a separate document that is given to the potential borrower before he or she signs the contract.

Any Store U.S.A.

MAIN STREET—ANY CITY, U.S.A.

(Customer's name here)

AMT. PAID $ _____

TO INSURE PROPER CREDIT RETURN THIS PORTION WITH YOUR PAYMENT

PREVIOUS BALANCE	FINANCE CHARGE 50 CENT MINIMUM	PAYMENTS	CREDITS	PURCHASES	NEW BALANCE	MINIMUM PAYMENT

FINANCE CHARGE IS COMPUTED BY A "PERIODIC RATE" OF   % PER MONTH (OR A MINIMUM CHARGE OF 50 CENTS FOR BALANCES UNDER $) WHICH IS AN **ANNUAL PERCENTAGE RATE** OF   % APPLIED TO THE PREVIOUS BALANCE WITHOUT DEDUCTING CURRENT PAYMENTS AND/OR CREDITS APPEARING ON THIS STATEMENT.

NOTICE

PLEASE SEE ACCOMPANYING STATEMENT(S) FOR IMPORTANT INFORMATION.

PAYMENTS, CREDITS OR CHARGES, RECEIVED AFTER THE DATE SHOWN ABOVE THE ARROW, WHICH IS THE CLOSING DATE OF THIS BILLING CYCLE, WILL APPEAR ON YOUR NEXT STATEMENT. TO AVOID ADDITIONAL FINANCE CHARGES PAY THE "NEW BALANCE" BEFORE THIS DATE NEXT MONTH.

ANY STORE, U.S.A.   MAIN STREET, ANY CITY, U.S.A.

This form, distributed by the Federal Reserve System, shows how a creditor may comply with the disclosure requirements of the Truth in Lending Act for revolving credit accounts.

Revolving Charge Accounts. The consumer opening a new account must receive a statement disclosing certain facts. Some of these facts include the monthly service charge used in computing the finance charge, the time period for paying a balance without incurring a finance charge, and information as to whether the lender will use any of the goods bought as security for the loan.

In addition, the regular monthly billing statements must contain an itemized account of all the transactions during the billing cycle, a detailed breakdown of the finance charge, and the rates and special

A house mortgage is one of the kinds of loans covered by the Truth in Lending Act, where the total amount of the finance charges and the true annual percentage rate must be disclosed. (*Ted Feder, Editorial Photocolor Archives*)

fees used to compute the charge. Study carefully the example of the form for a revolving credit account shown above.

At the present time, the law permits different methods of figuring finance charges on revolving charge accounts. A wise consumer should examine carefully the method used by the stores with which he or she does business because some methods require the consumer to pay more money. Some common methods are listed here.

- *Previous-Balance Method.* When there is a balance in the account at the end of the current billing cycle, the interest rate is figured on the balance outstanding at the beginning of the billing cycle. The previous-balance method does not take into account any payments, returns, or purchases during the billing cycle.

  The previous-balance method is the costliest method from the viewpoint of consumers. An example will illustrate how costly the method can be. Assume that one month you buy a product costing $500 and you pay $499 before the next billing date. The store's interest rate is 1½ percent a month. When you receive your bill next month, you find that you owe a total of $8.50—$1 owed on the balance and $7.50 for interest on the previous balance of $500. The previous-balance method is used by some charge account creditors.
- *Average Daily Balance Method.* Under this method, the cred-

itor adds up the actual amounts outstanding each day during the billing period and then divides the sum by the number of days in the period. The result is the amount that the interest rate is figured on. Payments are credited on the day they are received. Purchases are excluded in figuring the average daily balance.

- *Adjusted-Balance Method.* Of the three methods, the adjusted-balance method is the most advantageous to consumers. The interest charge is figured on the balance in the account after deducting payments and credits. Thus, if you owed $400 at the beginning of the cycle and paid $300 at any time during the cycle period, you would be charged interest on $100. Remember that under the previous-balance method you would pay interest on the entire $400.

A consumer who uses a revolving charge account plan should, by all means, check on the store's billing method, which the store is now required to explain. There is some concern in Congress about whether the previous-balance method should be banned. Many retailers, of course, are opposed to banning the method, asserting that such a ban would mean that they would have to increase their merchandise prices to make up for the money they would lose by using another method, such as the adjusted-balance method. In the meantime, the law does give stores their choice of methods, and the choice of a store is the consumer's business.

Checking Your Reading

1. Describe briefly the extent to which consumer credit has increased since 1945.
2. What are some major developments in the economy that have made the use of consumer credit more popular?
3. List and describe five advantages of buying on credit.
4. List and describe four disadvantages of buying on credit.
5. Explain why a consumer is really paying interest at a rate of nearly 12 percent when he or she borrows $1000 and repays $1060 (the principal plus interest at 6 percent) in 12 equal monthly installments.
6. What is the discount method of figuring installment interest?
7. What is the add-on method of figuring installment interest.?
8. What is a rough rule that consumers can use for determining the actual rate of interest on installment loans?

9. What is the intent of the Truth in Lending Act?
10. List eight disclosures that the Truth in Lending Act requires lenders to make.
11. Describe the previous-balance method of figuring finance charges on revolving charge accounts.
12. Describe the average daily balance method of figuring finance charges on revolving charge accounts.
13. Describe the adjusted-balance method of figuring finance charges on revolving charge accounts.

Consumer Problems and Projects

1. Compare the credit arrangements available from stores in your community that sell microwave ovens. Get figures on 12-month, 18-month, and 24-month plans. Report your findings to the class.
2. Assume that a family's automatic washer is broken and cannot be repaired. The family can save money for six months and pay cash for a new washer, or they can buy a new washer immediately by using credit. If they decide to wait until they have enough cash, the family will have to use a laundromat for six months. What are the advantages of each approach? Explain how you can determine which approach would be cheaper. In addition to money, what other factors should be considered in deciding which approach would be better for the family?
3. Write a report on the legal aspects of installment contracts. Books on business law can be helpful sources of information. You may also refer to later parts of this textbook.
4. Assume you are buying a home-entertainment center that will cost $1400. You plan to make a $200 down payment and pay the remaining $1200 over a 24-month period. The interest charge is 6 percent of $1200 times 2 (two years), or $144. Thus, the monthly installments will be $56—$50 on the principal (1/24 of $1200) and $6 on the interest (1/24 of $144). Compute the true annual interest rate using the formula shown on page 399.
5. Refer to problem 4, and assume that a service charge of $10 is added to the interest charge of $144. Compute the true annual interest rate using the formula given on page 399.

24

Sources and Types of Consumer Credit

Credit has been a part of our way of life for the past several decades. Does it seem strange, then, to learn that Congress had to act in 1975 to stop discrimination against women in the granting of credit? Our government has acted to protect consumers in other ways, too, where credit is involved.

Before discussing consumer credit protection, however, this chapter will examine the sources of credit, the kinds of credit available, and how our own credit reputation is built.

Where do consumers go to get credit? From banks and other financial institutions, from insurance companies, and sometimes perhaps from unlicensed lenders (although it is now a federal offense for lenders to practice without a license). Consumer credit also comes from retail stores, credit card companies, oil companies, airlines, and from many other sources. Let's begin by looking at where we borrow money.

WHERE TO BORROW MONEY

Some institutions are in business to lend money. The main ones are commercial banks, credit unions, savings banks, savings and loan as-

sociations, sales finance companies, and consumer finance companies.
In addition, money can be borrowed from the cash value of a person's
life insurance policies.

Commercial Banks

At one time commercial banks lent money only to business firms. Now
consumer loans make up a good part of their lending business. In fact,
at the end of the 1970s these banks held more installment credit than
any other type of financial institution. At the beginning of 1977 the
total amount of installment credit outstanding in the United States was
$178.7 billion, and commercial banks held $85.4 billion of that total.

For most of us, looking into the possibilities of a bank loan should
be one of the starting points when cash is needed. Personal finance
counselors say that often people confess that they did not shop for a
loan at a commercial bank because they were scared by the imposing
facade on the building and were not quite sure that they would be

Christmas shopping is one expense consumers can now borrow money for from a
commercial bank, although at one time such banks lent money only to business firms.
(*Susan Berkowitz*)

welcomed at the loan officer's desk. Actually, bankers estimate that they grant about 90 percent of the loans asked for by consumers. You are doing the bank a favor by investigating the possibility of being one of its customers. If you have a job and a record of prompt payment of debts, you should have no difficulty in obtaining a loan from a commercial bank.

Terms and interest rates vary from area to area and from bank to bank, so it is important to visit several banks to find the most favorable deal. Banks offer different types of loans. The loans can be small, such as a few hundred dollars to pay for some expected expense or to buy Christmas gifts. Or the loan may be as high as several thousand dollars to buy an expensive car. A congressional staff report surveyed commercial banks in late 1975 and found that in major cities around the country, interest rates ranged from about 9 percent to about 18 percent. The lower rates usually are for secured loans, where the value of the security covers the amount of the loan. For example, some people use stocks or bonds as security, and this permits them to borrow usually 60 to 70 percent of the market value of the stocks or bonds. The bank holds the stocks or bonds until the loan is repaid, and they are then returned to the borrower. If the borrower cannot repay the loan, the bank sells all or part of the security in order to collect the debt.

When loans are made for large amounts, for example, to buy an expensive appliance or a car, the bank may ask for a *chattel mortgage* as security. A chattel mortgage is recorded at the courthouse and indicates that the borrower has a claim against the goods. State laws vary regarding the use of chattel mortgages.

Most bank loans are made on the installment basis. To some clients, however, banks will offer loans on unsecured, short-term notes. Such a loan means simply that the borrower agrees to pay back a certain sum of money at a prescribed interest rate within a limited period of time, such as three months. No installments are made; the principal is paid all at one time. These short-term notes are usually figured on a simple interest basis, and the rates are generally quite favorable. For example, a commercial bank may offer a loan of $1000 at 9 percent per year for 90 days. The interest charge in dollars for the 90-day period would be computed by multiplying the principle P ($1000) times the annual rate R (0.09) times the loan period or time T ($90/365$). $I = PRT$; $I = 1000 \times 0.09 \times {}^{90}/_{365}$.

Thus, $22.19 would be the cost of borrowing $1000 at 9 percent for 90 days. Banks usually give short-term unsecured loans only to clients with good to excellent credit ratings, and they may give their regular customers extra consideration. The bank that consumers should start with when a bank loan is wanted is the bank with which they have been doing business in the past.

Credit Unions

Credit unions had their beginning more than a hundred years ago in Europe. The aim of the organizers was to protect working people from the high interest rates usually charged by moneylenders. The first credit union in the Western Hemisphere was organized in Canada in 1900, and nine years later a credit union was started in the United States.

What are credit unions? They are consumer cooperatives. They are formed by members of a closely knit group, such as employees of a business firm or members of a labor union, church, or club. (In fact, by law there must be some sort of "common bond" between credit union members.) A credit union is owned by its members and operates for the benefit of its members. They accept savings from members, and they make low-cost personal loans to members.

Credit unions grew slowly until about 1950, but since then they have grown rapidly. In 1950 the total assets (worth) of credit unions was about $1 billion. By 1968 their assets had grown to $12 billion, and by 1975 their assets had shot up to $38 billion! The number of savings accounts at credit unions has grown faster than savings at any type of competing institution, although the total amount saved is still small when compared with banks.

The outstanding installment credit of credit unions has been increasing recently. By the end of 1976, for example, their outstanding installment credit was $30.5 billion, a gain of 20 percent during the year. In fact, credit unions accounted for nearly one-third of the 1976 rise in installment loans.

Credit unions are an ideal source of credit for people who have an opportunity to join one. Because of low operating costs and certain tax advantages, credit union rates are usually among the lowest available.

How do credit unions keep operating costs low? For one thing, the members themselves often help hold down costs. Officers, except for perhaps the treasurer, may serve without pay. If the credit union is made up of employees of a company, the company often provides free office space and, in some cases, free clerical help. Since the members often know each other, costs of loan investigations and collection are reduced. Any person who has an opportunity to join a credit union should look into the advantages of joining. If the credit union is well managed, it could prove to be an excellent way to borrow or save money.

At a credit union a member may be able to borrow up to $2500 on a signature alone, and even more can be borrowed in some cases with the proper security pledged. Annual interest rates vary; in the late 1970s they were often as low as ¾ of 1 percent per month (or 9 percent a year). No extra fees are charged, and credit life insurance usually is included in the stated interest rate. Another advantage of borrowing from a credit union is that you are dealing with co-workers or friends who have a special interest in your financial welfare. On the other hand, you may not want to reveal your borrowing needs to the committee of co-workers who must approve the loan request.

Savings Banks and Savings and Loan Associations

Savings banks and savings and loan associations are good sources from which to borrow money for certain purposes. The laws governing these institutions vary from state to state. However, the consumer who wants to borrow money would be wise to check these institutions as a possible source, because they do grant several types of loans.

All savings banks and savings and loan associations grant mortgage loans. Many grant home-improvement loans, personal loans, and loans for education. Most also grant passbook loans to their depositors.

A person who takes out a passbook loan is, in a way, borrowing his or her own money. This type of loan cannot exceed the amount that is deposited in the borrower's account. But when funds are needed for only a short period of time, it is sometimes to the depositor's advantage to take out a low-cost passbook loan rather than lose the interest on savings, because the interest that must be paid on the loan is less than the interest that the borrower would lose by taking the money out of his or her account. For example, this type of loan can sometimes be used profitably to make payments that will later be reimbursed by insurance or to buy goods that would otherwise be purchased on a short-term installment basis.

Sales Finance Companies

Although sales finance companies do not actually lend a consumer cash in the same way as a bank might, they represent an important source of loans. These lenders supply credit through auto dealers, mail-order outlets, and other retailers. Essentially what happens is that when you buy an item such as an automobile on credit, the signed contract is sold by the retailer to a sales finance company for cash. The sales finance company has a legal interest, known as a "lien," in the item to ensure that complete payment will be made. You, as the consumer, must make your payments to the sales finance company. In the late 1970s only commercial banks held more installment credit than sales finance companies. Most of the credit extended by sales finance companies has been for the purchase of automobiles.

Consumer Finance Companies

Consumer finance companies, also called small-loan companies and personal finance companies, operate under state laws. In 1916 the Russell Sage Foundation cooperated with the National Federation of Remedial Loan Associations to draft a model law regulating interest rates and practices in the making of small, personal loans. In most states, the laws governing consumer finance companies are modeled after this Uniform Small Loan Law. Originally, the maximum loan permitted by licensed small-loan companies was $300, but legislative action in the various states has increased this figure so that most states permit them to make loans of $1000 or more.

Consumers may find it easier to walk into a friendly small-loan company and walk out with a $500 or $600 loan than they would to get the same money from a commercial bank. Small-loan companies keep longer hours—some stay open evenings and Saturdays—and they may ask fewer questions. But in return for such service, the borrower will usually pay a higher rate of interest. Consumer finance companies make chiefly small loans, and they are usually more willing than other credit institutions to lend money to someone who may be a poor risk. Thus, their business expenses are greater than those of more conservative institutions. These companies generally charge interest rates as high as state laws allow for various loan amounts. The typical charge is from 18 to 42 percent per year, depending on the size and nature of the loan and the state in which the firm is located. Before agreeing to pay these rates, consumers should check with other lenders.

Insurance Companies

Most Americans own life insurance policies. Many policies combine life insurance with savings. After a few years insurance policies with a savings feature have a cash surrender value, which may be used as a basis for borrowing money. An insurance company will lend a policyholder any amount up to the cash value of a policy. This value is always shown in tables that are included in the policy. Today, borrowing on life insurace is a bargain, since most credit is comparatively expensive. The interest rate for loans specified in most policies currently being issued is 5 to 6 percent. The interest is charged on the unpaid balance, so this is a true annual interest rate. There is no specified time for repayment. This absence of a time limit may be an advantage for persons who cannot make regular payments, but it can also be a disadvantage. If the borrower does not attempt to hold to some schedule for repayment, the cost of the loan will be high, for the borrower must pay interest charges as long as he or she has the money. It is well to remember, too, that an insurance policy is decreased by the amount of the loan. If, for example, a man who borrowed $1000 on a $10,000 life insurance policy died before he had repaid the loan, the insurance company would pay only $9000 to his beneficiary. Of course, the net value of his estate would be the same as if he had any other loan of $1000.

A loan from an insurance company is obtained easily. The insurance company provides loan forms. After they have been completed and returned, the loan will be made.

Other Sources

Pawnshops are not a usual source for loans, and their role as lenders is relatively small. Yet people do borrow from pawnbrokers because they find borrowing a small amount of money is quick and simple. The interest charge, however, is extremely high. You must pledge something valuable, such as jewelry or a musical instrument, to get a loan from a pawnshop. The pawnshop keeps the pledged article, and if you pay back the sum borrowed plus interest within the agreed period of time, you get the article back. If you do not pay back the loan at the agreed time, the pawnbroker will sell the pledged item.

Reputable loan companies operate under state license. Lenders who operate without a license are called "loan sharks," and the name is appropriate because they can and often do "devour" their victims. Since the passage of the Consumer Credit Protection Act in 1968, loansharking is a federal offense, but such lenders will no doubt continue to operate as long as they can find persons who will borrow money from them. They do well in places with inadequate small-loan laws, but they can also be found in almost any city, preying on the unwary, the timid, and the ignorant.

Why does anyone ever try to do business with an unlicensed lender? Only through ignorance or desperation. Many borrowers have overextended their credit or want to keep their affairs secret from family and friends. They take what to them seems an easy way out. The lender may make what seems like a good offer, but the heavy credit charges pile up on the borrower a little at a time. Soon the borrower is in serious financial trouble. The person who has borrowed from a loan shark is often afraid to report to the proper authorities for fear of the strong-arm tactics that the money lender threatens.

PLANS FOR BORROWING MONEY

Since the Truth in Lending Act, consumers can find out how much they pay for credit and how the credit charge is figured. However, finding out who offers credit and what kinds of credit plans best fit each person's needs is still the job of the consumer. The two basic types of credit plans are open account and service charge. *Open-account credit* does not usually require paying interest. *Service-*

Your dentist generally grants you open-account credit, in which monthly statements are mailed and you have about a month to pay without interest charges. (*New York University School of Dentistry*)

charge accounts, as the name implies, do require paying interest. However, there are many different kinds of service-charge accounts, and some of these plans include some features of open-account credit.

Open-Account Credit

The oldest type of credit for consumers is the open account, sometimes called *regular account*. The customer can buy in person, by telephone, or by mail, and the store transfers the goods—usually with no down payment or interest charge. A statement is mailed to the customer, usually monthly, and the customer typically has 25 or 30 days in which to pay the bill without interest charges. Open-account credit is granted not only by retail stores but also by doctors, dentists, television repair firms, plumbers, other professional people, and other types of service firms.

Service-Charge Accounts

Service-charge types of accounts have become popular over the years, and there is a variety of plans used. Names of accounts vary from store to store, and it is difficult to say which name fits which plan. But the important thing to remember is that the following kinds of accounts involve an additional cost to the consumer.

Revolving Credit Accounts. Under a revolving credit plan, the maximum amount that may be owed to the store at any one time is determined at the time the account is opened. For example, if your credit level is $500, you may charge goods up to the amount of $500 and pay for purchases over a period of time. The part that must be paid monthly depends on the terms set up by the store. You pay either a set amount or a percentage of the amount owed. For example, a store could specify that for a credit limit of $500 the monthly payments shall be $20. Or the minimum monthly payment could be set at 10 percent of the amount owed each month. The unpaid portion of the bill is subject to an interest charge, of course, and the amount is typically 1½ percent a month, or an 18 percent annual rate. New purchases may be charged to the account at any time as long as the total amount owed does not exceed the established maximum of $500.

Optional Revolving Credit. Many stores combine the features of open-account credit with revolving credit. That is, you can treat the account as open credit. The store bills you monthly, and you can decide to pay the entire bill within the agreed number of days after billing, usually 25 days. In that event, you pay no service charge. If, however, you do not wish to pay the entire bill that month, the account is treated as a revolving credit account, and you must make at least the agreed upon monthly payment and be subject to a percentage service charge.

Easy Payment Plans.   Some stores set up installment plans that do not have the optional open-account feature. The customer buys a product and agrees to pay a predetermined amount each week or each month until the item is paid for. Interest rates vary, of course, and so do the time periods that are involved in such agreements.

Consumers should consider carefully the amount of the carrying charge they are paying for charge purchases. The Truth in Lending Act makes comparison shopping for credit easy, and armed with the dollar cost of credit from various sources, the consumer can select the source of credit wisely. In some instances, money can be saved by getting a personal loan from a credit union or a bank and then paying cash for the goods. A large first payment may reduce the period of time during which the payments will be made, and this can reduce the charges. An ad reading "No Down Payment—Three Years to Pay" may have appeal, but remember that interest charges add up because payments are spread out over time. Paying quickly reduces credit costs.

Installment Credit.   When a person obtains credit from the seller of an expensive or big-ticket item, such as an appliance or a car, it is called *installment-sales credit*. If the buyer borrowed the money from a lender and then used the cash to pay for the purchase, this buyer would be getting an *installment cash loan*. In either case, the buyer may end up making the installment payments to someone other than the seller because retailers often "sell" their interest in installment-sales contracts to a sales finance company or have an open agreement with such a company.

Purchases on credit for products such as cars, refrigerators, television sets, and the like are handled differently from purchases on credit for small appliances, clothing, and relatively inexpensive goods. The bigger item serves as a guarantee for repayment. When you buy a refrigerator, for example, you are asked to sign a contract in which that refrigerator is pledged as security. If you fail to make the payments, the refrigerator could be recovered or repossessed by the creditor and then sold. The money from the sale is used to pay off your debt. How the creditor is protected is, of course, quite important to those who buy on an installment plan.

Usually, the seller is protected by asking the buyer to sign one of several types of contracts. The most used contracts are the chattel mortgage and the conditional sales contract. The provisions of each vary from state to state and from creditor to creditor. The important thing for buyers is to read the fine print carefully and to question the seller or the finance company on all doubtful areas until they are satisfied that they understand.

Chattel Mortgage.   When a chattel mortgage contract is used, the seller gives title to the goods to the buyer and then takes the mortgage as security. The seller must make the mortgage a matter of public record. The seller has a proportionate interest in the mortgaged property, which is always movable goods such as furniture and automobiles. If the buyer fails to live up to the obligations under the contract, the seller can ask in court to have the property sold at a sheriff's sale for the seller's benefit.

Conditional Sales Contract.   When a conditional sales contract is used, the title to the merchandise stays with the seller until full payment is received. When payments are not made according to the agreement, the merchandise can be repossessed. Depending on state law, the payments that had been made may be regarded as rent for use of the product, or part of the money may be refunded. Usually, the procedure in states that have laws patterned after the Uniform Conditional Sales Act is to sell the goods at an auction. After the creditor takes the unpaid balance and the expenses of repossessing and selling the property, any money remaining is given to the debtor. If the money received from the sale at the auction is not enough, the creditor may take legal action against the buyer for the remaining amount owed. In that event, the buyer may find himself paying money for a product he or she no longer has.

In some cases the auction sale is rigged so that only the creditor's friends or relatives are present to bid on the property. Thus, a $3000 car on which the debtor still owes $2600 may be sold at such an auction for $800 and the debtor would still be required to pay the difference of $1800. The creditor ends up with the car and the money. The debtor ends up with nothing.

Installment purchase contracts can be full of booby traps, and the buyer should read the contract with care before signing it. Some of the things to watch for are the following:

- *Acceleration Clause.* When the contract has an *acceleration clause,* all payments are due if one payment is missed. Then if the buyer is unable to pay the total unpaid balance, the goods may be taken and resold.
- *Add-on Clause.* An add-on clause enables the seller to keep title to a whole list of items you are buying on credit until all payments have been completed (for example, an eight-piece set of furniture). Even though you have already paid for some of the items, if you fail to make a single payment on time, the seller can repossess the entire set. An add-on clause can also permit the seller to add more purchases to your original installment contract. Then if you fail just once to make a payment on time, the seller can repossess the whole collection of items bought.
- *Balloon Clause.* Some contracts provide for a blown-up final payment. For example, a contract may call for 11 monthly payments of $60 and a final payment of $300. If you, as the buyer, do not realize that you agreed to that big final payment, you can easily end up in trouble with the creditor. Balloon payments are sometimes used to get the consumer to enter into a contract by offering invitingly small installment payments. Then at the end of the contract the consumer is faced with a balloon payment too large to pay. In some states today, balloon payments can be used only where the consumer has seasonal income. The federal Truth in Lending Act requires that if any payment is more than twice the amount of other scheduled payments, that payment must be identified as a balloon payment.
- *Wage Assignment Clause.* A wage assignment clause allows the store or finance company to force the borrower's employer to deduct payments from the borrower's paycheck. This is the legal process known as *garnisheeing wages,* and the Consumer Credit Protection Act restricts the weekly garnishment to whichever of these is the least amount: (1) 25 percent of a wage earner's take-home pay, or (2) take-home pay minus 30 times the federal minimum hourly wage. Some states have garnishment legislation that provides even more protection for borrowers than that provided by the federal Consumer Credit Protection Act. The Consumer Credit Protection Act says that where state restrictions are stronger, it will be state law which regulates.

CREDIT CARDS

How far are we from the day when a plastic card will replace cash? We have not yet reached the point where cash is not used, but the growth in the use of credit cards during the past two decades has been tremendous. By the mid-1970s nearly 12,000 banks were participating in credit card plans and more than 65 million bank cards were in circulation. Other kinds of credit cards are available too. A few years ago it was estimated that there were 250 million credit cards of one kind or another in circulation.

Colleges and universities in many places throughout the country now permit students to pay their tuition with credit cards. In some places, property taxes and car registration fees can be paid with a credit card. *Changing Times* magazine reported in December 1976 that just two bank credit cards, Master Charge and BankAmericard, represent about 20 percent of all outstanding credit.

Types of Credit Cards

Credit cards are generally divided into three categories: single-purpose cards, travel and entertainment cards, and bank credit cards. As the companies that offer these cards expand their services, and as new companies enter the field, these categories will become less accurate. For example, many so-called single-purpose cards can now be used to pay for a variety of goods and services, and one might be able to charge books offered by a book club on a travel and entertainment card. These categories are still helpful, however, since they tell you something about the company that offers the card and give some idea of its usefulness.

Single-Purpose Cards. The major oil companies have issued credit cards for quite some time, and department stores have identified their credit customers by issuing cards. No charge is made for the credit card. The customer simply makes application, and if he or she is credit-worthy, a card is issued. The purpose of the card, of course, is to encourage the cardholder to make most or all purchases from the firm issuing the card. Oil company cards have proved to be quite convenient, especially when you are traveling. Throughout the country, at any service station franchised by the company whose credit card you hold, oil, gas, tires, accessories, and repairs can be charged by simply using the card.

In some cases cooperative arrangements have been made between major oil companies and motel chains, airlines, and car rental companies so that motel charges (including meals), airline tickets, and car rental charges can be charged to oil company cards. Still another use for oil company credit cards has developed recently, and that is the

Oil company credit cards not only are a convenience but also make it easier to budget monthly auto expenditures. (*Susan Berkowitz*)

purchase of consumer goods sold by direct mail. The holder of an oil credit card might receive an advertising brochure through the mail that offers such merchandise as tools, cameras, radios, and so on. To buy the goods offered, the consumer returns a card indicating that he or she accepts the offer and agrees to have the selling price added to the account.

Restaurants, hotels, telephone companies, and airlines are among other firms that issue credit cards for their customers. From the consumers' point of view, the card furnishes all the advantages of open-account credit. Many of the firms issuing these cards also provide for revolving credit, which can be used if the customer does not want to pay the bill in full within a certain period of time after the billing date. The credit charge is typically 1½ percent a month, or 18 percent a year.

Travel and Entertainment Cards. Diners Club issued the first travel and entertainment card shortly after the Second World War. Other companies, such as American Express and Carte Blanche, quickly followed their lead. These cards in effect opened charge accounts for the cardholders at specific businesses throughout the country, particularly hotels and restaurants. The cards, which were designed with travelers and business people in mind, proved to be convenient items. People could more easily keep records of their expenditures on business trips, and they did not, of course, have to carry a lot of cash.

The person applying for a travel and entertainment card is given a quite thorough credit investigation. The annual fee that the cardholder must pay for the privilege of having this credit available throughout the country, and indeed the world, is about $20. An additional credit card for use by others, such as a wife or husband, costs an additional fee.

A business person who has a travel and entertainment card can take a client to lunch or dinner, pay the tab and the tip with a credit card, and have a convenient receipt of the expenditure. If a business person is away from home, he or she can pay for a hotel room and the airline ticket with the same card. The cards are used mainly for travel, but increasingly they are being accepted in all types of retail stores.

The participating restaurants, hotels, and other firms pay a discount fee as high as 7 percent to the credit card companies. That is, if the bill comes to $40, the restaurant collects $37.20 from the card issuer.

Bank Credit Cards.   Because of the success of travel and entertainment credit cards, banks decided to get into the business. The real credit card revolution has been due to the rapid expansion of these bank credit card plans. While in 1975 travel and entertainment cards numbered about 6 million, the number of bank cards issued at that time was 65 million. The bank cards began as small, local plans but have grown into large regional systems nationally interlinked by two major networks, BankAmericard (now known as "Visa") and Master Charge.

Under the bank card system, merchants do not have to extend credit in order to permit customers to charge purchases. The bank extends the credit, so the merchant does not have to take the risk of losses due to bad debts. Nor does the merchant have to go through the mechanics of sending out and collecting bills. The bank does this for the merchant.

In most cases, bank credit cards enable the customer to treat the charges as open-account credit or as revolving credit. If the bill is paid in full within a specified period of time after the billing date, no service charge is made. If the customer prefers to pay a smaller amount each month, an amount not less than the minimum payment specified on the monthly bill received can be paid. The interest charge is usually 1½ percent a month, or 18 percent a year. Thus, banks earn their money from both the merchants and the cardholders.

Most consumers who have a bank credit card can use it free. That has been one of the advantages of bank credit cards over travel and entertainment credit cards. But that may be changing. In the late 1970s some banks started charging credit card users a fee. For example, New York's Citibank, a major issuer of Master Charge cards, begain in 1976 charging its cardholders a fee of 50 cents for any month in which they pay their accounts on time and thus avoid any interest charge. Other banks have started charging the cardholder an annual fee. Some lawmakers are opposed to fees for bank cards, other than finance charges and late-payment penalties, and at least one member of Congress has considered introducing legislation to prohibit monthly or annual fees.

When a bank credit card is issued, the bank usually assigns to the cardholder a maximum amount of credit, based on the person's credit reputation, and the card is usually good for one year. The credit available might range from $100 to $1000 or even more. Also, most banks set a ceiling on the amount that can be charged without having the store check with the bank. Some banks also permit cardholders to borrow cash up to their maximum amount of credit. The amount borrowed is added to the customer's bill, and interest is charged beginning at the time the money is borrowed.

Bank cards are designed primarily for retail purchases at stores in a person's own community. In many instances, retail stores have discontinued their own credit cards and instead rely on the bank credit cards. As bank cards have become more popular and have become part of major card networks, they have gradually gone into the travel and entertainment business as well. In fact, many hotels and restaurants will accept bank credit cards, so the holders of these cards have many, if not most, of the advantages of holders of travel and entertainment cards. One would think that the increased use of bank cards would reduce the use of travel and entertainment cards, but thus far this has not happened.

GOOD NEWS AND SOME POSSIBLE BAD NEWS

One all-purpose credit card, such as a bank card or a travel and entertainment card, has the advantage of enabling consumers to carry just one card. Some of the other advantages of credit cards are listed here:

- Budgeting is made simpler because the consumer receives one monthly bill on which monthly purchases are itemized.
- The consumer makes out one check for many of the purchases made during the month. In some cases this might reduce a checking account service charge.
- Charge privileges are available at many stores without the necessity of filling out a multitude of credit applications.
- Credit cards are convenient and relatively safe. Travelers do not have to carry large sums of cash with them, and they need not worry about the embarrassment of running out of cash at inopportune times.
- Credit card receipts make good expense account and tax records.
- Even when a consumer's bank account may be low, he or she can take advantage of sales by using a credit card. In the case of an emergency expense, a credit card can be used and the payment does not have to be made until the bill is received in about a month. In effect, the consumer has received a short-term, interest-free loan if the bill is paid within the specified period of time.
- The cash-advance feature of some bank cards gives consumers access to money in emergencies without the red tape of securing a regular bank loan.

Some people have been critical of the increased use of credit cards, citing the fact that merchants increase the cost of their products to compensate for the discount fees they must pay to the credit card issuers. If prices are increased, then people who pay cash will also be paying higher prices for merchandise. But credit card issuers point out that the discount fee is no more, and often less, than the normal costs of extending credit. The merchant who relies on credit cards for charge sales does not have the bookkeeping expenses that would be necessary if he or she handled the credit. Then, too, losses due to bad debts are suffered by the credit card issuer rather than the merchant. At this time, it is difficult to assess the influence on prices that credit cards have, but the relationship certainly bears watching.

Another major criticism of credit cards is that credit purchases can be made so easily that it is possible to go too far into debt before realizing it. This criticism is no doubt well founded, and consumers who have credit cards should learn to use them wisely. Sales slips should be kept, and purchases should be recorded and tallied so that the cardholder knows exactly how much has been spent for various items. Some cardholders limit the use of their cards to certain types of expenditures so that they will not buy more than their incomes can bear at the time. Actually, for consumers who overbuy and go too far into debt, any kind of credit can be harmful. But, credit cards may be especially dangerous because they make credit purchases especially easy.

Unauthorized Use of Credit Cards

Consumers should take especially good card of their credit cards. When a credit card is lost or stolen, the chance exists that it will be used—and used to run up big bills! In one case a person was arrested with thousands of dollars in his possession. He had bought airline tickets with other people's credit cards, and then turned in the tickets for refunds. Unfortunately, credit card theft has become an organized crime. Thieves steal credit cards and then use them or sell them on the black market.

Fortunately, a 1970 amendment to the Consumer Credit Protection Act limits your maximum liability in case of unauthorized use of any credit card to $50 for each card. You are liable for no more than $50, even if you fail to discover the loss for a considerable period of time and even if you fail to notify the card issuer promptly. Actually, the card issuer can collect up to $50 for unauthorized use only if the issuer has satisfied certain requirements stated in the law. The five requirements that must be met by the issuer of the credit card are listed below.

1. The card must have been accepted by the cardholder. The law forbids the mailing of credit cards to persons who have not asked for them.
2. Adequate notice of the potential liability must be furnished to the cardholder.
3. The issuer of the card must provide an addressed notice which the cardholder may return in case the card is lost or stolen.
4. The unauthorized use must occur before the cardholder has notified the card issuer of the loss or theft.
5. All cards must provide a means of identification, such as the cardholder's signature or photograph.

CREDIT RATINGS AND GOVERNMENT HELP

A good credit reputation is a valuable asset for a consumer. When you apply for credit, you are asking someone to judge your ability and your desire to make payments on your debt. In order to make this judgment, the lender will probably ask you to give a great deal of information about yourself—information about such things as your income, your employer, your education, your home address, your previous address, your bank, and your other credit accounts. If you have used credit before, a local credit bureau no doubt has a file on you, and that file will be used by merchants and lenders. The credit bureau keeps information on your payment record and will watch personal matters that bear on your ability to pay debts. The most important piece of information about you, of course, is your past record of paying off debts. Lenders assume that people who have paid promptly in the past, particularly the recent past, will probably continue to do so.

A credit bureau exists to find out as much as possible about those who request credit and to circulate the information among clients. Some credit bureaus are profit-making business firms; some are mutual organizations supported by a group of merchants. Once you have established a credit record, it will stay in effect for many years. If you move from one city to another, the credit record will follow you as soon as you make a credit application in the new city to which you move. Credit records are maintained mostly for retail merchants, banks, and mortgage lenders, but the information may also be used by prospective employers.

Fair Credit Reporting Act

The thought of an organization knowing so much about you can be a bit frightening. To make certain that the information is used properly, Congress passed the Fair Credit Reporting Act, which became effective in 1971. The Fair Credit Reporting Act specifies the purposes for which reports can be used. It also limits the issuance of the reports to anyone who intends to use them for evaluating individuals for credit, insurance, or employment or for a legitimate need in connection with a business transaction. Reports can also be issued to an agency of the government if that agency is required by law to consider the consumer's financial status before granting a license or other benefit. Otherwise a report can be issued only in response to a court order or in accordance with the written instructions of the consumer. It is important that consumers be aware of this provision.

The Fair Credit Reporting Act includes other provisions. For example, anyone who orders an investigative consumer report (one for insurance company or employment purposes) must notify the consumer a report is being developed within three days after ordering the report. A basic credit report contains only identifying and factual information, as opposed to an investigative consumer report done for insurance or employment purposes. An investigative report contains subjective information with opinions obtained through interviews with various persons who know the person being investigated. The act requires that the reporting agency have reasonable procedures to ensure maximum possible accuracy of the information it reports. "Reasonable procedures" can be interpreted to mean that employees must be properly trained before handling information.

An additional provision of the act that is important to consumers is that the credit bureau, upon proper identification, must disclose the following to the consumer:

- The nature and substance of all information in its files concerning the consumer
- The sources of information on file
- The name of anyone who has been given the report within the past six months

Disclosure must be made to the consumer in person at the office of the credit bureau or by telephone if the consumer has previously submitted a written request. If the consumer challenges any of the information on file, the act requires the credit bureau to reinvestigate the consumer's record. Then, if it is still challenged by the consumer, the bureau must accept a statement of any length from the consumer and make the statement a permanent part of that person's file. Further, if the consumer requests, the credit bureau must send a copy of the consumer's statement to everyone who has received this person's credit report within the past six months. This important provision enables the consumer to avoid an unfavorable credit record if he or she has refused or delayed payment for just cause. It gives the consumer the opportunity to tell his or her side of the story.

Ending Discrimination

During the 1970s discrimination against women in the granting of credit received a great deal of attention. Based on testimony which it heard in 1972, the National Commission on Consumer Finance found that women have more difficulty than men in obtaining credit. The Commission identified these five problem areas:

1. Single women had more trouble than single men in obtaining credit.
2. When a woman married, she was usually required by creditors to

reapply for credit, usually in her husband's name. Men were not asked to do this when they married.

3. Creditors were often unwilling to give credit to a married woman in her own name.
4. The wife's income was often not counted when a married couple applied for credit.
5. Women who were divorced or widowed had trouble re-establishing credit. Women who were separated had an especially difficult time, since the accounts were often still in the husband's name.

By the mid-1970s more than half of the states passed legislation to end discrimination in the extension of credit. The federal government also acted. In 1975 Congress passed the Equal Credit Opportunity Act, and in the language of that act, it is now "unlawful for any creditor to discriminate against any applicant on the basis of sex or marital status with respect to any aspect of a credit transaction."

The Equal Credit Opportunity Act does not define discrimination, but it did authorize the Federal Reserve Board to set forth proper regulations. The law aims at such things as making sure that in the

The Equal Credit Opportunity Act of 1975 aims at making sure that a woman will be judged on the same basis as a man when applying for credit. (*First National Bank of Arizona*)

area of credit a woman is judged on the same basis as a man, and that husband and wife joint credit accounts will provide each of them with an independent credit history.

The regulations concerning equal credit opportunity include some specific things that creditors cannot do. For example, they cannot assign a value to sex or marital status in evaluating applications. They cannot stop giving credit, ask for another application, or change the terms of credit solely on a change of name or marital status. Creditors are also prohibited from discounting all or part of the income of the applicant or the applicant's spouse.

The regulations are also specific as to required practices. Every application must use only "married," "unmarried," or "separated" when referring to marital status. They may not use the words divorced or widowed. In addition, every application must state that if titles are requested (Mr., Mrs., Ms., or Miss), the designation is optional. In the late 1970s Congress was considering expanding the Equal Credit Opportunity Act to cover both race and age discrimination.

WHAT TO DO IF TROUBLE STRIKES

Building and maintaining a record for paying promptly is extremely important for establishing a good credit rating. Credit managers and loan officers constantly stress the importance of good communication between the borrower and the creditor—especially when the borrower has hit upon hard times and may have difficulty for a while making full payments. Consumers who have borrowed too much or who have had their incomes cut because of sickness, unemployment, or other problems should speak with their creditors at once. Often if you have a plan for taking care of the debt, even though it means that you will make smaller payments or will not make payments at scheduled times, the creditors will want to know about it. Usually they will do all they can to help. Silence on the part of a debtor when bills are past due makes creditors uneasy. They understand that any person can experience financial problems, and if they know you are sincere about paying off the obligation, they will usually cooperate fully.

When debt obligations are not met, say, on an installment plan for a piece of furniture, the creditor may take legal action and repossess the furniture. Most merchants dislike doing this, however, and they may find that the market for used furniture is not particularly good. They much prefer to work out a plan whereby the debtor can pay for the goods—even though the payments are late. The best advice for consumers, of course, is not to get so deeply in debt. If this advice is followed, a financial crisis will not occur.

Credit bureaus do make mistakes, so whenever you have difficulty getting credit, you should ask the lender which credit bureau supplied information so that the situation can be straightened out before further damage is done to your credit reputation.

Checking Your Reading

1. Give the names of six institutions that lend money to consumers.
2. Why are rates generally lower on secured loans?
3. Explain why credit union rates are usually among the lowest rates for borrowing money.
4. How do credit unions keep their operating costs low?
5. Consumer finance companies typically charge interest rates considerably higher than credit unions or commercial banks. How do consumer finance companies attract customers?
6. Explain why borrowing money on your life insurance policy is advantageous.
7. What is open-account credit?
8. Under a revolving credit plan, when is the maximum amount that may be charged at any time determined?
9. When a conditional sales contract is used, when does title to the merchandise pass on to the buyer?
10. Describe what is meant by a "balloon clause" in a conditional sales contract.
11. How do the issuers of travel and entertainment credit cards earn money?
12. List several advantages of credit cards.
13. Give two criticisms of credit cards.
14. What are the five requirements that must be met by the issuer of a credit card before the issuer can collect up to $50 for unauthorized use of the card?
15. What is the aim of the Equal Credit Opportunity Act of 1975?

Consumer Problems and Projects

1. Lawrence Friesen needs to borrow $600. Dinero Finance Company will lend him $600 for 12 months with payments of $55 a

month. What is the true annual interest rate being charged by the finance company?

2. What other lending agencies would Mr. Friesen be wise to consider before he borrows the money from Dinero Finance Company?

3. Compile information that will help you answer the following questions about credit unions. When did credit unions begin operating and for what reason? Where and when did credit unions begin in our country? How rapidly have credit unions grown during the past few decades? Why are operating expenses of credit unions relatively low? What are some advantages of credit unions from the consumer's point of view? Note: Obtain the data by interviewing credit union officers in your community and by using library resources.

4. Sharon Mancelli has missed five weeks of work because of illness. She is now behind in the payment of certain bills. She owes a department store $85, an oil company $48, and her physician $120. Her monthly rent payment of $190 will be due in one week. What action should Sharon take?

5. Make a comparison chart of the various agencies that lend money to consumers. Compare the amount each agency is generally willing to lend, the true interest rate, and the ease of securing a loan.

6. Using the *Readers' Guide to Periodical Literature*, make a list of articles about the Fair Credit Reporting Act and the Equal Credit Opportunity Act that have appeared recently in magazines available in your library. Locate the articles, and construct an annotated list of selected readings on the topics.

25

Government Services

Up to this point we have been looking mostly at consumers' choices in the marketplace. There are, however, many things we consume which we do not buy directly as individuals. Instead, they are things which we decide on together as citizens and ask government to provide.

These government services can have an important effect on the quality of our lives. They affect our safety, our health, our education, and our financial security. We can see the importance of good government services right in our own communities. Good fire and police protection, adequate recreation facilities, and well-run schools and hospitals all play an important part in making a community a pleasant place to live.

Government services can be an important resource which can help us in achieving our goals. The local library can, for example, help us with our schoolwork, help us to develop new hobbies and interests, and provide exciting novels and adventure stories for recreational reading. One of the reasons public services are such an important resource is that they are available to everyone, usually without any direct cost. When fees are charged, they usually are small and cover only part of the expense of providing the service.

432

Government services, of course, have to be paid for somehow. The bill is a sizable one. Federal, state, and local government spending in a year totals over $2000 per person. We pay this bill with our taxes—sales taxes, income taxes, real estate taxes, and so on.

The taxes we pay reduce our purchasing power as individuals. After we have paid our taxes, we have less to spend and our range of individual choices is reduced. But taken all together our taxes provide a sizable sum and can provide a wide variety of public services.

WHAT FUNCTIONS DOES GOVERNMENT SERVE?

Our taxes and expenditures for government are high because of the wide variety of functions that we have assigned to government. These functions can be classified into four general categories: (1) service functions, (2) income transfer functions, (3) market regulation functions, and (4) economic stabilization functions. Let us take a look at these four categories.

Service Functions

Service functions of the government include the conservation of natural resources, national defense, and the administration of justice. *Service functions* are services that business enterprises cannot or will not supply effectively. Almost three-fourths of all government spending goes to pay for the services provided by government. Part of this spending goes for equipment and supplies (for example, missiles, research facilities, and gasoline), and part goes to employees (including members of the armed forces and Congress). These expenditures are classified as *exhaustive expenditures* by economists because they use up goods and services supplied to government by the private economy. Once these resources have been used up by the government, they are no longer available for use in other ways.

Income Transfer Functions

Income transfer functions shift money and resources from some groups in our economy to others. They redistribute income among individuals, business enterprises, and state and local governments. Transfer payments are an important part of government expenditures and account for about 25 percent of total spending.

Income transfers are paid on the basis of need rather than as a

The administration of justice is one of the service functions of the government that we, as taxpayers, have collectively decided to buy. (*Sylvia Johnson, Woodfin Camp & Associates*)

payment for services. An example of income transfers to individuals is the welfare payments made to low-income families that include young children. A federal grant-in-aid to a community to assist it in financing a new sewage system is an example of a transfer to a local government. Another kind of income transfer is grants to business enterprises. These grants, or *subsidies*, are given to encourage particular activities. State and local governments, for example, sometimes promise companies who locate plants in their area special low tax rates. These lower tax rates are a type of subsidy.

Government expenditures for income transfers differ from government expenditures for services in that they are not exhaustive expenditures. Instead, income transfers are classified as *nonexhaustive expenditures.* This is because they do not use up any goods or any labor services. Income transfers instead shift purchasing power from the federal government to individuals, state and local governments, and business.

Market Regulation Functions

One of the important functions of government is to ensure that dealings in the marketplace are fair and honest. In the early years of our nation, the government had little responsibility for regulating dealings in the marketplace. It was not considered either necessary or appropriate for government to protect consumers. *Laissez faire*, a French expression which means "let people do as they choose," was the philosophy of the day. The chief involvement of the government in the marketplace was its role in enforcing contracts through the courts.

In the 1800s a series of crises and problems convinced most people that more direct regulation of the marketplace was needed. In order to protect competition in the marketplace and limit the power of large corporations and trusts, the government was given *antitrust powers*. (These powers will be discussed in Chapter 28.) The government also was given increasing power to set *standards*, or rules, controlling products, advertising, and the production process itself. These rules include regulations on auto safety, advertising claims, and smoke emissions from factories. The government also has been given increasing power over the kinds of *information* which must be provided to consumers. It has, for example, a good deal of power over product labeling and safety warnings on dangerous products.

Economic Stabilization Functions

Economic stabilization functions involve government regulation of the level of economic activity. The chief goals of these efforts are to maintain full employment and to control the rate of inflation. In working toward these goals, the federal government uses its power to regulate governmental spending, taxes, and interest rates.

Many government programs serve more than one function. For example, when government builds and operates public housing projects, it is providing a service—housing—and redistributing income, because of the reduced rents charged the tenants. Government spending can also serve both the service function and the economic stabilization function. In times of unemployment, the government may develop new park and recreation facilities, which provide a useful service. By hiring unemployed workers for the project, the government reduces unemployment. Because the workers hired have more money to spend, they contribute to increasing the level of business activity, and in this way the project serves an economic stabilization function. In this chapter we will focus on government activities which are designed to serve service and income transfer functions. Government's market regulation functions will be examined in more detail in Chapter 30. Government economic stabilization functions fall chiefly in the field of economics and are not discussed in this book.

WHY DOES GOVERNMENT PROVIDE SERVICES?

We rely on business to supply a major part of our consumer wants. Business people, attracted by the chance to make profits, set about supplying these wants. There are, however, certain situations in which the marketplace cannot, or does not, supply the kinds of things the public wants. If we relied on private business to supply these wants, we would find that the amounts provided would be too large or too small or priced too high.

Collective Goods

There are certain kinds of goods and services that cannot be divided up and sold to individual customers. These have been labeled "collective goods." Because of the nature of collective goods, there is no way to control who uses them or make users pay for them. Suppose, for example, that a private company built a flood-control dam and asked the people in the valley below it to pay for the protection they received. Everyone in the valley would be protected whether they paid or not. There would be no way to limit protection only to people who paid.

Collective goods are given this label because they are consumed by groups of people rather than single individuals and because all the members of the group benefit from them whether they pay or not. The only way this kind of goods and services can effectively be supplied is by government. As we saw in the example of the flood-control dam, there is no way a private company can make a profit supplying such services. A private company cannot force people to pay for flood-control service if they do not want to. And since those who pay and those who do not are all protected, there is no reason for anyone to pay.

Because private companies cannot make a profit from providing flood control, we can see that flood-control dams would never be built if government did not step in and build them. When government undertakes this kind of project, it can finance it by using its power to tax the people who receive the service.

Another example of a collective good is national defense. It is not the kind of service that can be provided by a private business and divided up and sold to individual customers. For this reason, it also is best provided by government.

Spillover Benefits

Government activity is also desirable in cases where a service provides benefits to others besides those who use it directly. An example of this kind of service is education. While education is an important benefit to the student who receives it, education also provides benefits to the entire community. It provides better-educated and more productive workers and more informed citizens and voters.

Suppose the decision about how much to spend on education were left just to individual students and their families. Their decisions would be guided by how much education would be worth to them. These decisions might ignore the value of education to the community. If the decision were left up to individuals, we might find them

If the decision about how much to spend on education were left up to individuals, society might lose spillover benefits not immediately apparent or not of concern to individual students and their families. (*George Aolla, Black Star*)

spending less for education than would be desirable from the standpoint of the community as a whole. Because of the value of education to society, it is in the interest of us all to encourage education and provide tax money to finance it. The extra benefits gained by society or by people other than those who directly use a good or service have been labeled *spillover benefits*.

Spillover Costs

Government activity may be necessary in cases where the use of a product creates problems that affect other members of society. In case of spillover benefits, which we discussed in the section above, society benefited from the consumption of a good or service. When a product or service creates *spillover costs*, society is instead harmed.

An example is the situation which occurs in many rural areas. Small towns and individual households along the banks of a river dispose of sewage in the easiest and cheapest way—by dumping it directly into the river without treatment. This creates a costly and dangerous pollution problem for people downstream. Here we have a situation in which one group's desire to cut sewage disposal expenses involves serious costs for another group.

We can see that government action is needed. It would be to the advantage of society as a whole if the dumping of raw sewage into rivers were stopped. In this case, society as a whole would gain if the government helped those living upstream to build sewage treatment facilities.

It also is often argued that there are spillover costs involved in the use of alcoholic beverages. Consumption of alcohol may harm the individual. It also can involve costs to society, such as the deaths, injuries, and property damage resulting from accidents caused by drunken drivers. The heavy taxes placed on liquor in most states grow out of a recognition of the social problems and costs that result from its use.

Inadequate Incomes

The marketplace provides income only to people who have goods or services (including their labor) to sell or money to invest. People who have nothing to sell and no investments receive no income. If these people are to survive, government must step in to help them. This help may come in the form of welfare payments, food stamps, or medical assistance. Each of these services involves redistributing income.

Tax money taken from people with higher incomes is transferred to people who need help.

Natural Monopolies

Government often is involved in providing or regulating utility services such as telephone, electricity, and water and in providing mass transit. Services such as these, which can be provided most cheaply by a single seller, are called *natural monopolies*. If the government did not control the number of companies producing these services, there would be wasteful duplication of equipment and competition for customers. The enterprise supplying a market can be operated by the government itself or by a private company. In this country, utilities most frequently are operated by private companies but are regulated by government to help ensure reasonable prices for customers.

Convenience

In some cases, government may provide services simply because it is more convenient to have it do the job. This is one of the reasons for public highways. Highways could be built by private companies and tolls charged; many roads were built in this way in earlier times. In general, however, it is easier and more convenient to have the government build and maintain roads and finance them out of tax money.

Other Types of Market Failures

All the situations we have discussed above are examples of "market failures." They are cases in which, if we relied solely on the market, the amount of services produced would not be ideal from society's point of view. As we have seen in cases of spillover costs, too much would be produced. In other cases, such as spillover benefits and collective goods, too little would be produced. In cases of natural monopolies, prices would be higher than necessary if several producers were allowed to provide the service.

There are other situations in which the competitive market does not work well. Market competition does not necessarily ensure that consumers will get all the information they need to make good decisions. For this reason, government services have been developed to ensure that consumers get certain kinds of information. An example is the agency activities which check to make certain that "truth-in-lending" information is provided.

HOW DOES THE GOVERNMENT PROVIDE SERVICES?

Government does not necessarily always provide needed services itself. This is only one of the ways such services can be provided. Another approach is to encourage the provision of a service by granting government *subsidies*. For example, the federal government may give a community funds to help finance its bus system. This subsidy allows the community to charge lower fares and helps to encourage use of the bus system. The government may use a reverse of this strategy to discourage certain activities. It does this by taxing them. An example is a proposed tax on automobiles based on the amount of air pollution they produce. Those who produced more pollution would be charged more. The owners whose cars were serious polluters would have the choice of getting their cars repaired or adjusted to reduce pollution, selling them, or just paying the tax. This type of tax, in effect, forces car owners to bear some of the spillover costs of the pollution their cars produce.

There is a third way that government can provide a service. This is by regulating the private producers who provide it. An example is the activities of public utility commissions. We have seen that utility services are a natural monopoly. They are most cheaply provided by a single producer. The government, instead of providing utility services itself, can grant this right to a private company. This company will be allowed to operate as a monopoly in its area. It will be the only seller of electricity, gas, or telephone services. The company granted this monopoly privilege is, however, subject to public controls. Public utility commissions are created to supervise the operations of utility companies, their services, and their rates.

Deciding on Government Versus Private Enterprise

There has been a continuing controversy in this country over the proper extent of government activity. Some people feel the government should take a larger role in providing goods and services, while others feel it already is doing things that would be better left to private enterprise.

The decision about whether a service is to be provided by government or private enterprise is determined, in part, by economic considerations. We have discussed the cases in which government activity is most appropriate. Only part of the decision about whether government or private enterprise will provide a service is economic, however. Part of the decision is a political one and is decided by citizens and legislators.

Arguments Against Government Programs

A number of arguments have been offered against having the government involved in providing public services. Some people argue that all government activities force people to do things they may not want to do. When services are provided by government, everyone is forced to support the service with their taxes, even though they may object to it. When the government moves into the field of social insurance, for instance, everyone is forced to join the program. This, it is argued, denies people the right to make individual decisons about providing for their own future.

Another argument is that individual citizens seldom have a real opportunity to express their opinions on a particular program. Many issues are involved in each election, and instead of voting on each issue, we vote for candidates supporting the program we consider most important. It is also difficult for voters to indicate how much of one service, relative to another, they would like. It is hard, for example, for voters to indicate that they would like more spending for education and less for highway construction.

Another criticism of government activity is that spending decisions are influenced too much by the actions of pressure groups. Some people argue that government decisions are influenced too much by powerful small groups, not public needs. They claim that projects are judged on their value to a small group with political power instead of their value to the public as a whole.

Arguments for Government Programs

Assigning government the responsibility for providing certain services does have certain advantages. The marketplace gives the most attention to those with the most money to spend. Their wants decide what kinds of goods and services will be produced, even though these may not meet the needs of everyone. The political process, however, differs from the marketplace. Each citizen has one vote and a more equal voice in deciding the kinds of good and services that will be provided.

In considering whether government or private industry should

Voting gives each citizen a more nearly equal voice in decisions about desirable goods and services than does the marketplace, since the marketplace gives the most attention to the people with the most money. (*UPI*)

supply a particular service, we need to remember that the market does not always operate effectively. Certain kinds of goods and services might never be provided if we had to depend solely on private corporations.

Government activity may be necessary in certain other special instances, such as cases involving large risks and high costs. The development of nuclear reactors for electric power production is one such case. The costs of development were so large and the possibilities of commercial applications so uncertain that no individual private firm could take the risk. Instead, the government took the risk, since the development of peaceful uses of atomic energy was considered to be important for national progress.

WHAT SHOULD WE EXPECT OF GOVERNMENT SERVICES?

When business produces products and services, it is controlled by the pressure of competition and the desire for profits. Because of their desire for profits, managers try to run their businesses as efficiently as they can. Costs are watched closely. In contrast, when government provides services, it is not under the same pressure to operate efficiently. There is no need to be concerned about profits. Government operations are financed by tax dollars, and the services produced are usually given away free. As a result, government agencies are not under the same pressure to operate efficiently that businesses are.

Another difference between business operations and government is that government is not under pressure to serve customers well in order to keep their business. In many cases, government is the only provider of the service. It has no competition. If the public does not like what is being provided, it has no other place to go. Sometimes, of course, there are other alternatives, such as private schools and private guard services. But these are usually so expensive that they are out of reach for most of us.

There is a third difference between business and government operations. The desire to make profits and to keep customers encourages business to develop new products and improve old ones. If a new product does not prove popular, it is dropped. Government is not under the same pressure. Nor is it under the same kind of pressure to drop old services, even if the demand for them has shrunk.

Because government is not controlled by the need for profits and the pressures of competition, we have to find other ways to make certain that it does its job well. We will discuss some of the methods which can be used to control the quality of government services in the next section. First, we will look at what we should expect of government as a provider of services.

As citizens and as consumers of public services, we have a right to expect certain things of the government:

- In deciding how to spend public funds, government should try to set priorities which reflect the public's views on the areas of most urgent need.
- Each program run by government should be managed carefully. With efficiency, more services can be produced per dollar spent.
- Programs should be developed so that they will meet the needs of the people to be served. For example, recreation facilities should be open at times which will permit everyone, including students and workers, to enjoy them.
- Everyone should have equal access to government services and receive fair and equal treatment. Requests for services should get careful and prompt attention.
- When people have problems in getting or using government services, they should have some place to turn for help.
- Consumer needs and interests should be taken into account in

Bread is a product whose price is affected by the government's agricultural program. Because so many prices are affected, it is important that consumer interests be taken into account in all such programs. (*Susan Berkowitz*)

the development of *all* government programs. Consumers are affected by a wide variety of government programs. They should have a voice in how these programs are organized and run. Farmers, for example, are not the only ones affected by the government's agricultural programs. Because these programs affect food prices, consumers should have a voice in them too.

This list suggests two key problems in providing government services:

- *The Problem of Consumer Representation.* There is a need to make certain that the interests of consumers are represented in planning and carrying out government programs.
- *The Problem of Consumer Redress.* There is a need to make certain that people who have problems in getting or using government services are able to get assistance.

Let's now look at some of the ways to deal with the problems of consumer representation in government and redress for users of government services.

CONTROLLING THE QUALITY OF GOVERNMENT SERVICES

Because government services are so important to the quality of our lives and affect us in so many ways, we want to have a say in how they are planned and run. As taxpayers and consumers of public services, we want the best quality possible. It is, however, difficult for consumers to know how to go about making their views known or how to complain when they are dissatisfied.

Representing Consumer Interests in Government

One of the ways that consumers can make their views known is a familiar one. It is by contacting members of Congress and of state legislatures when new laws are being considered. We all have the opportunity to express our views in letters.

However, it is not easy for consumers to express their views when Congress or state legislatures are considering new bills. It is often difficult to keep track of where bills are in the legislative process and to know when comments will do the most good. One of the important services which consumer organizations such as the Consumer Federation of America perform is to keep their members informed about new legislation.

When regulatory agencies like the Federal Trade Commission and Consumer Product Safety Commission are considering new regulations, they hold hearings and seek comments. This is supposed to give everyone a chance to present their views. However, this procedure does not guarantee that consumer interests will be represented. Consumers do not always know when key issues are being considered. When agencies want comments or are holding hearings on a proposed regulation, a notice is published in the *Federal Register*. The *Federal Register* is an official government publication in which new regulations are published and proposed regulations and hearings are announced. Since most consumers do not see the *Federal Register*, notices of opportunities to comment on new regulations affecting consumers and of hearings are now being published in the *Consumer Register*. The *Consumer Register* is part of the *Consumer News*, published by the Office of Consumer Affairs.

New "sunshine laws" also have made it easier for consumers to know what is going on within government bodies at all levels— national, state, and local. These laws open meetings to the public, make more documents available to the public, and provide for advance notice when important issues are being considered.

Knowing what is going on is only one of the problems consumers have in making their views known to government. There also are problems in making certain there is someone who can present consumer views to government. Officials have the responsibility to be fair and impartial. They count on the different interests involved to present their views. The officials then use the information presented to help them make the best decision. When business interests are affected, they usually are well represented. They cannot afford not to be. Consumers often are not represented. One reason is that while a regulation may be important to all consumers as a group, its value to an individual consumer may not be large. Keeping informed and voicing an opinion take time. Most consumers feel these costs outweigh the benefits they might get from making their individual opinions known.

Consumer Advocates.   Clearly, we need to find ways to make certain that consumers' viewpoints are heard in government hearings. We need consumer advocates who can keep informed on key issues and present consumer views. In recent years we have begun to see several different kinds of advocates appear to represent consumer interests. Some of these advocates represent consumer groups, such as Consumers Union. Others represent public-interest law firms, which specialize in representing the interests of the public or consumers in government hearings and proceedings. To help assist consumer groups in presenting their views, some government agencies have begun granting expense money and attorneys' fees to groups which contribute to the hearing process.

The government has taken other steps to help make certain that consumer interests are represented. Some agencies have created consumer advocate positions within their organizations. The advocate, who is a regular government employee, has the duty of representing consumer interests within the agency. This type of arrangement has been most common in public utility commissions. The effectiveness of a consumer advocate of this type depends, of course, on an adequate staff and budget.

Another method of providing consumer representation is to appoint a consumer advocate who is located outside the regulatory agencies. At the state level, positions of this type are usually located in the Department of Justice. They also may be located in a separate department. New Jersey uses this approach. It has a separate Department of the Public Advocate. This department represents consumer interests before regulatory agencies and also handles complaints from citizens about state government services, along with other duties.

Calling on the Public for Its Views. Government agencies use other methods to help them stay in touch with the public's opinions and needs. One way they do this is through advisory boards and committees which include representatives of different public and consumer interests. They also may hold open meetings to provide the public an opportunity to ask questions and express their views on important new proposals.

The idea of providing consumers special representation in government is still rather new. It is not clear which methods will work best. Right now several different approaches are being used. After these different methods have been tried for a while, we will be in a better position to decide which ones work best.

Providing Redress to Users of Government Services

In addition to being concerned about how government rules are made and programs planned, we also are concerned about how the rules are enforced and programs are run. When we are dissatisfied with government services, it is not easy to know where to turn for help. Dissatisfied consumers may find that the channel for complaints is through the same official they believe is responsible for their problems. As this problem has become recognized, new steps have been taken to help consumers.

Established Sources of Assistance. Legislators traditionally have played an important role in obtaining government services for people in their districts and in making certain that they are treated fairly by government. Legislators serve as a link between citizens and government agencies. Members of Congress, for example, help people in their districts obtain veteran's and social security benefits. Such services are an important part of the legislator's role, and legislators are expected to look after these problems.

Because of their control over agencies' budgets, legislators generally are effective in getting action. The number of problems coming to the individual legislator is large, and handling them shifts the legislator's attention from other duties. As a result, there has been interest in finding other ways to handle citizens' problems with government agencies.

The courts also have provided a channel for the complaints of citizens who feel they have been treated unfairly by government. The delays and expense of legal action make the courts useful only in the most important cases. The use of the courts is also complicated because of the limitations that are placed on suits against the government. The ancient Anglo-Saxon principle that the government cannot be sued without its permission has been modified over the years. However, it still limits the usefulness of the courts to citizens who feel they have been treated unfairly by government agencies.

New Channels for Complaints. The need for a better channel for citizens' complaints against government has created widespread interest in a new kind of official, the ombudsman. *Ombudsman* is a Swedish word for an official appointed by a legislative body to receive and investigate citizens' complaints about unfairness, dishonesty, and inefficiency in government agencies. The problems handled include consumer problems but also can include problems related to military service and the performance of prison and police officials. Ombudsmen do not have the power to reverse the decisions of government agencies. They do, however, report to the legislative body they serve and often have the power to publicize the results of their investigations. Because of these powers they usually are able to get government agencies to change their decisions in cases where they feel a citizen has been treated unjustly.

The ombudsman helps both to protect individual rights and to ensure efficiency in government operations. Examination of complaints about an agency gives the ombudsman a good picture of how well it is serving the public and whether any changes in its operations are needed.

The idea of the ombudsman has been adopted by many democratic countries outside Scandinavia, including Great Britain, New Zealand, and several provinces of Canada. The first ombudsman office in the United States was created by the state of Hawaii in 1967. The Hawaii ombudsman office handles a wide variety of complaints. Among the leading categories of complaints were public housing (including problems of getting a place in public housing and difficulties with other tenants), enforcement of pollution laws, highways and highway safety, and public education (including overcrowded school buses and problems in getting schooling for a handicapped child). State ombudsman offices more recently have been created in several other states, including Oregon, Nebraska, and Iowa.

The term "ombudsman" has also sometimes been applied to offices in the executive branch of government. An example of such an office is the public protector appointed by the county executive in Nassau County, Long Island, New York. This official has authority to "protect the public and individual citizens against inefficiency, maladministration, arrogance, abuse and other failures of government."

Some political scientists have expressed concern about the way the ombudsman concept is developing in the United States. Many of the offices created have been in the executive branch rather than in the legislative branch. The political scientists feel that these offices will be less independent and effective than the ones connected with a legislative body. Offices in the executive branch can be effective in resolving citizens' complaints. However, it seems unlikely that they will be as effective as ombudsmen in the legislative branch in pressing for government efficiency and in bringing about needed changes in government procedures.

Checking your Reading

1. What are the four functions we ask government to serve?
2. Why is the money spent by the government to provide services considered an exhaustive expenditure?
3. What are income transfers? Subsidies?
4. Why are income transfers classified as nonexhaustive expenditures?
5. What are collective goods? Why is national defense a collective good?
6. What are three different methods the government uses to regulate the marketplace?
7. What are spillover costs?
8. Why is pollution considered to create spillover costs?
9. Why are electrical companies and city transit lines permitted to operate as monopolies?
10. How does providing free public services financed by tax dollars shift income and benefits to lower-income people?
11. If the government wants to encourage the production of a par-

ticular good or service, does it have to produce the good or service itself? Explain.

12. What is the problem of consumer representation in government? What is the problem of redress for users of government services?
13. What do consumer advocates do?
14. What are some of the different types of consumer advocates?
15. Why are legislators usually effective in helping consumers with problems in obtaining public services?
16. What is an ombudsman? What functions does this person perform?

Consumer Problems and Projects

1. Seven situations in which the marketplace does not provide well for consumers' needs were discussed in this chapter. What are these situations? Why does private enterprise fail to meet society's needs in each of these situations?
2. When it provides a service, government often does not give individuals a choice about whether or not they will use it. People may be forced to use city water and sewer service even though they do not want it. Families may be required to send their children to school even though they do not want them to go. Why does government force these kinds of consumption on people?
3. Examine the discussions about a proposed piece of social legislation in newspapers and new magazines. *U.S. News & World Report* is likely to be especially useful. Who will benefit from the proposed program? How is it to be financed? Does the program involve the shift of income or benefits from one group to another? From whom and to whom? What are the arguments for and against this shift of income?
4. Check recent issues of the *Consumer Register* for notices of proposed regulations. Choose an issue which concerns you and prepare a letter with your comments on the proposal.
5. Check your local newspaper for public notices of hearings by government bodies. List hearings which are scheduled. Which are on issues which affect consumers? Exactly how would consumers be affected in each case?

26

Introduction to Taxes

During the past month, what have you used or consumed? Before you read further, spend a few moments thinking about an answer to that question.

You probably thought about such things as food, clothing, toothpaste, magazines, and gasoline. You may also have thought about larger, more expensive items such as housing, cars, insurance, furniture, and appliances.

Did you think about police and fire protection, highways, libraries, national parks, education, national defense, and sewage disposal? Most of us forget about such things, but they are consumed by us and they contribute to our welfare. Government—local, state, and federal—pays for them and a host of other things that we want and need. Where does government get the money? By collecting money from us, and this is called taxation, of course.

People certainly do not enjoy paying taxes, but they do enjoy a great many of the goods and services that are supplied by the government at no charge beyond the taxes they pay. We all share in consuming the goods and services made available by government. It is intended that they be made available to everyone at all times. Simply by being a citizen of the United States, you consume your share of the security provided by national defense spending. You may never travel on a national highway or visit a national park, but they are there waiting for you. You may never have occasion to call upon the police or the fire department directly, but they nevertheless protect you. You may or may not attend a public school, but the privilege of a free public school education is available to you.

TYPES OF TAXES

Taxes can be classified as either direct or indirect, depending on how they are paid to government. You pay your income taxes and your car license fees directly to the various levels of government. Thus, these are *direct* taxes. On the other hand, you pay the jeweler a tax on luxury items such as rings, and the jeweler then pays the tax to the government. For you, such taxes are *indirect*.

The way taxes relate to the taxpayer's income is another way to classify taxes. When taxes are described in this way, they are said to be proportional, progressive, or regressive.

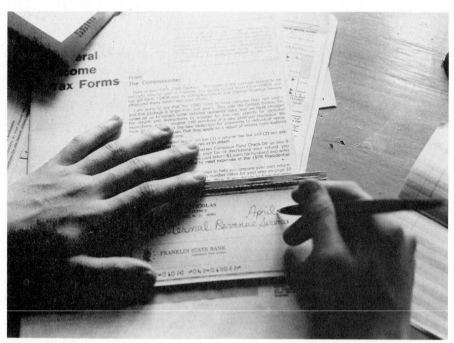

When you pay a tax directly to the government, you are paying a direct tax. (*Kip Peticolas*)

Proportional Taxation

If we could assume that each individual or each family benefits about equally from government services, then a simple solution to determining how much taxes each should pay would be to divide the taxes equally. The trouble with this solution, however, is that the tax burden does not have an equal effect upon each individual or each family.

By the late 1970s the average tax bill per family exceeded $4000. A family with an income of $4500 would have its income wiped out by such a tax, while a family with an income of $45,000 would find the tax burden relatively light. Thus a system that would tax people equally is not possible in our society. Most people agree that a person's tax contribution should, to at least some extent, reflect his or her ability to pay. The simplest way to tax people according to ability to pay is to use a system in which taxpayers pay a fixed percentage of every dollar of income. Such a system is called *proportional taxation*. When a taxpayer's income goes up, the taxes this person pays go up. If the tax rate is 10 percent, families earning $6000 a year would pay $600. Families earning $60,000 a year would pay $6000.

Progressive Taxation

Under a proportional tax system, the tax burden still falls more heavily on poor families. For example, a family earning $6000 may need all of this money just to buy such essentials as food and clothing. A $600 tax bill might mean a hardship. On the other hand, a family earning $60,000 could no doubt pay its $6000 tax bill and still easily afford many luxuries. As a result of this line of reasoning, many believe we need a tax system in which the tax rate is higher on higher incomes. Such a system is known as *progressive taxation.*

A progressive direct tax would be any income tax or any tax on money inherited by you or given to you. This tax would increase according to the increase in income or in the value of the inheritance or gift, and the tax would be paid directly to the appropriate government agency. There are no progressive indirect taxes because it would be impossible to administer them. The government would have to know the income of a customer, for instance, before the government's agent (the shopkeeper) could decide how much to tax that person.

Regressive Taxation

The term "regressive" refers to the fact that such taxes take a higher percentage of income from the poor than they do from the rich. They

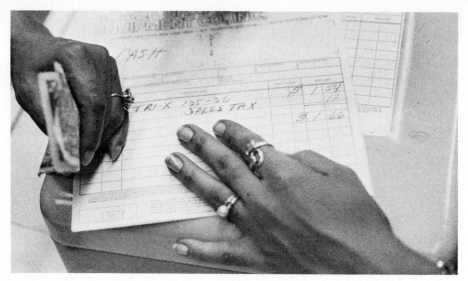

Indirect taxes like sales taxes cannot be progressive, since the person collecting the tax has no way of knowing the taxpayer's income. (*Kip Peticolas*)

are the reverse of progressive taxes. If a person earns $800 a month and buys $400 worth of goods upon which there is a 5 percent sales tax, that tax takes 2½ percent of this person's income for that month ($400 × 5% ÷ $800). Another individual, who earns $4000 a month, may buy the same goods for the same price of $400. This person will be paying only ½ of 1 percent of his or her income ($400 × 5% ÷ $4000) in taxes.

A Look at Our Taxes

When taxes are classified, they are usually considered either progressive or regressive. Sometimes the tax on houses is given as an example of a proportional tax because the rate is the same whether the house is large or small. But the property tax is considered by most persons to be a regressive tax because it is based upon the value of what is owned, not upon the ability to pay.

Other direct regressive taxes, as you can see in Table 26-1, include fees paid to register cars, dogs, or luncheonettes.

The federal income tax is essentially a direct progressive tax. It is paid directly to the government, and its rates are higher for larger incomes than for smaller ones.

You should remember that every tax has two kinds of classification:

TABLE 26-1
Characteristics of Taxes*

| Progressive Direct | Regressive | |
	Direct	Indirect
Personal Income Tax	State	Business Taxes
Federal	Property Tax	Federal
State	Motor Vehicle Licenses	Import Duties
Local	Personal Property Tax	Excise Taxes
Estate and Gift Tax	Business Licenses and Permits	State
Federal	Local	Excise Taxes
State	Property Tax	Sales Taxes
Corporate Income Tax	Business Licenses and Permits	State
Federal		Local
State		

*The classifications are meant to be general. Different laws and methods of assessment may sometimes modify the progressive or regressive nature of a tax.

it may be direct or indirect, and it may be either progressive or regressive. There are no progressive indirect taxes, however.

All sales taxes, import duties, and excise taxes are indirect and regressive. Corporate taxes, however, like those paid by individuals, are usually progressive. That is, the more profits a corporation earns, the higher the percentage of its earnings it must pay.

The states tax corporations according to their own laws, and these laws vary from state to state. Some corporation taxes, therefore, are progressive; others are regressive; and many are combinations of both forms.

Some Payments to Government May Not Be Taxes

Some government functions are not easy to classify with respect to their financing. The nickel you put into a parking meter can be called direct payment for a service, and it can also be considered a direct, regressive tax. The toll you pay for traveling over a bridge is similar, as is the fee for use of a park or recreational facility.

Social security taxes and unemployment insurance premium payments are unlike other taxes, since they do not benefit the entire population. They are taxes, though, because every wage earner must pay them, because governments collect them, and because they are paid at a flat rate based upon your earnings (and are therefore direct and regressive in nature). However, such funds are not used as other taxes are used—for the purchase of goods and services. Instead, they are paid out again to unemployed persons, the elderly, and widows and dependents of wage earners who have died.

THE CITIZEN AND TAXES

Along with other factors that cause taxes to rise, the demand for goods and services supplied by government continues to increase. There is no reason why a citizen who insists upon good police protection, for instance, should balk at paying the taxes necessary to supply salaries and equipment for the police force.

Behind the story of taxation lies a contradiction that has long puzzled citizens. On the one hand, we insist that no individual shall be taxed so heavily that this person cannot enjoy the use of some of the money he or she has earned. On the other hand, we believe that every citizen is equal under the law. We believe that everybody, therefore, should receive the same benefits from the governments. The first principle limits the amounts of money that are available as tax revenues. The second places unlimited demands upon the tax revenues. Somewhere between the two extremes we must constantly strive to be as fair as possible in order to reduce the injustices that must occur.

WHERE DO THE TAX DOLLARS GO?

In the fiscal year ended June 30, 1975, the federal government collected almost $279 billion and spent almost $313½ billion, which resulted in a budget deficit of about $34½ billion. (The previous year the deficit was $3.5 billion.)

While the greater part of the tax expenditures of federal and state and local governments went to pay for goods and services, the federal government was spending $106.7 billion for social security and similar programs, $14.7 billion for education and workforce development, and $31.3 billion just for interest on its many debts. The graphs on page 457 show where the federal government and the state and local governments get money and how that money is spent.

Each level of government spends most where its greatest interests lie. The federal government is concerned with the welfare and safety of all the states, so it spends a large amount of its income on *national defense*. The governments of states, on the other hand, are concerned with the welfare and education of their citizens, so they pay a large amount of their tax revenues for education and welfare.

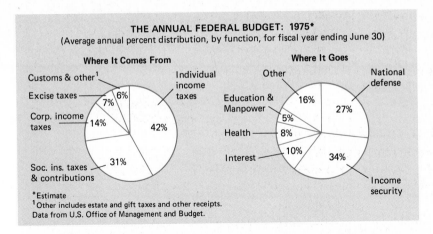

THE ANNUAL FEDERAL BUDGET: 1975*
(Average annual percent distribution, by function, for fiscal year ending June 30)

Where It Comes From

Customs & other¹
Excise taxes — 7%
6%
Corp. income taxes — 14%
Individual income taxes — 42%
Soc. ins. taxes & contributions — 31%

Where It Goes

Other
Education & Manpower — 16%
5%
Health — 8%
Interest — 10%
National defense — 27%
34%
Income security

*Estimate
¹Other includes estate and gift taxes and other receipts.
Data from U.S. Office of Management and Budget.

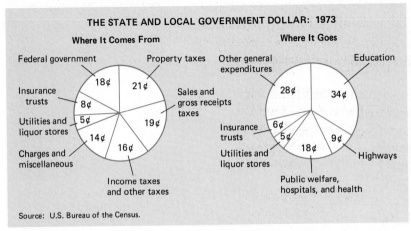

THE STATE AND LOCAL GOVERNMENT DOLLAR: 1973

Where It Comes From

Federal government
Property taxes
Insurance trusts — 8¢
18¢
21¢
Utilities and liquor stores — 5¢
Sales and gross receipts taxes
14¢
19¢
16¢
Charges and miscellaneous
Income taxes and other taxes

Where It Goes

Other general expenditures
Education
28¢
34¢
Insurance trusts — 6¢
5¢
9¢
Utilities and liquor stores
18¢
Highways
Public welfare, hospitals, and health

Source: U.S. Bureau of the Census.

Federal and state sources of income and where that income is spent.

FEDERAL TAXES

As a consumer of government goods and services, you are entitled to know how they are paid for and how the money was raised. As with all matters of taxation, your votes can change the systems. You owe it to yourself to learn about taxation practices and to change them if they do not seem fair or appropriate.

Every year the Internal Revenue Service finds mistakes made by individuals when they are reporting their incomes for tax purposes. With the use of computer systems and their accompanying data bases—storehouses of vast amounts of information—the federal government can find such mistakes. Very often they are mistakes that, if corrected, will lead to a refund of overpayments on the part of the

The federal government spends a large part of its income on national defense, since the welfare and safety of all the states is one of its major interests. (*Shel Hershorn, Black Star*)

taxpayer. In such situations, the citizen is lawfully and correctly avoiding taxes that should not be paid. Lawful tax avoidance is not only a way for you to save money, it is absolutely necessary if the system of taxation is to be fair. You should neither want nor be allowed to pay more taxes than the law requires.

On the other hand, *tax evasion*, which is the conscious attempt to escape paying taxes required by law, is illegal. Just as it is fair for people to pay only what they do owe and no more, it is also fair for people to pay at least what they do owe. As the Internal Revenue Service ties together its data sources and crosschecks the financial information of every American citizen, the chances for successful tax evasion are reduced. Those who would try to receive many benefits without paying for them through taxes are discovered and encouraged to pay their way.

It should be obvious that information systems are a source of great power. There are instances of abuse of that power, where a government agency has used the tax information of individual citizens against them. There are many who claim that as much danger exists from possible government abuse of information as from evasion of tax responsibilities by individuals. The problems suggested by this difference in positions must be the concern of all voters.

The Personal Federal Income Tax

As income rises, the personal income tax rate goes up. You have no doubt heard people refer to their income tax bracket. For example, a person might say that she is in the 50 percent tax bracket. Many students think that this means the person is paying 50 percent of her income in taxes. This is not true. The tax rate increases at certain levels of income, but the rate applicable to previous lumps of income remains the same.

Let's take the 1975 tax rates as an example. If the taxable income of a childless couple is $20,000, they would pay an income tax of $4380. How much would the tax be if they earned $22,000? The additional $2000 is taxed at 32 percent. The couple would probably say that they are in the 32 percent tax bracket because the last dollars they earned were taxed at 32 percent. A more accurate way to describe their tax bracket would be to say that their *marginal* tax rate is 32 percent. If they earned $22,000, they would pay $4380 on the first $20,000 and $640 on the next $2000 (32 percent of $2000). Their total tax bill would be $5020, or about 22.8 percent of their taxable income.

So when you hear that a family is in the 50 percent tax bracket, that means they paid 50 percent of the last, or marginal, dollars that they earned. The income made before that last bracket is taxed at progressively lower and lower rates. Even in the 50 percent tax bracket a childless couple would pay only about 33 percent of their taxable income to the government.

Who Pays Federal Income Taxes?   For the tax year 1976, an American citizen under 65 years of age who had a gross income of $2450 or more during the year must file a federal income tax return. Anyone 65 years or older on the last day of the tax year is not required to file a return unless that person had a gross income of $3200 or more during the year. A taxpayer with income of less than $2450 (or less than $3200 if 65 or older) should file a return to claim the refund of any taxes withheld.

Withholding Taxes and Paying Estimated Taxes.   The tax bite can be a big one, and experience has shown that taxpayers may not be entirely careful about setting aside enough money to pay their taxes when they come due. For this reason, and in order to have available a flow of cash, the federal government is empowered to collect and to withhold money from the salaries of individuals.

At the end of each year, every employer sends a record of wages paid and taxes withheld to the Internal Revenue Service. Each employee receives a copy of the same statement and then uses this statement to prove his or her own report of income and tax due.

After computing the income tax, the taxpayer pays the difference if his or her employer has withheld too little money. If the employer has withheld too much, the taxpayer applies for and obtains a refund. Naturally there are many people who file their returns early to get their refunds as soon as possible, but all citizens must settle their tax accounts before the April 15 deadline or be liable for interest charges on taxes due.

Students who have summer jobs with earnings totaling less than $2450 may have had federal income tax withheld from their pay. They are entitled to a refund of the amount withheld, and they should file a tax return form to obtain the refund. If you are such a student, call your nearest Internal Revenue Service office for instructions. You will find it listed under "United States Government" in your local telephone directory.

Those who have very large salaries or income from which the government does not withhold taxes (as would be the case for a professional person who is hired by a number of persons, such as a doctor, a lawyer or a consultant) must do their own withholding and paying in advance. This is accomplished by the use of the Declaration of Estimated Tax, a system of reporting and paying in advance four times a year, which, like withholding, is required by law.

Everybody who is likely to be a taxpayer receives tax forms and detailed instructions for completing them. These documents are mailed by the Internal Revenue Service just after the first of each year. Also, every citizen can get free individual assistance from the IRS or can get help in completing tax forms from a small army of people who specialize in this activity—advertising widely, setting up temporary offices in tax season, and charging either a flat rate or some percentage as a fee.

For those who prefer to work out their tax obligations themselves, there are, in addition to the instructions distributed free with the forms, low-cost comprehensive tax guides published by the Government Printing Office and a number of privately written and published tax guides that are prominently displayed for sale in the first four months of every year. These publications are updated annually to include the latest regulations. You should make a point of reading at least one such tax guide. Keep in touch with taxpayer hints published in newspapers and magazines. Above all, keep careful records of your income and expenditures so that when tax time comes, you can supply the necessary information with the least amount of confusion and inconvenience.

If you were given the responsibility for finding enough tax dollars to cover each year's federal budget, you would look in every direction for sources of tax money. One of the best sources, you would discover, would be the money of wealthy people. The money is represented, of course, by property, investments, and other possessions; these things are known as the person's estate. When these people die, their estates are transferred to their heirs. The federal government takes some of that money from estates.

One way to avoid leaving a large estate on which the taxes to be paid could be quite high would be to give the money away during your lifetime. Until January 1, 1977, the government had one tax rate for estates and a smaller tax rate for gifts. By setting a smaller tax rate on gifts, of course, the government encouraged people to make gifts during their lifetimes. The Tax Reform Act of 1976, which became effective at the beginning of 1977, changed this, however, by combining estate and gift tax rates into a single rate schedule.

The single rate schedule for estate and gift taxes is known as the *unified rate schedule.* The unified rates start at 18 percent and increase to 70 percent on amounts exceeding $5 million. The new law does provide, however, for certain deductions to be made from a person's gross estate in determining that person's taxable estate. For example, such items as the following can be deducted from the value of the estate: funeral expenses, various expenses needed to administer the estate, debts of the deceased person, and marital deduction for property passing to the deceased person's spouse. This marital deduction is equal to the greater of (*a*) one-half of the gross estate, or (*b*) $250,000. In addition to the deductions, the new law allows a credit, known as "unified estate and gift tax credit." The credit was $30,000 in 1977, and it will increase by steps each year through 1981.

Excise Taxes and Custom Duties

The consumer can avoid some taxes with no feelings of guilt. Among those most easily avoided are the taxes placed upon goods which are not really needed: tobacco, liquor, and imported goods and commodities, for instance.

The federal tax on specific commodities and services originating in this country is called an *excise* tax. You pay an excise tax whenever you pay for a long-distance telephone call. Excise taxes do not always apply only to luxury items such as liquor. New tires are sold at prices to which the "federal" (that is, the excise) tax must be added. The government is free to add to or remove from the list of items that bear an excise tax.

The excise tax is an indirect tax, which, you will recall, is collected by the merchant and passed on from the buyer to the government. Sometimes excise taxes are referred to as "hidden" taxes. There is no deceit or cheating implied by the term. The taxes are not really hidden, as a glance at any gasoline pump will show. The gasoline distributors are eager to prove that the price they are charging for gasoline is made up in large part of various excise taxes.

Taxes on imported goods are called *customs duties* or *tariffs*. When the government wishes to restrict the importing of any goods to protect American jobs or industries, it imposes very high tariffs on imported goods. Since these taxes drive prices up so that the imported items cost more than those made in this country, tariffs tend to discourage foreign competitors from bringing their products into the American market. Tariffs that do this are called *protective tariffs*. They can cause much disagreement and tension between countries.

The federal tax you pay on every gallon of gas is an excise tax, a special tax placed on certain goods and commodities. (*Susan Berkowitz*)

American citizens should keep in mind the need for trade with foreign countries, and therefore the need for using protective tariffs with caution. Exports of farm products and raw materials are very important to the prosperity of our economy, but in order to have money to buy such things from the United States, other countries must be able to sell their own products in this country.

At the same time, American goods often face very high tariffs in countries to which we hope to export them. Consumers have an important interest in free trade. *Free trade* is trade with few or no protective tariffs on either side. The competition provided by imported goods helps keep down the prices of goods produced in this country. High tariffs on foreign goods protect the profits of some businesses and the jobs of their workers, but they do so at the cost of higher prices for American consumers.

As a consumer you should know what excise taxes or customs duties you will be required to pay when you make purchases. If you can find goods or services that do not carry these excise taxes or customs duties, you can save money on many of your purchases.

STATE AND LOCAL TAXES

Most local governments, as well as state governments, need tax money to pay for local projects. The taxpayers pay for benefits they can see and experience directly.

Property Taxes

Although most property taxes are based upon real estate alone, many states and communities charge taxes based upon the value of other kinds of property, such as home furnishings, paintings, sculpture, and jewelry. Property such as money invested in stocks and bonds may also be taxed.

Real estate taxes are based upon the value of the property as decided by tax assessors. The tax rate itself is set by the local government as a percentage of the value set by the tax assessor. Communities vary widely in their assignment of tax rates and assessments. Some may prefer to charge a low rate based on the actual cash value of the property. Others may charge a higher rate, but apply it to only part of the value of the property. No doubt psychology enters into the setting of tax-rate practices. Here is an example showing how, by juggling the assessment and the tax rate, one community can get more money from a low tax rate than a similar community can get for equally valuable property.

Community A

Tax rate: $35 per $1000 of assessed valuation
Assessment: 50% of market value
The tax on property worth $40,000 is computed as follows:

$40,000 × 50% = $20,000
$20,000 ÷ $1,000 = 20
20 × $35 = $700 tax

Community B

Tax rate: $30 per $1000 of assessed valuation
Assessment: 70% of market value
The tax on property worth $40,000 is computed as follows:

$40,000 × 70% = $28,000
$28,000 ÷ $1,000 = 28
28 × $30 = $840 tax

Sales Taxes, License Fees, and Other Taxes

Nearly all states, and many cities, too, charge sales taxes. Combined state and local sales taxes can raise the price of products considerably. The sales tax in some states is as high as 6 percent. Such taxes are regressive, of course, because they hurt people with little money more than they hurt people with a lot. However, most sales taxes do not apply to staple items such as food, clothing, and medicines. People with low incomes spend a large proportion of their incomes for these tax-exempt necessities. Because of this fact, such exemptions help to ease the burden created by a sales tax on other items.

If you want to sell hot dogs or practice medicine, cut hair or drill for oil, tie up a ship at a public dock or sell turnips in a public market, hunt deer or listen to a singer in a nightclub, then you will be taxed or charged fees that, in effect, are taxes.

About one-sixth of state and local revenues comes from such sources as license fees and entertainment taxes. In this category of taxation there are many different kinds of taxes and ways of taxing. All the taxes are necessary for the state and local governments, and the revenues from them are all used for the people who benefit from the goods and services the tax dollars provide. Hunting license fees, for instance, are used to support state and local game control and the development of recreational facilities. Charging fees only to the users of specific services is a fundamental principle of taxation and one that you as a consumer should appreciate. It is up to you to see that governments use their taxing power to give the most benefits to the people.

Checking Your Reading

1. List several things that government "buys" with the taxes collected from its citizens.
2. Explain the differences between direct and indirect taxes.
3. Explain what is meant by proportional taxation.
4. What is meant by a progressive tax? Give two examples.
5. Give an example of how a tax can be regressive.
6. What is the best-known direct progressive American tax?
7. When consumers demand more goods and services from governments, what effect should they expect their demands to have on taxation?
8. Compare federal and state expenditures. What is the largest spending category for each level of government?
9. "A person in the 50 percent tax bracket does not pay 50 percent of his or her taxable income in federal income taxes." Explain what this statement means.
10. With more than 217 million people in our country, how can the Internal Revenue Service find mistakes made in individuals' income tax returns?
11. What is a customs duty? A protective tariff?
12. The property tax rate in one community is $40, and in a neighboring community it is just $35. Why is it not possible to say that the second community mentioned has lower property taxes?

Consumer Problems and Projects

1. We often hear or read that our governments act as nonprofit purchasing agents for consumers. A purchasing agent in a business firm is accountable to someone who is competent to evaluate the agent's performance. When governments act as purchasing agents, to whom are they accountable? Who evaluates their performance? Be prepared to explain your answer.
2. Continued increases in a particular tax rate can sometimes result in lower total tax revenues because of consumer reaction to the increase. That is, the tax can be so high that demand for the product goes down. In that case, tax revenue for the government also may go down. Prepare a short report on one of the following

taxes that describes how continued increases in the tax rate could influence consumer behavior and thus result in less rather than more revenue: (a) property tax, (b) city sales tax, (c) tax on tobacco, (d) tax on alcoholic beverages.

3. Governments sometimes provide services that directly benefit small groups of citizens rather than consumers generally. Prepare a report on one such service, and describe the group or persons who benefit from the service. Why is it provided? Does it indirectly benefit all consumers?

4. The basic purpose of requiring some type of licenses and permits is to enable local or state governments to exercise some control over those areas of activity. Do you believe this is a good reason for this type of tax? Why? Give an example of this type of tax.

5. Even though real estate taxes bring in the most revenue for local governments, many people do not consider the property tax to be the most satisfactory form of taxation. Explain why you agree or disagree with this point of view.

6. What might you suspect about the federal government's attitude toward private borrowing, considering that you deduct interest paid out from your taxable income?

PART SIX
Protecting and Assisting Consumers

27

Principles of Consumer Law

Consumers are protected by laws in many different ways. Laws regulate such things as advertising, sales techniques, and interest charges. Laws also help to control the quality of certain products, and they specify packaging and labeling requirements. But those are just a few of the ways in which laws help us. Laws of many kinds have been worked out over the years, and laws are constantly being developed for the benefit of consumers.

This chapter explains the background and the intent of some of the laws that affect consumers. It also shows how businesses operate within the framework of the laws and explains how you can use these laws for your benefit and protection. Remember, this chapter is merely an introduction to the subject of consumer law. When you need or want legal advice, be sure to get it from a licensed attorney. Later in this chapter, you will be given information about when, how, and where to get professional legal advice and help.

SOME KINDS OF LAW

Law is the sum total of the rules men and women live by. Without rules there would be no order and our society could not long exist. Where do laws come from? What kinds of laws exist? The law is found in four forms: constitutional law, statute law, case law, and administrative law. The following paragraphs summarize each of these four forms of law.

Constitutional Law

The basic laws of the land are contained in the United States Constitution and the constitutions of our 50 states. A "constitution" is a written document that sets forth the basic principles, aims, and laws of the government. Our federal and state constitutions establish not only the form and powers of government, but they also limit those powers and spell out the rights of citizens.

Constitutions can be amended, or changed, when necessary. But amendments are not made very often. The first ten amendments to the United States Constitution became effective in 1791, and they are referred to as "The Bill of Rights." The purpose of these ten amendments was to make clear certain individual and state rights not named in the Constitution. In the nearly 200 years since that time, just 16 additional amendments have been made.

An amendment being considered in the 1970s is the proposed Equal Rights Amendment (ERA). The ERA states that "Equality of rights under the law shall not be denied or abridged by the United States or by any State on account of sex." Congress proposed the ERA on March 22, 1972. The legislatures of 38 states must ratify (approve) the amendment before the deadline of March 22, 1979.

Statute Law

The lawmaking branches of federal, state, and local governments are known as "legislatures." The Congress of the United States, a state assembly, and a city board of commissioners or a city council are all legislatures. The main function of the legislative branch of government is to decide what laws ought to be passed (or amended or repealed) and then act upon these proposed laws. The laws enacted by federal and state legislatures are called *statutes*. Laws enacted by local governments, such as cities and counties, are called *ordinances*. At any given time, therefore, we are subject not only to the statute law of our nation, but also to the laws of our state, county, and city.

Case Law

The recorded decisions of judges are known as "case law." Case law is based on the earlier decisions of courts in similar situations. It comes down to us in the form of written court decisions. The principles set forth in these earlier decisions must be applied to the facts in every individual case that comes before a court. The first judge's ruling is called a *precedent*. The precedent serves as an example for the second judge and for judges in the future.

Administrative Law

Because of the complexities of modern life, legislative branches of government cannot provide all necessary or desirable law. Then, too, many technical matters require regulation that is often beyond the understanding of most legislators. Thus, legislative bodies have, by statute, created a large number of administrative agencies to carry out some of the functions of government. These agencies generally have the right to make rules, establish rates, and determine the rights of certain persons or business firms. Examples of these agencies on the federal level are the Federal Trade Commission and the Food and Drug Administration. The regulations and rules of these administrative agencies have the force of law because they have been given authority by statute law. These regulations and rules are known as "administrative law." In the next three chapters, you will read more about these agencies and how they help protect consumers.

THE LAW OF CONTRACTS

Contracts are involved in one form or another in nearly every business transaction. If you buy a suit that requires alterations, you complete an order. You have then actually made a contract by which you promise to pay for the suit and the store promises to deliver it to you, altered to fit you. Even simple transactions such as riding on the bus, going to the movies, or using the lights in your home are contracts that, if necessary, can be enforced by law.

To accomplish its purpose, any contract must be binding upon all

Even simple transactions such as paying money to ride on a bus are contracts that can be enforced by law. (*Art Zollo*)

parties. No one will be allowed to wriggle out. Another way of putting the same idea is to say the contract must be enforceable; that is, if somebody tries to escape, the courts, under the law, can force that person to perform as promised.

Some contracts must be written and signed by all the persons involved so that they are legally binding. This is true of many leases for the rental of property, of agreements for the sale of real estate, and of most installment-plan purchase contracts. Other less formal contracts may be oral and unwritten, and a few may even be unspoken. Still other agreements have no legal significance and thus do not constitute contracts. Personal agreements you make with friends, such as agreeing to go to a party, to attend the movies, or to visit a neighbor, are examples of agreements that are not legally enforceable contracts.

Mutual Assent Is Necessary

To be legally binding, a contract must be accepted by all parties involved. There can be no disagreement at all. When disagreement can be shown, this is proof that the parties did not agree. In such situations contracts cannot exist and thus cannot be binding.

In order to show and to prove mutual assent, two things are required by law, and they are absolutely essential: (1) a valid offer and (2) acceptance. These two essentials illustrate how useful the commercial laws are in setting up and maintaining a structure for business transactions.

There Must Be an Offer.   An offer is good only if it is made in such a way that it shows obvious intention on the part of the person making the offer to enter into legal agreement with the person to whom the offer is made.

The offer must be clear and definite, and it must be properly communicated.

A retail store placed an advertisement in the newspaper: Portable TV Sets, $89.50—Today Only. Because the dealer did not have sufficient quantity to meet all demands, there was no *obvious intention* to sell a TV set to everyone who responded to the advertisement. Therefore, the offer was not valid or legally binding; it was more in the nature of an "offer to make an offer."

Henry, who owns several cameras, offered to sell one to Jack for $20. Because Henry did not specify which camera he would sell for $20, the offer was not clear and definite. It could not result in a contract until there was an agreement on the specific camera offered.

Harris posted a public notice offering a reward of $25 for the return of her lost briefcase. Hanson, who had not seen the notice, found the briefcase and returned it. Because the offer was not *communicated* to Hanson, his return of the briefcase was not an acceptance of the offer. The offer was valid but not properly communicated.

A valid offer may be terminated in one of three ways: through lapse of time, through revocation, or through rejection. Only acceptance of the offer results in a contract.

Lapse of time can terminate an offer when a time limit has been set for acceptance.

Bob offered to sell his car to June and gave her three days to think it over. Unless June accepted the offer within the three-day period, the offer was automatically terminated.

The lapse of a reasonable length of time can terminate an offer when no time limit is specified for acceptance.

Bob offered to sell his car to June but set no time limit for the acceptance of his offer. The offer terminated after a reasonable length of time. However, since there can sometimes be disagreement about what constitutes a reasonable length of time, it is usually wise to specify a definite period.

Revocation of an offer terminates it at any time prior to its acceptance. (In the example above, Bob could have decided not to sell his car to June at any time before June decided to buy or not to buy it.) However, if there is an agreement to keep the offer open for a given period of time—this is called an *option* and is itself a type of contract—the offer cannot be withdrawn during the specified time period. To terminate an offer by withdrawing it, the revocation must be communicated to the offeree prior to acceptance.

The *rejection* of an offer terminates the offer immediately. If Bob had offered to sell his car to June and June had replied that she was not interested, the rejection would have terminated the offer.

There Must Be an Acceptance. Once a valid offer is made, the other parties either reject or accept it. Acceptance of an offer results in a contract. However, the acceptance must be unconditional to survive, and it must fit exactly with the terms of the offer. Finally, the acceptance must be signified by words, actions, or both.

Bob offered to sell his car to June if June would pick it up from the repair shop and pay the repair bill. If June picked up the car and paid for the repairs, she would indicate her acceptance of Bob's offer by this action.

You can accept an offer by mail or by telegram. The time of your acceptance will be that of the postmark on your letter or the time your telegram is accepted by the telegraph company. Some persons may insist that they have your acceptance in hand to satisfy the acceptance rules, however.

Consideration Is Necessary

To be legally binding, a contract must be supported by valuable consideration from each person. Consideration may be in the form of an object of value, a promise, or a performed act. If one person is to receive something for nothing, the contract cannot be enforced by law.

Jim promised to build a table for Tom if Tom would pay him $10 immediately. Tom paid Jim the $10. Tom could hold Jim to his promise because he had given consideration in the form of the $10, an *object of value*.

In exchange for Addison's promise to sell and deliver his car to Jenkins for $500, Jenkins promised to pay Addison on delivery. In this case, the consideration for Addison's promise to sell and deliver his car was the *promise* made by Jenkins to pay $500 on delivery.

Salazar promised to give her nephew John $2000 if John would obtain a college degree before his twenty-first birthday. The consideration for Salazar's promise to pay was her nephew's *performed act* of obtaining a degree. An enforceable contract would only arise if John obtained his degree before his twenty-first birthday.

Ralph promised to take Arthur on a three-day hunting trip but failed to do so. There was no contract because no consideration had been given by Arthur. Arthur had given nothing of value, done nothing, nor promised to do anything.

The Parties Must Be Competent

A contract is enforceable when it is made by two or more persons who can give sane and intelligent assent. This rule protects those who are not able to protect themselves because they are mentally ill or otherwise incapable of knowing what will happen if they agree to do or not to do some action.

Minors Are Not Considered Competent. At what age are you capable of "looking out for yourself"? The age at which society assumes you are capable is decided by law, and that law varies from state to state. Where formerly it was generally the practice to call people "minors" until they were twenty-one years old, there is now a common lowering of this age. This is indicated by the extension of voting privileges, which were formerly denied to those under twenty-one, to eighteen-year-olds.

No matter what the age ceiling for minors is in your state, until you reach it you have a special status. You can void (cancel) most contracts you make because you are assumed not to have full maturity of mind and judgment until you reach the age of majority. Although minors can walk away from a contract, claiming youth and inexperience as a defense for breaking it, the adult who makes a contract with a youth must perform his or her obligations. The law assumes that adults, at least, have the intelligence and the maturity to know and understand what they are doing.

Exceptions to the defense of minors occur when minors contract for necessities such as food, clothing, medical care, and education. Either the minor or the minor's parents must pay for necessities; if this were not so, merchants would be justified in refusing to sell such necessities to minors, fearing that they would suffer financial losses because of irresponsible young customers. If you are a minor, remember this exception to minority defense when you want to buy a wild item of dress.

Other People May Be Incompetent. Persons who are insane or who have faulty reasoning because of illness or other disability are not considered legally competent to make contracts. Just as youth and inexperience can be defenses against unfair contracts, so also can the disabilities resulting from advanced age. Rulings of incompetence serve to protect all parties, of course.

The Purpose Must Be Legal

Contracts must be made for legal purposes. If they are not, they are not legally binding. Contracts that involve actions against the law or public policy are considered illegal. They are not enforceable.

Tom promised to pay Ruth $20, if she would steal a typewriter for him. Ruth stole the typewriter and gave it to Tom, who refused to pay. Ruth could not collect because the agreement was unlawful. It called for a criminal act.

Carol bet Barbara $10 that the Midland High School team would beat Rutland High in Saturday's football game. Carol lost the bet but refused to pay. Barbara could take no legal action because the law enforces only legalized gambling contracts, such as bets made at race tracks.

Documents Must Have the Proper Elements

There is no particular form for written contracts, but they should contain the following elements: the date of the agreement, the names of the contracting parties, the purpose of the contract, the consideration, and the signatures of all parties or their agents.

Although you do not need written contracts for some business arrangements, there are many arrangements that demand written words. Among the arrangements that absolutely demand written contracts are (1) those that cannot be performed within one year, or (2) those that involve the sale of real estate or personal property of substantial value, or (3) those that guarantee to pay the debt of another person.

NEGOTIABLE INSTRUMENTS

Pieces of paper carrying promises to pay or requests for delivery of money are called *negotiable instruments*. Because so much commerce is carried on with the help of negotiable instruments, it is not in any way surprising that they are called *commercial paper*. The kinds of negotiable instruments most often used by consumers are checks and promissory notes.

Checks

The writer, or *drawer*, of a check is obligated to have enough money in his or her account to cover the check. The person to whom the drawer makes the check payable is the *payee*. The drawer may also make the check payable to "cash" or to him- or herself as "bearer." The check is then payable to whoever presents it for payment.

The drawer's bank is the *drawee*. It is required to honor or pay any properly drawn check if funds are available to cover it.

There are several plans now available whereby a person can write a check for a sum larger than his or her account holds. Through the magic of computers, any such "overdrafts," which are ordinarily illegal, are quickly converted to loans. The secret of such an arrangement is a type of standing promissory note that authorizes the bank to turn any overdraft into a consumer loan. The banks are delighted to have such agreements because they charge interest on such loans. Apparently, bank customers like the plans too. For one thing, the plans give you the feeling of having a little reserve of money at all times. For another, they are very convenient. Financial counselors may tell you they are too convenient for your own good.

The bank must refuse payment of any check that has been altered or forged. If the bank allows forged or altered checks to be paid, the bank is required by law to cover the loss. Thus, if you draw a check and then immediately ask the bank to stop payment, you are protected and the burden of stopping payment falls upon the bank.

Banks are not required to pay postdated checks before the date written on them. If you wrote a check on March 15 and dated it March 20, the bank would not pay the amount on the check until March 20.

When you must write a very large check, the payee may ask for a "certified check." *Certified checks* contain a statement by the bank that there is enough money in your account to cover the check and that the bank will honor that particular check. However, the bank does charge a small fee to make a certified check.

Promissory Notes

A promissory note is a written promise to pay a definite sum of money to the order of a designated person or to the bearer of the note at a specified or determinable time. It is a legal document, and payment can be enforced by law. The person who writes and signs the note is the *maker*. The person to whom it is payable is the *payee*. The promissory note is normally used in borrowing money from a bank, finance company, or credit union.

In some cases, creditors require cosigners or collateral as security for payment of a note. A *cosigner* is a person who promises to pay the note if the maker fails to pay. The cosigner's signature and that of the maker appear on the note. A *collateral note* is a promissory note that permits the payee to hold certain personal property of the maker— usually stocks or bonds—as security for payment of the note. If the maker fails to pay, the payee has the legal right to sell the collateral in lieu of payment.

Legal Requirements

In most states, negotiable instruments are governed by a modification of the Uniform Negotiable Instruments Law or by the Uniform Commercial Code. These laws are designed to protect the rights of all parties involved in the use of negotiable instruments. To be negotiable, an instrument must conform to the following requirements:

- It must be in writing and must be signed by the maker or drawer. No particular form of writing or signature is necessary. Any mark regarded by the drawer as his or her signature is legally valid. An authorized agent may sign the drawer's name followed by "per" or "by" and his or her own name to indicate that this person is the agent and not the drawer.

- It must contain an unconditional promise to pay a definite amount of money.
- It must be payable on demand or at a fixed or determinable future date.
- It must be payable to order of a particular person or to bearer.
- It must be delivered to the payee.

If an instrument meets these requirements, it is negotiable, even if it is not dated or does not specify the value given (consideration) or the place where it is payable.

Negotiation

A large part of the banking industry involves pushing tons of paper back and forth, delivering it to one place or another, as a convenient substitute for money. When a negotiable instrument is turned over from one payee to another, the process is called *negotiation*. This may be carried out in either of two ways: delivery or endorsement.

You can negotiate transfer of funds from yourself to another payee by *delivery* if the check is made payable to "bearer."

If a check is made payable to a specific person, however, that person must *endorse* the check by writing his or her name on the back before the check can be negotiated.

If Brown gives you a $10 check made out in your name and you want to transfer it to Horowitz, you must endorse the check and deliver it to Horowitz in order to transfer the title.

The person who endorses an instrument with intent to transfer the title is the *endorser*. The person to whom the instrument is transferred is the *endorsee* or *holder*. The endorser generally pledges credit for payment of the instrument if the maker fails to pay. There are several types of endorsements.

A *blank endorsement* is merely the signature of the endorser on the back of the instrument without comment or notation. Instruments with a blank endorsement can be negotiated subsequently by delivery from one person to another just as instruments made payable to bearer or cash.

A *special endorsement* is the signature of the endorser preceded by the words "Pay to . . ." or "Pay to the order of . . ." on the back of the instrument. The endorsee, whose name appears after "Pay to" or "Pay to the order of," must then endorse the instrument to negotiate it further or to cash it.

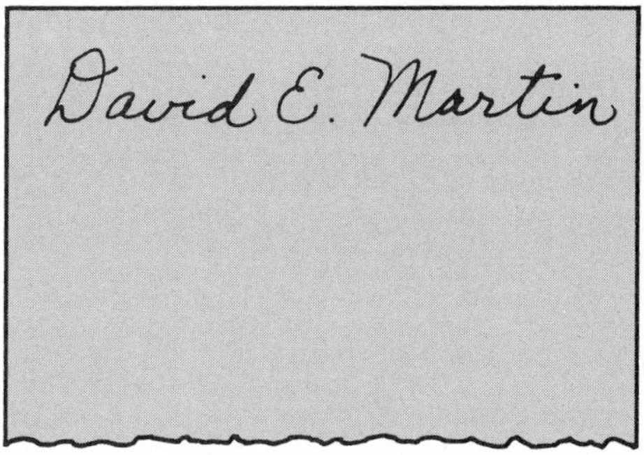

Blank Endorsement

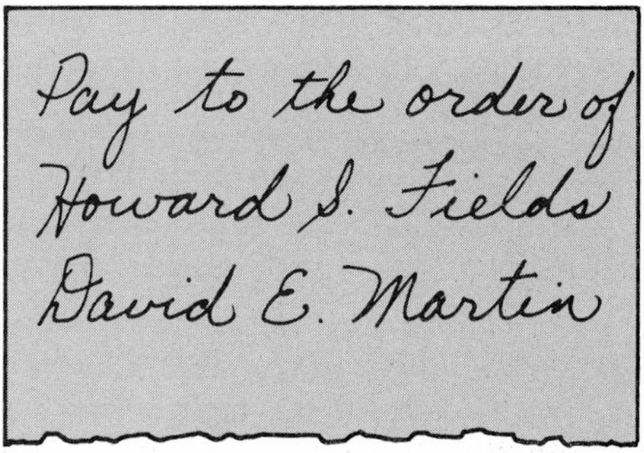

Special Endorsement

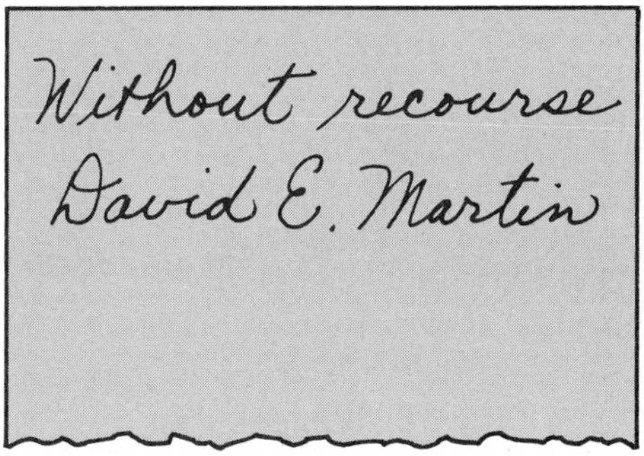

Qualified Endorsement

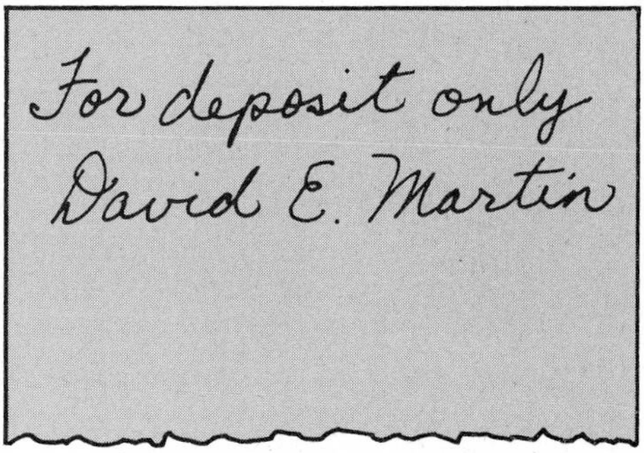

Restrictive Endorsement

A *qualified endorsement* is one that limits the liability of the endorser. An endorsement is qualified when the endorser writes the words "without recourse" on the back of the instrument before the signature. This means that the endorser assumes no responsibility for payment by the maker or drawer of the instrument.

A *restrictive endorsement* is one that restricts further negotiation of the instrument to the purpose specified by the endorser. Restrictive endorsements reading "For deposit only" with the endorser's signature are frequently used when checks are mailed to a bank to be deposited in the endorser's account.

WARRANTIES

Warranties are agreements or promises that give you special rights in case something you buy turns out to be defective or in some specified way fails to satisfy you. Whether the warranty is an express warranty (stated orally or in writing) or an implied warranty (assumed to exist), the warranty is not a safeguard against a poor buying decision on your part. It cannot guarantee that you will like what you buy; it can only promise to protect you if the merchandise fails to live up to the specified standards.

A consumer must be very careful to avoid being influenced too much by advertising claims that are merely statements of opinion. "Trade talk" and "puffing" are mildly persuasive ways of describing merchandise to influence the buyer; they are not warranties. Such statements as "This is the best car on the market," "You won't find a better suit for the money," or "This item is moving so fast you had better buy it now" are advertising claims, not warranties. These statements do not make specific promises regarding title, identity, performance, or quality. Learn to look for the two kinds of warranty, express and implied.

Express Warranties

An express warranty is an oral or written guarantee of a specific quality or performance feature. If a manufacturer makes a written promise that a shirt will not shrink more than 1 percent, that is a warranty. If a seller makes an oral promise that a shirt is washable, colorfast, and shrink-proof, and if the shirt fades and shrinks out of size on the first washing, the seller is responsible for the warranty.

It is difficult to prove an oral warranty, so it is preferable to get a written guarantee. This is especially true when you are buying clothes. Look for the manufacturer's tags specifying the kind of fabric used and the performance to be expected from the fabric.

Implied Warranties

An implied warranty is a guarantee that the buyer has a legal right to expect a degree of fitness or quality in what is purchased. There are several kinds of implied warranties. Some of the main ones are warranty of title, warranty of fitness for purpose, warranty of fitness for human consumption, and warranty of salability.

Warranty of Title. By the very act of selling an item the seller tells potential customers that he or she has a right to sell the item and that title will pass to the buyer at the time of sale. If you find that you were sold goods for which the seller did not have title or for which the title was defective, you may claim monetary damages by suing the seller for breach of warranty of title.

When you buy food, there is an implied warranty of fitness for human consumption, and you have a right to get your money back if foodstuffs are not as they should be. In cases of gross negligence, the seller may be held criminally liable. (*Kip Peticolas*)

Warranty of Fitness for Purpose. When you tell a seller your purpose in buying a particular item and rely on the seller's skill and judgment, there is an implied warranty of fitness for purpose. For instance, you tell a seller that you want a heavy-duty vacuum cleaner to clean wall-to-wall carpeting. After buying the cleaner recommended by the seller, you discover that the cleaner is only effective for light cleaning. In this case you can hold the seller liable on an implied warranty of fitness for purpose.

Warranty of Fitness for Human Consumption. When you buy foodstuffs from a food merchant, the food is covered by an implied warranty of fitness for human consumption. Both seller and buyer fully understand that the food is to be eaten. The seller is liable for any illness or injury to the buyer or the buyer's family that results from eating the food. This warranty applies to the sale of drugs as well as to the sale of food. In addition to the obligation imposed by the implied warranty, the seller may be held criminally liable in cases of gross negligence.

Be sure your own food market will take back food that does not live up to your expectations. You may not have a criminal case against the manager if your roast is tough, but if it was sold to you as tender meat, the manager made an implied warranty. Therefore you are entitled to get your money back.

Warranty of Salability. By the act of selling goods, merchants imply that what they sell will meet at least minimum standards of acceptability. When the buyer inspects goods and fails to notice defects that an average person could be expected to discover, there is no implied warranty of salability; but for goods that the average buyer cannot be expected to evaluate, such as a radio with complicated parts and construction, buyers are protected by an implied warranty of salability.

The Magnuson-Moss Warranty Act

On July 4, 1975, the Magnuson-Moss Warranty Act became effective. In proposing the legislation, Senator Moss stated that warranties have ". . . confused, misled, and frequently angered American consumers." The purpose of the act is to promote understanding. It is basically a disclosure statute. Sellers and manufacturers are not required to make any express warranties at all. If, however, they do choose to issue a "written warranty," it must comply with the disclosure requirements of the act.

Under the Magnuson-Moss Warranty Act, if any manufacturer or seller does use a written warranty in connection with the sale of a product costing more than $5, the firm must "fully and conspicuously disclose in simple and readily understandable language the terms and conditions of such a warranty." Furthermore, all written warranties of consumer products costing more than $10 must be labeled clearly and conspicuously as either "full" or "limited." A warranty can be designated as full only if it completely complies with certain requirements of the act.

Buying Goods "As Is"

Secondhand or damaged goods may be sold to consumers without either an express or an implied warranty. To protect his or her interest, the seller inserts the phrase "as is" into the written contract to warn the purchaser that the articles are being sold in the condition in which they are found at the time of sale. The burden of finding out what

The phrase "as is" protects the seller by making it the customer's responsibility to find out the item's actual condition. (*Kip Peticolas*)

condition the article is in falls upon the buyer. However, if the seller makes any fraudulent misstatements of facts in describing the "as is" condition and the buyer relies upon those statements, the contract may be voided by a court. This could happen if you bought a used car in obviously poor condition and the dealer told you that you would need only to repair the transmission to get the car in perfect running condition. If it turned out that the car needed a new front end, a ring job, four new tires, and a complete electrical system before it would start, the court might be sympathetic to your subsequent claim for damages.

LEGAL SERVICES AND THE CONSUMER

Although consumers are protected by laws, they occasionally require specific legal services to prevent legal problems from arising, to protect their interests, or to enforce their rights. Legal services, in one form or another, are available to every consumer. You will be in a better position to benefit from these services if you know when to seek legal aid and how to obtain it.

When to Seek Legal Aid

Almost everyone occasionally gets into a situation where legal aid is wanted or needed. The situations that are listed below normally call for the advice of a legal expert.

- Entering into a contract for the sale or purchase of real estate
- Entering into a sales contract involving a large sum of money
- Signing written agreements or contracts that are not presented in standard form
- Carrying out adoption proceedings
- Appearing in court as plaintiff or defendant
- Filing income tax returns if there is any possibility that the return will be questioned or if there are nonstandard deductions involved (Either an accountant or an attorney can perform this service.)
- Bringing charges or accusations against another person or defending charges brought against you, particularly if there is a possibility that a charge of libel or slander will be raised
- Drawing up wills, settling estates, or setting up trusts
- Entering into or setting up any type of business

How to Obtain Legal Aid

There are several ways to obtain legal aid when you need or want it. Your choice of legal services will depend on the situation, the services available in your area, and the amount you can pay. Legal services are available from many sources, such as lawyers, government agencies, and small claims courts.

Lawyers   You can get help from lawyers, but it takes time, effort, and thought to find the right person to help you. Simply finding a lawyer in the first place can be a puzzling problem to many people. If you have a legal problem and you have any doubts about its solution at all, your wisest move is to call the local bar association or the lawyers referral service and ask for the name of a lawyer who handles that kind of problem. You can also ask your friends for advice, although it is probably true that a friend's advice on professional recommendations is likely to be so colored by personal preferences that it may not be wise for you to follow it.

Choose your lawyer carefully; you may want to entrust this person with many different problems over the years, just as the doctor you choose equally carefully may help you through several illnesses. Above all, pick a lawyer you feel you can trust.

If you do not have enough money to pay for a lawyer's assistance, call on the local legal aid society—an organization usually sponsored by the local bar association and staffed by volunteers. The legal aid societies do more than provide legal assistance in criminal cases. Their members may give counseling in simple cases. At all times the societies stand ready to refer a person to another agency that can handle the problem more directly or more efficiently.

In any event, if you do work with a lawyer—and the chances are good that you will at several points in your life—be sure to be honest; take the advice you are given; avoid becoming involved in professional tactics and work; and do not make anxious telephone calls, but let your lawyer work on your problem for you. Finally, be prepared to discuss fees and to pay them. Your lawyer's services are valuable to you (how valuable you may never really know), and the protection offered you is one of the most valuable services you can consume.

Government Agencies. Certain government agencies in your state and city can give you direct legal aid when you need it. These agencies might include the office of the district attorney or the state's attorney, a department of insurance, a department of consumer frauds, and the department of banking. Check in your community to find out what kind of legal services are available through government organizations and officials.

Small Claims Courts

Much consumer fraud involves thousands of little claims involving amounts such as $10, $50, or $200. If a mechanic replaces a part incorrectly and the result is considerable damage to your car, what can you do when the mechanic won't take the blame but says that the car can be fixed for only $225? What remedy do you have when a dry-cleaning establishment ruins your dress and then refuses to replace it? When a large retail firm offers a fraction of what the warranty promises and tries to make you think you are lucky to get anything, what can you do? One remedy is to sue in a small claims court.

For many consumers, the law and the courts seem remote and priced too high for their relatively minor legal problems. In fact, the

Small claims courts give the ordinary person recourse to a court of law without great expense and inconvenience. (*Sylvia Johnson, Woodfin Camp & Associates*)

cost of our civil courts in terms of money, time, and inconvenience is usually high. For many consumers recourse to a court of law may be a mere theoretical right. But small claims courts are neither remote nor expensive. It is for giving the ordinary person "a day in court" in small matters otherwise not worth going to court for that these "people's" courts were started.

Small claims courts have a ceiling on claims—generally about $500. Their advantages include the relatively small fee (often $5) for the court services, the speed with which the case is heard, and the fact that there is no need to have a lawyer. In regular courts, the case may not be heard for months or years, while in small claims courts the waiting time may be just a few weeks. Small claims courts are quite informal. They are presided over by the same judges who handle cases in other courts, but in a small claims court the judge ordinarily dresses more informally and doesn't wear a robe. The consumer does not need a lawyer—in fact, some courts bar lawyers. The discussion of the case is informal and in easily understood language.

Some critics contend that small claims courts have deteriorated into little more than collectors courts for business firms. Such a development is unfortunate, and surely it is now time that people become more aware of the services that these courts can provide for consumers.

Checking Your Reading

1. Explain what is meant by a constitution.
2. What is the main function of the legislative branch of government?
3. Explain what is meant by case law.
4. Why do the regulations and rules of administrative agencies, such as the Federal Trade Commission, have the force of law? What is this law called?
5. What is a contract?
6. What are the two essential elements of a valid contract?
7. List three types of contracts that must be in writing to be legally binding.
8. Define a negotiable instrument. Give two examples of a negotiable instrument.
9. What term is used to refer to the person who writes a check? The person to whom the check is payable? The bank on which the check is written?
10. List four types of endorsements.
11. What is an express warranty?
12. Name four types of implied warranties.
13. Explain briefly the purpose of the Magnuson-Moss Warranty Act of 1975.
14. When goods are purchased "as is," what is the responsibility of the seller? The buyer?
15. List five situations that normally call for the advice of a legal expert.
16. Explain why small claims courts were started.

Consumer Problems and Projects

1. Write a report on the origin of the Constitution of the United States. Include in your report such things as the time at which the

convention was held, the names of the states appointing delegates, the number of delegates who signed the Constitution, and the dates that the various state conventions ratified the Constitution. Use library resources such as encyclopedias and almanacs to locate information for your report.

2. Make a list of the amendments to the Constitution of the United States from Amendment XI to the most recent. Indicate the date on which each amendment was ratified.

3. "Put it in writing" is the practice of many business people. Is this a sound practice? Is the extra work involved justified, or would an oral agreement be as satisfactory? Does this apply to most of the contracts we make each day? Explain your answer.

4. A minor is unable to make many contracts since, from a legal point of view, a minor is considered incompetent. Is this to the advantage of a minor? When is it disadvantageous to a minor? Is it fair that an adult must carry out the obligations in a contract even though the minor is not required to do so? Explain your answer.

5. Although a check is a substitute for money, it is *not* always as readily accepted. Describe the procedure that you would follow in order to make your check as acceptable as money.

6. Would you accept a negotiable instrument endorsed to you by a qualified endorsement? What is the legal effect of this endorsement?

7. If you received a large check with a blank endorsement, what could you do to decrease your risk in carrying it?

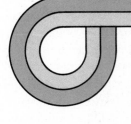

28

The Development of Consumer Protection

Concern with improving consumer protection has come in three waves. The present period of concern about protecting consumers follows two earlier ones—the early 1900s and the 1930s. The three periods have had several common features.

- In each period consumer prices, especially food prices, were increasing rapidly.
- In each period many consumers joined together and agreed they would not buy food items they thought were priced too high. These boycotts rapidly spread across the country.
- Consumers' concerns were increased by magazine and newspaper stories reporting the dangers of widely used food and drugs. These reports produced demands for new protective legislation.
- New consumer organizations developed to help consumers deal with their problems and voice their concerns.

All three periods occurred in times of widespread social unrest and economic difficulties. These social and economic problems led people to look critically at both business and government to see how well they were performing. In each period the public's concern with these problems, along with the pressure of rising prices on their purchasing power, caused them to look more carefully both at business's practices and the quality of its products.

ISSUES IN THE EARLY 1900s

The economic life of the country changed rapidly in the last 40 years of the nineteenth century. In 1860 most people lived in rural areas and were involved in farming. By the end of the century, 40 percent of the population lived in urban areas and most worked in industrial jobs. The population had doubled. A nationwide network of railroads had been completed. This made it possible for manufacturers to sell their products throughout the country. A few manufacturers recognized the opportunity. They gave their products brand names and began to advertise them in magazines, newspapers, and on signboards.

The rapid growth of cities and industry created a new set of problems for the nation. They were problems it had never been concerned about before: urban poverty, the growth of urban slums, dishonesty in city government, unsafe working conditions, jobs which took advantage of women and children with long hours at low pay, and a variety

Unsafe working conditions and jobs that took advantage of women and children were among the problems created by the rapid growth of cities and industry toward the end of the last century. (*UPI*)

of consumer problems. In about 1900 a new group of political reformers appeared which was concerned with these problems. These reformers, the Progressives, wanted to use the power of government to
bring about the social and economic reforms they felt were needed.

The increasing numbers of urban workers worked for wages. They
did not produce crops to sell, and only a few grew food for their own
use. Their economic welfare depended on the wages they and their
families were able to earn and on the prices they had to pay to get the
food, clothes, and other things they needed. Consumer prices had
fallen during the years after the Civil War. But in 1897 the money
supply began to increase, and this set off a long chain of increases in
consumer prices.

Workers were worried by the new price increases. Because of these
worries many joined the labor union movement, which grew rapidly.
With the help of their unions, many workers were able to improve
their wages and get ahead of inflation. For most people, the years at
the turn of the century were a time of comfort and prosperity. But
some who had fixed incomes, such as government employees and
clerical workers, suffered as rising prices cut their purchasing power.

The public blamed both the giant new corporations which were
growing up and the union movement for the price increases. The
growth of corporate *trusts* began to concern the public. The trusts
were groups of companies under the same central management which
controlled production and fixed prices. Newspaper and magazine investigations of the trusts increased the public's concern.

Magazine editors found that exposés on the trusts, dishonesty in
government, and unsafe products helped to sell magazines. A new
style of hard-hitting, investigative journalism was born. It soon got the
label "muckraking." Life insurance companies, railroads, and politi-
cians all were investigated by the "muckrakers," and the demands for
reform grew.

Early Antitrust Legislation

Toward the end of the nineteenth century, both the public and the
government began to realize that new rules were needed to control
business practices. Some companies were using unfair practices to
destroy their business competitors. Others were joining together in
agreements about how much they would produce so that they could
charge higher prices. Others made agreements about sales territories
which gave each company a territory of its own in which it would have

no competition. The businesses which used these practices hoped to reduce competition and get control of markets which they would keep all to themselves. Without any competition they would be free to raise prices as they chose. They would have the power which comes with being the only seller in a market, the power of a *monopoly*.

The first law regulating competitive practices was the Interstate Commerce Act of 1887. It set up a government commission to supervise the behavior of the railroads and the setting of rates. The passage of the ICC Act marked the beginning of government regulation of interstate commerce. It was followed in 1890 by the Sherman Antitrust Act. This act prohibited business combinations to fix prices and limit competition.

At the turn of the century, a new group of giant corporations were formed, including Standard Oil, United States Steel, General Electric, and American Telephone and Telegraph. These mergers led to new "trust-busting" action by the administrations of Theodore Roosevelt (1901–1909) and William Howard Taft (1909–1913). The Supreme Court order to split Standard Oil into a number of smaller companies, the breakup of the beef trust, and other antitrust action helped slow the growth of giant corporations.

During the administration of Woodrow Wilson (1913–1921), additional government machinery for controlling unfair business practices was created. The Clayton Antitrust Act of 1914 spelled out in more detail the specific practices that were considered in restraint of trade. The Federal Trade Commission Act of 1914 created the FTC. The act gave the FTC power to investigate unfair trade practices and to issue cease-and-desist orders to stop unfair practices and violations of antitrust laws. In its early years the chief concern of the FTC was protecting business firms by maintaining competition rather than protecting consumers.

Purity and Safety of Food and Drugs

In the early days of our country, many food products were *adulterated*, that is, cheap ingredients were mixed in to replace the ones which were supposed to be there. Tea was adulterated with ground-up leaves, and lard was added to butter. Products often were unsanitary or unsafe. The food-processing industry was new and had little idea about the dangers of some of the chemicals they used to preserve and color food. Copper salts were added to canned peas to dye them to a fresh shade of green. Formaldehyde, a poisonous chemical used to preserve specimens in biology labs, was added to canned meat to keep it from spoiling.

The development of the nationwide rail network and refrigerated cars opened a national market to the food processors and meat packers. Unsanitary conditions, unsafe additives and preservatives, and adulteration became less and less acceptable to the public as they came to depend on store-bought processed foods. Beginning in the 1890s, a number of attempts were made to get a federal pure food and drug law. Muckraking journalists, women's groups, and concerned food chemists worked hard to get a law passed, but had no success.

A Pure Food and Drug Act was finally passed in 1906, after a scandal created by Upton Sinclair's book *The Jungle*. The book gave a sickening picture of conditions in Chicago's meat-packing plants. The public and President Theodore Roosevelt demanded that Congress take action. The meat-packing industry ended its opposition when it realized government inspection was the only way to restore the public's confidence in its product. Earlier bills had been opposed by business and by those concerned about increasing the power of the federal government. The new legislation was a milestone in consumer protection. It firmly established the federal government in the role of regulating the safety and purity of consumer products.

The battle with the trusts, the fight for pure food and drugs, and the increasing volume of advertising all helped to make the public more aware of their interests as consumers. The public began to realize their interests as consumers were separate from their interests as workers or as business people. The growth of this idea among consumers was another of the important results of the first wave of concern about consumer protection.

ISSUES OF THE 1930s

World War I and the prosperity of the 1920s shifted the public's attention away from consumer issues. The good times of the 1920s were not, however, without their problems. Consumers were faced with the problem of choosing such new and unfamiliar products as radios, refrigerators, vacuum cleaners, and automobiles. To influence them, advertisers began to put ads everywhere—in magazines and newspapers, on billboards and electric signs, and on the new medium of radio. Some people began to wonder whether consumers who were bombarded by ads could make good decisions. Their concerns were expressed in a book published in 1927 by Stuart Chase and F. J. Schlink.

MECHANICAL EXERCISE—A MEANS OF CURE.

RHEUMATISM, STIFF JOINTS, SCIATICA, LUMBAGO, PARTIAL PARALYSIS, SPINAL CURVATURE, FEEBLE CIRCULATION, CONSTIPATION, CORPULENCE, &c.

ALSO USEFUL IN PROMOTING THE PHYSICAL DEVELOPMENT OF YOUNG PEOPLE AND CHILDREN.

PROVIDES AN AGREEABLE EXERCISE WITHOUT FATIGUE FOR THOSE LEADING SEDENTARY LIVES.

UPWARDS OF 400 PATIENTS TREATED LAST YEAR, ON THE RECOMMENDATION OF THE LEADING PHYSICIANS AND SURGEONS, BOTH IN LONDON AND THE PROVINCES.

HOURS:

GENTLEMEN, 8 to 10.30 a.m.; 3.30 to 7 p.m.

LADIES, 11 a.m. to 2.30 p.m.

INSPECTION OF THE MACHINES FREE, AND INVITED.

The above Engraving represents one of the Fifty Machines in use at the Institution, and is of great value in cases of Stiffness and Loss of Power at the Shoulder Joints.

ZANDER INSTITUTION, 7, SOHO SQUARE, W.C.

Inflated advertising claims and other advertising abuses were among the factors leading to the formation of Consumers' Research, Inc., the first consumer-supported product-testing organization, in 1929.

The book, entitled *Your Money's Worth: A Study in the Waste of the Consumer's Dollar*, attacked advertising and high-pressure sales tactics. It called for scientific testing and product standards to give consumers the information they needed. The idea won widespread support and led to the founding of Consumers' Research, Inc., the first consumer-supported product-testing organization, in 1929.

With the Depression of the 1930s consumers again became concerned with their problems as consumers. Even those who still had jobs often had to adjust to income cuts. Consumers were forced to consider the problem of spending wisely more carefully than they ever had before. Public attention also focused on the economic system. The public wanted to know what had happened to the economy and why.

Although the public was not very concerned with consumer problems in the 1920s, educators began to recognize the need for educating consumers. Home economists began to give more attention to research on the economic problems of families to get the information they needed to improve teaching. Other educators used new scientific findings on food, clothing, and housing needs to develop plans for consumer education programs.

The Depression gave a new importance to consumer problems, and consumer education topics found their way into the schools for the first time. Emphasis was given to ways to identify the best buys and careful money management. Students were taught to "use it up, wear it out, make it do, or do without." Classes practiced making their own toothpaste and face creams as a way to save money. Budgeting was studied as a way to cut expenses, rather than as a way to plan spending to get the things wanted most.

Product Testing

During the Depression the problems of consumers were made worse by the appearance of a flood of poor-quality products at bargain prices. In the early 1930s real bargains were offered by merchants who were in financial difficulty. As these supplies were sold, they were replaced with low-quality products which took advantage of the belief that real bargains were still available. These false bargains in shoes, clothing, and sheets wore out quickly. This created new support for the testing and grade labeling of consumer products. The demand for product information brought Consumers' Research and its offshoot, Consumers Union (CU), into their own. In addition to product testing, Consumers Union concerned itself with a wide variety of issues affecting consumers. With the founding of CU, the consumer movement had its first solid organizational base. CU helped provide leadership, staff, and money for the fight for consumer protection.

The reports of CU and CR stripped away inflated advertising claims and gave consumers the facts they needed. For the first time consumers had their own source of information and no longer had to depend only on what manufacturers told them.

Antitrust Action

During the 1920s and 1930s large corporations continued to grow at the expense of smaller firms. In the 1920s the larger firms had found it easier to get the money needed to expand and to develop and market new products. The Depression destroyed many smaller firms and strengthened the position of the large ones.

In the early years of Franklin Roosevelt's New Deal, efforts were made to discourage excessive competition and price cutting. It was felt they could slow economic recovery. By 1938 government officials had decided that more competition would be desirable. Congress investigated monopoly problems and the Antitrust Division of the Justice Department stepped up its activities. Little real progress was made, and with the beginning of World War II, antitrust activity slowed.

The main result of the new interest in antitrust action was to strengthen the powers of the Federal Trade Commission. In its early years the FTC could act only when a business was injuring a competitor by using unfair business practices. With the Wheeler-Lea amendment to the FTC Act in 1938, the FTC was given power to deal with cases in which unfair practices injured consumers. It also was given power to act against false advertising of food, drugs, and cosmetics.

Consumer Representation in Government

Consumer interests gained representation in a major government agency for the first time in the 1930s. This came about when a Consumer Advisory Board was appointed in the National Recovery Administration (NRA), the government agency set up to coordinate economic recovery efforts. The board found its role difficult, however. General Hugh Johnson and the other NRA officials saw no need for the board. They argued that the consumer interest was the public interest and that they represented the public interest. The board countered with the argument that consumers, workers, and sellers each have separate interests and that the public interest is the balancing of these different interests. This argument provided a logical basis for consumer representation in government.

Modernizing the Pure Food and Drug Act

The need for revising the Pure Food and Drug Act was widely recognized by the early 1930s. The old law had been weakened by court decisions and outdated by new technology. The New Deal administration offered a new bill that would have given the government many new powers, including controls over labeling and advertising. The new bill also proposed placing cosmetics under Food and Drug Administration (FDA) regulation and requiring the labeling of foods with quality grades. The need for new legislation was dramatized in a series of exposé books. The first, *100,000,000 Guinea Pigs* (100 million was the size of the United States population at that time), was a bitter report on dangerous products and on advertising and wasteful increases in the number of brands. Another, *The American Chamber of Horrors*, illustrated the need for new legislation with reports of injuries and deaths resulting from unsafe products.

There was strong opposition to the proposed bill, especially to the portions regulating advertising and calling for the creation of a grade-labeling system for food. A new law was finally passed after a tragedy created public demand for action. In 1937 a liquid form of a new sulfa "wonder drug" was placed on the market without testing. Although the drug was safe in capsule form, its liquid form, elixir sulfanilamide, was deadly. Over 100 people died after taking it.

The new law passed in 1938 extended FDA control to cosmetics and required that safety be tested and established before a product was offered on the market. The new law updated the government's regulatory efforts and brought them into line with advances in technology. Advertising controls were established, but responsibility for enforcing them was given to the FTC instead of to the FDA. The failure of the proposals for strong controls over labeling and the creation of a system for grade labeling was, however, a disappointing defeat for the idea of the consumer's right to product information. The 1930s showed again that major new consumer legislation often comes only after tragedy or scandal dramatizes the need for more consumer protection.

RECENT ISSUES

President Kennedy often is credited with beginning the present period of concern with consumer protection with his 1962 Consumer Message to Congress. In it he set forth a consumer bill of rights:

- The right to choose among a variety of products
- The right to be informed
- The right to safety
- The right to be heard through representation in government

Because of international crises, the problems of recession and inflation at home, and congressional resistance, the Kennedy administration had only limited success in getting passage of the legislation that had been outlined in the Consumer Message of 1962.

Early in his administration, Lyndon Johnson recognized that increasing public and congressional interest in consumer problems had improved the possibilities for passing legislation. He offered his own program in February 1964 in a consumer message to Congress urging passage of 12 new laws. President Johnson did not, however, push his program strongly, and there was little action on it.

In 1966 the pressure of rising food prices increased consumer unrest. After a gradual increase in the early 1960s, food prices jumped 5 percent in 1966. In October supermarket boycotts spread throughout the country. At about this same time, President Johnson began to push his consumer legislation proposals harder. One of the appealing features of his program was that it offered important reforms that cost relatively little. This was an important consideration because of the rapidly increasing costs of the Vietnam war. As a result of Presidential interest and support, a number of new bills were passed in 1966. Their passage created a momentum that continued into the early 1970s.

The Consumer Advisory Council

To implement the fourth right of his consumer message, the right to be heard, President Kennedy asked the Council of Economic Advisers to appoint a Consumer Advisory Council. Although the functions of the council were strictly advisory, the consumer interest never before had been represented at so high a level of government. In its first report the council recommended that the President appoint a special advisor on consumer affairs to his staff.

President Johnson acted on this recommendation, and in early 1964 he appointed Esther Peterson as Special Assistant to the President for Consumer Affairs. This action brought a consumer representative into the highest levels of government. Esther Peterson was followed in this post by Betty Furness and Virginia Knauer. In 1977 President Carter appointed Esther Peterson to the job again. The Special Assistants for Consumers Affairs have headed the Office of Consumer Affairs and have performed a variety of duties. They have advised the President about consumer problems and on new legislation affecting the consumer. They have testified before congressional committees on the need for new legislation and have rallied support for bills offered by the administration. They have also developed consumer education materials and advised schools on consumer education programs. In addition, they have assisted in the organization and development of state and local consumer organizations throughout the country.

As Special Assistant to the President for Consumer Affairs, Mrs. Esther Peterson is a voice for the consumer at the highest levels of government. Her duties include advising the President, testifying before congressional committees, and working with consumer organizations throughout the country. (*Dennis Brack, Black Star*)

Product Safety

The regulation of food and drugs was one of the areas singled out by President Kennedy for special attention in his 1962 consumer message. The weaknesses of the existing laws in ensuring that drugs on the market were both effective and safe had become clear during hearings on the regulation of the drug industry. The new legislation was passed only after news of the tragic affects of a new sleep-inducing drug in parts of Europe forced action upon Congress. It was learned that this drug, called thalidomide, could cause malformation in babies whose mothers had used it during the early months of pregnancy. Word of the thalidomide case reached the public in June. By August 1962, legislation expanding the powers of the FDA had been passed and signed into law.

After President Johnson's landslide election in 1964, more new consumer legislation seemed likely. In 1965 hearings began on tire and auto safety. As the auto-safety hearings went on, attention shifted from the manufacturer's responsibilities for auto safety to the driver's.

This view was challenged a few months later when Ralph Nader's book *Unsafe at Any Speed* appeared. In it Nader presented evidence of the role of faulty engineering, construction, and design in auto accidents and injuries. Public concern mounted, and in his State of the Union message in January 1966, President Johnson promised new legislation.

New hearings on the administration's proposed Highway Safety Act began in March 1966, with Ralph Nader as a key witness. When news broke that General Motors had hired investigators to check Nader's background and habits, members of Congress became angry. They felt General Motors was interfering with a congressional witness. The auto-safety bill passed later that year was far stronger than the original one proposed. The auto-safety hearings brought Ralph Nader onto the national scene for the first time and firmly established his position as a spokesperson for consumers.

After the auto-safety bill was passed, Nader focused his attention on the National Highway Safety Bureau, which the bill created. Later that year he helped lead a campaign for stricter inspection in meat-packing plants which sold meat only within state lines. In late 1967 a new law was passed which extended federal inspection standards to intrastate plants. Nader then turned his attention to other safety issues—gas pipeline safety, radiation hazards, and poultry inspection.

In the late 1960s people became aware of the dangers of other consumer products. They were concerned about accidental poisonings of children who had swallowed household cleaners. They were worried about unsafe toys and dangerously designed cribs. They were concerned about injuries and accidents to older children and adults too. They were aware that clothing which met the government standards on flammable fabrics could burn dangerously and result in painful or even fatal burns. They knew many people were injured by walking into glass doors they had not seen. Concerned members of Congress knew that the government's product safety rules were a "patchwork" which left many problem areas uncovered. In 1967 a study commission was set up to investigate the problem and possible remedies. The result was the creation of the Consumer Product Safety Commission. The new commission, which began operation in 1973, was given responsibility for most of the existing safety programs except those for food, drugs and cosmetics. It also was given broad responsibilities for making consumer products safer and power to ban any products which it judged to carry unreasonable risks.

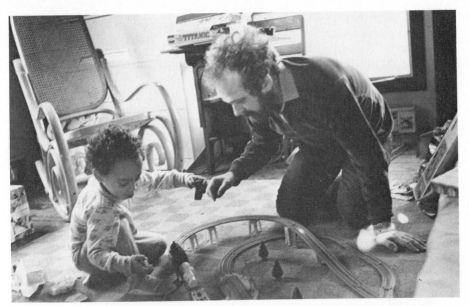

Unsafe toys and other consumer products dangerous to children and adults became a focus of concern in the late 1960s, resulting in the creation of the Consumer Product Safety Commission in 1973. (*Helena Frost*)

The Formation of Consumer Organizations

Nader's independent operating style and the air of mystery which surrounded him led him to be called "the Lone Ranger of the consumer movement." In about 1968 Nader decided to expand his one-person operation in order to attack more problems. His first step was to organize a group of law students to investigate the Federal Trade Commission. It had become clear that new laws were not enough; strong enforcement by the government agencies responsible also was essential. The FTC investigation was followed by investigations of the Interstate Commerce Commission and the Food and Drug Administration. The law student investigators were hard-working and hard-hitting. They soon got the nickname "Nader's Raiders," and their study results got wide attention.

Nader and other consumer activists recognized that investigations by themselves would not win the reforms they wanted. Other kinds of action were needed. The result was the creation of a new public role—the *public interest lawyer*. Public interest lawyers' chief concern is to protect the public and its rights rather than to make profits for themselves. In doing this, they engage in a variety of activities:

- Investigating suspected violations
- Publicizing conclusions about needed reforms in news conferences, press releases, and speeches
- Petitioning government agencies to take action on problems.
- Undertaking lawsuits against government agencies and private firms
- Organizing citizen groups to support needed legislation
- Lobbying legislators to win their support for legislation
- Testifying before Congress in support of legislation

In 1971 Nader organized Public Citizen Inc. to carry on these activities and to solicit money from the public to support them. It has worked on such issues as energy policy, antitrust regulation, tax reform, and the creation of an Agency for Consumer Advocacy.

The muckrakers of the early 1900s and the authors of the exposé books of the 1930s hoped to get reform by calling the public's attention to the problems they wrote about. The public interest lawyers of recent years have gone further. They have proposed legislation, pressured for its passage, and watched its enforcement carefully. As a result, the public interest lawyers have had a great deal more impact than many earlier reformers.

During the 1960s consumers' associations were organized in most states and in a number of major cities. These organizations developed information on local and state problems and lobbied for new protective legislation. In addition, some pressured merchants they felt were abusing consumers. In 1967 a national organization was formed to bring the state associations and other groups with consumer interests together under one roof. The organization, the Consumer Federation of America, is a national federation of over 200 organizations. Besides the state and local consumer associations, it includes rural electrical co-ops, credit union leagues, labor unions, and other groups with consumer interests, such as the National Council of Senior Citizens. It lobbies in support of consumer legislation and has been active in supporting the creation of an agency for consumer protection. The organization also is involved in fact-finding and the analysis of such issues as energy policy. It also provides an information clearinghouse on the activities of the state and local consumer associations.

Growing Interest in Consumer Redress

During the 1960s it became clear that consumers had another serious problem which had not been fully recognized before. It was the problem of having their complaints heard and having their difficulties set right—the problem of *redress*. President Nixon recognized the importance of the problem when he included it in a "Buyer's Bill of Rights" which was part of his 1969 Consumer Message to Congress. In it he said, "the buyer has the right to register his dissatisfaction and have his complaint heard and weighed, when his interests are badly served." Businesses which recognized the problem moved to improve their handling of complaints. They set up "hot lines" and consumer service offices to receive complaints and tried to make complaint-handling procedures faster, fairer, and more systematic.

Consumers, as individuals and groups, increasingly have used legal action as a way to get redress. One of the techniques used has been to join together in a *class action*. This is a suit brought by a group of individuals who all have the same problem or complaint and who have joined together as a class to sue a firm or government agency. Class actions have been used by groups of consumers only in recent years. They have been used in cases in which large numbers of consumers have suffered small losses in dealing with the same company. No one consumer could afford legal action because one person's losses usually are too small. But when they join together, legal action becomes possible. For example, a group of consumers who have been overcharged by a drug company which illegally joined with other companies to fix prices can join together to get back the overcharges. Federal court rules have discouraged suits in federal courts. As a result, consumer class actions usually are brought in state courts. Congress has considered several bills which would have made it easier for consumers to bring class actions. Although none have been passed, class actions have become an important tool for consumers seeking redress.

Another important improvement in consumer redress in recent years has been the stepped-up activity of consumer fraud bureaus within the state attorney generals' offices. These agencies have worked both to educate consumers about fraud schemes and to help them with complaints. Telephone hot lines and branch offices have been set up to make it easier for consumers to contact the agencies. Some of the agencies focus chiefly on helping individual consumers get their money back or get contracts canceled. Others put more emphasis on getting businesses to discontinue practices which are considered deceptive and pay less attention to the problems of any one individual. In both cases, the consumer fraud bureaus provide an important avenue of redress for consumers.

New Emphasis on Consumer Information and Education

Important gains have been made in getting recognition of consumers' rights to information. The Truth in Lending Act (1968) forces lenders to spell out credit costs in such a way that interest rates can be compared more easily. The Truth-in-Packaging law (1966) resulted in better label information and an attempt to reduce the number of different package sizes to simplify shopping.

Government as well as business has been forced to provide more information. Under the Freedom of Information Act, the government has been forced to release the results of product tests made by government agencies. The results of product tests by the National Bureau of Standards and the General Services Administration have been adapted and published for use by consumers.

In the early and mid-1960s a new surge of interest in consumer education occurred. Educators and the public both came to recognize that consumer education is an important and useful subject for all students, college-bound and vocational, men and women alike. In a number of states, laws were passed requiring consumer education courses in the schools. Consumer education, with its real-life problems, was found to be a useful way to arouse interest in topics in English, math, social studies, and science. The new curricula continued to stress both buyer techniques and money management and also gave new emphasis to the problems and uses of installment credit. New emphasis was also given to the idea that one's spending should reflect personal goals rather than someone else's idea of a good budget.

CONSUMER PROTECTION: A CONTINUING PROBLEM

It seems clear that consumer protection is likely to be a continuing issue in this country. This seems likely because of the consumer problems which continue to arise out of three areas:

- Unwise uses of new technology that result in unsafe products
- Changing ideas about the social responsibilities of business
- The operations of a dishonest fringe of the business community and lapses by some of those in it

There is little reason to believe any of these problem areas will ever disappear completely.

The history of consumer protection shows that new technology often has been used without full understanding or concern about its dangers. The automobile had been around for 70 years before Ralph Nader got the public to recognize that autos included unsafe design features and sometimes were poorly engineered. Although the dangers of unwisely used new technology have been most dramatic in the area of food and drugs, new legislation to control these dangers has come only after scandals and tragedy have focused public opinion on the problems. Legislation often has come long after the problems were first recognized.

Consumers no longer judge business on its products alone but also on the social costs of producing them. The public's ideas of what constitutes a social cost have evolved rapidly in the past 70 years. The passage of the Pure Food and Drug Act and the Meat Inspection amendment in 1906 was a recognition of the social costs of injurious drugs and adulterated food. In the early 1900s the public came to recognize that unsafe working conditions, long hours, and the ex-

The automobile was around for 70 years before Ralph Nader brought the attention of the consumer public to the role of faulty engineering and design in auto accidents, resulting in the auto safety bill of 1966. (*UPI*)

ploitation of child and female labor also have social costs. Gradually the public view expanded again to include air pollution and water pollution as social costs. Now new factors which may seem even less tangible are coming to be regarded as social costs. These include discriminatory hiring practices and unfair treatment of less educated and low-income consumers.

Checking Your Reading

1. What features do the three periods of concern about consumer protection have in common?
2. What do we mean when we speak of a corporate or business "trust"? Why did the public feel it was necessary for the government to regulate trusts?
3. What events led up to the passage of our first federal pure food and drug law? Why was its passage considered a milestone?
4. What important service have Consumers' Research and Consumers Union provided consumers?
5. How did the Wheeler-Lea Act expand the power of the FTC?
6. When did consumer interests first win representation in a major government agency? In what agency?
7. What are the four points in President Kennedy's consumer bill of rights?
8. How did Ralph Nader first become established as a spokesperson for consumers?
9. What are public interest lawyers? What do they do?
10. When was the Consumer Federation of America organized? What are the activities of the organization?
11. How can consumers use consumer class actions to gain redress?
12. What is meant by the "social cost" of producing a product?

Consumer Problems and Projects

1. How do you feel consumer interests can best be protected? With consumer information and education? With new protective laws? With stricter enforcement of existing laws? By making it easier for consumers to seek redress? By organization of consumer

groups? What are the strengths and weaknesses of each of these approaches?

2. What are some of the consumer protection issues which are important currently? Select one and prepare a report on it. Your report should answer the following questions: What is the problem? What remedies have been suggested? What arguments have been offered for and against these proposals? Who will benefit? Who will have to bear the costs? The *Readers' Guide to Periodical Literature* will help you locate useful articles on your problem. The decision-making process outlined in Chapter 2 will help you organize your report.

3. Read one of the books which has had an important effect on the development of consumer protection and prepare a report on it. Evaluate the evidence presented and the conclusions reached. What effect did the book have? What information can you find about criticisms made of the book? You may choose one of the books mentioned in this chapter or select another one with the approval of your teacher.

4. Prepare a brief report on an individual, group, or law which has been important in the development of consumer protection. Some possible topics are listed below.

The Muckrakers	Federal Meat Inspection Program
Ralph Nader	Consumers Union
Pure Food and Drug Act	Consumer Class Actions
Antitrust Laws	

There are a number of individuals and groups which were not included in this chapter. You may wish to investigate one of them.

Rachel Carson	National Consumers League
Dr. Harvey Wiley	Florence Kelley

5. Prepare a paper supporting or opposing some consumer protection proposal about which you feel strongly. What evidence can you offer to back your arguments? Draft a letter to the editor or to a legislator outlining your views.

6. Draw up your own list of consumers' rights and responsibilities. What rights do you feel consumers should have? What responsibilities?

29

Sources of Assistance for Consumers

In the last few years we have heard a great deal about consumer problems and complaints. When consumers complain to government and business, what kinds of things do they complain about? The lists of consumer complaints received differ among agencies, but these are some of the problems that appear most often:

- Unsatisfactory repairs and service—poor construction, excessive charges, and difficulties in obtaining spare parts, especially for automobiles, appliances, and televisions
- Defective merchandise, especially automobiles and appliances
- Misleading packaging, labeling, and advertising
- Merchandise that was ordered, paid for, and never received
- Computerized billings, including complaints about the procedures for calculating interest charges and errors in billing
- Warranty problems—difficulties in obtaining repairs promised and disagreements about who is responsible for paying for them under the terms of the warranty

The reason automobiles and appliances are a frequent subject of complaint is that they are expensive items and difficulties with them usually involve major financial losses. Some reports of consumer problems also indicate complaints about purchases from door-to-door salespeople that seem out of proportion to the number of purchases most of us make this way.

COMPLAINING TO GET RESULTS

Consumers who feel a particular firm has not treated them fairly may be torn between a desire for revenge and the hope that by making a complaint they can get better treatment. Seeking revenge is certain to create even more problems and do little to correct the original situation. What is needed is a cool head and an organized plan for remedying the problem.

When Should You Complain?

You should consider making a complaint whenever you feel a product does not live up to claims or reasonable expectations. If there has been a mistake or a misunderstanding, the honest and reputable firm will want to know about it. In a real sense, you are helping them when you call a problem to their attention. Reliable dealers and manufacturers want to know about problems customers experience with their products and want to keep their customers satisfied. When you complain to less careful or less honest merchants, you are also performing a service. Your complaint will help to convince them that they cannot afford to mistreat customers.

Before making a complaint, it is wise to check over product use and care instructions. This may save you time, embarrassment, and money. A review of the instructions may eliminate the need for returning the product or a service call. Check the warranty too. Is it still in effect? Does it cover the problem?

To Whom Should You Complain First?

The firm from whom you made your purchase is the best place to turn first. If the company is in your local area, it usually is easier to reach than most other sources of help. Also, other sources of help expect consumers to try to help themselves by first going directly to the merchant from whom the purchase was made. You should make an effort to make your complaint promptly. Stores are more likely to act on problems with recently purchased items.

Before going to the store, think carefully about what is bothering

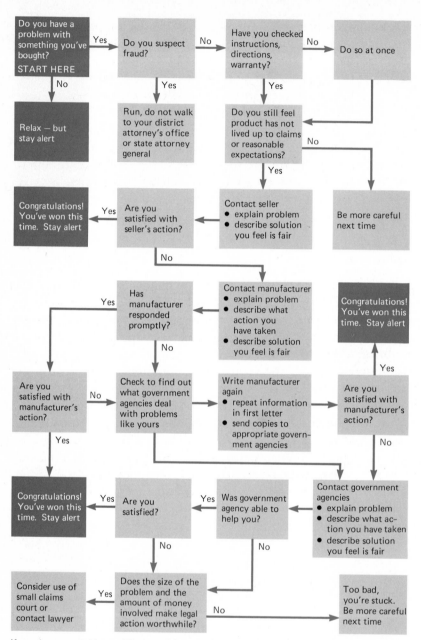

If you have a problem with something you bought, there are a number of things you can do to get the problem corrected.

you and what you plan to ask them to do. What is the problem? Can you give a description of what is wrong? What would you like done about the problem? Do you want a refund or do you want to exchange the item? Or do you want a replacement or repairs? Next you should assemble your receipts and records relating to the purchase. It is also helpful to have the original package, tags, and so forth, if the item is a new one.

Find out who in the store you should speak to about your problem, then state your case. Be fair and reasonable, but do not be timid. If the item is left for repairs or for a refund, be sure to get a receipt for it. If you are not satisfied with the results you get, contact the owner or manager, either in person or by letter.

What Do You Do Next?

If the store cannot or will not help you, you should consider complaining to the manufacturer. This is especially appropriate if the problem concerns defects in the product, problems in getting repairs, or disagreements over warranty terms. Reliable manufacturers want to know about customers' problems in getting service in stores that sell their product.

Most products now carry the name of the manufacturer and their address and ZIP Code. It may speed things up somewhat to write directly to the appropriate official or department. The names of company officers and their addresses are available in business directories that are available in most local libraries. One standard reference is *Standard & Poor's Register of Corporations, Directors and Executives,* which is published annually. If you cannot find it, ask the librarian for other references. If you do not direct your letter to a particular company officer, send it to the "Consumer Service Department."

What should you include in your letter? Here are some suggestions:

- A clear statement of your problem, along with a description of the item, including model and serial numbers and the date and place of purchase.
- A description of what steps you already have taken to solve your problem, including contacts with the store which sold you the item.
- A statement of the remedy you believe would be fair. This may include refund, repair, or replacement. You may also want to ask to be paid for your extra expenses or inconvenience.

- Photocopies of receipts, and canceled checks if appropriate. Keep the originals for your records.
- Your name, address, and phone number. (This information is too often forgotten.)

Your letter should be neat, easy-to-read, and typewritten if possible. Be sure to save a copy in case future correspondence is necessary. One advantage of putting your complaint in letter form is that it gives you a record for future use.

If you return an item, be sure to insure it. If you would like a postcard receipt as a record that it was received, the service costs only a small fee.

Allow two to three weeks for a reply to your letter. Most major companies have special departments to handle customers' problems more quickly. In large firms these departments have to handle as many as 1000 letters a week, so you may need to be patient.

If your problem is a result of misleading advertising or claims about a product, your best second step probably is not a letter to the manufacturer. In such cases, a call to your local better business bureau or chamber of commerce is more appropriate. If you suspect out-and-out fraud, contact local law enforcement officials.

What Stronger Measures Should You Take?

If you have had no action on your letter within a month, you probably will want to consider some stronger measures. The next step involves a second letter, but this time copies should be sent to a number of government and business agencies that are concerned about consumer problems.

Your second letter should restate your problem and point out that your earlier letter, of such and such a date, has not been answered. In the letter list the agencies to whom you are sending copies. These could include one or more of the following:

- Office of Consumer Affairs (OCA) in the Department of Health, Education, and Welfare
- U.S. Federal Trade Commission
- U.S. Consumer Product Safety Commission
- U.S. Postal Service
- U.S. Food and Drug Administration
- Office of your state's attorney general
- Local law enforcement officials
- Appropriate business trade associations such as the National Automobile Dealers Association, Grocery Manufacturers of Amer-

ica, Association of Home Appliance Manufacturers, Gas Appliance Manufacturers of America, American Movers Conference, and the Mobile Homes Manufacturers Association
- Your senators and representatives in Congress

We will discuss the kind of help that some of these officials and agencies can give in the following section. While some of these agencies can handle a wide variety of problems, others can provide help only on certain special kinds of problems.

AGENCIES THAT ASSIST CONSUMERS

If the store and the manufacturer involved fail to solve your problem, there are additional sources of help to which you can turn. Some of these sources were mentioned briefly in the section on how to make complaints. The kinds of problems with which each agency deals are set by law or the rules of the organization. A clearer understanding of who can provide help will aid you in reaching the best source more quickly.

You must be prepared to be told your complaint is unjustified. Some consumers are unreasonable; some misunderstand what was told them; and some are too impatient about deliveries. Some are dishonest and try to take advantage of firms' desire to please their customers. If you double-check all the details about your purchase before you complain, you can be more certain of avoiding the embarrassment of being told your complaint has no basis.

Better Business Bureau

The agency that most consumers with problems think of first is the Better Business Bureau (BBB). We discussed the information and education activities of the better business bureaus in Chapter 5. Another important role of the better business bureaus is handling complaints. The bureaus handle complaints free, but insist that they be submitted in writing. Usually a standard form is provided for this purpose. This helps better business bureau staffs to be certain they have the facts straight before they begin action on a problem.

The consumer with a problem should understand the particular types of problems with which the better business bureaus will deal. Their chief concern is in working out misunderstandings and disagreements arising from misleading advertising and misrepresentation. This is the purpose for which they originally were founded. The bureaus will not handle complaints about unsatisfactory merchandise in cases where misleading advertising or misrepresentation is not involved. They refuse to pass judgment on the quality of goods or services or on the fairness of the prices charged for them. They also refuse to give legal advice and will not handle cases involving disagreements over the terms of the contracts.

After receiving a complaint in writing, the BBB sends a copy of it to the company involved. It asks the company to investigate the problem and to attempt to solve it. Most companies contact the consumer and try to reach an agreement. Some companies ignore the BBB's requests. When this happens, the BBB will suggest other sources of assistance or legal action. BBBs have no power to force a company to do anything. Companies who are members of a BBB may be criticized if they fail to settle too many complaints and may even be expelled. BBBs have had little or no control over nonmember companies.

We discussed some of the problems in the performance of local better business bureaus in Chapter 5. Even though some local organizations are perhaps not all they could or should be, the better business bureaus are one of the few local sources of help for consumers. Because of the bureaus' long experience and their recent efforts to improve their services, consumers with problems relating to misleading advertising and product claims should turn first to their local better business bureau. Most smaller towns and cities do not have them. In many cases, local chambers of commerce perform the same types of service for consumers, with the same types of rules.

Office of Consumer Affairs (OCA)

This office is part of the Department of Health, Education, and Welfare and is located in Washington, D.C. The OCA has no power of its own to use in resolving consumer complaints. Instead, it works through the agencies in whose jurisdiction problems fall. When the OCA receives consumer complaints, it may also contact the company involved directly. Many complaints have been resolved in this way. All consumer letters are acknowledged. Each complaint writer is sent a letter which tells what action the OCA has taken, and a carbon copy of the letter is sent to the company involved.

Letters concerning problems may be sent to the Office of Consumer Correspondence, Office of Consumer Affairs, Washington, D.C. 20201.

Federal Trade Commission

Consumer problems arising from misleading advertising and illegal business practices fall under the jurisdiction of the Federal Trade Commission. Some typical problems include:

- Deceptive pricing claims—for example, the advertisement of "Brand X Pens—Retail Value $15, Our Price $7.50," when the stores in the area are in fact charging only $10 for brand X pens
- Deceptive guarantees—for example, advertising a battery as guaranteed for 36 months when it normally could be expected to last for only 18 months
- Deceptive information about credit charges and abusive debt-collection practices

The FTC has new powers given it in 1975 to seek redress for certain types of problems. These powers probably would not be used to help an individual consumer with a special problem. They would, however, permit the FTC to go to court to seek redress for groups of consumers with a similar problem. It should be recognized that most of the FTC's efforts are focused on stopping companies who are using unfair or deceptive practices, rather than on helping individual consumers. The FTC, in effect, concentrates on "locking the barn door before more horses are stolen."

The FTC now maintains consumer protection specialists in its regional offices throughout the country to assist consumers in making complaints. Both the main FTC offices in Washington and the regional offices serve as clearinghouses for consumer complaints. When a problem falls outside the jurisdiction of the FTC, they will forward the problem to the appropriate agency.

Complaints for the FTC may be made through its regional offices or sent to its Washington office, Secretary, Federal Trade Commission, Washington, D.C. 20580.

Consumer Product Safety Commission

The Consumer Product Safety Commission (CPSC) deals with complaints about the safety of most consumer products. Food, drugs, and cosmetics are handled by the Food and Drug Administration. Problems with automobile safety are handled by the National Highway Traffic Safety Administration. Products under CPSC's jurisdiction include toys, flammable fabrics, bicycles, and power lawn mowers. The CPSC receives complaints about safety problems and product-related

Safety problems with many products, including bicycles, toys, flammable fabrics, and power lawn mowers, can be reported to the Consumer Product Safety Commission over a free nationwide "hotline." (*Art Zollo*)

injuries over a free, nationwide telephone "hot line." It also provides answers to questions about product safety over the hot line.

Complaints about the safety of a product are followed up by an investigation. If the commission decides the product is a serious hazard, the manufacturer is informed. The manufacturer is expected to notify purchasers of the product, either by mail or with radio and TV ads. Manufacturers are required to correct the problem by either repairing or replacing the product or by taking it off the market and making refunds to those who purchased it.

The CPSC can be contacted over its toll-free hot line: dial (800) 638-2666, in Maryland dial (800) 492-2937. The CPSC also can be contacted through its area offices in major cities or in Washington: Bureau of Information and Education, Consumer Product Safety Commission, Washington, D.C. 20207.

U.S. Postal Service

The postal inspectors of the U.S. Postal Service want to know about all kinds of fraudulent schemes involving use of the mails. The Postal

Inspection Service has successfully combatted ads for "King-Sized Western Estates" that turned out to be in the middle of the desert and miles from town. They have also staged successful crackdowns on fake contests used to lure the so-called "winners" into making purchases. For example, one promoter who used this scheme informed "winners" that they had won a new sewing machine. All they had to do to get the machine, the promoter said, was to buy a cabinet for it. On investigation, the price charged for the cabinet was more than the usual price of the sewing machine and the cabinet together.

While the Postal Inspection Service has been successful in fighting outright fraud, it has had less success in dealing with mail-order operators responsible for a leading consumer complaint—failure to receive merchandise that has been ordered and paid for. One of the problems seems to be that under existing law it must be proved that the firm knowingly made false claims. Mail-order operators can avoid prosecution by sending out some orders and pocketing the money for others. If questions arise, they can claim a "mistake" had been made.

The Postal Service also has the power to return to the senders all

Failure to receive mail-order merchandise that has been paid for is a leading consumer complaint. Under existing law, however, the Postal Inspection Service must prove that the firm knowingly made false claims before it can take action. (*Kip Peticolas*)

mail addressed to a promoter of a scheme judged to be deceptive. These "mail blocks" have been useful in protecting consumers.

The Postal Inspection Service has had a record of some success in obtaining refunds for consumers. It makes informal inquiries by phone and letter in behalf of consumers and is reported to have had good results. It does not, however, have any legal power to force companies to make refunds. Postal inspectors are stationed in most major cities and can be contacted through your local postmaster.

Other Federal Agencies

The federal agencies we have mentioned are not the only ones which can help consumers obtain redress. The National Highway Traffic Safety Administration is concerned about automobile safety defects and can order "recalls" for the replacement of defective parts. The Civil Aeronautics Board can assist airline passengers who have had difficulties. For example, airlines are required to give "denied boarding compensation" in the form of cash payments to passengers who are "bumped," that is, refused seats even though they had reservations and arrived at the gate on time.

Many other federal agencies want to receive complaints, but have no power to help consumers get redress. The Food and Drug Administration, for example, welcomes reports about unsafe food, drugs, and cosmetics. It has no power, however, to help consumers who have been injured or want the purchase price refunded. The only power the FDA has is to take action to stop future sales of unsafe products so as to protect other consumers. The only alternative open to injured consumers who want redress is to sue the manufacturer on their own. Other federal agencies have similar limits on their power to help consumers. They are able to protect consumers from loss and injury by regulating the making and sale of products and services. They have, however, few powers to help individual consumers who actually have been injured or have suffered losses.

State Attorney Generals

At the state level, the best source of help is the attorney general's department. More than half the states now have special consumer fraud or consumer protection bureaus within this department. The principal concern of these offices is with frauds and misleading advertising and product claims. Most serve as clearinghouses for consumer complaints. When a problem does not fall within their jurisdiction, they refer it to other agencies. Most also are active in educating consumers about fraudulent schemes.

Some bureaus have been very effective in helping consumers. Branch offices, mobile units, and telephone hot lines have been set up to make it easier for consumers to make complaints. The bureaus often are able to solve problems without court action. Most are settled with a phone call or a hearing in the agency's offices. Effective bureaus, such as those in Illinois and the states of New York and Washington, have been able to get millions of dollars refunded to consumers each year.

Some of the agencies focus most of their attention on helping individual consumers get their money back or get contracts canceled. Others have put more emphasis on getting business to stop deceptive practices than on helping individual consumers with problems. They concentrate on getting companies to promise to discontinue practices which are considered deceptive. If a company fails to keep its promise, the agency then will begin court action.

There is a good deal of difference between states in the real legal power given to the consumer fraud bureau. Many bureaus have only limited powers and must rely on getting companies to cooperate voluntarily. Most have fairly good success in getting such cooperation. Regardless of the basis of their success, the state bureaus are an important source of assistance for consumers.

State Regulatory Agencies

In each state there are agencies responsible for regulating many different kinds of businesses and professions. These agencies have the principal responsibility for supervising the conduct of local retail and service firms, independent professionals such as physicians and lawyers, and corporations operating within the state. Agencies in the various states are organized differently and have different names. However, they carry on most of the same functions.

State departments of insurance supervise the activity of insurance firms operating in the state and often can provide assistance on such problems as unexplained cancellations of auto insurance, difficulties in obtaining a settlement with a company, or questions concerning rates. Questions concerning the conduct and operations of banks should go to the state department of banking.

State bureaus of weights and measures deal with questions about the accuracy of grocery scales, gasoline pumps, and other weighing and measuring devices. In many states this bureau is part of the state department of agriculture.

Consumers' problems in getting honest and competent appliance and auto repairs have led several states and cities to institute systems of licensing repairers and repair shops. One of the most active agencies of this type is the Bureau of Repair Services in the California Department of Consumer Affairs. One of the activities of this bureau is to contact television repair shops in behalf of consumers with complaints. If it appears that the shop is at fault, the bureau requests the shop to correct the problem.

When repeated complaints about a particular shop pile up, the bureau places a "rigged" television set in a private home near the shop under suspicion. All the parts in the set are secretly marked so that when the shop services the set, the bureau can quickly determine which parts actually were replaced. If it appears that a shop is cheating, the bureau repeats the check in other homes with other rigged television sets. When there is enough evidence, the bureau conducts a hearing on the case. If the agency decides a shop has been dishonest, it can cancel its registration, putting it out of business.

Many other types of business, business people and professionals are licensed by the state. Some examples are barbers, physicians, and auto dealers. The state boards regulating their activities usually can provide some assistance or advice on consumer problems. It should be recognized that the members of these boards usually are members of the profession they regulate. Most boards seem reluctant to take strong action on complaints. Recently action has begun to get more consumer members on state boards and to make them more responsive to consumer interests.

Local Government Agencies

In some metropolitan areas the district attorney's office has a separate division to handle complaints about consumer fraud. Some offices have been very successful in getting large numbers of complaints settled without legal action, but they also do take legal action where necessary. The Consumer Fraud Division of the Cook County (Chicago) District Attorney's Office receives a large volume of complaints—about 40 a day. One of the major weapons of this agency is its power to call offending merchants to informal hearings in its offices. In many areas, the district attorneys are too often poorly informed about consumer problems or are understaffed and feel they must devote their time to prosecuting violent crimes such as robbery and murder.

Several cities and counties have set up special consumer protection offices. The activities of the City of New York Department of Consumer Affairs have attracted national attention. The department is concerned with such matters as false advertising, improper labeling and pricing, and weights and measures. Other cities with special consumer protection offices include Boston, Chicago, Detroit, Dallas, and St. Louis. Counties with special county offices include Nassau County in New York (Long Island), Dade County in Florida (Miami area), and Allegheny County in Pennsylvania (Pittsburgh area).

Local News Media

As consumer problems have come more and more into the news, many local newspapers and radio and TV stations have established consumer complaint centers. These centers handle consumers' problems with business and help them to obtain services from government

Media-run consumer complaint centers, such as this television broadcast, not only help solve individual problems but also perform an educational role by letting people know where they can turn for help if they have a similar problem. (*Courtesy of NBC*)

agencies. Some of the problems handled are reported in a regular column or broadcast. An example of such a complaint center is the one run by *The Washington Star* in Washington, D.C. The center has several full-time staffers, plus others on part-time assignments. Some of the results of the center's efforts are reported daily in the *Star's* "Action Line" column.

In addition to helping individuals with problems, the media-run complaint centers also perform an educational role. They inform the public about where they can turn for help if they have a similar problem. They also identify frauds and deceptive offers which should be avoided.

LEGAL ASSISTANCE

It should be clear, from the previous section, that government agencies and the better business bureaus have only limited power to get redress for consumers. The only power many have is to *request* firms who have mistreated consumers to refund their money, replace a product, or cancel their contract. Only in a few cases do they have power to order such actions.

Consumers who are unable to get their problems corrected by the means we have discussed in this chapter will have to turn to the courts for help. If the amount involved is not too large, they can sue in small claims court (see pages 485–487). Lawsuits in small claims courts can be conducted without the help of a lawyer. If the problem is a more serious one, a lawyer's help will be needed (pages 484–485).

DIFFICULTIES IN IDENTIFYING PROBLEMS

We are just beginning to get a full picture of consumers' problems and complaints. For years consumer problems were handled on an individual basis. No attempt was made to classify them into categories in order to determine what kinds of problems are most frequent. In the past few years several agencies have begun systematic computerization of consumers' problems in order to get an overview of the situation. We now will have a better idea of the areas in which action is most urgently needed.

Even after the full range of consumer complaints has been analyzed, another problem still remains. This problem is the consumer with a problem who fails to complain—the silent victim. No one knows or can even guess how many silent victims there are. Some are silent because they do not even know they have been deceived. Others are ashamed to admit their problems. Some do not know where to turn for help. Others do not believe any real relief for their problems is available. All consumers must be encouraged to make complaints they consider valid. By doing this, they can help themselves and other consumers as well.

Checking Your Reading

1. When should you make a complaint about a product or service?
2. Why is it important to review product use and care instructions before making a complaint?
3. In general, where should you go first with a complaint? Why?
4. What documents and items should you have with you when returning a product or making a complaint?
5. What sources are available for locating the address of a business firm when you want to make a complaint by mail?
6. List five essential pieces of information that should be included in a letter of complaint.
7. If your letter of complaint is not answered, what follow-up should be taken next?
8. What types of consumer problems are better business bureaus concerned with? What types of problems do they refuse to handle?
9. How does the Office of Consumer Affairs assist consumers who have complaints?
10. What kinds of consumer problems fall under the jurisdiction of the Federal Trade Commission?
11. To what agency would you complain if you ordered some records through the mail and paid for them, but never received them?
12. Which state agency has chief responsibility for handling complaints about consumer frauds?
13. What kinds of business activities are state regulatory agencies responsible for supervising?
14. On what kind of consumer problems can local district attorney's offices often provide assistance?
15. What kinds of complaints are handled by the consumer complaint centers run by local news media?

Consumer Problems and Projects

1. What consumer problem have you or your family had recently? Draft a letter of complaint to the business firm involved, complete with the address. Be sure you include all the essential information.

2. Prepare a follow-up letter that would be appropriate for use if you did not receive a reply to the complaint letter you prepared. Include a list of agencies to whom copies should be sent.

3. If your complaint letters written for projects 1 and 2 were not answered, what agency would you ask for assistance? Why do you feel it would be an appropriate choice? Draft a letter, complete with address, to the agency stating your problem and requesting help.

4. The new hair dryer Jackie Hamilton bought at a local department store broke the first time she used it. She was so angry that she wrapped it up and mailed it back to the manufacturer without even a letter of explanation. "Let them figure it out!" she said. What do you think of the way Jackie handled this problem? What approach might have been more effective?

5. Some people shop at stores that charge high prices just because they feel that if they have a problem or complaint it will be handled quickly and politely. Do you think this makes sense?

6. Check recent issues of *Consumer News*, published by the Office of Consumer Affairs, for listing of product recalls. Make a study of five recent recalls. In each case, what was the problem? What company was involved? What government agency ordered the recall? What should consumers who purchased the product do? What will be done for those who bought the product—repairs, replacement, refund, or what?

7. Do any of your local media have columns or programs which assist consumers? Study the problems reported for a period of several days. Prepare a study listing each problem, the company or government agency involved, and the final results. Do you feel the column or program is handling all kinds of complaints or just the easy ones which do not involve local companies?

30

Government Agencies that Regulate the Marketplace

The federal government is involved in regulating a major part of everything that goes on in the marketplace—from the price of airline tickets to the amount of peanuts in peanut butter. Twenty or more federal agencies are involved in regulating things which consumers buy. We already have discussed some of the activities of a few of these agencies. In this chapter we will take a closer look at the government's regulatory activities and their effectiveness.

WHY DOES GOVERNMENT REGULATE THE MARKETPLACE?

The government has several reasons for regulating the marketplace. One of its chief concerns is to protect and promote fair competition between businesses. As we saw in Chapter 1, competition has many important benefits. It helps to ensure that prices are fair. Competition also enables consumers to have a choice among a variety of products offered by different sellers. It also helps ensure that customers will be well treated by firms who want to keep their business.

In addition to stepping in to protect competition, the government also may get involved in regulating the marketplace in two other types of situations. These are cases involving spillover costs or cases where natural monopoly exists. In such cases, the market, if allowed to operate on its own, might not produce satisfactory results.

We discussed both spillover costs and natural monopolies in Chapter 25. In discussing spillover costs, we saw that sometimes a product or service will affect others besides those who produce or sell it and the people who buy and use it. An example is air pollution created by automobiles. This air pollution has costs which fall partly on people who own cars, but some of its cost spills over on others and affects everyone in the community. Home gardens, shrubbery, and agricultural crops are injured; paint and the exteriors of buildings are damaged; and the health of almost everybody in the community is affected. We can see that when these spillover costs are large, it may be desirable for government to step in and regulate the design and use of automobiles. Government action may be desirable to control other kinds of spillover costs too. Pollution, auto safety, and product sanitation are a few of the cases in which spillover costs exist.

The government also may become involved in regulating the market in cases in which there are natural monopolies. These are cases in which it is most efficient to have a product or service supplied by a single enterprise rather than to encourage competing firms. An example of a natural monopoly is electrical service. It is cheaper and more efficient to have electricity supplied by one company, than it is to have several companies operating in the same area. If there were several companies, each would have to maintain its own generating equipment, its own lines, and its own service forces. Clearly, it is cheaper for consumers to have only one company operating in an area. When a service or product seems to be a natural monopoly, government may step in and allow only one company to operate. Since there is no competition to help control prices, the government also regulates prices to ensure they are fair. Utilities are one example of natural monopolies. Transportation is another area in which natural monopolies are believed to exist.

We have identified three reasons why government regulation may be necessary:

- To ensure competition
- To control spillover costs
- To regulate natural monopolies

Let us now look at the techniques and procedures the government uses.

HOW DOES GOVERNMENT REGULATE THE MARKETPLACE?

We saw in Chapter 1 that there are four different methods the government can use to regulate the marketplace. We saw that one of these methods is to protect competition. If there is a danger that an entire industry is coming under the control of one or only a few sellers, antitrust action to protect fair competition may be necessary. A frequent type of antitrust action is control of mergers (the joining together of several smaller companies into a large one). This is done when there is a danger that the new company will be so large and powerful that competition will be affected.

Another method that the government uses to control the marketplace is to regulate the information which is available. It controls the use of fraudulent or untrue claims and makes certain that consumers are provided with the kinds of information they need. In some cases the government itself provides information and educational materials to help consumers choose more wisely. An example is the pamphlets of the Cooperative Extension Service. In other cases, it requires manufacturers or sellers to provide needed information. Examples of this approach are clothing care labeling and the statements of interest rates on an annual percentage basis which lenders must provide.

A third method of regulating the marketplace is to set standards. As we have seen, standards are rules or models against which something can be judged. There are all types of standards. Standards set crash-safety requirements for automobiles and care-labeling requirements for jeans. Standards also set the requirements for safety and effectiveness in medicines.

A fourth method of regulating the marketplace is to help consumers get redress when they have problems in the marketplace. We saw in the last chapter that some government agencies can help consumers get refunds, repairs, and replacements when they have problems. Others can do little to help individual victims, but are able to take action to stop companies who are using unfair or unsafe practices. Another way in which consumers can get redress is to use the courts to sue for damages. They may sue either as individuals or sue in a class action, along with other consumers who have had the same problem. Suits may be based on claims that sellers have deceived the buyers or have failed to live up to the terms of a contract. They also may be based on claims that a manufacturer has been negligent or careless in producing a product.

The use of these four methods of regulating the marketplace by different government agencies is summarized in Table 30-1.

TABLE 30-1
Major Federal Government Regulatory Programs

MAINTAINING AND ENSURING COMPLETION

Civil Aeronautics Board—regulates mergers and competitive practices of airlines including rates, schedules, and services

Federal Communications Commission—regulates number and type of radio and TV stations and community antenna television (CATV) services; regulates content of radio and television programs; regulates foreign and interstate telephone rates and services.

Federal Energy Regulatory Commission—regulates interstate transmission of electricity, natural gas, and oil; regulates mergers

Federal Trade Commission—enforces antitrust laws; regulates unfair and deceptive business practices that interfere with competition

Interstate Commerce Commission—regulates operations and rates of interstate rail, bus, truck, and water carriers including household movers; regulates mergers

Justice Department—enforces antitrust laws aimed at preventing restraint of trade and mergers that may lead to monopoly power and unfair pricing.

PROVIDING AND REGULATING INFORMATION

Providing Consumer Information

Food Safety and Quality Service, Department of Agriculture—performs grading of meat, poultry, eggs, dairy products, fruits, and vegetables.

Cooperative Extension Service—provides publications and educational programs on buying and money management

Food and Drug Administration, Department of Health, Education, and Welfare—provides educational programs on food and drug safety and labeling

General Services Administration—provides information on services available from government through Federal Information Centers; distributes government consumer information publications through the Consumer Information Center

Government Printing Office—distributes government publications

National Bureau of Standards, Department of Commerce—prepares consumer publications based on its testing results

Office of Consumer Affairs, Department of Health, Education, and Welfare—prepares consumer information materials; coordinates government consumer education and information activities.

Office of Consumers' Education, Department of Health, Education, and Welfare—provides financial aid for state and local consumer education programs.

Ensuring Accurate Product Information Is Provided

Food Safety and Quality Service, Department of Agriculture—ensures accurate labeling of meat and poultry products

Consumer Product Safety Commission—regulates safety labeling of hazardous household chemicals

Federal Trade Commission—ensures accurate labeling of wool, fur, and textile products

Food and Drug Administration, Department of Health, Education, and Welfare—regulates labeling of food, drugs, cosmetics, and medical devices; takes action against medical and nutritional quackery

Office of Interstate Land Sales Registration—ensures reports on subdivision lots and condominiums are available to prospective buyers

TABLE 30-1 (continued)

Controlling Advertising Content

Civil Aeronautics Board—regulates airline advertising

Federal Communications Commission—places some controls on advertising on radio and television

Federal Deposit Insurance Corporation—regulates advertising by insured banks

Federal Trade Commission—has power to take action against most kinds of deceptive and misleading advertising

Food and Drug Administration, Department of Health, Education, and Welfare—regulates advertising of prescription drugs

Securities and Exchange Commission—regulates advertising of investment securities

U.S. Postal Service—takes action against fraudulent advertising sent through mails

Ensuring Credit Cost Information Is Available (Truth in Lending)

Bureau of Federal Credit Unions, Department of Health, Education, and Welfare—federally chartered credit unions

Comptroller of the Currency, Treasury Department—national banks

Federal Home Loan Bank Board—savings and loan associations

Federal Reserve Board—state banks that are members of Federal Reserve System

Federal Trade Commission—small-loan companies, retail stores, and service establishments

SETTING REGULATIONS AND STANDARDS

Product Safety

Food Safety and Quality Service, Department of Agriculture—inspects fresh and processed meat and poultry products

Consumer Product Safety Commission—sets and enforces safety standards for most consumer products except food, drugs, cosmetics, pesticides, and automobiles

Environmental Protection Agency—regulates pesticide sales and use

Food and Drug Administration—checks to ensure safety of food, drugs, cosmetics, and medical devices.

Transportation Safety

Federal Aviation Administration, Department of Transportation—promotes air transport safety and provides air-traffic control services

National Highway Traffic Safety Administration, Department of Transportation—develops safety performance standards for new vehicles

HELPING CONSUMERS GET REDRESS

Civil Aeronautics Board—handles complaints against airlines

Consumer Product Safety Commission—requires manufacturers of hazardous products to repair or replace them or refund purchase price

Federal Trade Commission—can seek redress for groups of consumers who have experienced losses because of deceptive advertising or illegal business practices

Interstate Commerce Commission—handles complaints on household movers, bus lines, and railroad lines

Office of Consumer Affairs, Department of Health, Education, and Welfare—receives consumer complaints and works with appropriate agencies to solve them

U.S. Postal Service—helps resolve problems with mail-order purchases

FEDERAL REGULATORY AGENCIES

General policies on regulating the marketplace are set out in laws passed by Congress. Congress gives the responsibility for administering these laws to different agencies and leaves the details of regulation up to them. They decide which problems are most pressing and how best to deal with them.

The regulatory agencies have the power to make new rules and regulations and to enforce them. These powers are called *quasi-legislative powers,* since they are like the lawmaking powers of a legislative body. Using these powers, agencies can regulate business practices and tell firms what they may and may not do. When a new rule is to be issued, an agency first publishes the proposed regulation in the *Federal Register,* an official government publication containing important legal notices. Hearings then are held on the regulation to allow the industry and the public to make their comments. After taking these comments into account, the agency issues the regulation in final form.

Most regulatory agencies also have *quasi-judicial powers,* that is, judicial powers like the courts. Agencies can use these powers to make investigations, bring charges when they believe rules have been violated, and then make decisions and enforce them.

Some of the regulatory agencies are offices within regular cabinet departments. The Food and Drug Administration, for example, is part of the Department of Health, Education, and Welfare. Others, such as the Federal Trade Commission, are independent commissions and are separate from the three branches of government. Since there are so many different agencies involved in regulating the marketplace, we will focus our attention on only a few of the key ones: the Federal Trade Commission, the Consumer Product Safety Commission, and the Food and Drug Administration.

Federal Trade Commission

The Federal Trade Commission is one of more than 40 independent boards and commissions. Many of these agencies, like the Interstate Commerce Commission, the Securities and Exchange Commission, and the Civil Aeronautics Board, are involved in consumer protection activities. The independent boards and commissions all are headed by a group of board members or commissioners rather than by a single administrator. The FTC, for example, has five commissioners, one of whom is named as chairperson. When it created these agencies, Congress felt it was desirable to have them headed by a group of people rather than by a single person. It felt that this would allow different interests and points of view to be represented. The commissioners, or board members, are appointed by the President and must be approved by the Senate.

Congress also felt that since commissions and boards have quasi-legislative and quasi-judicial powers, they should be protected from political pressures and from party politics. One way they tried to do this was by giving the board members and commissioners long-term appointments. FTC commissioners, for example, are appointed for seven-year terms.

The Federal Trade Commission was created in 1914 to control unfair business practices that affected competition and to handle anti-trust problems. In 1938 its responsibilities were expanded to include fraud, deception, and other practices that injure consumers.

When the FTC operates as a quasi-judicial agency, it proceeds much like a law court does. When a questionable practice is discovered, there is an investigation to find out whether federal laws have been violated. If it appears that there has been an important violation,

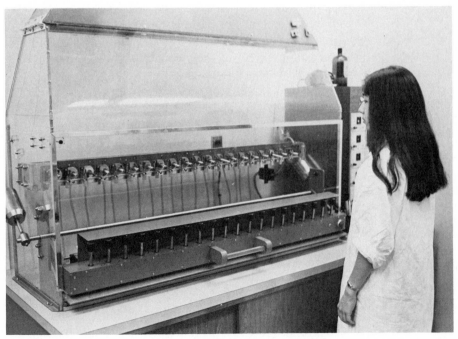

One of the FTC's responsibilities in protecting the consumer is testing tar and nicotine levels of cigarettes. (*Federal Trade Commission*)

proceedings are begun. Most cases are settled with a promise of *voluntary compliance* from the business firm involved or a *consent agreement* between the FTC and the firm. In these agreements the firm promises to stop engaging in the practice the FTC has challenged. When a case is settled this way, the firm is not fined or punished and does not have to admit it did anything wrong. Handling cases in this way has important advantages. It saves the FTC time and effort and gets questionable practices stopped quickly. It also permits firms to avoid the expense and publicity of formal proceedings.

The chief difference between voluntary compliance and consent agreements is that the FTC includes specific orders in consent agreements. These orders describe the practices the firm must stop. The orders may also require the firm to take some affirmative action, that is, to *do* something. Sellers may, for example, be required to include certain key facts in future advertising or to return money to deceived customers. These orders have the force of law. If they are disobeyed, the firm can be fined.

When a case is not settled by voluntary compliance or a consent agreement, it moves to the next stage. This involves a formal hearing before one of the FTC's administrative law judges. Depending upon the judge's decision, a *cease-and-desist* order may be issued. Such an order requires the firm to stop engaging in the challenged practice. It may also require some affirmative actions by the firm, such as refunds. Cease-and-desist orders carry no fines or punishment. However, if they are disobeyed, fines can be imposed.

In addition to its quasi-judicial powers, the FTC has important quasi-legislative powers. It can use these powers to develop new regulations, which have the force of law. These *trade regulation rules* cover entire industries and deal with unfair methods of competition and unfair or deceptive practices which affect consumers. An example is the rule which requires gasoline dealers to post octane ratings on gas pumps. The FTC has made increasing use of trade regulation rules in recent years. One of the chief reasons for their use is that they make it easy for the FTC to impose new regulations on entire industries, instead of going after individual firms on a case-by-case basis. Some people, in fact, have become concerned that the authority to issue trade regulation rules gives the FTC too much power. They argue that Congress should review new regulations and veto ones it objects to.

In the late 1960s the FTC was strongly criticized by Nader's Raiders and others who had reviewed its activities. They felt the agency had done little and that when it had done anything, it had tended to focus on minor problems. They felt it had spent too much effort on fighting deceptive fur labeling and deceptive schemes which claimed you could make money at home raising chinchillas. Not enough time, they felt, was spent on major consumer problems or on antitrust enforcement.

Under new leadership, the agency plunged into action with antitrust suits and new trade regulation rules. Congress has reacted favorably to this new activism, and the FTC budget and staff have increased sharply in recent years. The FTC's new activism has produced new critics—mostly business people. They are concerned that the agency has tremendous power but is subject to no real control by Congress or by anyone else. The FTC seems certain to continue to be a center of controversy.

Consumer Product Safety Commission

The Consumer Product Safety Commission began operation in 1973. This makes it the newest major federal agency regulating the marketplace. Like the FTC, it is an independent commission. It has five commissioners named by the President for seven-year terms and approved by the Senate. One of these commissioners is the chairperson.

The CPSC has power to issue safety standards for most common household products. Only a few products, including food, drugs, cosmetics, pesticides, and motor vehicles, are not under its control. A major portion of the products covered by the CPSC was not previously covered by any safety law. When it was created, the agency was given responsibility for enforcing some laws that previously had been enforced by other agencies. These include the Flammable Fabrics Act and the Federal Hazardous Substance Act covering household chemicals and toys.

The CPSC has the power to issue safety standards which have the force of law. It does this when it feels a product involves unreasonable risks of injury to consumers. These regulations are issued only after hearings and the rest of the rule-making process has been completed. The rules issued by the CPSC can cover product performance, composition, and design and packaging, as well as warnings and instructions for use. An example of the standards issued by the CPSC is the recent one covering bicycles. It covered brakes, chain guards, sharp edges, and other safety risks. Its most visible result is the use of more reflectors.

The CPSC also has power to ban hazardous products which it feels cannot be made in a way that will ensure the user's safety. The agency also has power to order manufacturers to replace or repair or make refunds and to notify purchasers when safety defects are discovered after a product has been sold. In addition to its power to ban defective products, the CPSC also has power to go to court to seek fines and jail sentences for business executives who do not comply with its regulations.

Information and education are an important part of CPSC's program. The agency believes it can reduce injuries by making the public more aware of product hazards. It has used a variety of methods to inform the public: news articles, pamphlets, radio and TV spot announcements, films, and even coloring books on playground safety for children. As part of this program, the agency operates a consumer hot line to handle consumers' comments about safety matters and requests for information. The number is (800) 638-2666 [in Maryland (800) 492-2937].

One of the problems facing the CPSC as a new agency is to decide on its priorities for action. Since it is responsible for ensuring that a wide range of products do not involve unreasonable risks, it must decide where to focus its efforts. One of the bases for these decisions is the information the CPSC collects on injuries associated with the use of products. This information is collected through The National Electronic Injury Surveillance System (NEISS) from hospital emergency rooms throughout the nation. This information is used to prepare the Product Hazard Index.

Because it is still a relatively new agency, the CPSC has had to

TABLE 30-2
Consumer Product Hazard Index: A Listing of Products Most Frequently Involved in Serious Injuries

1. Bicycles and bicycle equipment, including accessories.
2. Stairs, steps, and ramps.
3. Football activities, equipment, and apparel.
4. Baseball activities, equipment, and apparel.
5. Swings, slides, seesaws, and other playground equipment.
6. Tables, not including glass tables.
7. Swimming activities, pools and equipment.
8. Beds, including springs and frames, not including mattresses and box springs.
9. Liquid fuels including gasoline, kerosene, charcoal starter, etc.
10. Nails, carpet tacks, screws, thumbtacks.

Source: Consumer Product Safety Commission.

devote a good deal of effort to organizing itself and developing a set of priorities to guide its program. The agency has developed several major new regulations in recent years, including ones covering flammability of children's sleepwear and bicycles. It has found the going difficult in many areas, however. The proposed standard for power lawn mowers developed for the CPSC by Consumers Union created a storm of controversy.

When the CPSC was created, some people felt its powers would make it the most powerful regulatory agency ever established. The CPSC has not yet fulfilled this prediction. It remains to be seen whether the prediction will come true as the agency grows and develops.

Food and Drug Administration

A third major agency involved in regulating consumer products is the Food and Drug Administration. Its organization differs from the FTC and the CPSC. It is not an independent commission. Instead, it is part of the Public Health Service in the Department of Health, Education, and Welfare. It is responsible for enforcing laws and regulations to ensure the following:

- Drugs and medical devices are safe and effective
- Food is safe, wholesome, and nutritious
- Cosmetics are safe to use

It has been estimated that 20 cents of every dollar consumers spend goes for products regulated by the FDA.

Control of the marketing of new drugs is one of the FDA's chief responsibilities. When manufacturers apply for permission to market new drugs, they must provide evidence that they are both safe and effective. The FDA reviews these scientific test results. When it is satisfied, it gives its approval for the drug to be sold. The FDA recently was given more control over the safety and effectiveness of medical devices—including everything from tongue depressors to heart pacemakers.

Most processed foods, except for meat and poultry products, are also a responsibility of the FDA. In regulating food marketing, special attention is focused on *misbranding* and *adulteration*. By law, foods and other products under FDA regulation are considered misbranded when their labeling is false or misleading. Food products would be considered misbranded if they did not conform to official standards of identity, were not the quality indicated, or were not properly filled.

The FDA is responsible for ensuring that drugs are safe. This agency was instrumental in keeping thalidomide, a sleep-inducing drug, from being marketed in this country even though it was available in other countries. Thalidomide was eventually found to be a cause of birth defects like those which affect this boy. (*UPI*)

Products are considered adulterated when a valuable or important ingredient has been left out or taken out. Strawberry jam, for example, would be considered adulterated if it had fewer strawberries in it than called for in the standard of identity. Products also are considered adulterated if they contain filth or are contaminated in any way. The FDA also is responsible for checking the safety of food additives, including food colors, preservatives, and artificial sweeteners.

In its enforcement activities the FDA uses both in-plant inspections and laboratory testing. FDA inspectors check food-processing plants, warehouses, and drug-manufacturing plants which make products for sale in interstate commerce.

The FDA has only a few hundred inspectors in the field to check the thousands of facilities producing food and drugs. Because of its limited number of inspectors, the FDA has been placing more emphasis on helping plants to develop quality-control programs. These programs identify possible causes of problems and develop procedures for checking products during the production process. On their inspection visits, FDA inspectors review the firm's efforts. This method is felt to provide a better check on a firm's activities than judging it only on problems observed on the particular day of an inspection visit.

In addition to in-plant inspections, the FDA conducts laboratory tests of products obtained from retail stores and from consumers with complaints. It also conducts its own laboratory tests of new drugs and chemical food additives to determine their safety. These tests provide a check on manufacturers' reports of their tests of product safety.

The FDA has a variety of enforcement procedures that it can use. It can ban products from the market, request manufacturers to recall them, seize and destroy products, and in extreme cases, request the Justice Department to prosecute offenders.

In large part, the FDA relies on firms to cooperate voluntarily. Much of the FDA's enforcement efforts are devoted to informing firms about regulations and helping them to comply with them. Some of the FDA's critics say it relies too much on voluntary compliance. They say it seems to take legal action only against the worst offenders. Too many firms, they argue, are let off without punishment if they promise to stop using a questionable practice.

One reason for the FDA's reliance on voluntary compliance may be its budgetary problems. Getting voluntary compliance is a good deal cheaper than lengthy legal actions.

The FDA has been given many new responsibilities in recent years, but it is handicapped by limited funds. At least part of the criticisms of the FDA grow out of problems created by an inadequate budget. Improvements will require more funds. Consumers and their representatives will have to decide how much improved regulation of product safety is worth to them.

CRITICISMS OF THE REGULATORY AGENCIES

In the last few years we have heard an increasing volume of criticism of the regulatory agencies. We have heard accusations that the regulatory agencies have been "captured" by the industries that they are supposed to regulate. There also have been widespread claims that regulation has destroyed competition in some industries, such as the airline industry; these critics call for de-regulation to restore competition. Others have argued that the problem is that the regulatory agencies are not really responsible to anyone and offer suggestions to change this. Let's look more closely at these three different kinds of criticism.

"Capture" by the Regulated Industry

Many political liberals, including Ralph Nader, are concerned that the regulatory agencies have been "captured" by the industries they are supposed to regulate. They claim that the agencies have forgotten their responsibility to the public and instead focus their attention on protecting the industry they are supposed to regulate. Instead of controlling the industry, the agency treats it as a client whose interests come first.

The development of this kind of orientation comes about for several reasons. Links between an agency and the industry it regulates are strong and contacts are frequent. Many agency officials are former industry executives. Often government officials take jobs in the regulated industry when they leave their government jobs. Government officials see industry representatives frequently and work closely with them on a variety of projects. It is hardly surprising in these circumstances that government officials come to share industry viewpoints. Another factor is the small army of business representatives and lobbyists who work to influence government decisions. They are constantly at work pressing their viewpoints on industry problems on government officials.

Some attempts have been made to deal with the problem of "capture." These efforts attempt to reduce industry influence on regulatory agencies. Part of this effort has been stronger conflict-of-interest rules, limiting financial links between government officials and regulated industries. There also have been increased efforts in recent years to recruit officials from outside the regulated industries. Consumer and public interest groups, universities, and government all have been used as sources of officials, in the hope that their thinking will be more independent. Another step is restrictions on taking jobs in the regulated industry. For example, senior CPSC officials are not allowed to take jobs in a regulated industry for 12 months after they leave the commission.

Another step in controlling industry influence is the efforts being made to make it easier for consumer, environmental, and other public interest groups to express their views in agency proceedings. New laws make it easier for the public and consumer advocates to keep track of what is going on in an agency. This makes it easier for them to express their opinions at times which will have the most influence on agency decisions. The "Sunshine Act" opens up meetings and hearings in the regulatory agencies which previously often were closed. The Freedom of Information Act makes agency reports, files, and documents more readily available. In addition, some agencies are providing financial assistance to groups who otherwise could not afford to come to testify at hearings.

Regulation Destroys Competition

Some critics feel that the problem is not the capture of the regulatory agencies, but the whole idea of regulation. They argue that too often regulation interferes with competition. This viewpoint has gotten strong support from several different political quarters—from leaders in the recent Republican administration to Ralph Nader.

These critics argue that the regulatory agencies sometimes have limited the number of sellers in a particular market too much. This has been done because the regulation agency wanted to keep competition "orderly" and prevent the kind of cutthroat competition which would destroy weaker companies. The result of these kinds of policies, critics argue, is to limit competition so much that it is almost destroyed. They point out, as an example, that when the Civil Aeronautics Board

Critics of the regulatory agencies, such as Ralph Nader, feel that too often the regulation interferes with and limits competition, and that the regulators are too closely related to the industries they regulate. (*UPI*)

limits the number of airlines which can operate between Chicago and Atlanta and sets the rates, it has pretty much destroyed any chances of real competition on the route. When one airline on this route tries to win passengers away from another, it cannot cut prices — price competition is prohibited. All it can do is offer minor extras — in-flight movies, colorful flight attendants' uniforms, and more comfortable seating.

The solution, according to this group of critics, is to deregulate some of the industries which are now regulated. One of their special targets is the transportation industry and the agencies which regulate it, especially the Interstate Commerce Commission and the Civil Aeronautics Board.

Lack of Accountability

There is still another group of critics of the regulatory agencies. They are less common than the first two, but they have some strong arguments to offer. Their chief concern is that the regulatory commissions and boards are not really accountable to anyone. Because most of them are independent, they do not have to answer to anyone and are not directly responsible to either the President or Congress. They are not responsible to the public either.

In fact, the public often has had a difficult time knowing how and why the regulatory commissions come to particular decisions. The new "Sunshine Act" will make it easier for the public to hold the agencies accountable for their decisions.

Some of the critics who feel the regulatory commissions should be made more accountable want to make them more directly responsible to the President. Some also have proposed the idea of a "sunset act" for regulatory agencies. Such a law would require an agency to justify its existence to Congress periodically. Every so often, perhaps every 10 years, it would have to prove it was having some useful effect. If it could not prove this, it would be disbanded or reorganized.

ENSURING CONSUMER INTERESTS ARE REPRESENTED

Over the years there have been a variety of suggestions for new agencies to protect consumers. Starting in the 1930s, some people argued that what was needed was a new Department of Consumers. Such an organization, they said, would bring all the consumer protection activities of government under one roof. This, they believed, would give consumers the representation they needed in government.

Others, including Ralph Nader, opposed this idea. They believed that all the problems which have limited the effectiveness of regulatory agencies in the past would be problems for any new department too. Instead, they favored the idea of a Consumer Protection Agency which could represent consumers' interests in regulatory actions and in court cases. Bills to create such an agency have come close to approval several times since 1969.

The chief responsibility of the proposed organization would be to present consumer views before the various regulatory agencies of government. The new agency would have no regulatory power of its own. Instead it would help make certain that the decisions made by regulatory agencies were well-informed ones which took consumer interests into account.

The new agency would participate in rule making by the departments of the executive branch and the independent regulatory commissions. It also would participate in court actions that affect the interests of consumers. There are certain government activities in which the agency probably would not be involved. These include actions by the FBI, the CIA, and the Defense Department and the settlement of labor-management disputes. Proposals also call for the new agency to be given authority to handle consumer complaints sent to the government.

Some business people have opposed the idea of a Consumer Protection Agency. They feel it is unnecessary and would only increase the amount of government bureaucracy and red tape. They argue the new agency would do what the regulatory agencies are already supposed to be doing. Critics also have questioned whether one agency can speak for all consumers. They argue that consumer problems and needs are too varied for that. Supporters of the new agency respond that it probably would not attempt to speak for consumers in all cases. Instead, it probably would focus its attention on cases in which consumer interests are clear-cut and whose economic impact would be greatest.

Checking Your Reading

1. What are the three cases in which it may be necessary for the government to regulate the marketplace?

2. What are the four methods the government can use to regulate the marketplace? Give an example of each method.
3. What do quasi-legislative powers and quasi-judicial powers permit regulatory agencies to do?
4. How do the independent commissions and boards differ from other government agencies?
5. What do we mean by voluntary compliance? Why does the FTC rely heavily on it?
6. What are trade regulation rules?
7. What types of products does the CPSC control?
8. When can the CPSC issue a safety standard?
9. What is NEISS? How does the CPSC use the information it collects?
10. What products does the FDA control?
11. What do we mean by the term "misbranding"? "Adulteration"?
12. Why does the FDA rely heavily on getting voluntary compliance from firms?
13. What are some of the reasons why a regulatory agency might be "captured"?
14. Why do some people argue for deregulation?
15. How do Sunshine Acts and sunset laws help to make agencies more accountable to the public?
16. Why have some people opposed the idea of a Department of Consumers?
17. What functions could the Consumer Protection Agency have?
18. Why do some people favor the creation of a Consumer Protection Agency? What arguments did others offer against it?

Consumer Problems and Projects

1. How does government regulation affect the things you use? Name 10 products and services you have used recently, and indicate how regulation affects the production, sale, or use of each one.
2. Prepare a report on one of the regulatory agencies which controls the market for consumer goods and services. Try to answer the following questions:

Why was the agency formed?

How have its responsibilities and powers changed
over the years?
What problems has it had to deal with in recent
years? What action has it taken on them?
What criticisms have been made of the agency?
Do you feel they have any basis?

3. Certain areas of government regulation are the subject of continuing controversy. Prepare a report on what has happened recently in one of the following areas:

Food and food additive safety
Drug safety
Automobile safety
Safety of products under control of CPSC
Transportation regulation
Antitrust regulation

Check the *Readers' Guide to Periodical Literature* for recent news on your subject.

4. Some of the critics of the idea of regulation say we do not need so many laws to protect consumers, as long as consumers who are injured or defrauded can sue for damages. Do you see any weaknesses with this argument? Can you think of any situations in which it would not be reasonable for consumers to spend the money required to sue? How could consumers deal with cases in which they did not know how to reach the company involved, such as cases involving fly-by-night operators?

5. Some critics of regulation feel that it is not desirable or necessary to ban dangerous products. The best approach, they say, is to tell consumers the risks involved and let them decide for themselves whether or not to use the product. Do you see any problems with this approach? Can we estimate the risks of every type of product? How can we be sure that consumers understand the risks they are taking? What about spillover effects on others?

Index